Journal of the Early Book Society
For the Study of Manuscripts and Printing History

Edited by Martha W. Driver
Volume 28, 2025

Copyright © 2025
Pace University Press
41 Park Row
New York, NY 10038

All rights reserved
Printed in the United States of America

ISBN: 978-1-9652246-10-8
ISSN: 1525-6790

Member

Council of Editors of Learned Journals

™ The paper used in this publication meets the minimum requirements of American National Standard for Information Sciences—Permanence of Paper for printed Library Materials
ANSI Z39.48—1984.

The *Journal of the Early Book Society* is published annually. *JEBS* invites longer articles on manuscripts and/or printed books produced between 1350 and 1550. Special consideration will be given to essays exploring the period of transition from manuscript to print. Collecting and evaluation of essays for *JEBS 29* begins in November and continues through May 2026. Authors are asked to follow the *Chicago Manual of Style*. Longer papers with endnotes and a full Works Cited list (substantial essays of 8000 words or more) on any aspect of the history of manuscripts and/or printed books, with emphasis on the period between 1350 and 1550 should be sent electronically and in hard copy with an abstract to Martha Driver, 333 East 53 St, Apt 12B, New York, NY 10022 (mdriver@pace.edu). A limited number of illustrations may be included with complete captions and permissions citations; authors are responsible for acquiring publishable images and permissions. The *Nota Bene* section features shorter essays that include only endnotes (not a Works Cited list). Please submit shorter essays (under 8000 words) to Michael P. Kuczynski (mkuczyn@tulane.edu) and copy to Martha Driver (mdriver@pace.edu). Send brief notes about little- or lesser-known collections and libraries of interest to the Society to Martha Driver. Members of the Early Book Society who are recent authors may send review books to Susan Powell, Reviews Editor. Sue can be contacted at S.Powell@salford.ac.uk. Her current mailing address is Pear Tree Cottage, Church Road, Blythburgh, Halesworth, Suffolk IP19 9LL UK. Subscription information can be obtained from Pace University Press.

Those interested in joining the Early Book Society or with editorial inquiries may contact Martha Driver by post or e-mail (mdriver@pace.edu). Information can also be found at <www.nyu.edu/projects/EBS>. For ordering information, call Pace University Press at 212-346-1405 or visit http://www.pace.edu/press. Institutions and libraries may purchase copies directly from Ingram Library Services (1-800-937-5300).

The editor wishes to thank Gill Kent, Mark Hussey, Kaitlyn Tenorio-Gravesande, Kianna Swingle, and Manuela Soares of Pace University Press for their help and advice on this issue.

Journal of the Early Book Society
For the Study of Manuscripts and Printing History

Editor:
Martha W. Driver, *Pace University (emerita)*

Associate Editors:
Michael P. Kuczynski, *Tulane University*
Susan Powell, *University of Salford (emerita)*

Editorial Board
Matthew Balensuela, *DePauw University*
Julia Boffey, *Queen Mary, University of London*
Cynthia J. Brown, *University of California, Santa Barbara*
James Carley, *York University*
Joyce Coleman, *University of Oklahoma*
Margaret Connolly, *University of St Andrews*
Helen Cooper, *Magdalene College, University of Cambridge*
Consuelo Dutschke, *Columbia University*
Susanna Fein, *Kent State University*
Ann M. Hutchison, *Pontifical Institute of Mediaeval Studies and York University*
William Marx, *University of Wales, Lampeter*
John McQuillen, *The Morgan Library & Museum*
Carol M. Meale, *Bristol University*
Ann Eljenholm Nichols, *Winona State University*
Judith Oliver, *Colgate University*
Veronica O'Mara, *University of Leeds*
Steven Partridge, *University of British Columbia*
Lucy Sandler, *New York University*
Alison Smith, *Wagner College*
Sebastian Sobecki, *University of Toronto*
Helena Szepe, *University of South Florida*
Jane Taylor, *Durham University*
Toshiyuki Takamiya, *Keio University*

John Thompson, *Queen's University, Belfast*
Robert F. Yeager, *University of West Florida*
Daniel Wakelin, *University of Oxford*
Ronald Waldron, *King's College, University of London*
Edward Wheatley, *Loyola University*
Mary Beth Winn, *SUNY Albany*

Contents

Articles

Another Manuscript by the Hammond Scribe of Legal Works in English   1
    DANIEL WAKELIN

Nicole Gilles and the Turquam-Gilles Manuscript and Printed Book Collection, ca. 1499   29
    SARAH DYER MAGLEBY

A 1555 German Gift Book for Queen Mary I   63
    VALERIE SCHUTTE

Special Essay Cluster

Constructing Community in Late-Medieval French Lyric   83
    LUCAS WOOD, ELIZAVETA STRAKHOV, S. C. KAPLAN

Homosociality, Life-Writing, and the Claim to Coterie Authorship in the *Livre des Cent Ballades*   87
    ELIZAVETA STRAKHOV

"*Oncques ne vy plus plaisant compaignie*": Jubilant Poetry as Record of Women's Puissance   121
    S. C. KAPLAN

Inscribing Poetic Fellowship in the Personal Manuscript of Charles d'Orléans   149
    LUCAS WOOD

Nota Bene: Brief Notes on Manuscripts and Early Printed Books
Highlighting Little-Known or Recently Uncovered Items or Related Issues

An Unrecorded Prayer of St. Edmund of Abingdon in Madrid, Biblioteca Nacional MS 6422   191
    R. F. YEAGER

Aristotle in Pieces 197
    LISA FAGIN DAVIS

Philological Missing Links: The "*-Manuscripts" in the Stemma of the German 213
Translation of Lanfranc's *Chirurgia magna*
    CHIARA BENATI

A New Middle English Fragment of John Arderne's Extracta Hemorroidarum: 231
Evidence for the Surgical Readership of Translation T
    CALEB PRUS

More Messing With Old Books: The Rewards of Bodleian Library, MS Laud 241
Misc. 603
    RALPH HANNA

Unpublished Latin Quatrain of John Gower in a Lincoln College Manuscript 265
    DAVID R. CARLSON and JAMES M. W. WILLOUGHBY

Descriptive Reviews

Sara J. Charles 273
The Medieval Scriptorium: Making Books in the Middle Ages
    MARTHA RUST

Laura Cleaver, Danielle Magnusson, Hannah Morcos, and Angéline Rais, eds. 277
The Pre-Modern Manuscript Trade and its Consequences, ca. 1890–1945
    VIRGINIA BLANTON

Richard Gameson, Andrew Beeby, Flavia Fiorillo, Catherine Nicholson, Paola 281
Ricciardi, and Suzanne Reynolds
The Pigments of British Medieval Illuminators: A Scientific and Cultural Study
    KATHRYN A. SMITH

Kathleen E. Kennedy and Melek Karataş, eds. 285
Manuscripts in Bristol Collections: A Descriptive Catalogue
    RALPH HANNA

Steven W. May 287
English Renaissance Manuscript Culture: The Paper Revolution
    MATTHEW SULLIVAN

Corinne Saunders and Diane Watt, eds. 291
Women and Medieval Literary Culture: From the Early Middle Ages to the Fifteenth Century
    JENNIFER N. BROWN

Anna Dlabačová, Andrea Van Leerdam, and John J. Thompson, eds. 295
Vernacular Books and their Readers in the Early Age of Print (c. 1450–1600)
    MARY MORSE

John Goldfinch, Takako Kato, Satoko Tokunaga, eds. 299
Production and Provenance: Copy-Specific Features of Incunabula
    SUSAN POWELL

Thomas C. Sawyer 307
The Making and Meaning of a Medieval Manuscript: Interpreting MS Bodley 851
    RALPH HANNA

Misty Schieberle, ed., with Amanda Bohne 311
Medieval Manuscripts, Readers & Texts. Essays in Honour of Kathryn Kerby-Fulton
    JULIA BOFFEY

About the Authors 315

Another Manuscript by the Hammond Scribe of Legal Works in English

DANIEL WAKELIN

In the early twentieth century, Eleanor Prescott Hammond identified six English literary manuscripts written in full or in part by the same scribe.[1] He (it is assumed) has since then taken her name: the Hammond Scribe. The list of his manuscripts was later extended by A.I. Doyle, Richard Firth Green, Jeremy Griffiths, and Linne R. Mooney.[2] He copied one work that must postdate 1459 and others that refer to Edward IV as living, so before April 9, 1483, or to people in ways that seem unlikely to have been said after 1484. Some of the watermarks in his manuscripts, all in paper, recur in other sources dated from around 1465 to the mid-1480s. So it seems that he was working during the reign of Edward IV and perhaps a few years before or after.[3] It was at one point suggested that he might be the London stationer named in records as John Multon, for the phrase "quod Multon" appears in one of his books, but that has been disputed; "quod Multon" looks more like the name of an author whose work was being copied.[4] For now, this scribe is most safely known as the Hammond Scribe.

The list of manuscripts identified as his handiwork has, since the year 2000, stood at fifteen.[5] Those manuscripts are:

1. Cambridge, Trinity College MS O.3.11: a miscellany largely of political, civic and legal prose in or translated into English.

2. Cambridge, Trinity College MS R.3.21, fols. 34r–49v: religious poems in a miscellany otherwise largely by another scribe and largely of verse in English, much by Lydgate.

3. Cambridge, Trinity College MS R.14.52: a miscellany largely of medical and scientific prose in or translated into English.

4. London, British Library MS Additional 29901: a miscellany largely of heraldry and royal precedent in Latin and French.

5. London, British Library, MS Additional 34360: a miscellany largely of verse in English, much by Lydgate.

6. London, British Library, MS Arundel 59: Hoccleve, *The Regiment of Princes*, and Lydgate and Burgh, *The Secrees of Old Philisoffres*.

7. London, British Library, MS Cotton Claudius A.viii, fols. 175r–197v: Fortescue, *The Governance of England*.

8. London, British Library, MS Harley 78, fol. 3r: a fragment from a probably incomplete copy of *Piers the Plowman's Creed*.

9. London, British Library, MS Harley 372, fols. 71r–112r: a long fragment from a copy of Hoccleve, *The Regiment of Princes*.

10. London, British Library, MS Harley 2251: a miscellany largely of verse in English, much by Lydgate.

11. London, British Library, MS Harley 4999: *Nova statuta* up to 18 Henry VI in English translation.

12. London, British Library, MS Royal 17.D.xv, fols. 167r–301v: a large part of Chaucer, *The Canterbury Tales*.

13. London, Royal College of Physicians MS 388: Chaucer, *The Canterbury Tales*.

14. Oxford, Bodleian Library, MS Rawlinson D.913, fol. 43r–v: a fragment from a copy of an English prose work on Merlin.

15. Worcester, Cathedral Library MS F.172: a miscellany largely of devotional prose and ecclesiastical constitutions in or translated into English.

To this list I here add a sixteenth manuscript, entirely in the Hammond Scribe's handwriting, which has not hitherto been identified as such:

> 16. Cambridge, University Library, MS Ee.1.2: Littleton, *Tenures*, in French, and the old *Natura brevium* in French and Latin, each with a unique accompanying translation into English.

This additional manuscript gives a little more information about the engagement of the Hammond Scribe in copying practical works for everyday use, which were increasingly written in or translated into English in the second half of the 1400s.

This manuscript, Cambridge, University Library, MS Ee.1.2 (hereafter MS Ee.1.2), has two of the standard works on England's common law, indispensable to lawyers in training. The first is *Tenures* by Sir Thomas Littleton (d. 1481), a guide to property law, which replaced an older work on the subject (fols. 2r–165r). The second is one of the works, this one likely late fourteenth-century, on particular kinds of writs, a *Natura brevium* (fols. 166r–264r). Littleton's *Tenures* was first printed in 1482/3, and this work on the *Natura brevium* in 1494. Each, as well as older and newer texts on the same topics, was frequently reprinted thereafter, and Littleton's *Tenures* was the law book written in England that was most often printed.[6] Both were owned by many lawyers in the later fifteenth century and sixteenth century. Littleton's work became the standard guide to property law for the young men who studied at the Inns of Court, whether to become lawyers or simply to master enough law to manage their lands.[7]

From the 1520s, translations of each were printed more than once by John Rastell.[8] This manuscript by the Hammond Scribe also presents translations, however, not those printed by Rastell nor that of Littleton edited in the seventeenth century by Edward Coke. Instead, those in MS Ee.1.2 are unique and seemingly the earliest translation of each work. For Littleton's *Tenures*, the manuscript gives each section in the original law French and then immediately gives a translation of that section, switching back and forth thus throughout the work. For this *Natura brevium* it does the same but, as is usual for that work, it also gives a sample writ or "brief" in Latin before its commentary in French, and the English translation is of both the Latin and the French.

A manuscript of treatises on the common law fits neatly among the volumes copied by the Hammond Scribe. He often made books of legal interest, whether for himself or for customers or patrons. His oeuvre includes a copy of the more recent English statutes, the *Nova statuta*, also in a unique English translation; a work by the lawyer Sir John Fortescue on *The Governance of England*; and many works on legal precedent and governance more broadly defined, in civic, heraldic, and ecclesiastical settings. He also copied a wide range of scientific, religious, and literary works, including Thomas Hoccleve's poem on good governance, *The Regiment of Princes*, and John Lydgate and Benedict Burgh's version of the *Secreta secretorum* among others. Holly James-Maddocks speculates that, from his output and collaborations, "we might imagine the Hammond scribe as a well-connected 'hand for hire,' a freelance scribe associated with drapers, heralds, and a mayoral household." A little more is learned about the world he served if we first identify his involvement in MS Ee.1.2 and then consider how close he was to the origins of the legal works he copies there.

Identifying the Hammond Scribe

The Hammond Scribe's handwriting is instantly recognizable among that of fifteenth-century scribes.[11] What first raises the alert that one might be reading one of his books is that he tends to use very long, tapering extensions that slope to the right for over a centimeter before trailing off at the tops of the letters **f** and **s**. He does this on the top lines of pages or sometimes the top lines of sections after a space left on the page (that is, where such extensions are possible).[12] MS Ee.1.2 has one or more of these tapering extensions on a majority of its pages.

Of course, this is just the sort of oddity that would be easily imitated, whether by the Hammond Scribe as apprentice following his master, by the Hammond Scribe's dutiful apprentice following him, or more widely by somebody thinking that it looks stylish.[13] (This and other features mentioned here can be seen in Figs. 1 and 2.) It cannot alone be a marker of his work. But further scrutiny then suggests less imitable features of ductus and aspect as well as other "shibboleth" letterforms that confirm a clear identification in this case. Comparisons can be made to all of his manuscripts, many of them helpfully illustrated on the website *Late Medieval English Scribes*.[14] His copy of another legal work in English, a translation of the *Nova statuta*, is the most alike.

First, his handwriting is modeled on secretary script, which by this period had spread beyond royal writing offices and aristocratic correspondence and was widely used for copying entire books. The overall ductus is that of a variety of secretary script as it was used in contemporary handwriting for letters and documents, a variety that became more common in the later 1400s and replaced anglicana for these functions during the 1500s. As in other current specimens of secretary from the mid-1400s, the body of letters is tightly curled, and the ascenders slope to the side. (M.B. Parkes described this variety of secretary as looking as though the letters were being squashed from above.)[15]

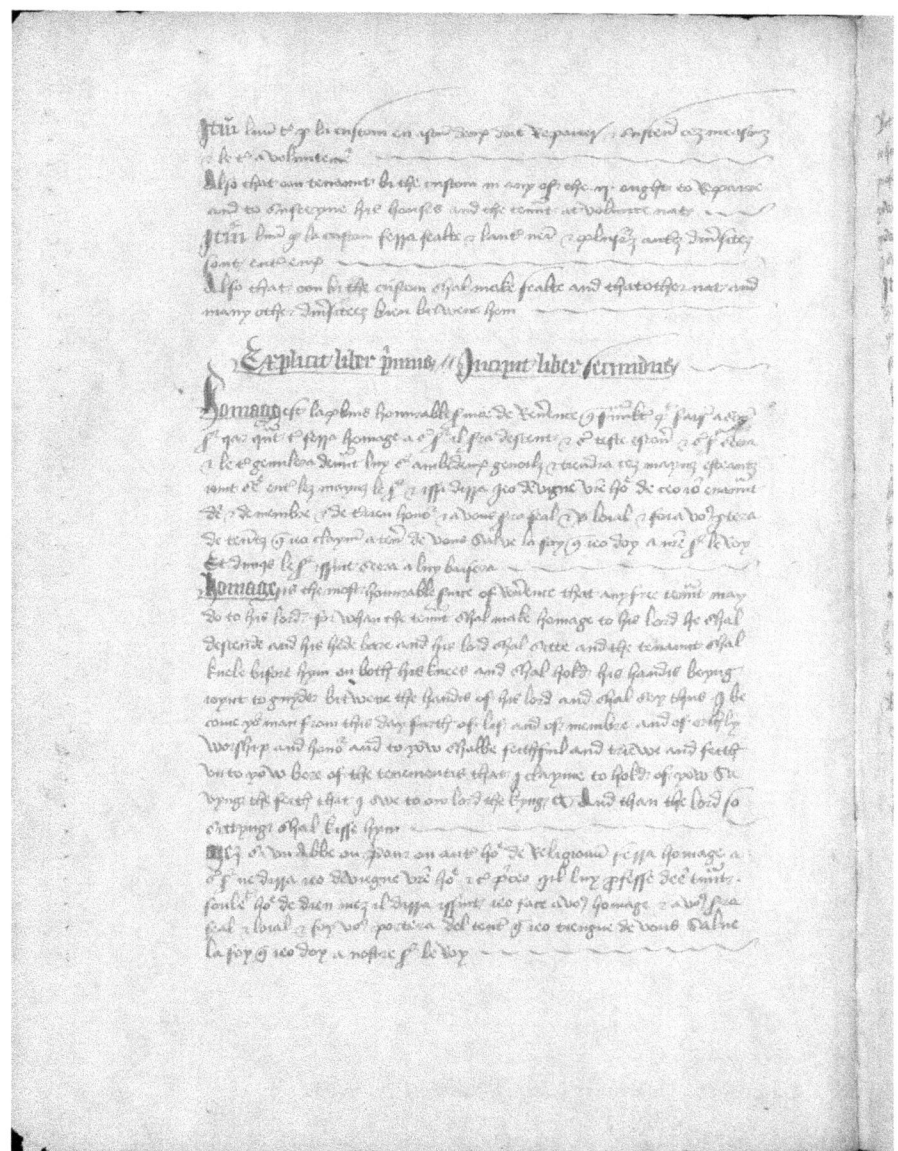

Figure 1: Cambridge, University Library, MS Ee.1.2, fol. 17v.

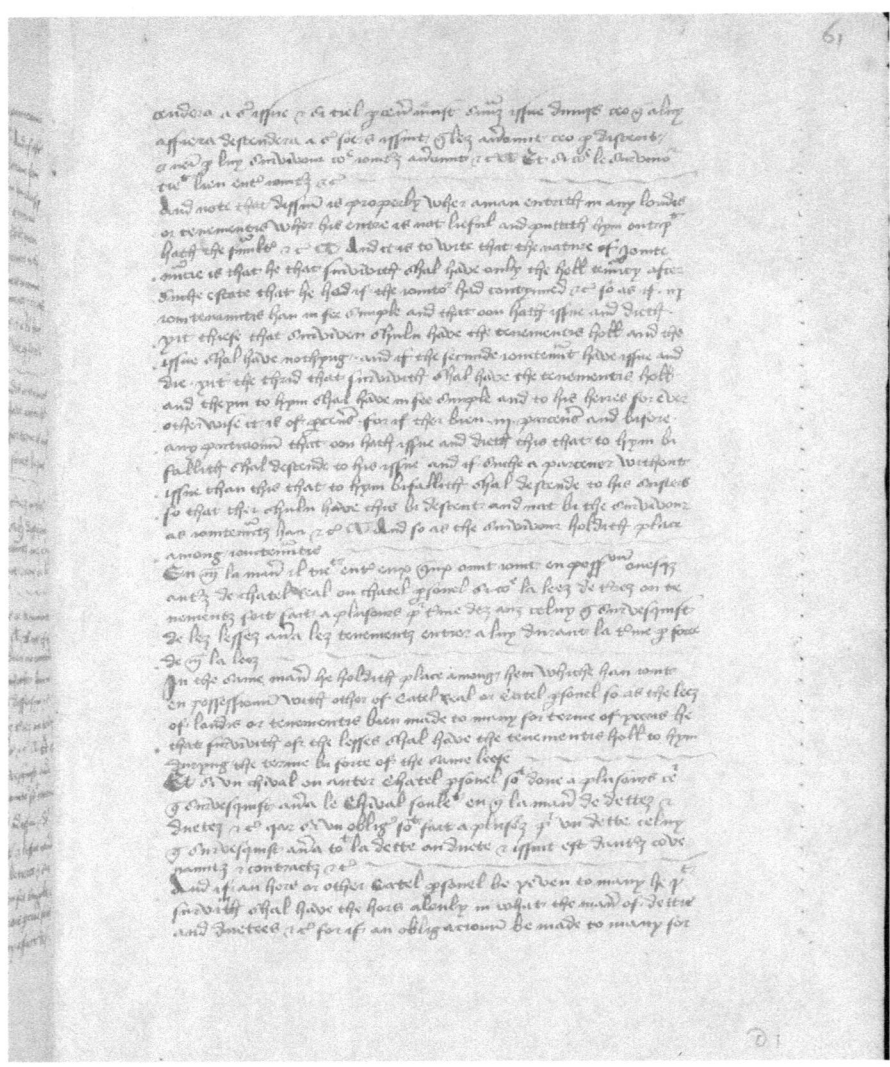

Figure 2: Cambridge, University Library, MS Ee.1.2, fol. 61r.

Indeed, for the Hammond Scribe the ascenders are long, from baseline to top more than double the *x*-height, and they often slope rightwards at about 70 degrees from the baseline. Many of those ascenders have loops, sometimes clearly emerging from fast movements of the pen from one graph to the next, but loops formed by a tight jerk of the pen at their top rather than a wide rounded curve. There is also a long approach stroke, again doubling the *x*-height, on the start of **v** or **w** (the latter of which is formed of two **v** shapes), albeit that this approach stroke slants leftward instead, countervailing the ascenders. In a few places, the approach stroke on **v** or **w** seems to be added as an extra stroke. (zooming in on a digitized page reveals such overlapping strokes and changes of ink.)[16] Overall, his handwriting gives greater visual emphasis to what comes above the body of the letter than what comes below; his tendency to lengthen strokes decoratively on the top lines of pages (noted above) continues that visual emphasis.[17] There is also a slope at a similar angle and similar length to the ascenders in one descender, too, on **p**, strengthening that angle as one distinctive element of the aspect of his writing. This is what Eleanor Prescott Hammond put so well—almost providing a guide to identifying *any* scribe—when she said that "the relative proportions and the general character persist."[18]

His execution in this legal prose is a little more current than in some of his poetic manuscripts, where either the prestige of the poem or the process of pausing every few words for a line break has slowed down his writing. Also, in this manuscript, there are very few of the broken strokes found in more calligraphic grades of secretary during this period. Nonetheless, the ductus or movement of the pen often leaves gaps in letters. One gap occurs in one-compartment **a**, leaving a slight space in the top of the letter; another occurs in **d**, where a small upward spike suffices to demarcate the left-hand side of the lobe and does not join to the looped ascender above to close that lobe; another occurs in **e** formed from two separate strokes, one long below, one short above, a typical feature of this variety of secretary (and one which comes to predominate in the 1500s); and another in **p**, where the top of the curl for the bowl often does not connect with the sloping descender. These gaps seem to occur because, overall, his handwriting is fairly current, with minims often joined in a zigzag movement.

Although modeled on secretary script overall, the handwriting shows an admixture of influences from anglicana, the variety of cursive that had been used in England for longer. That is common to many other specimens of secretary script of the third quarter of the 1400s in England. A few of the Hammond Scribe's letterforms would be more canonical in what we now categorize as anglicana: while his final **s** is usually kidney-shaped, as in secretary models, the sigma-shaped **s** that in anglicana is used at the end of words here occurs at the start of them.[19] His **g** usually has two compartments, with the tail joined to the lobe, and the lower loop is long and narrow, as it increasingly becomes in anglicana in the final quarter of the century. He mostly favors the zetoid **r**, which fifteenth-century secretary shares with textualis, done in a narrow cursory form resembling **i** (confusingly for the transcriber), as prevails in secretary handwriting from Scotland and in the 1500s. But he also often occasionally uses long **r**, especially where double **rr** is required or in word-final position, in English, French, and in *Natu-*

ra brevium in Latin alike; this is a letterform far more usual in anglicana.[20]

A few other letters stand out: notably, word-final **t**, which tends to end with a crossbar projecting right, from which a separate stroke jerks downward and leftward diagonally. It is an unusual otiose flourish in handwriting marked by an effort more at speed than calligraphy.[21] His majuscules—though we should beware that these self-conscious forms are more easily imitated—are also distinctive, especially his flamboyant rendering of **E** in both his main handwriting and his display script.[22] Most striking is **R**, where the left-hand vertical stroke is in effect omitted, and it is the diagonal right-hand lower stroke that continues upwards to form the left-hand side of the lobe at the top. (Doyle called this "footless.")[23]

With a scribe of English of this period, it is sometimes still just about possible to identify distinctive habits of spelling, too. The many terms borrowed directly—often calqued—from law French in the two works copied in MS Ee.1.2 are less susceptible to dialectal variation of the kind found in English, but a few features arise.[24] Most commonly, there is a strange habit of orthography that was typical of the Hammond Scribe: a tendency to use <ie> where other scribes would use <e>. For instance, the plural of the third person verb *to be*, notionally *been*, is spelled <bien>, and *true* is spelled here <triewe>.[25] There is also what Simon Horobin calls the "interchangeable" use of <c> and <s>, where the other might be expected, as in <choise> for *choice*, or <licens> for *licence*.[26] Other spellings typical of this scribe, though less unusual, include <chirche> with medial <i>, <moche>, <nat>, <suche>, <to guyder> with <to> separated and a medial <d>, and <yit>.[27] Overall, the orthography is akin to that in his other known manuscripts.

The Hammond Scribe was polygraphic and could also produce a variety of textualis that he used in this manuscript, as in some others he made, as a display script for headings or highlighted words.[28] It is best called by Continental palaeographers' preferred term *textualis*, perhaps using the modifying term *textualis media*, rather than by the term *textura*, which has misleading connotations of only the higher grades of execution.[29] For the Hammond Scribe's rendering of this script does not have crisp serifs, as in uses of it influenced by carved inscriptions in the 1400s, but has pronounced rightward ticks curving up from the feet of minims and of other letters such as short **r**. Such flowing movements of the pen might suggest that he formed his textualis fast, almost with currency, rather than in its usual set execution. That upward tick very occasionally reaches the next vertical in an untidy way, the antithesis of the careful placement of strokes more customary in the smartest textualis.[30]

A similar currency is suggested by a few other letterforms that occur in his textualis and which make his display script distinctive: he leaves the tail of **g** in his textualis open, unconventionally for this script and more typical of secretary (and, paradoxically, unlike his use of a closed tail for **g** in his secretary script).[31] In textualis, his long **s**, a straight vertical stroke topped by a short sloping one, often has a slightly too-long top stroke, as though edging towards his sloped or even his tapering form in his secretary handwriting; very rarely, he does indeed use his sloping form of **f** or long **s** with a tapering extension into the space above.[32] His rendering of textualis is, then, confident but a little unconventional in details. That might suggest that this is somebody who copied for a living but was not one of the textwriters who specialized in liturgical books in textualis; it suggests that this was, rather, somebody trained in cursive handwriting originally for documentary production who could imitate textualis, a little imperfectly, when required.

In addition, some features of layout circumstantially corroborate—though such design elements cannot sufficiently confirm—that this book was made by the Hammond Scribe. He tended to create books that were not deluxe but were well ordered, with careful deployment of graphic design to articulate the structure of texts; he was highly competent. This manuscript shows features of logical design similar to his others. For instance, the mode of underlining Latin passages in red, framed by a curved upward stroke on the left and a straight dash on the right, is the same in *Natura brevium* here and in the Latin annotations on his copy of Hoccleve's *The Regiment of Princes*.[33] The textualis is not only typical in its style but in its deployment for the first few words of sections, as in his copy of the *Nova statuta* in English, or for key words under discussion, as in his copy of a glossary of Old English legal terms.[34] Among other decorative elements, his use of a wavy red line-filler at the end of paragraphs recurs in his copy of heraldic treatises, and the scale of the waves and the way that these line-fillers stray over the right-hand ruling into the marginal space are identical (Fig. 2).[35]

Overall, the copy of *Tenures* and *Natura brevium* is very similar in size and decor to that of *Nova statuta* by the Hammond Scribe. *Tenures* and *Nova statuta* are not identical: for instance, *Tenures* has forty rules for thirty-nine lines of text, but *Nova statuta* has forty-five rules for forty-four lines; *Nova statuta* does not have the red wavy line-fillers when paragraphs end mid-line. But these texts would look broadly harmonious together, similar in scale, in the use of display script, and in an absence of sidenotes from the *Nova statuta* and Littleton's *Tenures*.[36] In addition, the watermark in *Tenures* and *Natura brevium* in MS Ee.1.2 seems to be identical with a watermark that appears on only one leaf—strangely—in *Nova statuta* in London, British Library, MS Harley 4999. It is a hand with **A** or maybe **LA** on its cuff and a six-petaled flower on a stalk above its fingertips.[37] A similar but not identical watermark, where the fingers differ in arrangement and the seed-head of the flower is less distinct, also appears in the Hammond Scribe's manuscript of civic regulations and works of political governance; it might be paper from the same supplier, using variations of a house style in his mold at different times or in a different ream of paper.[38] But the likenesses between the manuscripts of *Nova statuta* and the two legal treatises, newly identified as his work, are close in materials, layout, and kinds of text.

The Closeness of the Scribe to the Legal Works

There are questions to ask about the closeness of the Hammond Scribe to the translations he copied in MS Ee.1.2. These questions are prompted by the second work, *Natura brevium*, ending incomplete. Throughout this work there is a Latin writ or brief expounded in French, then an English translation of both the Latin and the French. But at the end is the Latin writ of intrusion and then seven lines of exposition in French which end mid-sentence at the foot of the page, a recto, with the commentary incomplete and without any translation into English. This point is only two thirds of the way through the work as found in roughly contemporary manuscripts of the Latin and French.[39] That interruption is made stranger by two features of the quiring and ruling of the manuscript.

The quiring is mostly regular throughout, in large quires of ten bifolia, giving twenty leaves.[40] Then the Hammond Scribe used a smaller quire of three bifolia, giving six leaves, to end the copying, and in fact he only wrote on the first three and a half leaves of that quire. The text ends at the foot of the fourth recto of that quire, and the remainder is left blank. When a final quire is much shorter, one would normally deduce that a scribe made it so deliberately, because he had looked ahead and seen that the text was soon going to finish. That was standard practice for planned endings.[41] Given such common methods, and given that a final short quire of six leaves would not be enough to complete all of the older French *Natura brevium*, it is likely that the Hammond Scribe knew that the English translation was not finished at the time of writing.

Moreover, it is possible—though unprovable—that the Hammond Scribe began his final quire with twenty leaves, like the others, but only realized during the first three leaves that he was running out of text to copy. If so, he could have removed fourteen of the remaining leaves in the middle of the quire and thereby turned the eighteenth leaf of a regular twenty into the fourth leaf of an irregular quire of six, written what little text he had left, and stopped. After all, if he had wanted to make a smaller quire from the outset and avoid wasting paper, an experienced scribe might have calculated that he only needed four leaves, as he in fact used, rather than six, of which he then left, two and a half blank.

A sense that the ending was abrupt is borne out by the ruling. The manuscript was pricked throughout for ruling, but the ruling switches at several points earlier in the book from drypoint to lead and back again, and midway through quires, so that sometimes half a bifolium is lead, half drypoint.[42] The ruling must not, therefore, have been applied to bifolia all at once in advance, as was the usual way of saving labor and standardizing presentation, but sequentially as copying progressed. Such a process of ruling is rare but not unheard of, and an example can be adduced from the milieu around this scribe.[43] As this scribe was ruling only as he went along, when he ended *Natura brevium* mid-sentence at the foot of a recto, he left the verso and the subsequent extant leaves of this last quire unused, pricked but not ruled.[44] Evidently, the Hammond Scribe had been supplying only as much ruling as he needed as his copying progressed, and then here stopped abruptly, perhaps unexpectedly. Whether he planned a quire of only six leaves or reduced a larger quire to six leaves, it seems that he was aware that the translation was unfinished; this was not an accidental interruption of his copying by some external event.

The Hammond Scribe's awareness that the text was incomplete is suggested, further, because it would be a remarkable coincidence—albeit not an impossibility—that his exemplar was incomplete exactly where his copying reached a page break. It seems more likely that he realized that the exemplar was incomplete at some point a little further ahead and so stopped at a page break for tidiness, and perhaps reduced his quire, until he knew whether the rest was going to arrive—which it evidently did not.[45] A similar tidy page break occurs in another manuscript by the Hammond Scribe. This too is a legal work in translation: the English rendering of the *Nova statuta*. His copy in London, British Library, MS Harley 4999, ends mid-sentence, in the middle of Chapter 17 of the statutes issued in the eighteenth year of the reign of Henry VI, and again, neatly at the foot of a page, albeit there a verso, and with the following and final leaf that survives ruled.[46] It has been suggested that this translation once continued to the statutes for the twentieth year of the reign of Henry VI, but I can see no evidence of how much more translation, if any, was completed and not copied.[47]

Likewise, in a different genre and in a scenario less clear, there survives the last page of a copy by the Hammond Scribe of the poem *Piers the Ploughman's Creed*. All that remains is one leaf, starting at line 172 and ending at line 207, again at the very foot of a page. As A.I. Doyle puts it, this page of the poem "could have been in continuation of a longer portion or copy of the *Creed*, interrupted perhaps by failure of the exemplar or other external factor, involving coincidence with the foot of the page."[48] That page of poetry had frame-ruling only, but the verso had not been thus ruled and was left blank by the Hammond Scribe. (It was only later filled with unrelated texts by others.) It is striking that he made one poetic and two legal copies that stopped short precisely at page breaks, twice without ruling the following page; this looks like a deliberate method of dealing with problems in incomplete exemplars or with breaking his stints of work and for some reason not returning to them.

It is another interesting coincidence that the two legal texts in which he does this are both unattested in other copies, complete or otherwise. The translation of the old *Natura brevium* is not that printed in the 1500s (as noted), and that of the *Nova statuta* is not one of those found in other manuscripts of the second half of the 1400s. There is no other evidence that the particular translations of *Nova statuta* and *Natura brevium* nor of Littleton's *Tenures* copied by the Hammond Scribe circulated elsewhere, as no other copies of them survive, even though the numbers of manuscripts of the original French and of other translations of *Nova statuta* suggest that there was a demand for such works. As such, there arises the suspicion—but one not proven—that both *Nova statuta* in London, British Library, MS Harley 4999 and *Natura brevium* in MS Ee.1.2 are copies of translations still in progress; that the Hammond Scribe was copying them close in time and milieu to their origin; and that he paused for more to be done that was not, in the end, done. This is an overextended hypothesis, but it would be worth testing further by detailed work on the texts of these translations. For instance, errors of incomplete translation, such as leaving French "Et" instead of *and* in the English ("nat bi lyneal ascencioun Et in suche cas wher"), might suggest that this is a copy made from a still-rough draft.[49] A full study of the text and translation would be a useful project to examine this hypothesis.

Beyond the translations, the involvement of the Hammond Scribe also raises questions about the origins of the original French not of *Natura brevium*, which likely dates from the later 1300s and survives in multiple copies, but of Littleton's *Tenures*.[50] Littleton claims that he is writing *Tenures* for one of his three sons, addressed in the conclusion repeatedly as "mon fitz" or "my sone" (in this early translation).[51] This was a convention for instructive works, as in Chaucer's *Treatise on the Astrolabe*, so its reliability in dating is uncertain, but if it were true, it would help to date *Tenures*. Littleton's eldest son, Sir William was born around 1450/1 and later entered the Inner Temple; the third and youngest son's birth date is unknown, but he entered Lincoln's Inn in 1477.[52] For *Tenures* to be useful to one of the sons as a lawyer in training, it was presumably written no earlier than the adolescence of the eldest in the mid-1460s, and of course before Littleton's death in 1481.[53]

Then the identification of the Hammond Scribe as copyist of Littleton's French *Tenures* in MS Ee.1.2 strongly suggests an earlier date for this manuscript than was thought. Previous sources suggested around 1500 and "s. xv. ex" as its date; it contains a note of ownership by the lawyer Sir John St.

Peire (d. ca. 1505).[54] But the datable parts of the Hammond Scribe's known output range between 1459 at the earliest and 1484 at the latest (as said above). While a scribe might well work for longer than twenty-five years, that range suggests that this manuscript is among the earliest copies of Littleton's *Tenures* and perhaps dates close to Littleton's composition of the work, perhaps before his death in 1481 or before the first printed edition by John Lettou and William de Machlinia around 1482/3. Interestingly, samples of collation suggest that the Hammond Scribe's French text of Littleton's *Tenures* was not copied from that first printed edition of 1482/3; as well as small divergences in grammar and spelling, it contains a few phrases not in the printed edition and larger omissions of passages that were in the print. Thus MS Ee.1.2 adds to our sense of how Littleton's work was circulating in his own lifetime or immediately after, which only a few other manuscripts have yet suggested.[55]

One other early manuscript is illuminated by an artist who is connected to the Hammond Scribe, at a few degrees of separation, and who has an oeuvre datable to around 1470 to around 1490; that book has an Oxford binding found on books printed in the 1480s. Its colophon names Littleton as "unum justiciariorum Communis Banci" ("one of the judges of the Common Pleas"), without any word such as *nuper* which would suggest that he had died.[56] Two other manuscripts were apparently written in 1481/2 and 1482, though with some uncertain evidence.[57] (An early date for another early manuscript should be discounted: London, Inner Temple, MS Barrington 82, once dated to the mid 1400s, seems to me to be by a scribe who copied statutes in the 1490s.)[58] And the copy by the Hammond Scribe in MS Ee.1.2 probably dates within Littleton's life or within a few years of his death. Indeed, the Hammond Scribe's manuscript is headed with the name "Litelton Iustice".[59] This inscription could show either knowledge of the author or willingness to tie the work to him, whether because he was still alive or as an act of posthumous piety. (Above "Litelton Iustice" is the monogram "ihc" for *ihesus*, though it is common for scribes to write this at the start of their copying and need not suggest a piously memorial interpretation of "Litelton Iustice".) It might or might not be relevant that he is entitled *justice*, which he became when appointed to the bench of the Court of Common Pleas in 1466, and not *sir*, which he became when made a Knight of the Bath in 1475. Either way, the presence of the author's name also suggests some closeness to the text's origins, perhaps in networks around the Inns of Court.

From this closeness in date to Littleton's day, it would be dangerously tempting to speculate whether Littleton himself had made the translation of his *Tenures* and of the old *Natura brevium*. He did use English: his will records "my grete English boke" among his otherwise Latin, and not legal, books, and indeed he was among those in the fifteenth century who made the shift to compose their will in English.[60] It is interesting that the town government of Coventry, for which he served as recorder from 1448 to 1455—a prestigious role for a lawyer at this time—was an innovator in using English for records of its Leet Court, long before the mayor and aldermen's court in London, for instance.[61]

But rather than speculate about the author, it is safer to say that the translation is typical of works copied by this scribe, for the Hammond Scribe copied other unique manuscripts of translations into English of works for law and government: the aforementioned *Nova statuta*, Nicole Oresme's *De moneta*, London civic records and regulations, even brief ecclesiastical constitutions.[62] Nor is that to assert that this scribe was himself the author of those translations to which his handwriting is the only witness—though of course that is possible. Rather, it is simply to note that he was moving in a milieu, linked to London's knightly and mercantile circles, especially the mayor, Sir Thomas Cook, and his secretary, John Vale, where such translations were made and read of many works of law and government, not only of Littleton's *Tenures*.[63] A question for further research, perhaps through stylometrics, dialectology, or the study of methods of translating, would be whether the translations of *Tenures*, *Natura brevium*, and *Nova statuta* were an interrelated project or one person's work.

The Hammond Scribe was originally of interest for the evidence his manuscripts gave of the transmission of *The Canterbury Tales*, in which his attempts to solve problematic gaps in the text are intriguing, and of Lydgate's poems.[64] With the addition to his output of translations of Littleton's *Tenures* and the old *Natura brevium*, it is his writing of works of everyday use, for various professions and activities, that becomes more prominent. In this, his output is typical of writing in English done in the second half of the 1400s, when there was an ever-growing use of English for law, as here, precedent, heraldry, military advice, civic rules, political thought, to say nothing of everyday administrative accounts and letters. These volumes serve a distinctive set of interests and might be compared to the series of legal works, some in law French, some in English translation, some with French and translation side-by-side, printed by John Rastell between around 1513/14 and 1531, including the later translation afresh of Littleton's *Tenures*, in order to serve the "commyn welth".[65] The Hammond Scribe's copying of works of common law in translation marks that shift to English for everyday writing decades before Rastell, even for the rarefied world of the law.[66]

University of Oxford

Acknowledgments
I am grateful to the Leverhulme Trust, which funded the research of which this is part, and to Dan Haywood and Charlotte Ross for advice.

NOTES

1. Eleanor Prescott Hammond, "Two British Museum Manuscripts (Harley 2251 and Adds. 34360): A Contribution to the Bibliography of John Lydgate," *Anglia* 28 (1905):1–28; Eleanor Prescott Hammond, "Some Notes and Additions to 'Two British Museum Manuscripts etc.'" *Anglia* 28 (1905):143–144; Eleanor Prescott Hammond, "A Scribe of Chaucer," *Modern Philology* 27 (1929):27–33.
2. A. I. Doyle, "An Unrecognized Piece of *Piers the Ploughman's Creed* and Other Work by Its Scribe," *Speculum* 34 (1959):428–436; R. F. Green, "Notes on Some Manuscripts of Hoccleve's Regement of Princes," *British Library Journal* 4 (1978):37–41; Linne R. Mooney, "More Manuscripts Written by a Chaucer Scribe," *Chaucer Review* 30 (1996):401–407; Linne R. Mooney, "A New Manuscript by the Hammond Scribe Discovered by Jeremy Griffiths," in *The English Medieval Book: Studies in Memory of Jeremy Griffiths*, ed. A.S.G. Edwards, Vincent Gillespie, and Ralph Hanna III (London: British Library, 2000), 113–123.
3. For dated works, see Hammond, "Scribe of Chaucer"; Daniel W. Mosser, "Dating the Manuscripts of the 'Hammond Scribe': What the Paper Evidence Tells Us," *Journal of the Early Book Society* 10 (2007):31–70, at 42–43; Linne R. Mooney, "The Scribe," in *Sex, Aging and Death in a Medieval Medical Compendium*, ed. M. Teresa Tavormina, 2 vols. (Tempe, AZ: Arizona Center for Medieval and Renaissance Studies, 2006), 1:55–63, at 55–56. For an overall range, Mooney, "More Manuscripts," suggests 1460–1488; Holly James-Maddocks, "Scribes and Booklets: The 'Trinity Anthologies' Reconsidered," in *Scribal Cultures in Late Medieval England: Essays in Honour of Linne R. Mooney*, ed. Margaret Connolly, Holly James-Maddocks, and Derek Pearsall (Woodbridge: Boydell, 2022), 146–179, at 147, suggests 1458–1480. One text in Worcester, Cathedral Library, MS F. 172, fol. 166r, which I have not seen myself, ends with a date, but the roman numeral is transcribed as "milesimo CCCCxlvij" by R. M. Thomson, *A Descriptive Catalogue of the Medieval Manuscripts in Worcester Cathedral Library* (Woodbridge, UK: Brewer, 2001), 115, which could conceivably be a date for translating or for copying, but as "milesimo cccxlvij" by Valerie Edden, *The Index of Middle English Prose: Handlist XV: Manuscripts in Midland Libraries* (Cambridge, UK: Brewer, 2000), 68. Either way, it could not be the date of the text being translated, as that is a set of constitutions of Robert Winchelsey, archbishop of Canterbury, who died in 1313.

4. As clarified by Mooney, "More Manuscripts," 405, correcting Margaret Lucille Kekewich, Colin Richmond, Anne F. Sutton, Livia Visser-Fuchs, and John L. Watts, eds., *The Politics of Fifteenth-Century England: John Vale's Book* (Stroud, UK: Sutton, 1995), 57, 107–112, which notes that this John Multon died in 1475. The Hammond Scribe is named Multon by Anthony Gross, *The Dissolution of the Lancastrian Kingship: Sir John Fortescue and the Crisis of Monarchy in Fifteenth-Century England* (Stamford, UK: Watkins, 1996), 105–122. Aage Brusendorff, *The Chaucer Tradition* (Copenhagen: Møller, 1925), 181, suggests that the heading to a poem in London, British Library [hereafter BL], MS Additional 34360, fol. 59r, "quod Richardown," might reveal his name; such a phrase does not appear in his other copy of the same poem in BL, MS Harley 2251, fol. 1r. But Mooney, "Scribe," 58, suggests that Richard Down was the brother-in-law of the Hammond Scribe's repeated patron or customer, Sir Thomas Cook.
5. The list appears in Linne R. Mooney, "New Manuscript," 113–114; Mooney, "Scribe," 56–57; and Holly James-Maddocks, "Scribes and Booklets," 147, n. 4. The list on the website by Linne Mooney, Simon Horobin, and Estelle Stubbs, *Late Medieval English Scribes*, Centre for Medieval Studies, 2011, www.medievalscribes.com [hereafter LMES], omits Oxford, Bodleian Library [hereafter BodL], MS Rawlinson D.913, fol. 43r–v. I am grateful to Linne R. Mooney and Holly James-Maddocks for confirming (personal communication, November 8, 2023) that they were not aware of further identifications made subsequent to those lists.
6. The earliest editions were Sir Thomas Littleton, *Tenores nouelli* (London: John Lettou and William de Machlinia, [1482/3]; STC 15719); Sir Thomas Littleton, *Tenores nouelli* (London: William de Machlinia, [ca. 1484]; STC 15720); and *Natura brevium* (London: Richard Pynson, [1494]; STC 18385), with a colophon in English but the rest in the original French. I follow the datings in Lotte Hellinga, *Catalogue of Books Printed in the XVth Century Now in the British Library (BMC). Part XI: England.* (Leiden, Netherlands: De Gruyter Brill, 2007), 16–17, 248–249, 252–253 (for Lettou and de Machlinia); and in Alan Coates, Kristian Jensen, Cristina Dondi, Bettina Wagner, and Helen Dixon, *A Catalogue of Books Printed in the Fifteenth Century Now in the Bodleian Library*, 6 vols. (Oxford; Oxford University Press, 2005), 4:1834 (for Pynson). See Joseph Henry Beale, *A Bibliography of Early English Law Books* (Cambridge, MA: Harvard University Press, 1926), T.3 to T.61, for an overview of the printing of these works, albeit the details are superseded by *STC*.

7. John H. Baker, *Collected Papers on English Legal History*, 3 vols. (Cambridge, UK: Cambridge University Press, 2013), 2:612, 621–622, 627–630, 633, and for copies, e.g., 616–617. For more on Littleton, see, e.g., Thomas Garden Barnes, *Shaping the Common Law: From Glanvill to Hale, 1188–1688*, ed. Allen D. Boyer (Stanford, CA: Stanford Law, 2008), 32–45; Margaret Hastings, *The Court of the Common Pleas in Fifteenth Century England* (Cornell, NY: Cornell University Press, 1947), 14, 30–34, 64, 76–77, 84–92, 187, 198.
8. E. J. Devereux, *A Bibliography of John Rastell* (Montreal: McGill-Queen's University Press, 1999), 111–112, 116, 139, 141 (nos. 14, 17, 34, 36: *Natura brevium* along with *Exposiciones terminorum*), 117–118 (nos. 18 and 19: Littleton). See STC 15759.5, 15760, 20701, 20703.3, 20703 (in fact two editions, according to Devereux).
9. John H. Baker and Jayne Ringrose, *A Catalogue of Legal Manuscripts in Cambridge University Library* (Woodbridge, UK: Boydell, 1996), 160, identify the translations as unique. Compare Coke's version as reprinted by Eugene Wambaugh, ed., *Littleton's Tenures in English* (Washington, DC: Byrne, 1903). As precise translations of technical works, the translations are very similar in legal lexis, but syntactical differences are frequent and go beyond what might have been updating, and there are larger divergences (e.g., passages printed by Coke, in Wambaugh, ed., *Littleton's Tenures in English*, 13–16, not in CUL, MS Ee.1.2, fol. 8r). The works are calendared also by Margaret Connolly, *The Index of Middle English Prose: Handlist XIX: Manuscripts in the University Library, Cambridge* (Dd–Oo) (Woodbridge, UK: Brewer, 2009), 82.
10. James-Maddocks, "Scribes and Booklets," 175.
11. His handwriting has been described most fully in Doyle, "Unrecognized Piece," 429–430.
12. Mooney, "More Manuscripts," 406, uses the lovely term "flying ascenders," though ascender is more often reserved for upright strokes on **b**, **d** and **h**.
13. For similar strokes by two contemporary scribes, see, e.g., BodL, MS Ashmole 396, fols. 24r, 91r, copied in Oxford around the third quarter of the 1400s.
14. *LMES* (see n. 5 above).
15. M. B. Parkes, *English Cursive Book Hands* (Oxford: Clarendon Press, 1969), commentary on plates 10.(iii) and 12.(ii).
16. E.g., Cambridge, University Library [hereafter CUL], MS Ee.1.2, fol. 61r, the first **v** in "surviveth"; or fol. 264r, l. 4, "writ"; ll. 9 and 12, "have"; 19, "vel". Some of the Hammond Scribe's manuscripts use a downward curling approach stroke on **v** and **w**: e.g., Cambridge, Trinity College [hereafter TCC], MS R.3.21, fols. 34r–49v, where he varies between

that and the upward approach stroke, even within lines (e.g., fol. 39r, l. 20, "a wey" and "wikkednesse"). On the value of "DIY digitization" for paleographical analysis of ductus, see my "A New Age of Photography: 'DIY Digitization' in Manuscript Studies," *Anglia* 139 (2021): 71–93, at 85.
17. In TCC, MS O.3.11, the Hammond Scribe's ascenders are sometimes so tall that they cross the ruling for the line above.
18. Hammond, "Scribe of Chaucer," 27.
19. Another of his manuscripts, London, College of Physicians, MS 388, differs in using the sigmoid **s** in word-final position.
20. E.g., CUL, MS Ee.1.2, fol. 17v, l. 10, "faire"; l. 11, "ferra". Compare, e.g., BL, MS Arundel 59, fol. 8v (on *LMES*), l. 3, "array"; l. 8, "verray".
21. E.g., word-final **t** in CUL, MS Ee.1.2, fol. 61r, l. 17, "without"; l. 30, "that"; or fol. 184r, in a sidenote "impedit". Compare, e.g., BL, MS Harley 372, fol. 80r (on *LMES*), in a sidenote "est".
22. E.g., CUL, MS Ee.1.2, fol. 61r, l. 22, "En"; l. 32, "Et" (overlapping with "duryng" above); or fol. 17v, at the start of a heading in display script "Explicit". Compare, e.g., London, Royal College of Physicians, MS 388, e.g., fol. 143r (on *LMES*), in the heading "Explicit" there in cursive handwriting
23. E.g., CUL, MS Ee.1.2, fol. 17v, ll. 10, 17, "Reu*e*rence". See Doyle, "Unrecognised Piece," 429–430.
24. For lists, see Hammond, "Two British Museum Manuscripts," 10; Hammond, "Scribe of Chaucer," 27; Doyle, "Unrecognised Piece," 429–430.
25. E.g., CUL, MS Ee.1.2, fol. 17v, l. 8, "bien"; l. 23 "triewe". The spelling <bien> is very frequent, e.g., three times on fol. 40v: l. 18, "vileynes that bien Regardaunt"; l. 21, "han bien seised"; l. 27 "bien named". On this feature, see Simon Horobin, "Linguistic Features of the Hammond Scribe," *Poetica* 51 (1999):1–10, at 5, and Lister M. Matheson, "The Dialect of the Hammond Scribe," in *Sex, Aging and Death in a Medieval Medical Compendium*, ed. M. Teresa Tavormina, 2 vols. (Tempe, AZ: Arizona Center for Medieval and Renaissance Studies, 2006), 1:65–93, at 74–76.
26. CUL, MS Ee.1.2, respectively fol. 15r, l. 13; and fol. 31v, l. 2. See Horobin, "Linguistic Features," 5–6.
27. CUL, MS Ee.1.2, respectively, e.g., fol. 8v, l. 14, "chirche"; fol. 13v, l. 1, "moche"; fol. 17v, l. 4, "nat"; fol. 8v, l. 5, "suche"; fol. 17v, l. 21, "to guyder"; fol. 13v, l. 23, "yit". For present-day English *not*, the spelling <nought> also appears rarely (e.g., fol. 13v, l. 24). This follows the checklists of Horobin, "Linguistic Features," 5–6, and for *together* Matheson, "Dialect," 73.

28. BL, MS Harley 4999, a copy of *Nova statuta* in English, has the same design. By contrast, TCC, MS O.3.11, has headings in the Hammond Scribe's cursive handwriting, sometimes in red ink.
29. For these terms, see Albert Derolez, *The Palaeography of Gothic Manuscript Books* (Cambridge, UK: Cambridge University Press, 2003), 21, 72–73.
30. E.g., CUL, MS Ee.1.2, f. 17v, l. 9, on the minims in "secundus". Something also goes awry with a (perhaps not needed) tick at the baseline on **b** biting with **e** in the first *"liber"* on this line.
31. E.g., CUL, MS Ee.1.12, fol. 17v, ll. 10, 17, "Homage". Compare, e.g., BL, MS Cotton Claudius A.viii, fol. 175r (on LMES), ll. 2 and 3, "Regale"; l. 12, "Regem".
32. E.g., CUL, MS Ee.1.2, fol. 17v, l. 9, word-initial **s** on "secundus" (though contrast the more canonical textualis of long **s** in "secundus" on fol. 52v, l. 10). Compare, e.g., London, College of Physicians, MS 388, fol. 245v, l. 5, **f** on "fabula".
33. CUL, MS Ee.1.2, fols. 166r–264r passim. Compare BL, MS Arundel 59, e.g., fol. 61r, for Latin annotations on Hoccleve. I thank Charlotte Ross for suggesting the likeness of layout with this MS.
34. Respectively BL, MS Harley 4999, and TCC, MS O.3.11, fols. 65r–67r.
35. Compare CUL, MS Ee.1.2, fol. 61r, with, e.g., BL, MS Addition 29901, fol. 10v. There are different, shorter line-fillers in TCC, MS O.3.11, fol. 100v.
36. CUL, MS Ee.1.2, does have sidenotes naming the writs discussed in *Natura brevium*.
37. Mosser, "Dating," 36, 42–43, and 63, fig. 8b, reproducing BL, MS Harley 4999, fol. 198v. Mosser describes the hand as topped by a six-pointed star, but I would describe it as a flower, given what looks like a central seed head. Baker and Ringrose, *Catalogue*, 160, likewise describe it as a flower in CUL, MS Ee.1.2. Neither Mosser nor Baker and Ringrose identify it in published collections of watermarks; nor could I.
38. Compare Mosser, "Dating," 62, reproducing one from TCC, MS O.3.11, fol. 52r.
39. Comparing, e.g., TCC, MS O.3.56, fol. 101v, where it is 98 of 141 sections as divided in the table of contents on fols. 121r–v (dated to the reign of Edward IV on fol. 124r); or, e.g., BodL, MS Rawl. C. 289, fol. 51r, which a later hand numbered as 85 of 120 sections (though the main scribe is datable palaeographically to the third quarter of the 1400s).
40. There are no quire signatures or leaf signatures remaining, but the loose binding, replaced in 1954, makes it easy to see the quiring. The collation is: I^{20} (1st cancelled or wanting; 20th remounted and damaged),

II–XIV^{20}, XV^6 (5th cancelled). He uses quires of twenty leaves, with one shorter to end the copying of a text in BL, MS Arundel 59, i.e., fols. 1r–89v = I–II^{20}, III^{20} (1 leaf cancelled), IV^{20}, V^{12} (Hoccleve, *The Regiment of Princes*) | VI–VII^{12}, VIII^1 (Lydgate and Burgh, *The Secrees of Old Philisoffres*), according to Brusendorff, *Chaucer Tradition*, 181–182.

41. For this procedure, see Daniel Wakelin, *Immaterial Texts in Late Medieval England: Making English Literary Manuscripts, 1400–1500* (Cambridge, UK: Cambridge University Press, 2022), 119–120.
42. E.g., switches at CUL, MS Ee.1.2, fols. 6r–v, 86v–87r.
43. E.g., BodL, MS Laud misc. 557 fols. 66v–67v, of Lydgate's *The Siege of Thebes*, discussed in Wakelin, *Immaterial Texts*, 79–80. Roger Thorney (d. 1515), whose ownership note is on BodL, MS Laud misc. 557, fol. 66r, also owned TCC, MS R.3.21, containing copying by the Hammond Scribe. Thorney was part of London's mercantile elite, like the drapers who owned books by the Hammond Scribe. See Kathleen L. Scott, "Past Ownership: Evidence of Book Ownership by English Merchants in the Later Middle Ages," in *Makers and Users of Medieval Books: Essays in Honour of A.S.G. Edwards*, ed. Carol M. Meale and Derek Pearsall (Cambridge, UK: Brewer, 2014), 150–177, at 164.
44. CUL, MS Ee.1.2, fols. 264r–v and 266r–v. The intervening fol. 265 has been lost, leaving only a stub. (The modern librarian's foliation includes this lost leaf, as is common with foliation by Cambridge University Library.)
45. Charlotte Ross points out to me a similar interruption at a tidy page break in the copying of *Reson and Sensuallyte* in Oxford, Bodleian Library, MS Fairfax 16. Was such tidy pausing at page breaks standard scribal practice to avoid disruptive changes of handwriting, ink, or layout mid-page, if they or another scribe were ever able to resume?
46. BL, MS Harley 4999, fol. 227v. The following, ruled but originally blank fol. 228r at some stage became detached and is remounted by conservators, but so has been the cognate fol. 217 at the start of the quire, so this does seem originally to have been the leaf following the final page of text on fol. 227v.
47. Kathleen Kennedy, "Prosopography of the Book and Politics of Legal Language in Late Medieval England," *Journal of British Studies* 53 (2014):565–587, at 571–572, 583–584, suggests that the translation of Nova statuta copied incompletely in BL, MS Harley 4999, also existed in some other lost copy where it would have ended a little later, in 20 Henry VI. She suggests that the translation would have ended there, because she considers it identical to a translation printed in 1534, which changes the phrasing of its headings in that year 20 Henry VI. But comparing the passages that Kennedy, "Prosopography," 585–587,

helpfully prints in parallel from MS Harley 4999 and the 1534 print reveals many differences in syntax and vocabulary, whereas the likenesses are those which might be expected of two renderings of the same, highly formulaic legal text. Similar degrees of difference and likeness emerge in comparing, e.g., the same passage in BL, MS Additional 81292, fol. 259r–v, and what was formerly Schøyen collection, MS 1355, fol. 151v (sold at Christie's London, June 11, 2024, lot 39; I thank Eugenio Donadoni for the chance to examine it before its sale). I have compared only selected excerpts, but my preliminary hypothesis is that these three MSS and the 1534 print of *Nova statuta* in English offer four separate translations. (As it happens, the translation in BL, MS Additional 81292, ends, in a way that looks planned, at chapter 12 again of the year 20 Henry VI.)
48. Doyle, "Unrecognised Piece," 428–429, 433, describing and reproducing BL, MS Harley 78, fol. 3r, one of a collection of fragments gathered by the antiquary John Stow in the 1500s. This page begins with the word "And," which suggests that it followed other leaves of the poem.
49. CUL, MS Ee.1.2, fol. 2v, l. 30.
50. For the date and MSS of *Natura brevium*, see Baker and Ringrose, *Catalogue*, 160.
51. CUL, MS Ee.1.2, fols. 164r–165r.
52. John H. Baker, *The Men of Court 1440 to 1550: A Prosopography of the Inns of Court and Chancery and the Courts of Law*, 2 vols. (London: Selden Society, 2012), 2:1020–1023; John H. Baker, "Littleton [Lyttleton], Sir Thomas (d. 1481)," *Oxford Dictionary of National Biography* (Oxford: Oxford University Press, 2004), https://doi.org/10.1093/ref:odnb/16787. Wambaugh, ed., *Littleton's Tenures in English*, xlix, lix, suggests that *Tenures* was written for the second son, Richard.
53. Baker, *Collected Papers*, 2:612, suggests ca. 1460; *ODNB*, s.n. Littleton [Lyttleton], Sir Thomas (d. 1481), suggests a decade before Littleton's death in 1481.
54. CUL, MS Ee.1.2, fol. 165v; Baker and Ringrose, *Catalogue*, 160.
55. Baker and Ringrose, *Catalogue*, 117, list early manuscripts.
56. Cambridge, St. John's College, MS C.13, discussed by Baker and Ringrose, *Catalogue*, 117; James-Maddocks, "Trinity Anthologies," 159 and fig. 5; Strickland Gibson, *Early Oxford Bindings* (Oxford: Bibliographical Society, 1903), 23 (no. 24) and pl. XV, XVI. The connections are through the artists and scribes who collaborated on BodL, MS Douce 322, and TCC, MS R.3.21, the latter featuring the Hammond Scribe (as noted above).
57. CUL, MS Mm.5.2, and BL, MS Harley 5146, noted by Baker and Ringrose, *Catalogue*, 117, 490–493. MS Mm.5.2 is not included in P. R. Robinson, *Catalogue of Dated and Datable Manuscripts c. 737–1600 in*

Cambridge Libraries, 2 vols. (Cambridge, UK: Brewer, 1988), nor MS Harley 5156 in Andrew G. Watson, *Catalogue of Dated and Datable Manuscripts c.700–1600 in the British Library*, 2 vols. (London: British Library, 1979).

58. J. Conway Davies, *Catalogue of Manuscripts in the Library of the Honourable Society of the Inner Temple*, 3 vols. (London: Oxford University Press, 1972), 2:964, dates London, Inner Temple, MS Barrington 82, to the mid-1400s, but Baker, *Collected Papers*, 2:693–694, reviewing Conway Davies, and N. R. Ker, *Medieval Manuscripts in British Libraries*, 5 vols. (Oxford: Oxford University Press, 1969–2002), 1:88, date it palaeographically "s.xv.ex." As far as I can tell, London, Inner Temple, MS Barrington 82 is by the scribe who copied most of London, National Archives, E 164/11, the *Nova statuta* in French and English datable ca. 1495/6, illustrated by P. R. Robinson, *Catalogue of Dated and Datable Manuscripts c. 888–1600 in London Libraries*, 2 vols. (London: British Library, 2003), no. 132, pl. 226, 227. Ker, *Medieval Manuscripts*, 1:19, 190–191, notes a likeness between the main scribe of E 164/11 and of many other copies of *Nova statuta* and other legal texts; J. J. Griffiths, "The Production of Manuscripts in London at the End of the Fifteenth Century and the Introduction of Printing, with Particular Attention to Copies of the Statutes" (unpublished manuscript, 1979, in keeping of Daniel Wakelin), the winning essay of the Gordon Duff Prize, 1979, 3–4, and Robinson, *Dated and Datable... London*, no. 132, confirm that.

59. CUL, MS Ee.1.2, fol. 2r. Another early manuscript of *Tenures* contains an ascription to Littleton: San Marino, CA, Huntington Library, MS Ellesmere 34.B.60, fol. 132r.

60. Printed by Wambaugh, ed., *Littleton's Tenures in English*, xlvii–lvii, with books on liv–lvi.

61. Mary Dormer Harris, ed., *The Coventry Leet Book*, 4 vols., EETS os 134, 135, 138, 146 (London: Kegan Paul, Trench, Trübner, 1907–1913), 235 (Littleton's appointment); and, e.g., Harris, ed., *Coventry*, 263–264, 266, 271 (intermittent appearances). By coincidence, Anthony Fitzherbert, author of *La novel natura brevium*, a replacement for the older *Natura brevium* copied in French and in English translation in this manuscript discussed here, was also a later recorder of Coventry; see J.H. Baker, Fitzherbert, Sir Anthony (c. 1470–1538), *Oxford Dictionary of National Biography* (Oxford: Oxford University Press, 2004), https://doi.org/10.1093/ref:odnb/9602.

62. TCC, MS O.3.11, calendared by Linne R. Mooney, *The Index of Middle English Prose: Handlist VIII: Manuscripts in the Library of Trinity College, Cambridge* (Cambridge, UK: Brewer, 1995), 109–114; BL, MS Cotton

Claudius A.viii, fols. 175r–197v; BL, MS Harley 4999; Worcester, Cathedral Library, MS F. 172, fols. 155r–166r (only; the rest of this MS consists of devotional prose). Littleton's will bequeathed "*Constitutions Provincial*" to Halesowen Abbey (as transcribed by Wambaugh, ed., *Littleton's Tenures in English*, liv), but the phrasing sounds like William Lyndwood's larger collection.
63. On those links, see Mooney, "More Manuscripts," 404; Mooney, "A New Manuscript," 114; Kekewich, Richmond, Sutton, Visser-Fuchs, and Watts, eds.,, *John Vale's Book*, 107–112. The Hammond Scribe's books owned by Vale or naming Cook are TCC, MS O.3.11; TCC, MS R.14.52; BL, MS Harley 2251; and Worcester, Cathedral Library, MS F. 172. Littleton sat on a commission of *oyer et terminer* which tried Cook in summer 1468 (Hastings, *Court of Common Pleas*, 88–89), but that reflects Littleton's prominent legal position rather than proving a particular connection between the men. Also, Littleton is buried in Worcester Cathedral, where one manuscript by the Hammond Scribe copied for John Vale ended up, but this is a coincidence, as this manuscript, MS F.172, entered the cathedral's library only in the eighteenth century from a local antiquary (Thomson, *Worcester Cathedral Library*, 116).
64. Hammond "Scribe of Chaucer," 32–33.
65. Rastell's words quoted by Kathleen Tonry, *Agency and Intention in English Print, 1476–1526* (Turnhout, Belgium: Brepols, 2016), 55–56. For a full listing, see Devereux, *Bibliography*, 88–93, 101–104, 110–112, 115–118, 139, 141–152, 163–166 (nos. 3–4, 10–11, 13–14, 16–19, 34, 36–45, 50–52). Coincidentally, Rastell also began his legal career in Coventry (Devereux, *Bibliography*, 5–6).
66. Kennedy, "Prosopography," 566, makes a similar point about the translations of *Nova statuta*.

WORKS CITED

Manuscripts

Cambridge, St. John's College, MS C.13.
Cambridge, Trinity College, MS O.3.11.
Cambridge, Trinity College, MS O.3.56.
Cambridge, Trinity College, MS R.3.21.
Cambridge, Trinity College, MS R.14.52.
Cambridge, University Library, MS Ee.1.2.
Cambridge, University Library, MS Mm.5.2.
London, British Library, MS Additional 29901.

London, British Library, MS Additional 34360.
London, British Library, MS Additional 81292.
London, British Library, MS Arundel 59.
London, British Library, MS Cotton Claudius A.viii.
London, British Library, MS Harley 78.
London, British Library, MS Harley 372.
London, British Library, MS Harley 2251.
London, British Library, MS Harley 4999.
London, British Library, MS Harley 5146.
London, British Library, MS Royal 17.D.xv.
London, Inner Temple, MS Barrington 82.
London, National Archives, E 164/11.
London, Royal College of Physicians MS 388.
Oxford, Bodleian Library, MS Fairfax 16.
Oxford, Bodleian Library, MS Laud misc. 557.
Oxford, Bodleian Library, MS Rawlinson D.913.
San Marino, CA, Huntington Library, MS Ellesmere 34.B.60.
formerly Schøyen collection, MS 1355.
Worcester, Cathedral Library MS F.172.

Secondary Sources

Baker, John H. *The Men of Court 1440 to 1550: A Prosopography of the Inns of Court and Chancery and the Courts of Law*. 2 vols. London: Selden Society, 2012.

———.*Collected Papers on English Legal History*, 3 vols. Cambridge, UK: Cambridge University Press, 2013.

———. "Fitzherbert, Sir Anthony (c. 1470–1538)." *Oxford Dictionary of National Biography*. Oxford: Oxford University Press, 2004. https://doi.org/10.1093/ref:odnb/9602.

———. "Littleton [Lyttleton], Sir Thomas (d. 1481)." *Oxford Dictionary of National Biography*. Oxford: Oxford University Press, 2004. https://doi.org/10.1093/ref:odnb/16787.

———, and Jayne Ringrose. *A Catalogue of Legal Manuscripts in Cambridge University Library*. Woodbridge, UK: Boydell, 1996.

Barnes, Thomas Garden. *Shaping the Common Law: From Glanvill to Hale, 1188–1688*, ed. Allen D. Boyer. Stanford, CA: Stanford Law, 2008.

Beale, Joseph Henry. *A Bibliography of Early English Law Books*. Cambridge, MA: Harvard University Press, 1926.

Brusendorff, Aage. *The Chaucer Tradition*. Copenhagen: Møller, 1925.

Coates, Alan, Kristian Jensen, Cristina Dondi, Bettina Wagner, and Helen

Dixon. *A Catalogue of Books Printed in the Fifteenth Century Now in the Bodleian Library*. 6 vols. Oxford: Oxford University Press, 2005.

Connolly, Margaret. *The Index of Middle English Prose: Handlist XIX: Manuscripts in the University Library, Cambridge (Dd–Oo)*. Woodbridge, UK: Brewer, 2009.

Conway Davies, J. *Catalogue of Manuscripts in the Library of the Honourable Society of the Inner Temple*. 3 vols. London: Oxford University Press, 1972.

Derolez, Albert. *The Palaeography of Gothic Manuscript Books*. Cambridge, UK: Cambridge University Press, 2003.

Devereux, E. J. *A Bibliography of John Rastell*. Montreal: McGill-Queen's University Press, 1999.

Doyle, A. I. "An Unrecognized Piece of Piers *the Ploughman's Creed* and Other Work by Its Scribe." *Speculum* 34 (1959):428–436.

Edden, Valerie. *The Index of Middle English Prose: Handlist XV: Manuscripts in Midland Libraries*. Cambridge, UK: Brewer, 2000.

Gibson, Strickland. *Early Oxford Bindings*. Oxford: Bibliographical Society, 1903.

Green, R.F. "Notes on Some Manuscripts of Hoccleve's *Regement of Princes*." *British Library Journal* 4 (1978):37–41.

Griffiths, J. J. "The Production of Manuscripts in London at the End of the Fifteenth Century and the Introduction of Printing, with Particular Attention to Copies of the Statutes." Unpublished manuscript, 1979 (in keeping of Daniel Wakelin).

Gross, Anthony. *The Dissolution of the Lancastrian Kingship: Sir John Fortescue and the Crisis of Monarchy in Fifteenth-Century England*. Stamford, UK: Watkins, 1996.

Hammond, Eleanor Prescott. "Two British Museum Manuscripts (Harley 2251 and Adds. 34360): A Contribution to the Bibliography of John Lydgate." *Anglia* 28 (1905):1–28.

———. "Some Notes and Additions to 'Two British Museum Manuscripts etc.'" *Anglia* 28 (1905):143–144.

———. "A Scribe of Chaucer." *Modern Philology* 27 (1929):27–33.

Harris, Mary Dormer, ed. *The Coventry Leet Book*, 4 vols. EETS os 134, 135, 138, 146. London: Kegan Paul, Trench, Trübner, 1907–1913.

Hastings, Margaret, *The Court of the Common Pleas in Fifteenth Century England*. Cornell, NY: Cornell University Press, 1947.

Hellinga, Lotte. *Catalogue of Books Printed in the XVth Century Now in the British Library (BMC). Part XI: England*. Leiden, Netherlands: De Gruyter Brill, 2007.

Horobin, Simon. "Linguistic Features of the Hammond Scribe." *Poetica* 51 (1999):1–10.

James-Maddocks, Holly. "Scribes and Booklets: The 'Trinity Anthologies' Reconsidered." In *Scribal Cultures in Late Medieval England: Essays in Honour of Linne R. Mooney*, ed. Margaret Connolly, Holly James-Maddocks, and Derek Pearsall, 146–179. Woodbridge, UK: Boydell, 2022.

Kekewich, Margaret Lucille, Colin Richmond, Anne F. Sutton, Livia Visser-Fuchs, and John L. Watts, eds. *The Politics of Fifteenth-Century England: John Vale's Book*. Stroud, UK: Sutton, 1995.

Kennedy, Kathleen. "Prosopography of the Book and Politics of Legal Language in Late Medieval England." *Journal of British Studies* 53 (2014):565–587.

Ker, N. R. *Medieval Manuscripts in British Libraries*. 5 vols. Oxford: Oxford University Press, 1969–2002.

Littleton, Sir Thomas. *Tenores nouelli*. London: John Lettou and William de Machlinia, [ca. 1482/3]; STC 15719.

———. *Tenores nouelli*. London: William de Machlinia, [ca. 1484]; STC 15720.

Matheson, Lister M. "The Dialect of the Hammond Scribe." In *Sex, Aging and Death in a Medieval Medical Compendium*, ed. M. Teresa Tavormina, 1:65–93. 2 vols. Tempe, AZ: Arizona Center for Medieval and Renaissance Studies, 2006.

Mooney, Linne R. *The Index of Middle English Prose: Handlist VIII: Manuscripts in the Library of Trinity College, Cambridge*. Cambridge, UK: Brewer, 1995.

———. "More Manuscripts Written by a Chaucer Scribe." *Chaucer Review* 30 (1996):401–407.

———. "A New Manuscript by the Hammond Scribe Discovered by Jeremy Griffiths." In *The English Medieval Book: Studies in Memory of Jeremy Griffiths*, ed. A.S.G. Edwards, Vincent Gillespie, and Ralph Hanna III, 113–123. London: British Library, 2000.

———. 'The Scribe." In *Sex, Aging and Death in a Medieval Medical Compendium*, ed. M. Teresa Tavormina, 1:55–63. 2 vols. Tempe, AZ: Arizona Center for Medieval and Renaissance Studies, 2006.

———, Simon Horobin, and Estelle Stubbs. *Late Medieval English Scribes*. Centre for Medieval Studies, 2011. www.medievalscribes.com.

Mosser, Daniel W. "Dating the Manuscripts of the 'Hammond Scribe': What the Paper Evidence Tells Us." *Journal of the Early Book Society* 10 (2007):31–70.

Natura brevium. London: Richard Pynson, [1494]; STC 18385.

Parkes, M. B. *English Cursive Book Hands*. Oxford: Clarendon Press, 1969.

Robinson, P. R. *Catalogue of Dated and Datable Manuscripts c. 737–1600 in Cambridge Libraries*. 2 vols. Cambridge, UK: Brewer, 1988.

———. *Catalogue of Dated and Datable Manuscripts c. 888–1600 in London Libraries*. 2 vols. London: British Library, 2003.
Scott, Kathleen L. "Past Ownership: Evidence of Book Ownership by English Merchants in the Later Middle Ages." In *Makers and Users of Medieval Books: Essays in Honour of A.S.G. Edwards*, ed. Carol M. Meale and Derek Pearsall, 150–177. Cambridge, UK: Brewer, 2014.
Thomson, R. M. *A Descriptive Catalogue of the Medieval Manuscripts in Worcester Cathedral Library*. Woodbridge, UK: Brewer, 2001.
Tonry, Kathleen. *Agency and Intention in English Print, 1476–1526*. Turnhout, Belgium: Brepols, 2016.
Wakelin, Daniel. *Immaterial Texts in Late Medieval England: Making English Literary Manuscripts, 1400–1500*. Cambridge, UK: Cambridge University Press, 2022.
———. "A New Age of Photography: 'DIY Digitization' in Manuscript Studies," *Anglia* 139 (2021): 71–93
Wambaugh, Eugene, ed. *Littleton's Tenures in English*. Washington, DC: Byrne, 1903.
Watson, Andrew G. *Catalogue of Dated and Datable Manuscripts c. 700–1600 in the British Library*. 2 vols. London: British Library, 1979.

Nicole Gilles and the Turquam-Gilles Manuscript and Printed Book Collection, ca. 1499

SARAH DYER MAGLEBY

Nicole Gilles (d. 1503), a notary and secretary to King Louis XI and comptroller of King Charles VIII's treasury, was a known historian and bibliophile who accrued a substantial book collection throughout his lifetime.[1] Gilles's enthusiasm for books and book collecting becomes apparent through examination of notations he wrote in the surviving books identified as owned by him; his relationship with Antoine Vérard, *libraire de Paris*; his own book projects, including the *Chronique et annales de France*, which he authored, and his potential printing interests; and, most important, the manuscript and book collection described in the estate inventory of Gilles's wife, Marie, a prominent member of the Turquam family.[2] The extensive list of books detailed and evaluated in the family's inventory, completed over a year following Marie's death, unveils this couple's excitement in acquiring manuscripts as well as printed books; printing was a relatively new technology during their lifetimes.[3] This study explores the bourgeois book collection of Gilles and Marie, highlighting both extant manuscripts and the select rooms in which they were stored. This analysis reveals this couple's interests in book printing and binding, acquiring secondhand manuscripts alongside the latest printed books, separating their finest manuscripts and printed works for special appraisal, and commissioning brand-new manuscripts.

Following Marie's death on September 7, 1498, notaries and appraisers under the direction of Jean Turquam, Marie's brother, compiled a postmortem inventory of this couple's three residences in and outside Paris, which they completed in November 1499.[4] No inventory exists for Gilles specifically, but the objects listed would have been owned by Marie and Gilles together, even though Marie's death was the catalyst for creating this document. Indeed, the Turquam-Gilles family owned many other unlisted objects, either gone from the household before the notaries drew up the inventory, missed by the notaries, purposely excluded by the homeowners, or purchased following 1499, so this document captures only a partially reliable, frozen snapshot of a specific moment of Marie and Gilles's home. This twenty-six-folio document, though missing its preface, reveals that Marie and Gilles furnished their households with dozens of tapestries and textiles, precious metalwork, numerous painted and sculpted images, and, most important for this study, an extensive library.

In drafting the inventory, the notaries documented the couple's religious and secular book collection. In November 1499, the total number of books notaries identified amounted to over 116 items: fifty-six printed books, twenty-nine handwritten manuscripts, thirty unspecified books, and one scroll containing a genealogy of the kings of France. Unfortunately, these calculations are not entirely conclusive, even with precise numbers of books listed in the inventory, as the notaries sometimes employed more general terms or phrases to describe an unspecified number of books—such as "a bundle" or "other small volumes."[5] An exact calculation of the books belonging to Marie and Gilles falls even further from complete exactitude as other factors contributed to the number of manuscripts and printed books owned by the family at any given moment. For instance, some books may have been gifted, sold, borrowed by others, or misplaced before the inventory's creation following Marie's death. In addition, Gilles did not die until July 10, 1503, so any books purchased or commissioned after the inventory's completion date were likely not present.

According to the Turquam-Gilles inventory and other surviving documents, Gilles and Marie owned three households in France. The first two residences were found outside Paris, the *hôtel des Tournelles* in Chelles-Sainte-Baupteur and the *maison de Mesly* in Créteil, with the latter acquired by Gilles sometime in 1486.[6] Their Parisian residence was named the *hôtel du Moustier* and located in the parish of Saint Paul on the rue Saint Antoine and rue du Roi de Sicile, with a garden off the rue de Petit marivaux (modern rue Pavée) in Paris (Fig. 1). The inventory of Ma-

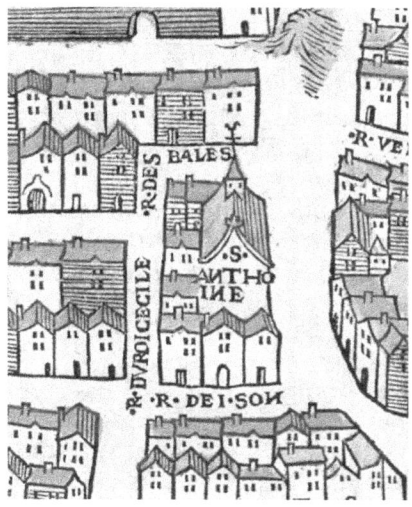

Figure 1. Section of houses between the rue du Roi de Sicile and rue Saint Antoine in Paris, from the plan by Truschet and Hoyau, ca. 1550, Basel University Library, Kartenslg AA 124. Photo: Basel University Library.

rie and Gilles's Parisian residence on the rue Saint Antoine and rue du Roi de Sicile fills twenty-two of the inventory's twenty-six folios, making it their most prominent household, at least in 1499.[7] The home was composed of two main buildings, one outwardly facing rue Saint Antoine and the other overlooking the rue du Roi de Sicile, surmounted by an attic, known as a *grenier*.[8] These two main structures were connected, and the home had views of a courtyard, garden, and stable. Le Maresquier-Kesteloot incorrectly describes this home as eleven rooms and spaces, with a range of storage rooms called "*comptoirs, galleries ou garde-robes*" (workrooms, galleries, or storage rooms).[9] While there are many storage rooms within this home, the *hôtel* apparently included seventeen main rooms (*chambres, salles, saletes*, and a *grenier*; that is, rooms, large and small reception rooms, and an attic), multiple smaller storage rooms (*comptoirs, galleries*, and *garde-robes*, or workrooms, galleries, and storage rooms), a kitchen, a stable, a treading mill, and a "*boutique*" (also called a *comptoir*) for public business, explicitly described as Gilles's by the notaries.

Three rooms of Marie and Gilles's Parisian home contained this couple's extensive library.[10] These spaces appear to have been primarily dedicated to housing their collected works, as most other objects in these areas were seemingly not as significant—furniture, stored items, or small decorative works. Additionally, each room contained a specific category of books, with only slight overlap in a few cases. The separation of unbound books, printed books and less expensive manuscripts, and luxury manuscripts denotes that Gilles and Marie organized their collection in a strategic and methodical manner.

Four books from the collection are known to be still in existence. They have been identified from Gilles's signature, but not all are recorded in the inventory: a compendium of French histories titled *Origo Francorum seu Chronicon Francorum* (*The Origin of the Franks or the Chronicle of the Franks*) bound with a contemporary legal document (Bern, Burgerbibliothek, cod. 70), a manual of Christian instruction known as *Le doctrinal des simples gens* (*The Doctrinal of the Common People*, Paris, BnF, Ms. fr. 17088), an Old French romance called *Le roman d'Alexandre* (Paris, BnF, Ms. fr. 789), and a French version of Ovid's *Metamorphoses* titled *Ovide moralisé* (Rome, Biblioteca Apostolica Vaticana, MSS Reg.lat.1686).[11] While other books may have survived through time, they are either unsigned (making their attribution difficult) or are still undiscovered. An examination of the three rooms and the collective and individual extant and nonextant books within them gives insight into Gilles and Marie's taste in books, how and where a bourgeois family would have kept popular and luxury books and manuscripts, and how these texts shaped the identity of Gilles, Marie, and their familial status.

Room 1: Bundles of Books

On Tuesday, November 26, 1499, the notaries arrived at the first of Gilles and Marie's libraries after three days of recording the estate inventory. The notaries first catalogued and evaluated all of the family's moveable furniture in the large chamber. The furniture in this room is described as rather impressive compared to other equivalent spaces; it included a chair with images of the Annunciation, a couch with a crest—all indications of this room's fineness and importance.

Following these relatively lengthy descriptions of furniture, the notaries arrived at the most significant items in the room: several printed books. This large chamber contained the fewest books in Gilles and Marie's collection. Two of the entries include multiple titles that are unbound in printed form, making it challenging to determine the exact number of books in this space. Six entries in the inventory provide basic information on the following works:

1. *(A lettre form) Item les* Croniques de France *en parchemin en grant volume et lettre d'impression non relyees prisees ensemble 6 livres parisis.*[12]

   [(In gothic script) Item, the *Croniques de France* on parchment, in a large volume, and printed, unbound, priced together at 6 *livres parisis.*]

2. *Item deux volumes en papier non relyez escriptz en lettre d'impression de Josephus faisant mencion de* la bataille Judayque *prises 24 solz parisis.*

   [Item, two volumes on paper, unbound, printed, of Josephus, making mention of *la bataille Judayque*, priced at 24 *solz parisis.*]

3. *Item une bote des livres de Cydrac imprimez en papier et y a sept livres en grant volumes prises ensemble 28 solz parisis.*

[Item, a bundle of the *Livres de Sydrach*, printed on paper, and there are seven books in large volumes, priced together at 28 *solz parisis*.]

4. *Item une aultre livre de Vincent L'istorial en grant volume aussy escript en lettre d'impression prisee 32 solz parisis.*

[Item, another book of Vincent's *Miroir historial* in a large volume, also printed, priced at 32 *solz parisis*.]

5. *Item les quatre volumes des Croniques Froissart escript en lettre d'impression en grant volume prises ensemble 64 solz parisis.*

[Item, the four volumes of the *Croniques de Froissart*, printed in a large volume, priced together at 64 *solz parisis*.]

6. *Item une bote de livres escriptz en lettre d'impression en papier non relies appellez les Cent nouvelles nouvelles en petit volume prisee ensemble 28 solz parisis.*

[Item, a bundle of books, printed on paper, unbound, called the *Cent nouvelles nouvelles*, in a small volume, priced together at 28 *solz parisis*.]

Aside from the furniture, this room's only other items were "*XXX mains de papier blanc en grant volume.*" A "*main de papier*" equaled twenty-five sheets of paper, meaning that there were 750 blank sheets in total, possibly prepped and ready for printing additional copies of previous projects or in anticipation of future publications.

The size of this room is significant, as the notaries described it as *grant* (large), a word only used for two of the rooms in the home. While there is enough furniture to fill this room, it is odd how few small, portable items are listed. It is possible that this room could have functioned as a workspace for Gilles in his printing pursuits, as bourgeois homes often operated as commercial spaces as well as domestic ones.[13] Notably, no binding tools are listed alongside the furnishings of the room (some bookbinding tools appear in the last room containing other books), so this space could have served more for storage of his projects. Overall, the inclusion of the fine furniture suggests the importance of this space. More significantly, the bundles of unbound books and blank paper indicate Gilles's engagement with this room, potentially for his hobby of making books, not just writing them.

Further evidence that this was a workroom, or potentially a working storeroom, for some of Gilles's side projects is shown by the book titles included in the room's listing. Roger Doucet did significant work on Parisian libraries of the sixteenth century, including Gilles's substantial book collection.[14] Doucet transcribed Gilles's entire library in the Turquam-Gilles inventory and connected each listed manuscript and printed book with extent texts and their published dates (if possible), in order to inform readers of the exact editions that would have been held in these libraries. Doucet identifies Gilles's books in this room in the following manner:

1. *Chroniques de France* called *chroniques de Saint-Denys, depuis les Troyens jusqu'à la mort de Charles VII, en 1461*. Paris, 1476, 3 vol.

2. Flavius Josephus. *De la bataille judaïque*, trans. Claude de Seyssel. Paris, 1492.

3. Sydrach. *La fontaine de toutes sciences du philosophe Sydrach*. Paris, 1486.

4. Vincent de Beauvais. *Le ... volume de Vincent, Miroir historial*. Paris, 1495–1496, 5 vol.[15]

5. Froissart. *Le ...volume de Froissart des Croniques de France*. Paris, no date, 4 vol.

6. *Les cent nouvelles nouvelles*. Paris, 1486.[16]

Doucet does not identify the printers of these books, but according to him, all except the first book appear to have been printed by Antoine Vérard, an early Parisian *libraire* and publisher at the forefront of hybrid manuscripts and printed books. It is likely that Doucet is incorrect concerning the first book, as Vérard also published a *Chroniques de France* in 1493, emphasizing Gilles's ties to the *libraire* through the printed works in this room.[17] Consideration of book printing in the late fifteenth century and Gilles's relationship and collaborations with Antoine Vérard offers further insight to the grouping of these texts, as several of these editions were products of a collaboration between this *libraire* and Gilles.

Vérard and Gilles had a significant relationship in the book industry.[18] Surviving documents and extant printed books reveal that Gilles collaborated on several book projects with Vérard, including the *Cent nouvelles nouvelles* and *Livres de Sydrach*. Vérard's early life is undocumented, but his name first appears in a Book of Hours from September 12, 1485.[19] According to this book's colophon, Vérard was already an established bookseller, making him one of the earliest *libraires* specializing in printed books in France.[20] The colophon also notes Vérard owned two shops in Paris, one on the Notre Dame bridge, part of the main quarter for book production, and the other in the Palais de la Cité, in front of the Sainte-Chapelle.[21] He is most famously known as the first bookseller to print a Book of Hours, of which he printed over eighty editions between 1485 and 1512. His productions certainly became a standard of elegance and a template for those who followed him in French production of this type of book.[22]

Vérard was a major bookseller in Paris and to the royal family, thus establishing a prestigious reputation. He became known for printing luxury books on vellum, which proved to be special volumes, or deluxe copies.[23] Vérard found in Gilles a financial backer who would support his early pursuits, and several documents clarify their relationship. Most of these documents are notarial accounts. One from May 1491 concerns certain amounts of money that Vérard owed and paid to Gilles.[24] Another document, dated February 3, 1490, explains that Vérard was required to deliver ninety-three missals for *"l'usage de Noyon"* to Pierre Ysabeau for Easter, and that if he failed to produce them, the sum of 300 *livres tournois*, which he received from Ysabeau, would not be repaid to Gilles, from whom Vérard had borrowed funds. Vérard ultimately did not meet this deadline but pledged to finish these missals by Christmas and indicated that he would pay Gilles six months following this expected completion.[25]

Gilles collaborated with Vérard on several occasions, although it is unclear the exact role each man played within this partnership. Evidence for this relationship appears in another record from the document of May 1491, in which Vérard paid off his debt of 140 *livres tournois* to Gilles.[26] This document from May 1491 also referred to *"autres livres qu'ilz avoient fait imprimer en societé"* [other books that they had printed in society], suggesting these men had other printing projects. Based on this document and the two books they published, *Cent nouvelles nouvelles*, published on December 24, 1486, and *Livres de Sydrach*, dated February 20, 1487, Mary Beth Winn posits that the relationship between Vérard and Gilles must have lasted approximately five years.[27] It is possible that this partnership lasted longer; a document from January 10, 1498, discusses a marriage gift from Gilles to Jean de Fontenay, the husband of Gilles's daughter Jehanne Gilles. This gift comprised a house and seventy-nine *arpents* (acres) of land at Pierrelaye, which the couple then sold for 200 *livres tournois* to Antoine Vérard.[28] Evidently, Vérard's connection to Gilles and his family did not end in 1491. Documents written after 1491 about Gilles's book-publishing relationship with Antoine Vérard do not survive, but the relationship between Vérard and Gilles may well have extended beyond five years.

All of these unbound texts in Gilles's large chamber were likely ready to be examined or purchased, waiting for potential customization by future customers, or they were older editions ready to be sold.[29] Additionally, these unbound books sat in this room for years after their publication date.[30] Most significantly, the *Cent nouvelles nouvelles* and *Livres de Sydrach*, both known collaborations between Gilles and Vérard, were in multiple copies, cited as unbound in this room. It is possible they were part of a future investment.

Room 2: An Affordable Library

The second portion of Gilles and Marie's book collection was housed several rooms away from the large chamber. The inventory begins, as usual, with the furniture in the room. Here, too, the Turquam-Gilles family kept many standard furniture pieces, most of them with distinctive elements yet not as fine as those in the previous workroom. Examples of these items were benches with a lockable chest or a table that could turn. This room also contained several decorative, potentially functional items associated with military action, including twelve heraldic panels of wood, weapons, and armor. There was also a small *tableau* that held a scroll containing a genealogy of the kings of France.[31] Following these items, the notaries listed another portion of Gilles and Marie's book collection: about seventy-one works, most of which were printed, and two of which have been identified in present-day collections.

To emphasize this section of the inventory, the scribe made a point to write the word *Livres* in the margin next to the beginning of these evaluations, noting their importance within the inventory (Fig. 2).[32] The notaries listed the books in this room in groupings, often combining several together with one price attached. The tastes of Marie and Gilles can be deduced through the titles of the books—they were interested not only in religious texts but in history, law, philosophy, and French romances as well.[33]

The first grouping in this room was comprised of eight books, all religious in nature. The notaries valued these books together at 7 *livres parisis* and described them as printed on paper and bound. Among these books are a Golden Legend, a Bible in the French language, a missal, a Roman breviary, and the life of Jesus Christ. The notaries then grouped together works by Roman historians, philosophers, and saints (Aristotle, Valerius Maximus, Saint Augustine), again printed on paper, all bound in leather and valued at 9 *livres parisis*. The collections of books continue with more religious volumes, including *Le doctrinal de la foy, la fleur des commandemans de Dieu*, and a *livre de la vie humaine* (*The Doctrine of the Faith, The Flower of God's Commandments,* and a *Book of Human Life*), all bound and written like the previous works but given a much lower value

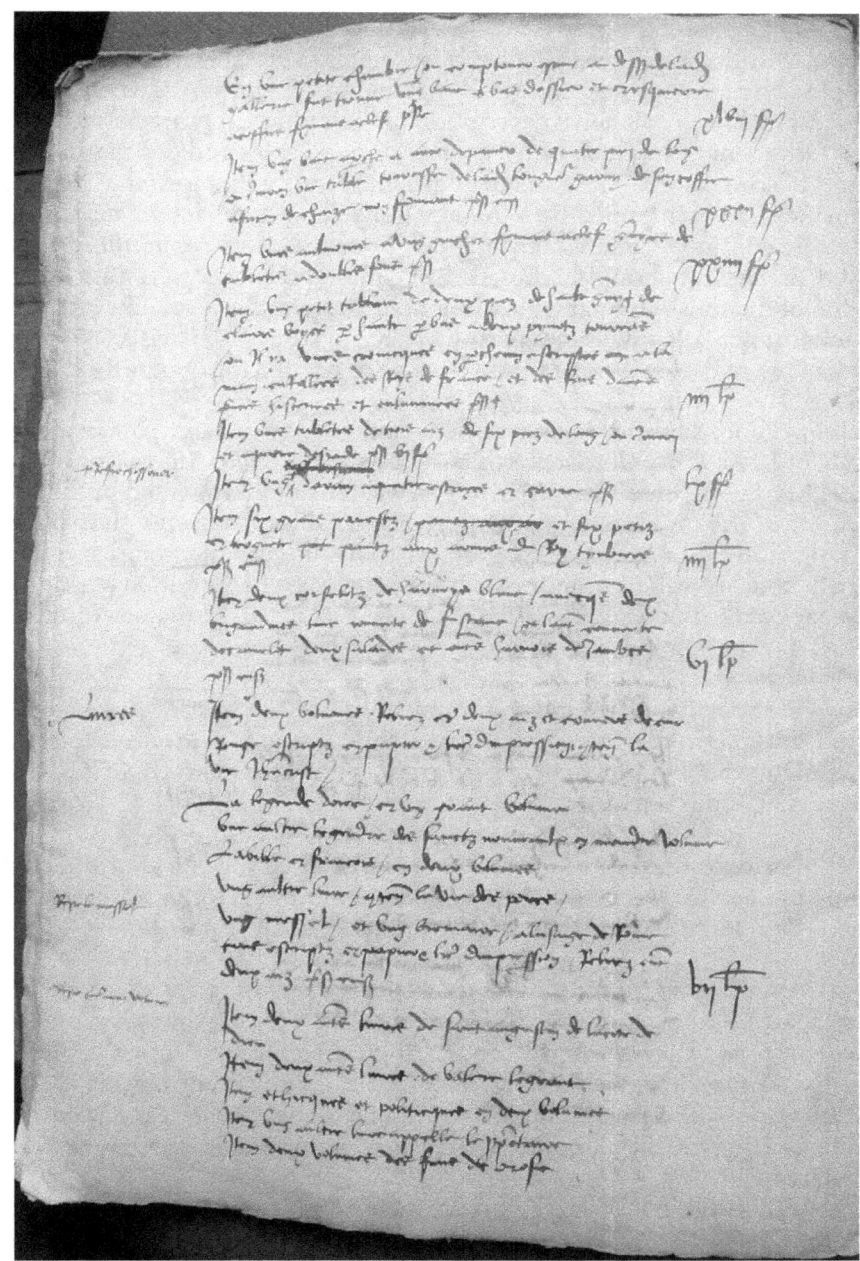

Figure 2. Archives nationales, MC/ET/XIX/66, novembre 1500, folio 17v. Photo: Sarah Dyer Magleby.

of 36 *solz parisis*. The next selection of books suggests interests in many popular works such as the *Roman de la Rose* and several works by Giovanni Boccaccio and Boethius, all priced together at 70 *solz parisis*; the notaries did not include a collective description of their physical characteristics.

Other entries include only one or two book titles and descriptions instead of six or more. These smaller entries indicate an interest in Arthurian romances, as exemplified by a three-volume set of *Lancelot du lac*, though there is continued interest in religious books such as *Les meditations de Saint Bernard*. It should be noted that Gilles and Marie were purchasing some of the most popular texts of the time, hot off the press, likely buying books immediately after initial printings. From Doucet's analysis, it appears that many of these editions would have been printed during the 1480s and 1490s.[34]

Two books from this inventoried space are still extant. First is a used copy of *Le roman d'Alexandre*, which also contains *Judas Maccabeus* (Paris, BnF, Ms. fr. 789). This manuscript was written and illuminated in the first quarter of the fourteenth century, predating Gilles's lifetime.[35] It includes the signature of Nicole Gilles, along with his title of notary and secretary to the king, as well as other inscriptions, such as a handwritten passage in the back of the manuscript stating that Gilles acquired the manuscript from Jean Dusseau in 1483:

> Pertinet Nicolao Gilles, domini nostri regis notario et secretario, ejusque in camera compotorum clerico, et emit Turonis a Johanne Dusseau, Belli Jochi prope Lochias, in mense januari M°CCCC° octuagesimo tercio.[36]

> [Belongs to Nicole Gilles, notary and secretary to the king and clerk in the chamber of accounts, and bought in Tours by Jean Dusseau, of Belli Jochi near Loches, in the month of January 1483.]

Dusseau came from Beaulieu-lès-Loches, approximately 30 kilometers southeast of Tours and close to Vendômois. As the possible *seigneur de la Grue en Vendômois*, Gilles was potentially a neighbor to Dusseau.[37] Keith Busby surmises that Gilles likely acquired the book from Dusseau when Gilles was on official assignment to Touraine in the winter of 1484; however, the script by Gilles, or one of his scribes, notes that it was purchased in January of 1483.[38]

While Gilles likely purchased the manuscript from Dusseau or traded for it in 1484, there were several other owners of the book before them. Dusseau signed the end of the book, along with the phrase *"mon tres honnore seigneur"* (my most honorable lord), and Gilles signed as well with the elaborate Latin notation cited above. Other hands appear in the book, either emphasizing certain sections of the manuscript in the margins ("*noms des autheurs de ce roman*"), providing the beginning of a date ("*anno domini*"), or suggesting a familiarity with Arthurian romances and the possessed manuscript ("*A l'aventure va Gauvania*").[39]

Doucet points out this entry in the Turquam-Gilles inventory as corresponding to this book:[40]

> Item ung aultre livre escript en parchemin en langaige de picart contenant les fais d'alixandre et de judas macabeus [sic] prise 16 solz parisis.
>
> [Item, another book written on parchment in the Picard language containing the deeds of Alexander and of Judas Maccabees, priced at 16 *solz parisis*.]

While this manuscript fits the description provided by the notaries—on parchment, in Picard—it also is illuminated with many miniatures as well as charming and entertaining marginal imagery, for example folio 1r (Fig. 3). What does this say, then, about the process or priorities of the notaries when writing about each book? Again, this could reflect a lack of consistency or other unknown aspects. Several entries in the inventory provide details when books have illuminations and historiated initials, and the absence of such details here could mean that older books such as this were not prized as much for their visual contents. The price of the book is low compared to others in Gilles's "*boutique*," the final location where Gilles kept all the most impressive books. This book did not make it into the more privileged book space, even though it is more densely illuminated than another surviving book that did, *Le doctrinal des simples gens*. Could it be the age of the book? The provenance? The condition? Unfortunately, it is unclear why this book was placed in this room rather than in the "*boutique*."

Another identified book is an edition of the *Ovide moralisé* (Rome, Biblioteca Apostolica Vaticana, MSS Reg.lat.1686), for which unfortunately the inventory provides even less information than for the previous manuscript. According to Ernest Langlois and the prologue from the manuscript, the author of this text was a Norman clerk living in Angers in the service of René of Anjou, the duke of Anjou and king of Naples.[41] The author, noting that he will stay unnamed to avoid any glory to himself, began translating the text from Latin into French verse in April 1466 and finished by September 1467. It is unclear when Gilles purchased or was given this unilluminated manuscript, but it likely was not long after the book's creation. Gilles

Figure 3. *Le roman d'Alexandre et autres poëmes français*, ca. 1280 (Paris, BnF, Ms. fr. 789), folio 1r. Photo: Sarah Dyer Magleby.

signed the manuscript on folio 2v, a folio and a half before the prologue, writing "*Pertinet Nicolao* Gilles" (Belongs to Nicole Gilles). Gilles's signature can also be found immediately under the end text of the final folio. Here he writes, "*C'est a moy N. Gilles*" (It is mine, N. Gilles). Interestingly, there is Latin script following this signature and a few blank pages, which says:

> Dampna fleo rerum, sed plus fleo dampna dierum
> Quisquis potest rebus succurrere, nemo diebus
> Quatuor debemus Deo
> Honorem, quia est creator
> Amorem, quia est redemptor
> Timorem, quia est judex
> Gratiarum actiones, quia est remunerator[42]

> [I weep for the loss of things, but I weep more for the loss of days
> Anyone can help with things, no one with days
> We owe God four:
> Honor, because he is the creator
> Love, because he is the redeemer
> Fear, because he is the judge
> Thanksgiving, because he is the rewarder]

These verses were used rather frequently in the Middle Ages, and according to Langlois, are also found in two manuscripts in the Bibliothèque nationale de France.[43] While the author of this poetic text was probably from the fifteenth century, it is unclear whether the inscription was written in the manuscript while Gilles owned the book.

This manuscript is also probably found in Gilles and Marie's inventory, identified as the *Metamorphoses*, though the description is rather brief. Moreover, this manuscript is not priced individually, but alongside a selection of other books. Notaries list this grouping as:

> Item ung aultre livre appelle *la dotrinal* [sic] *de la court*
> escript a la main
> Ovide *Mertamophoce* [sic] en francoys
> *Les cronicques abregees* et *les drois de la couronne*
> *de France* et ung aultre livre
> Le livre de *Prudence et Melibee*
> *Le Romant de la Roze*
> Neuf aultres livres de petite valleur
> Le tout prise ensemble 70 solz parisis

> [Item, another book called *La doctrinal de la court*
> written by hand
> Ovid's *Metamorphoses* in French
> *Les Chroniques abregees* and *Les drois de la couronne de France* and another book
> The book of *Prudence and Melibee*
> *Le Roman de la Rose*
> Nine other books of little value
> All priced together at 70 *solz parisis*]

Doucet assumes most of these books are printed, except the first entry, which the notaries confirm is handwritten. However, the survival of Gilles's *Ovide moralisé* suggests that the notaries may have bundled both printed books and manuscripts together in singular entries. This raises further questions: Why are these books combined? Are they thematically related, or simply placed next to each other in the room? Why were they priced together at all? Similar to Gilles's copy of *Le roman d'Alexandre*, his *Ovide moralisé* was much cheaper compared to the most expensive books in the collection, especially when considering the fifteen other books with which it is priced, suggesting that this room housed many of Gilles and Marie's more affordable, less valuable books. Even so, the presence of Gilles's signatures in his *Le roman d'Alexandre* and *Ovide moralisé* demonstrates their significance. Whether they were meaningful acquisitions, anticipated loans, or something else entirely is unknown.

Room 3: Precious Manuscripts and Printed Books

The last space in which books were inventoried is the "*comptouer dudict maistre Nicole Gilles*," or the "*boutique*" of Nicole Gilles. The notaries intentionally left Gilles's "*boutique*" to the end, as it held some of the finest possessions and required the most study and examination. While it is somewhat unclear what the purpose of this "*boutique*" was, it is likely that this was a public-facing workspace for business—potentially for both him and his clerks, who also resided in this household.[44] This room also faced the rue Saint Antoine, a main street in this sector of Paris, instead of the rue du Roi de Sicile, a much smaller road at the back of the *hôtel*.

Gilles's "*boutique*" included some of the most fascinating items, but Gilles may have moved some of these objects inventoried here for appraisal by the notaries. This "*boutique*" included the entire metalwork collection of the Turquam-Gilles family, from fine tableware such as goblets to elaborately decorated belts and jeweled rings, all of which comprised a majority of Gilles and Marie's material wealth. It is likely that most of these objects, particularly the metalwork, were brought into this "*boutique*" so that multiple appraisers could evaluate and weigh the more than four hundred exquisite items in gold or silver. Gilles may have regularly kept the thirty illuminated and historiated manuscripts in his "*boutique*" or he may also have brought them there for examination to more precisely determine each object's monetary value.

The inventory of Gilles's "*boutique*" does not mention any furniture. The notaries usually began by detailing each of the *biens meubles*, or moveable goods, in a room before examining smaller items. What does this say about this room? Could it mean that any seating, tables, or shelving present were built-in components, as in the fifteenth-century miniature from the *Livre des simples médecines* featuring a shop with precious stones (Fig. 4)? Another option could be that servants or members of the household removed all furniture from the room to accommodate the metalwork and valuable books for appraisal. Last, the lack of furniture could mean that the room was intentionally left empty—but this seems the most unlikely option, as it was a public-facing space.

The notaries and appraisers began their inventory of this space by recording each individual book in detail. However, unlike the inventory of the other spaces, the notaries listed other items awkwardly alongside Gilles's most prized books within the margins of this portion of the inventory, such as some knives and an awl—possibly objects for bookmaking. Since these objects are not cited in the body of the text, it is possible that they were unintentionally missed and added later.

The notaries recorded thirty manuscripts and printed books in this section of the inventory, of which twelve were printed books (*lettre d'impression*), and the other eighteen written by hand (*a la main*). While the notaries priced some of these books together, they evaluated others individually, and for these items they included more meticulous descriptions, indicating that they were especially precious. Besides noting if the books were printed or handwritten, the notaries also often indicated the type of writing within each book (*lettre batarde, lettre de forme*, for example), the material it is written on (almost always parchment), the type of book or its title (such as a Book of Hours, a psalter, or the Bible), the binding materials (leather, velvet, fur), if it closed with a clasp, if it contained historiated letters and illuminations, and, for six of these books, the incipits (first words) of the second folio following the calendar and beginning the final page of the manuscript or printed book.[45]

Dating many of these texts is difficult, but because book printing did not begin in Paris until the 1470s, most of the printed books were probably completed between 1470 and 1500. Gilles likely purchased many of these books himself, as the inscription in one of his surviving works (*Le*

Figure 4. *Livre des simples médecines*, 15th century (Paris, BnF, Ms. fr. 9136), folio 344. Photo: BnF.

doctrinal des simples gens, BnF, MS. fr. 17088) explains that he had a manuscript copied for his household or himself, but others may have been gifts. The manuscripts are more difficult to date; Gilles and Marie could have received them as gifts, commissioned them, or purchased them. One of the surviving works, *Le roman d'Alexandre*, discussed above, likely dates from the fourteenth century, so Gilles certainly collected earlier manuscripts, indicating his antiquarian interests. Like other contemporary collectors, he possessed both new and used books. Even so, one Book of Hours in this section indicates it was made during Gilles and Marie's lifetime, specifically customized with gold clasps formed in this couple's initials.[46]

The thirty books in the third room fall into several distinct categories: a Bible, two missals, five psalters, a collection of seven books on religious instruction, two volumes on the history of the world, and thirteen Books of Hours. The fact that Gilles and Marie owned thirteen Books of Hours—roughly 11 percent of their entire library—is a testament to the importance of that class of books.[47] The inventoried Books of Hours vary in price, with the cheapest, a grouping of six printed and handwritten versions (possibly hybrid editions?), costing only 8 *solz parisis*, while the most expensive one, illuminated and handwritten, was appraised at 20 *livres parisis*.[48] Seven of the thirteen Books of Hours were solely written by hand while the other six were all partially printed or part of a grouping of both printed and handwritten works. The printed Books of Hours were less expensive than the handwritten Books of Hours. It is interesting that Gilles had a taste not only for the fine and luxurious but also for the popular and more easily available.

Scholars have identified a surviving instructional religious text from the inventory in Gilles's "*boutique.*"[49] Titled *Le doctrinal des simples gens* ([The Doctrinal of the Common People]; BnF, MS. fr. 17088), this text was written originally by Guy de Roye, archbishop of Sens, between 1385 and 1390. In 1474, Gilles commissioned a copy to be written in French on parchment.[50] The explicit at the end of the manuscript (fol. 197v) reiterates the title and asserts Gilles's ownership:

> Explicit Doctrinale simplicium gencium—Ce livre est a moy N. Gilles et le feiz escripre a Paris l'an mil CCCC soixante et quatorze.
>
> [*Explicit Doctrinale simplicium gencium*—This book belongs to me, N. Gilles, and was written in Paris, the year 1474.]

Scholars have consulted the Turquam-Gilles inventory in order to see if this manuscript appears among the collection of books. Doucet and Scheurer both claim that this book was located in Gilles's "*boutique,*" described within a larger entry as:

Item ung a b c et unes pseaulmes reliees separement escriptz en parchemin et enluminez. Item ung *Chatonnei et Theodolei glosez* aussi escriptz en parchemin et enluminez. Item ung *Domiase* escript en parchemin relie entre deux aiz et enlumine. Item ung dotrinal [sic] aussi escripte en parchemin ystoriee et enluminee. Ung *Gressime* aussi escripte en parchemin enlumine et a lettres d'or prisez ensemble 4 livres 16 solz parisis.

[Item, an abc and a psalter, bound separately, written on parchment and illuminated. Item, a *Chatonnei et Theodolei glosez* (*Caton and Theodulus with Commentary*), also written in parchment and illuminated. Item, a *Domiase*, written on parchment, bound between two boards and illuminated. Item, a doctrinal, also written on parchment, historiated and illuminated. A *Gressime* (*Graecismus*), also written on parchment, illuminated and with gold letters, priced together at 4 *livres* 16 *solz parisis*.]

Scholars point to the doctrinal recorded in this entry as evidence for this surviving book.[51] While this is an imprecise description, the surviving manuscript does match the few words given in the account: written on parchment, historiated, and illuminated. The price assigned to the book can only be approximated, as it is bundled together with five other books at a total of 4 *livres* 16 *solz parisis*.

Though the description does mention that the book is historiated and illuminated, only a single illumination in this manuscript appears at the very beginning, on folio 1r (Fig. 5). This front page has an elaborate border, a historiated initial, and a large illumination that takes up a third of the overall page. Unfortunately, the illumination is not in excellent condition, as the faces of all the figures, including some of the objects they hold, have worn down and oxidized over time. In the center sits the Trinity, shown as three individual yet undivided figures, particularly represented by their shared red robe. Centrally, God wears the papal crown, while all three are adorned with golden halos. The Trinity sits on a wooden bench, decorated as a throne with the addition of a cloth backing. Below them rests the host and a chalice, and they are flanked on either side by saintly figures. Moses is the only other recognizable figure, as horns curve from his head, and he holds the tablets of the ten commandments. Throngs of red angels peacefully watch, receding far back into the distance. Beneath the illumination is a historiated initial in the form of a dragon, which begins the phrase "*ce present livre en francais*" [this present book in French]. The surrounding border depicts many red, pink, and blue flowers with interwoven forms embellished in gold leaf.

Figure 5. *Doctrinal des simples gens*, 15th century (Paris, BnF, Ms. fr. 17088), folio 1r. Photo: Sarah Dyer Magleby.

Figure 6. *Bible historiale*, 15th century (Paris, BnF, Ms. fr. 3), folio 3r. Photo: BnF.

The subject of the Trinity was popular, as is evident when comparing the doctrinal's illumination to similar illuminations with the same visual structure. For instance, on folio 3r of a *Bible historiale* (Fig. 6) the three members of the Trinity also sit on a long bench with a high back. In the center is God with his papal crown, and angels play instruments at the edges. The marginal work is familiar as well, with blues, reds, and greens mixed with gold leaf in a sharp foliage style outlined in ink.[52] Another example comes from an edition of *De proprietatibus rerum* (Fig. 7), which isolates the Trinity, moving it away from any other figures. Identical figures sit on their wooden bench as they seem to discuss or argue among one another, judging by the hand gestures. Instead of a single robe they wear identical clothing to unite them as one in their tight composition. Furthermore, an illumination of the same subject in a Book of Hours (Fig. 8) includes a similar style, as the illuminator has kept the linework soft and avoided strong lights and shadows; the marginal foliage is similar as well, especially the strawberries.

Figure 7. *De proprietatibus rerum*, 15th century (Paris, BnF, Ms. fr. 22531), folio 14r. Photo: BnF.

Figure 8. Book of Hours, 1445–1450 and 1460 (Paris, BnF, Ms. lat. 9473), folio 144r. Photo: Bnf.

Missing from the Inventory: The Last Identified Manuscript

The last known extant book owned by Gilles is the *Origo Francorum seu Chronicon Francorum ab anno Domini 380 usque ad 1308* (Bern, Burgerbibliothek, cod. 70). This manuscript does not appear in the Turquam-Gilles inventory.[55] As a result, scholars claim it must have been acquired after the notaries and appraisers compiled the inventory.[56] While this is possible, as Gilles lived about four more years following the drafting of the inventory, this is not the only explanation. For most inventories, it is rare for the notaries to include all the contents of the home; items may have been given away or accidently missed.

Composed of 195 folios on untrimmed paper, cod. 70 contains many texts and information provided by multiple owners.[57] *Origo Francorum seu Chronicon Francorum ab anno Domini 380 usque ad 1308* is a compilation of the histories of France: the Latin *Laudes Francorum* (fols. 1r–2r) and Guillaume de Nangis's Latin *Chronicon* (fols. 3r–201v), and one contemporary French document—bound in the manuscript upside-down, so it is read in that order—called the *Mémoire dressée par la commission de 36 notables, nommés par Louis XI* (fols. 205v–202r). A majority of the text as a whole covers French history from the Trojan émigrés aiding Emperor Valentinian in 375 BCE through Charlemagne and Saint Louis until 1308 CE, with Isabella of France and Edward of England.[58] The last of the pages, the *Mémoire*, discusses the Treaty of Conflans, which was meant to seek "renovations, provisions, and remedies suitable for the public good of the kingdom" from September 1466.[59] At the end of this document, Gilles wrote, in different ink and script, "Scriptum manu propria N. Gilles" (Written by N. Gilles's own hand). In fact, Gilles signed this manuscript multiple times: on folio Av and folio 11v as "*C'est à N. Gilles*," on folio 3r and folio Zr as "*C'est à moy N. Gilles*," and on the former title label (which today is glued on the back cover of the binding) as "N. Gilles."

One of the more fascinating parts of this manuscript is not necessarily the body of the text itself but the recycled portions, or pieces of unwanted and reused printed and handwritten papers, that later readers found in the binding of the manuscript. These scraps include pieces of printed books: a Latin Psalter, an exposition of the subject of the Psalms, Meditations on the Passion, Life of Saint Margaret, *Le viandier de Taillevent*, *Livres de Sydrach*, three different Books of Hours (including one counterproof), and a Latin grammar text.[60] One other text was used in the binding material, although handwritten, which was the journal of receipts of a Parisian bookseller clerk (*journal d'un commis de libraire parisien*); this journal gives details as when, at what price, and to whom were sold certain books, the kinds of books sold, and the sums paid to two scribes, an illuminator, and a binder whose names are noted.[61] Moreover, the clerk provides specific dates when transactions took place, dating the binding to around 1500.[62] The writer does not mention the bookseller's name, but because of the reference to certain shops and because this record was attached to a fragment of corrected proofs from Vérard's 1486 edition of Sydrach, it is likely that the clerk worked for Vérard.[63] While the inclusion of some pages of Gilles's and Vérard's collaborative Livres de Sydrach in the bookbinding may say something about the creators of the text, it is unclear if Gilles knew about the binding scraps—so the book may have been bound by a binder who worked for Vérard, or this may be just an interesting coincidence.[64]

The provenance of this manuscript is well documented, particularly within the manuscript itself. Gilles was the primary owner and made sure to display this via his signature throughout the manuscript's pages. Gilles then handed down this book to Jean de Fontenay, his son-in-law through marriage to his daughter Jehanne Gilles in 1497.[65] Fontenay also signed his name in the book, although only twice and always situated next to his father-in-law's signature. Underneath Gilles's signed name on folio Av, Fontenay wrote "*Et depuis à J. Fontenay des comptes 1504*" (And since then to J. Fontenay of the accounts 1504). Fontenay also wrote a date next to Gilles's name on this page, seemingly to document when Gilles acquired the text. With the same script as Fontenay's signature, Fontenay wrote the year 1502 by Gilles's name. If this was the correct date when Gilles obtained cod. 70, then its absence from the estate inventory of 1499 makes sense, and this also tells us that it may have been one of the final manuscript purchases by Gilles, as he died only a year later in 1503—a bibliophile and book collector until the end. Fontenay's second signature is found at the end of the book on folio Zr, which states "*Et à J. Fontenay an 1504*" [And to J. Fontenay [in the] year 1504], with again the addition of the date 1502 by Gilles's name above.

It appears that the manuscript came into the hands of another man in the mid-sixteenth century, who signed "*Ex libris T. Mallessei Castrilucii, Chastelluz*" on folio Zr under Gilles and Fontenay's signatures. This same hand wrote a brief paragraph on folio 195v concerning the use of the manuscript during the reign of Francis I, who, by his order, asked Paul Émile to write the history of France, for which the manuscript was used.[66] Lastly, the book was acquired by Jacques Bongars, who signed his name three times (fols. 1r, 3r, and 205v) and brought the book to Bern in 1632.

Conclusion

Examination of these books separately within the context of Gilles and Marie's library provides much information about their intellectual and religious priorities and pursuits. It appears that Gilles was especially interested in collecting as well as producing books, evidenced by the inventoried and identified books. This bourgeois couple selected specific spaces to keep their books, ensuring they were in rooms that facilitated their proper use. These rooms are certainly some of the nicer spaces in the home, equipped with fine furniture to make the study of these books an easy task. Though the final room of books is possibly not where Gilles and Marie initially kept their most precious manuscripts, their relocation to and inclusion in this space underscores their importance to the family's status and wealth, as the most expensive objects were placed in this room by the family for ease of evaluation by appraisers.

Gilles decided to sign his name at least once, and in some cases multiple times, on the pages of these four manuscripts, thus laying claim to possession of these volumes—and he may have done so with other books that are not identified in modern collections or do not survive. It is possible that Gilles's signatures indicate the books' preciousness to him, his plans to loan these books, or his excitement in claiming ownership. No matter the reason, Gilles's signatures tell us of his desire to mark his identity on these objects and personalize them for his own purposes. Interestingly, Gilles included multiple signatures throughout the Bern manuscript to mark his ownership, a practice its inheritors continued. Additionally, Gilles often signed these books in similar places, before the beginning of the text and immediately following its conclusion, possibly to ensure readers knew of his connection to these books. Through the ways Gilles and Marie acquired books, whether as secondhand purchases, gifts, or personal commissions, they collected a diverse assortment of manuscripts and printed books, indicating their literary expertise, personal interests, and elevated social status.

University of Kansas

NOTES

1. For further background information on Nicole Gilles and the family trees of the Turquam and Gilles families, see Jacques Xavier Carré de Busserolle, *Archives des familles nobles de la Touraine de l'Anjou, du Maine et du Poitou* (Tours, France: Suppligeon, 1889); Jacques Riche, "L'Historian Nicole Gilles (14..–1503). Sa vie, son manuscript original, les premières éditions de ses Annales et sa place dans l'historiographie française," 2 vols. (Thèse de l'École des chartes, 1930), Archives nationales, Pierrefitte-sur-Seine, AB/XXVIII/83; André Lapeyre and Rémy Scheurer, *Les notaires et secrétaires du roi sous les règnes de Louis XI, Charles VIII et Louis XII (1461–1515): Notices personnelles et généalogies* (Paris: Bibliothèque nationale, 1978), 1:149–151; Robert Descimon, "Élites parisiennes entre XVe et XVIIe siècle: du bon usage du Cabinet des titres," *Bibliothèque de l'École des chartes* 155.2 (1997):636;

Yvonne-Hélène Le Maresquier-Kesteloot, "L'ascension sociale d'une famille parisienne au XVe siècle: Les Turquam," *La Cité* 25 (2006):28–50. For documents discussing Gilles's relationship with those in book production, see Arch. nat., MC/ET/XIX/6, 7–9 mai 1491; Arch. nat., MC/ET/XIX/6, 6 juillet 1491; Arch. nat. MC/ET/XIX/12, 10 janvier 1498 (n.st.).
2. While Gilles's *Annales* does not make a significant appearance in this article, there are scholars researching his work on this text, most prominently Catherine Emerson. See Catherine Emerson, "Nicole Gilles and Literate Society," in *"Le Bel Épy qui foisonne": Collection and Translation in French Print Networks, 1476–1576*, ed. Catherine Emerson (Oxford: Peter Lang, 2019), 53–70; and Catherine Emerson, "Nicole Gilles's Presentation of the Death of Louis XI and the Collection of Symbols of Kingship," in *The Medieval Chronicle 14*, ed. Erik Kooper and Sjoerd Levelt (Boston and Leiden, Netherlands: Brill, 2021), 47–52.
3. Arch. nat., MC/ET/XIX/66, novembre 1500.
4. Madeleine Jurgens, *Documents du minutier central des notaires de Paris: Inventaires après décès, 1 (1483–1547)* (Paris: Archives nationales, 1982), 42; Lapeyre and Scheurer, *Notaires et secrétaires*, 1:149.
5. The term *"une bote"* appears twice in the inventory alongside groupings of books. Likewise, notaries wrote the phrase *"aultres petiz volumes"* three times in two entries, implying further unknown titles.
6. Lapeyre and Scheurer, *Notaires et secrétaires*, 1:149–150; Jurgens, *Documents du minutier central*, 42.
7. Jurgens, *Documents du minutier central*, 42; Lapeyre and Scheurer, *Notaires et secrétaires*, 1:149.
8. For common household reconstructions taken from probate inventories, see Pierre Couperie and Madeleine Jurgens, "Le logement à Paris au XVIe et XVIIe siècles," *Annales. Economies, sociétés, civilisations. 17e année* 3 (1962):488–500.
9. Yvonne-Hélène Le Maresquier-Kesteloot, "La maison médiévale parisienne, espace de relations, d'après les inventaires après décès," in *La maison, lieu de sociabilité dans des communautés urbaines européennes, de l'Antiquité à nos jours: Colloque international de l'Université Paris VII–Denis Diderot, 14–15 mai 2004*, ed. Florence Gherchanoc (Paris: Éditions le Manuscrit, 2006), 76.
10. In the Turquam-Gilles inventory, Room 1 is located on fols. 16r–17r, Room 2 is on fols. 17v–18v, and Room 3 is on fols. 19r–25r (although in Room 3 the books themselves are only on fols. 19r–20r).
11. Many thanks to my advisor and friend Anne D. Hedeman for bringing the *Ovide moralisé* to my attention.
12. The Turquam-Gilles inventory exclusively uses *livres parisis* for its monetary values. *Livres* could also be broken down into two further units:

solz/sous and *deniers*, where 1 *livre* is 20 *sous* and 1 *sous* is 12 *deniers*. Ronald Edward Zupko, *French Weights and Measures before the Revolution: A Dictionary of Provincial and Local Units* (Bloomington: Indiana University Press, 1978), 171; Katherine Baker, "Painting and the Luxury Arts in Paris, 1490–1515: Objects and Their Urban Contexts" (PhD diss., University of Virginia, 2013), 172.
13. Felicity Riddy, "'Burgeis' Domesticity in Late-Medieval England," in *Medieval Domesticity: Home, Housing and Household in Medieval England*, ed. Maryanne Kowaleski and P.J.P. Goldberg (Cambridge, UK: Cambridge University Press, 2008), 14–36.
14. Roger Doucet, *Les bibliothèques parisiennes au XVIe siècle* (Paris: A. et J. Picard, 1956), 12–13, 83–89.
15. Doucet notes here that this is only one of the volumes in this series. Doucet, *Bibliothèques parisiennes*, 83–84.
16. Ibid., 83.
17. It is unclear why Doucet chose the 1476 edition for the *Chroniques de France*, as Vérard also published an edition in 1493. Because Doucet does not explain his reasoning, it is possible that he was unaware of its existence. Other examples printed by Vérard from 1493 provide the same date range (through the reign of Charles VII) as the 1476 edition. "Le premier volume des croniques de France," Bibliothèque nationale de France, Gallica, https://gallica.bnf.fr/ark:/12148/bpt6k87131441; "Josephus, Flavius: De bello Judaico. [French:] De la bataille judaique. Tr: Claudius de Seysselo (?)," British Library, Incunabula Short Title Catalogue, https://data.cerl.org/istc/ij00489000; "Sydrach, Philosophe: La fontaine de toutes sciences [French] [Ed: Nicole Gilles]," British Library, Incunabula Short Title Catalogue, https://data.cerl.org/istc/is00878000; "Vincentius Bellovacensis: Speculum historiale [French] Miroir historial. Tr: Jehan du Vignay," British Library, Incunabula Short Title Catalogue, https://data.cerl.org/istc/iv00287000; "Froissart, Jean: Chroniques," British Library, Incunabula Short Title Catalogue, https://data.cerl.org/istc/if00322000; "Nouvelles: Les cent nouvelles nouvelles," British Library, Incunabula Short Title Catalogue, https://data.cerl.org/istc/in00277000. For a digital surrogate for these manuscripts, see Bibliothèque nationale de France, Gallica; and British Library, Incunabula Short Title Catalogue, in the bibliography. See also Mary Beth Winn, *Anthoine Vérard, Parisian Publisher, 1485–1512: Prologues, Poems and Presentations* (Geneva: Librairie Droz, 1997).
18. There are two main monographs on Antoine Vérard and his life as a *libraire*: John Macfarlane, *Antoine Vérard* (London: Chiswick Press, 1900); and Winn, *Anthoine Vérard*. Beyond these monographs, there are several articles and a doctoral dissertation that provide further in-

formation on Vérard: Rémy Scheurer, "Nicole Gilles et Antoine Vérard," *Bibliothèque de l'École des chartes* 128.2 (1970):415–419; Louis-Gabriel Bonicoli, "La production du libraire-éditeur parisien Antoine Vérard (1485–1512): Nature, fonctions et circulation des images dans les premiers imprimés illustrés" (PhD diss., 3 vols., Université Paris Ouest Nanterre La Défense, 2015); Cynthia J. Brown, "Paratextual Performances in the Early Parisian Book Trade: Antoine Vérard's Edition of Boccaccio's *Nobles et cleres dames* (1493)," in *Cultural Performances in Medieval France: Essays in Honor of Nancy Freeman Regalado*, ed. Nancy Regalado, Eglal Doss-Quinby, Roberta L. Krueger, and E. Jane Burns (Rochester, NY: D.S. Brewer, 2007), 255–264; Laura Weigert, "Antoine Vérard's Illuminated Playscript of *La vengeance nostre seigneur*: Marketing Plays and Creating the King's Image," in *The Social Life of Illumination: Manuscripts, Images, and Communities in the Late Middle Ages*, ed. Joyce Coleman, Mark Cruse, and Kathryn A. Smith (Turnhout, Belgium: Brepols, 2013), 251–293; Sheila Edmunds, "From Schoeffer to Vérard: Concerning the Scribes Who Became Printers," in *Printing the Written Word: The Social History of Books, circa 1450–1520*, ed. Sandra Hindman (Ithaca, NY: Cornell University Press, 1992), 21–40; Mary Beth Winn, "Printing the *Cent nouvelles nouvelles*: Anthoine Vérard's 1486 Edition and Its Sixteenth-Century Successors," in *The* Cent nouvelles nouvelles *(Burgundy-Luxembourg-France, 1458–c. 1550)*, ed. Graeme Small, Texte, Codex, & Contexte, 23 (Turnhout, Belgium: Brepols, 2023), 81–134.

19. Mary Beth Winn compiled other instances where the name Vérard generally appears in prior documents, but none strongly indicates familial ties to the fifteenth-century bookseller. See Winn, *Anthoine Vérard*, 15–17.

20. The following is Antoine Vérard's colophon from his first printing: Ces presentes heures on [sic] este acheueez/ le deuziesme jour de septembre. M. cccc./ quatrevingtz et cinq faictes īpmer p / āthoine verard libraire demourāt a pa/ris a lymaige saint iehan levangeliste sur le pont ñredame ou au palaiz au pmier pylier devant la chapelle ou on/châte la messe messeigneurs les psidēs. [These present hours were completed on the second day of September 1485 printed by Antoine Vérard *libraire*, who lived in Paris at the image of Saint John the Evangelist on the Notre Dame bridge or at the Palais at the first pillar in front of the chapel where they chant the mass *messeigneurs les presidens.*] Winn, *Anthoine Vérard*, 15–16.

21. Virginia Reinburg, *French Books of Hours: Making an Archive of Prayer, c. 1400–1600* (Cambridge, UK: Cambridge University Press, 2012), 22; Winn, *Anthoine Vérard*, 16.

22. Reinburg, *French Books of Hours*, 31.

23. Winn, *Anthoine Vérard*, 15.
24. Arch. nat., MC/ET/XIX/6, 7–9 mai 1491.
25. Winn, *Anthoine Vérard*, 19.
26. Arch. nat., MC/ET/XIX/6, 7–9 mai 1491.
27. Winn, *Anthoine Vérard*, 18.
28. An *arpent* equates to almost an acre. Arch. nat., MC/ET/XIX/12, 10 janvier 1498 (n.st.).
29. There were two editions of *Sydrach*, one from February 20, 1486/1487 and the other from ca. 1496. The second edition is considered a similar reprint of the first. Winn, *Anthoine Vérard*, 359. Also, it was often the responsibility of the buyer to bind the books. They could purchase a book and take it away or pay additional costs of binding. Graham Runnalls, "La vie, la mort et les livres de l'imprimeur-libraire parisien Jean Janot d'après son inventaire après décès (17 février 1522 n.s.)," *Revue Belge de Philologie et d'Histoire* 78.3–4 (2000):824.
30. These books may be unbound because Gilles decided to rebind them.
31. For more information on genealogical scrolls, see Joan Holliday, *Genealogy and the Politics of Representation in the High and Late Middle Ages* (Cambridge, UK: Cambridge University Press, 2019); Stefan G. Holz, Jörg Peltzer, and Maree Shirota, *The Roll in England and France in the Late Middle Ages* (Berlin: De Gruyter, 2019); Elizabeth Morrison and Anne D. Hedeman, *Imagining the Past in France: History in Manuscript Painting 1250–1500* (Los Angeles: J. Paul Getty Museum, 2010); Lisa Fagin Davis, *La Chronique Anonyme Universals: Reading and Writing History in Fifteenth-Century France* (Turnhout, Belgium: Brepols, 2015).
32. The only other places where notaries incorporate marginal headings and notations are alongside the tapestries and sometimes with the metalwork objects (although this is more involved since an appraiser is also recognized.
33. For the complete list of books in this section, see Doucet, *Bibliothèques parisiennes*, 13.
34. Ibid., 12–13.
35. Dating provided by François Avril; see BnF notecards in the *fichier Avril* in "Français 789," Bibliothèque nationale de France, Archives et manuscrits, https://archivesetmanuscrits.bnf.fr/ark:/12148/cc51038b. For a digital surrogate for this reference, see Bibliothèque nationale de France, Archives et manuscrits, in the bibliography.
36. Folio 218r. Scheurer, "Nicole Gilles et Antoine Vérard," 416; Keith Busby, *Codex and Context: Reading Old French Verse Narrative in Manuscript* (Amsterdam; New York: Rodopi, 2002), 2:718.
37. According to Jacques Xavier Carré de Busserolle, during the fifteenth century the Gilles family seemed to be new members of the nobility, as

Gilles's father, Marthurin Gilles, became the seigneur *de la Grue* upon his marriage to Julienne de la Chateigneraie in 1446. Carré de Busserolle, *Archives des familles nobles*, 38–39.

38. This seeming discrepancy in date may be due to medieval dating, as the new year began at Easter, which would have been April 18 of that year, making these dates line up. Busby, *Codex and Context*, 2:718.
39. Ibid., 2:719.
40. Doucet, *Bibliothèques parisiennes*, 83–89.
41. Ernest Langlois, "Une rédaction en prose de l'Ovide moralisé," *Bibliothèque de l'École des chartes* 62 (1901):251–252.
42. Langlois transcribed this text but made some errors that I have corrected.
43. Langlois cites these as *Notices et extraits de quelques manuscrits latins de la Bibliothèque nationale*, IV, 70. Langlois, "Rédaction en prose," 251.
44. Notaries named one room in Gilles and Marie's Parisian household as the "*couchent les clercs*," implying that clerks who assisted Gilles in his role at the royal chancellery not only worked with him but lived as part of his household as well. Le Maresquier-Kesteloot, "Maison médiévale parisienne," 76.
45. While most of these seemingly do not survive or may be unknown if they do not have Gilles's signature, it may be possible to identify some books in the future with this detailed information.
46. This manuscript is described as:
    Item, a Book of Hours, written on parchment in gothic script, illuminated and historiated, bound between two boards covered in black velvet, closes with two gold clasps, one with an N and the other an M and with two small chains and two buttons, all of gold, enameled with pansies, begins with the word a luminem on the second folio after the calendar and finishes at the penultimate folio with the word *affectionis*, priced at 20 *livres parisis*.
    Arch. nat., MC/ET/XIX/66, novembre 1500.
47. Reinburg, *French Books of Hours*, 20; Thomas Kren and Scot McKendrick, *Illuminating the Renaissance: The Triumph of Flemish Manuscript Painting in Europe* (Los Angeles: J. Paul Getty Museum, 2003), 121.
48. The notaries also describe the six Books of Hours as being in three pairs. This, along with their low cost, may suggest that Gilles and Marie purchased duplicates of similar Books of Hours. Arch. nat., MC/ET/XIX/66, novembre 1500.
49. For the most complete discussion of this book, see Léopold Delisle, "Documents parisiens de la Bibliothèque de Berne," *Memoires de la Société de l'histoire de Paris et de l'Ile-de-France* 23 (1896):248–265. See also Doucet, *Bibliothèques parisiennes*, 12–13; Scheurer, "Nicole Gilles et Antoine Vérard," 416.
50. Scheurer, "Nicole Gilles et Antoine Vérard," 416.

51. See Doucet, *Bibliothèques parisiennes*, 88; Lapeyre and Scheurer, *Notaires et secrétaires*, 1:150; Léopold Delisle, *Manuscrits latins et français ajoutés aux fonds des nouvelles acquisitions pendant les années 1875–1891* (Paris: Bibliothèque nationale, 1891), 181–183.
52. François Avril and Nicole Reynaud, *Les manuscrits à peintures en France, 1440–1520* (Paris: Flammarion-Bibliothèque nationale de France, 1993), 293–294.
53. Susie Nash, *Between France and Flanders, Manuscript Illumination in Amiens in the Fifteenth Century* (London: British Library, 1999), 127–128.
54. "Français 1661," Bibliothèque nationale de France, Gallica, https://gallica.bnf.fr/ark:/12148/btv1b90588532; "Français 820," Bibliothèque nationale de France, Gallica, https://gallica.bnf.fr/ark:/12148/btv1b10560227m; "Français 923," Bibliothèque nationale de France, Gallica, https://gallica.bnf.fr/ark:/12148/btv1b90596046. For a digital surrogate for these manuscripts, see Bibliothèque nationale de France, Gallica, in the bibliography.
55. Doucet, *Bibliothèques parisiennes*, 12.
56. Ibid., 12; Scheurer, "Nicole Gilles et Antoine Vérard," 416.
57. Delisle, "Documents parisiens," 248; "Cod. 70 (A) Laudes Francorum, Nangis, Guillaume de: Chronicon, lat., 1480 (ca.)–1500 (ca.) (Codex Produktionseinheit)," Burgerbibliothek of Berne, http://katalog.burgerbib.ch/detail.aspx?ID=130886.
58. The Burgerbibliothek's catalogue breaks down the significant figures discussed in this manuscript, including the folios on which each is discussed. "Cod. 70 (A) 2. Nangis, Guillaume de: Chronicon, 1480 (ca.)–1500 (ca.) (Codex Inhalt)," Burgerbibliothek of Bern, http://katalog.burgerbib.ch/detail.aspx?ID=134122; Delisle, "Documents parisiens," 248.
59. A full transcription of this text can be found in Delisle, "Documents parisiens," 256–262.
60. For further information on these fragments, see ibid., 266–270; and Bonicoli, "Production du libraire-éditeur," 1:17–32.
61. Delisle has transcribed this text and Bonicoli has adjusted this transcription's chronological numbering and completed a strong analysis on its contents to argue for Antoine Vérard as the master *libraire* mentioned in this journal. Additionally, I have further interpreted the information in this document, providing an analysis of the types of goods bought, sold, and stored at this business. Delisle, "Documents parisiens," 270–280; Bonicoli, "Production du libraire-éditeur," 1:17–32; Sarah Dyer Magleby, "A Day in the Life: The Lost Ledger of a Parisian libraire Clerk" (paper presented at Translating the Past: A Gathering of Students and Colleagues, University of Kansas, Lawrence, KS, October 14, 2023).

62. The clerk does not provide the year for any of his dates but does include the date, day of the week, and even time of day in some cases. Bonicoli has done a careful analysis of the possible dates, along with an examination of the fragments, and concludes that the clerk wrote this journal between 1490 and 1503, with a higher likelihood of a later date around 1500; Bonicoli, "Production du libraire-éditeur," 1:17–32.
63. Delisle, "Documents parisiens," 279; Winn, *Anthoine Vérard*, 24; Bonicoli, "Production du libraire-éditeur," 1:17–32.
64. Delisle identifies this edition of *Sydrach* as Vérard's but stops at the identification, noting a full surviving example at the BnF. Delisle, "Documents parisiens," 268–269.
65. Their marriage contract can be found in Arch. nat., MC/ET/XIX/12, 17 juin 1497.
66. Delisle, "Documents parisiens," 265. Transcription of the paragraph by Delisle:
    Le present volume et pluisieurs aultres avoient este mis par commandement du grand Roi Francois, premier de ce nom, entre les mains du seigneur Paul Emile, avecq pluisieurs anciens fragmens, instructions et memoires, par messire Marc le Groing, chevalier viconte de la Mothe au Groing, premier gentilhomme de la chambre du Roi, et despuis prevost de l'hostel et grand prevost de France pour dresser au vrai l'histoire de France, ce qui auroit este faict auecq l'aide du dict viconte et du Sieur de Langay, commis par le dict Roi ainsi qu'il appert par les lettres patentes sur ce expediees par le chancelier Du Prat. [This present volume and several others had been placed by command of the great King Francis, first of that name, in the hands of Lord Paul Emile, with several ancient fragments, instructions and memoirs, by Sir Marc le Groing, knight viscount of La Mothe au Groing, first gentleman of the king's chamber, and since provost of the *hôtel* and grand provost of France to draw up the true history of France, which would have been done with the help of the said viscount and of the Lord of Langay, commissioned by the said king as it appears from the letters patent on this sent by the chancellor Du Prat.]
    See also Franck Collard, "La bibliothèque de Saint-Victor au service des rénovateurs de l'histoire de France vers 1500? Nicole Gilles, Robert Gaguin et Paul Émile face aux ressources victorines," *Cahiers de recherches médiévales et humanistes* 17 (2009):227–240.

WORKS CITED

Primary Sources

Archives Nationales—Minutier Central des Notaires de Paris:
Arch. nat., MC/ET/XIX/6, 7–9 mai 1491.

Arch. nat., MC/ET/XIX/6, 6 juillet 1491.
Arch. nat., MC/ET/XIX/12, 17 juin 1497.
Arch. nat., MC/ET/XIX/12, 10 janvier 1498 (n.st.).
Arch. nat., MC/ET/XIX/66, novembre 1500.

Secondary Sources

Avril, François, and Nicole Reynaud. *Les manuscrits à peintures en France, 1440–1520.* Paris: Flammarion-Bibliothèque nationale de France, 1993.
Baker, Katherine. "Painting and the Luxury Arts in Paris, 1490–1515: Objects and Their Urban Contexts." PhD diss., University of Virginia, 2013.
Bibliothèque nationale de France. Archives et manuscrits. https://archivesetmanuscrits.bnf.fr/.
———. Gallica. https://gallica.bnf.fr/.
Bonicoli, Louis-Gabriel. "La production du libraire-éditeur parisien Antoine Vérard (1485–1512): Nature, fonctions et circulation des images dans les premiers livres imprimés illustrés." 3 vols. PhD diss., Université Paris Ouest Nanterre La Défense, 2015.
British Library. Incunabula Short Title Catalogue. https://data.cerl.org/istc/_search.
Brown, Cynthia J. "Paratextual Performances in the Early Parisian Book Trade: Antoine Vérard's Edition of Boccaccio's *Nobles et cleres dames* (1493)." In *Cultural Performances in Medieval France: Essays in Honor of Nancy Freeman Regalado*, ed. Eglal Doss-Quinby, Roberta L. Krueger, and E. Jane Burns, 255–264. Rochester, NY: D.S. Brewer, 2007.
Burgerbibliothek of Berne. Online Archive Catalogue. "Cod. 70 (A) 2. Nangis, Guillaume de: Chronicon, 1480 (ca.)–1500 (ca.) (Codex Inhalt)." http://katalog.burgerbib.ch/detail.aspx?ID=134122.
———. Online Archive Catalogue. "Cod. 70 (A) Laudes Francorum, Nangis, Guillaume de: Chronicon, lat., 1480 (ca.)–1500 (ca.) (Codex Produktionseinheit)." http://katalog.burgerbib.ch/detail.aspx?ID=130886.
Busby, Keith. *Codex and Context: Reading Old French Verse Narrative in Manuscript.* 2 vols. Amsterdam and New York: Rodopi, 2002.
Carré de Busserolle, Jacques Xavier. *Archives des familles nobles de la Touraine de l'Anjou, du Maine et du Poitou.* Tours, France: Suppligeon, 1889.
Collard, Franck. "La bibliothèque de Saint-Victor au service des rénovateurs de l'histoire de France vers 1500? Nicole Gilles, Robert Gaguin et Paul Émile face aux ressources victorines." *Cahiers de recherches médiévales et humanistes* 17 (2009):227–240.
Couperie, Pierre, and Madeleine Jurgens. "Le logement à Paris au XVIe et XVIIe siècles." *Annales. Economies, sociétés, civilisations. 17e année* 3 (1962):488–500.

Davis, Lisa Fagin. *La Chronique Anonyme Universals: Reading and Writing History in Fifteenth-Century France*. Turnhout, Belgium: Brepols, 2015.

Delisle, Léopold. "Documents parisiens de la Bibliothèque de Berne." *Memoires de la Société de l'histoire de Paris et de l'Ile-de-France* 23 (1896):15–280.

———. *Manuscrits latins et français ajoutés aux fonds des nouvelles acquisitions pendant les années 1875-1891*. Paris: Bibliothèque nationale, 1891.

Descimon, Robert. "Élites parisiennes entre XVe et XVIIe siècle: du bon usage du Cabinet des titres." *Bibliothèque de l'École des chartes* 155.2 (1997):607–644.

Doucet, Roger. *Les bibliothèques parisiennes au XVIe siècle*. Paris: A. et J. Picard, 1956.

Edmunds, Sheila. "From Schoeffer to Vérard: Concerning the Scribes Who Became Printers." In *Printing the Written Word: The Social History of Books, circa 1450-1520*, ed. Sandra Hindman, 21–40. Ithaca, NY: Cornell University Press, 1992.

Emerson, Catherine. "Nicole Gilles and Literate Society." In *"Le Bel Épy qui foisonne": Collection and Translation in French Print Networks, 1476-1576*, ed. Catherine Emerson, 53–70. Oxford: Peter Lang, 2019.

———. "Nicole Gilles's Presentation of the Death of Louis XI and the Collection of Symbols of Kingship." In *The Medieval Chronicle 14*, ed. Erik Kooper and Sjoerd Levelt, 47–62. Boston and Leiden, Netherlands: Brill, 2021.

Holliday, Joan. *Genealogy and the Politics of Representation in the High and Late Middle Ages*. Cambridge, UK: Cambridge University Press, 2019.

Holz, Stefan G., Jörg Peltzer, and Maree Shirota. *The Roll in England and France in the Late Middle Ages*. Berlin: De Gruyter, 2019.

Jurgens, Madeleine. *Documents du minutier central des notaires de Paris: Inventaires après décès*, 1 (1483-1547). Paris: Archives nationales, 1982.

Kren, Thomas, and Scot McKendrick. *Illuminating the Renaissance: The Triumph of Flemish Manuscript Painting in Europe*. Los Angeles: J. Paul Getty Museum, 2003.

Langlois, Ernest. "Une rédaction en prose de l'*Ovide moralisé*," *Bibliothèque de l'École des chartes* 62 (1901):251–255.

Lapeyre, André, and Rémy Scheurer, *Les notaires et secrétaires du roi sous les règnes de Louis XI, Charles VIII et Louis XII (1461-1515): Notices personnelles et généalogies*. 2 vols. Paris: Bibliothèque nationale, 1978.

Le Maresquier-Kesteloot, Yvonne-Hélène. "L'ascension sociale d'une famille parisienne au XVe siècle: Les Turquam," *La Cité* 25 (2006):28–50.

———. "La maison médiévale parisienne, espace de relations, d'après les inventaires après décès." In *La maison, lieu de sociabilité dans des communautés urbaines européennes, de l'Antiquité à nos jours: colloque inter-*

national de l'Université Paris VII—Denis Diderot, 14–15 mai 2004, ed. Florence Gherchanoc, 73–86. Paris: Éditions le Manuscrit, 2006.

Macfarlane, John. *Antoine Vérard*. London: Chiswick Press, 1900.

Magleby, Sarah Dyer. "A Day in the Life: The Lost Ledger of a Parisian *libraire* Clerk." Paper presented at Translating the Past: A Gathering of Students and Colleagues, University of Kansas, Lawrence, KS, October 14, 2023.

Morrison, Elizabeth, and Anne D. Hedeman. *Imagining the Past in France: History in Manuscript Painting 1250–1500*. Los Angeles: J. Paul Getty Museum, 2010.

Nash, Susie. *Between France and Flanders: Manuscript Illumination in Amiens in the Fifteenth Century*. London: British Library, 1999.

Reinburg, Virginia. *French Books of Hours: Making an Archive of Prayer, c. 1400–1600*. Cambridge, UK: Cambridge University Press, 2012.

Riche, Jacques. "L'Historian Nicole Gilles (14..–1503). Sa vie, son manuscript original, les premières éditions de ses Annales et sa place dans l'historiographie française." 2 vols. Thèse de l'École des chartes, 1930. Archives nationales, Pierrefitte-sur-Seine, AB/XXVIII/83.

Riddy, Felicity. "'Burgeis' Domesticity in Late-Medieval England." In *Medieval Domesticity: Home, Housing and Household in Medieval England*, ed. Maryanne Kowaleski and P.J.P. Goldberg, 14–36. Cambridge, UK: Cambridge University Press, 2008.

Runnalls, Graham. "La vie, la mort et les livres de l'imprimeur-libraire parisien Jean Janot d'après son inventaire après décès (17 février 1522 n.s.)." *Revue Belge de Philologie et d'Histoire* 78.3–4 (2000):797–851.

Scheurer, Rémy. "Nicole Gilles et Antoine Vérard." *Bibliothèque de l'École des chartes* 128.2 (1970):415–419.

Weigert, Laura. "Antoine Vérard's Illuminated Playscript of *La vengeance nostre seigneur*: Marketing Plays and Creating the King's Image." In *The Social Life of Illumination: Manuscripts, Images, and Communities in the Late Middle Ages*, ed. Joyce Coleman, Mark Cruse, and Kathryn A. Smith, 251–293. Turnhout, Belgium: Brepols, 2013.

Winn, Mary Beth. *Anthoine Vérard, Parisian Publisher, 1485–1512: Prologues, Poems and Presentations*. Geneva: Librairie Droz, 1997.

———. "Printing the *Cent nouvelles nouvelles*: Anthoine Vérard's 1486 Edition and Its Sixteenth-Century Successors." In The Cent nouvelles nouvelles (*Burgundy-Luxembourg-France, 1458–c. 1550*), ed. Graeme Small, 81–134. Texte, Codex, & Contexte, 23. Turnhout, Belgium: Brepols, 2023.

Zupko, Ronald Edward. *French Weights and Measures before the Revolution: A Dictionary of Provincial and Local Units*. Bloomington: Indiana University Press, 1978.

A 1555 German Gift Book for Queen Mary I

VALERIE SCHUTTE

During the English Reformation, there were many literary exchanges linked England and Germany.[1] One such manuscript is British Library, Royal MS 15 B XIII,[2] a Latin translation of Plutarch's *De virtute mulierum*, or *The Virtues of Women*, by German humanist Hermann Cruser. He dedicated his translation to Queen Mary I and gave it to her in spring 1555. Despite Cruser's influence and prolific production, he is the subject of few secondary works. One very brief biography and list of his printed works exists in German.[3] Marianne Pade has examined Cruser's translations of Plutarch, yet she makes no mention of his 1555 manuscript to Queen Mary.[4] Similarly, Katherine M. MacDonald discusses Cruser's 1561 translation of *Lives* but does not address any of his earlier manuscript translations.[5] Peter Ure only explores Cruser's translations to find the source text for George Chapman's plays of the late sixteenth and early seventeenth centuries.[6]

Scholars have, however, explored other dedications accompanying early-modern English translations of Plutarch's works.[7] Andrew Taylor has investigated John Christopherson's gift of Plutarch to Mary during her brother Edward's reign, while Jeremy Maule has examined Plutarch gift manuscripts made by Henry Parker, Lord Morley.[8] Fred Schurink has also looked at dedications added to several English-language translations of Plutarch in sixteenth-century England; for example, the dedications by Thomas Wyatt to Catherine of Aragon, Thomas Elyot to his sister, John Hales to Thomas Audley Lord Chancellor, and Thomas Blundeville to Queen Elizabeth.[9]

Schurink shows that English translators offered their translations for a variety of reasons, such as positioning themselves as learned counsel to a reigning monarch or making practical advice from antiquity available for non-Latinate English readers. Schurink also suggests that there is more to learn from Tudor translations of Plutarch, such as the social and political contexts in which these works were created, differences between manuscript and printed versions, and the role of patronage in the production of literary works.[10] This essay directly responds to Schurink's call for more work to be done on dedications. Although Cruser's manuscript translation is in Latin, not English, close study provides information about the differences between manuscript and print, the occasion of giving a translation, and client and patron relationships.

Hermann Cruser and Mary

Hermann Cruser was one of the most well-known and influential translators of Plutarch's work in the mid to late sixteenth century. Prior to Mary's reign, Plutarch's *Lives* consisted of small multi-authored manuscript gatherings.[11] But in 1564, Cruser finished a complete Latin translation of *Lives*, which to this day remains useful and significant to those studying Plutarch.[12] Cruser included a dedication to King Philip II of Spain at the beginning of the text; he further dedicated most of the individual Greek and Roman pairings to various Germans or those with German ties, such as bishops, archbishops, counts, dukes, princes, and various other secretaries and chancellors in Cleves, as well as Philip II and King Frederick II of Denmark and Norway. Later, in 1573, Cruser published a collection of his own single-authored translation of Plutarch's *Moralia* in Basel, replacing other multi-authored collections as the most authoritative Latin version available.[13]

Cruser was not only an eminent humanist scholar, however. He also served as a diplomat for Duke William of Cleves, brother of Anne of Cleves,[14] dedicating the pairing of Pericles and Fabius Maximus in his Plutarch edition to William in 1564. By June 1540, Cruser was at the court of Francis I, aiding in William's search for a bride.[15] After the death of Henry VIII in 1547, William sent Cruser to England no less than six times in response to Anne of Cleves's pleas for financial assistance.[16] On December 19, 1549, imperial ambassador François van der Delft reported to the emperor that William sent Drossart de Montjoye and Cruser to England to obtain payments of the pension that was previously granted to Anne.[17] The diplomats met with King Edward but did not achieve much to alleviate Anne's financial situation.[18] In the Acts of the Privy Council, it is recorded that:

> Thambassadours of the duc of cleve whose names be doctour harman Cruser and christopher van Rolshmisen toke their leave of the Kinge maiestie and the lordes and had passport for them and their x servante four horses or geldinges and their money.[19]

For this visit, Cruser was in England just over five weeks; either van der Delft was wrong about who accompanied Cruser, or van Rolshmisen was already in England and returned home with Cruser.

Cruser was dispatched to England again in March 1551, this time with the son of Henry Olisleger, vice chancellor of Cleves, to discuss Anne's financial situation with Edward's council and the possibility of Anne's having to return to Cleves.[20] Vice Chancellor Olisleger had previously participated in the marriage negotiations between Anne and Henry. Cruser regarded Olisleger so highly that in 1564 he dedicated the pairing of Demosthenes and Cicero to him, appreciating how Olisleger had devoted his life and career for the betterment of Cleves. He likens the vice chancellor's character to that of Cicero, as both were eloquent, learned, humane, tireless, and tender to their enemies. Cruser's translations of Plutarch's lives of Cicero and Demosthenes serve as Cruser's monument to Olisleger, their friendship, and shared experiences.

During Cruser's spring 1551 visit to England, imperial ambassador Jehan Scheyfve reported in April that the English wanted rid of Anne and she desired to return home, so long as she could keep her pension.[21] On June 2, 1551, King Edward wrote to the duke of Cleves, trusting that the duke would find his response, as conveyed by Cruser, to be just and fair.[22] Cruser must have stayed in England for another month, as Scheyfve again reported on Cruser's activities on July 6, 1551, noting that he had just departed for William's court a few days prior and that he had petitioned Edward's council several times about Anne's household and allowances. Scheyfve believed that Cruser and the council had reached a reasonable arrangement and that the archbishop of Canterbury showed Anne favor.[23] It is not clear if Cruser was in England for the third time in July 1551 or if he had been in England since he arrived that March. But it seems likely that Cruser was in England the entire time.

Cruser returned to London in October 1553, though not to discuss Anne's finances. Rather, he was one of several representatives sent to settle a new trade agreement between English merchants and the Hanseatic Towns; he also brought letters of congratulations for the new Queen Mary from Duke William.[24] Prior to his arrival, William's wife, Duchess Maria of Cleves, also wrote to Mary both to congratulate her on her accession and to recommend Cruser to her as "orator of the said lord and our husband," coming to handle the business of William's sister.[25] Mary wrote back to William on October 27, 1553, to tell him that though she was now queen, she would maintain her friendship with Anne, who had always been very dear to her, and that Cruser would give William further details.[26] As one nineteenth-century German historian notes, "Mary had always been kind to abandoned Anne," so it is likely that her sentiments to the duke were more than mere form.[27] Anne's situation in England was much improved at Mary's accession, and this was shown when she rode with Princess Elizabeth directly behind Mary upon the new queen's entry into London for her coronation.

On March 14, 1554, William wrote to Mary, apprising her that he must send Cruser to Anne to inform her of the deaths of their sister Sybille (d. February 21, 1554) and their brother-in-law, Sybille's husband, John Frederick of Saxony (d. March 3, 1554). William assured Mary that these affairs would be dealt with quickly.[28] On September 5, 1554, Duke William again wrote to Mary to accept the credentials of Cruser, who had returned to England to congratulate Mary on her marriage to Philip. Cruser was accompanied by his wife, and both stayed with Anne for a while, probably to advise on Anne's new place within the English royal family and check on her financial status.[29]

Cruser's final known visit to England occurred in May 1555.[30] This visit, however, was quite unpleasant for Anne, as Cruser came to remove two of Anne's servants at the behest of her brother. Jasper Brockehouse was Anne's cofferer, having held the post since 1547. He, his wife, Gertrude, and Otho Wylik were subjects of the duke of Cleves yet served in Anne's household. Beginning in 1552, when Anne's household expenses exceeded her income of £2,666 by £922 a year, Brockehouse and Wylik attempted to curb Anne's spending so that her household would be self-sufficient. This made the men incredibly unpopular with William, who believed that his sister was entitled to live the life of "Sister to the King," her position at the Tudor court since her divorce from Henry VIII, even if that meant outspending her income. William sent Cruser to handle the matter. Anne then allowed Brockehouse to travel to Cleves to defend himself, but she did not release him from her service. One year later, in spring 1556, because Cruser had not succeeded, William was so frustrated with Brockehouse and Wylik that he sent Anne's cousin Franz von Waldeck to persuade Anne to remove the men. She continued to refuse. In the meantime, Waldeck asked Cruser for his assistance, but it was of no use, for Cruser was no longer welcomed by Anne, and after that visit, it does not seem that Cruser ever returned to England.[31] However, Cruser apparently remained a diplomat, as in his 1564 dedications he mentions serving as a diplomat to Philip's court twice, as well as taking a brief leave from William's court that allowed him to work on his Plutarchan translations.[32]

The Virtues of Women

It must have been during this final spring visit to England that Cruser gave Queen Mary his Latin translation of Plutarch's *Virtues of Women* in manuscript, as the dedication is dated 1555. Cruser's manuscript is in Latin, including the dedication to Mary; all of Cruser's translations of Plutarch were from the Greek into Latin. Yet, since Cruser served as a diplomat to England at least six times, it is reasonable to believe that he spoke or read English, so he could have written his dedication to Mary in English. Perhaps he chose to write the dedication in Latin because there was a possibility that Philip would have access to the manuscript, and Philip did not read English well. At approximately the same time as Cruser, Richard Eden dedicated his translation from Spanish of *The Decades of the Newe Worlde* by Peter Martyr d'Anghiera to the royal couple in Latin, yet the remainder of Eden's translation was in English.[33] In his dedication, Eden writes that he also included an oration to his English readers, and:

> It is unnecessary to repeat the same thing here, and little necessary since English is your native language most Serene Queen, and you may think likewise it was written or spoken to you most illustrious King, not only because you are one in the flesh by the divine bond, but also by the same gentleness of spirit, humanity, affability, and virtues other, no less spirit of character than you are one by the bond of the flesh.[34]

Eden completed his translation in English so that it could be read by Mary, who could then pass it on to Philip and her people, yet he provided a Latin dedication so that it could be read by both Philip and Mary. Cruser may have used the same strategy.

The only copy of Cruser's manuscript is in the British Library. It contains forty-five folios and is made of paper, which is in good condition with only minor wear around the edges, suggesting that the book was not heavily used. There are no markings or signs of readership other than a "C" next to the beginning of the tale of Perlides and an "S" near the beginning of the section on Stratonice. The title page is undecorated, containing only the title and the year in the shape of an inverted triangle.[35] The body of the text is broken into twenty-six sections, each a tale of a virtuous woman, each with small illuminated capitals in gold, red, blue, and black metallic ink. The first line of the body text has an illuminated "D" within a red frame against a backdrop of green grass, blue water, and white clouds.[36] Within the letter "D" are two naked people: a dark-skinned bearded man carrying a fair-colored, blonde woman whose breasts are fully exposed. They appear to be on a cart that is being pulled by two horses or cows, one white, the other brown. The white horse is rearing up behind the vertical line of the "D," perhaps suggesting unsettled movement. This possibly represents the abduction of Europa. The dedication, spanning folios two through six, has an illuminated capital of a blue letter "F," set against a background of lush green grass, a blue sky, and a white cloud, all within a red frame.[37] Straddling the letter "F," as if trying to lift it out of the ground, is a shapely naked man, who has one arm around the base of the "F" and the other hand across the top of the letter.[38]

To begin his dedication, Cruser appeals to Mary, calling her by all of her titles: "Lady Mary Queen of England, France, Naples, Jerusalem and Ireland, Defender of the Faith, Princess of Spain and Sicily, Archduchess of Austria, Duchess of Milan, Burgundy, and Brabant, Countess of Habsburg, Flanders, and Tyrol."[39] Though Cruser uses this complete list of titles, some of which Mary inherited and others that were bestowed upon her through marriage, he does not jointly dedicate this manuscript to Philip. Philip was in England at the time, awaiting the birth of his and Mary's first child, but the subject matter of the text, brave deeds of virtuous women, was presumably not a subject of immediate interest to the king, even if he could read the dedication.[40] At approximately the same time, Mary and Philip were co-dedicatees of Eden's *The Decades of the Newe Worlde*, as well as Johann Slotan's *De retinenda fide orthodoxa*, a text that celebrated the return of Catholicism to England, both subjects more suitable Mary and Philip together.[41]

In Cruser's dedication, he introduces himself as a "councilor and ambassador" of William, Duke of Jülich and Cleves, of which Mary would have been aware since Cruser had previously been to England in this capacity.[42] After his introduction, Cruser immediately acknowledges that some people suggest that a ruling queen is not natural because women are weak in body and spirit. To this, he counters that these people do not understand the work of nature and would also complain that men are sluggish and thoughtless.[43] From his personal observation, Cruser notes that men desire the strength of lions and the swiftness of deer, yet they should really focus their minds on the heavens. Even men renowned for their strength or their wit, such as Scipio Africanus, the Roman general who defeated Carthage in the Second Punic War, and Cato the Wise, the Roman senator and historian, "were not of equal strength and disposition on every side."[44]

Cruser's inclusion of Scipio in his dedication to Mary is quite interesting. At least twelve *Lives* by Plutarch were lost by the late fifteenth century, including that of Scipio Africanus, who was "esteemed by Plutarch the greatest man Rome had produced."[45] However, a version of Scipio's life written by Donato Acciaiuoli had come to be mistaken for the lost Scipio text, and by the sixteenth century was readily accepted as a life by Plutarch.[46] Between 1522 and 1535, Henry Parker, Lord Morley, had given Henry VIII a manuscript pairing of Acciaiuoli's lives of Scipio and Hannibal.[47] That Cruser includes Scipio in Mary's manuscript shows that he was aware of Plutarch's great affection for the Roman general. Cruser later includes the lives of Scipio Africanus and Hannibal in his 1564 compendium, though it is one of the rare pairings that is not prefaced with a dedication. However, it remains unclear if Cruser considered Acciaiuoli's account of Scipio to be that by Plutarch.

After Cruser's mention of these important Roman men, he acknowledges that the differences between them were great, as one conquered through combat and the other ruled through prudence. Since there could be such a disparity in excellent qualities among men, Cruser questions "who can be surprised" that there are women who take precedence before men and "who are carefully educated from the earliest age" in all manner of things.[48] These women, though they are educated, are often confined to their homes, especially when they give birth, and are kept away from all contemplation and difficult affairs.[49] For Cruser, this is not satisfactory; he has chosen to "strive to draw them out of the shadow into the light and the sun, from the house to forum and the public."[50] To illustrate his point, Cruser asks, "why are the Amazon celebrated?"[51] He answers: because they traverse the world and wage wars to earn great victories. Further he cites Semiramis, the only Assyrian queen to rule over that empire, who had "genius, prudence, spirit, and prominence" in the ninth century BCE.[52] Similarly, he describes Tomyris, the Scythian queen, who defeats and kills her enemy Cyrus the Great when he invades her lands.

Here, Cruser seems to invoke the Power of Women topos, in which an author or artist brings together, "at least two, but usually more, well-known figures from the Bible, ancient history, or romance to exemplify a cluster of interrelated themes that include the wiles of women, the power of love, and the trials of marriage."[53] Importantly, the topos "singles out the most celebrated men of the past to prove the power of women," "disorderly women" who exercise power that no man, despite his abilities, is able to resist.[54] This essentially antifeminist concept was invented to condemn overreaching women, yet it could be subverted for "competing interpretive claims," such as that put forward here by Cruser.[55] For Cruser, the Amazons, Semiramis, and Tomyris were women who overpowered men, but they did so to protect their kingdoms and people in a way that should be celebrated. Clearly Cruser knew his ancient history, but his adoption of these themes shows that he also knew contemporary political events. The concept of a female monarch was not typical for England, and Cruser understood that in order to be a successful queen, Mary must act like classical warrior women by claiming power and authority usually only granted to men. Tomyris, queen and ruler of Scythia, was also used as an example for Mary in the pageantry created for her coronation.[56]

Cruser finds himself with no shortage of examples of powerful women for Mary. He recalls her own grandmother, Isabella of Spain, as "decorated with the insignia of virtue."[57] Cruser proudly boasts that Isabella did not concede her authority to her husband, King Ferdinand, accompanying him on both warlike and peaceful expeditions. She, "while the mighty city of Granada was being surrounded, endured in the camp in all the long and unrelenting heat" with her husband.[58] According to Cruser, Mary's mother, Isabella's daughter Catherine of Aragon, inherited this same virtue and fortitude. While Catherine's husband, "King Henry waged war with the French, the Scots, who thinking that the opportunity of his absence was in their favor, endeavored to invade England,"[59] Catherine herself "gathered together an army, repressed their legions, and slew their king," King James IV.[60] Queen Catherine behaved so wisely that she earned much praise and inspired the greatest admiration of her people, who missed her greatly after her death. Similarly, Cruser tells Mary that "your cousin Queen Mary of Hungary is from the same family," both a woman and a prince, with greatness of mind, equal to kings and emperors, and worthy to be a sister of Caesar.[61] To provide contemporary examples, Cruser cites Mary's family of strong ruling women, and he suggests that she is carrying on that tradition.

Cruser was not the only dedicator who appealed to Mary's relatives in a dedication. Prior to Mary's accession, dedicators mentioned her male relatives, specifically her father, King Henry VIII, and brother, King Edward VI, in an effort to gain patronage.[62] Similarly, Richard Eden, in his joint dedication to Mary and Philip, recalls their shared ancestors Emperor Charles V and King Ferdinand II of Aragon.[63] Making reference to the dedicatee's forebears seems to be a tactic that Cruser often used in his dedications, whether it was to show off his knowledge of the dedicatee or to make his dedication more personal. In Cruser's primary dedication to Mary's husband, Philip, in 1564, he calls Philip's father, Charles, "prudent" for once meeting with Philippe of Commines, a writer and diplomat at the courts of King Louis XI of France and Duke Charles the Bold of Burgundy, while passing through France.[64] Cruser continues to praise "the splendor of the remarkable virtues both of you and of your ancestors," such that "there is no need for the descendants of your Majesty to seek the lights of virtue abroad, but to seek them at home."[65] Furthermore, Cruser writes, "In the emperor Charles, your majesty's father, not one or the other virtue shone forth, but so many, and his deeds were so illustrious, that of no other emperor since Charlemagne."[66] This is a remarkable parallel to Cruser's own comments to Mary; he provides several examples of brave, virtuous, and wise women from Mary's own family to look to as examples of good queenship.

One can imagine Cruser understood the lessons these women could provide for a regnant queen as well. Cruser dedicates his work to Mary because there is no woman in her kingdom more worthy, as she has embraced the virtues of both her mother and grandmother when she "navigated a very stormy sea" and "prudently avoided the plots of many of the most cunning men."[67] Cruser views her reign as a signal of "hope for the future" for her subjects, and he claims, "there is no place in the middle of the Christian world which is not full of your heralds," singing her praises.[68] It is evident that Cruser greatly admired Mary as queen and understood the challenges that a female monarch faced.

Further, according to Cruser, Mary had married a noble and virtuous man, fulfilling both her political and dynastic duties. Cruser says that Mary's "most noble crown by which the whole world does not have better or more illustrious, multiplies through the fruit of your marriage."[69] Cruser must have been referring to Mary's pregnancy, expected to come to term in May 1555, coinciding with his visit to England, and implies that her child will unite the territories of England and Spain under one crown going forward. He says as much when he notes that "at the same time you are called into association with so many kingdoms, so that the might of your embrace happens in nearly the whole world."[70] This is an important point to highlight; by 1555 Mary was ruler over many kingdoms, not just England, all of which Cruser mentions at the beginning of his dedication. She was an important imperial queen, and her child with Philip was expected someday to rule over the English and Spanish empires.

The only other dedicator to make this same connection was Richard Eden, who dedicated his printed book to both Mary and Philip. In his dedication to the royal couple, Eden extolls "your royal virtues and names and splendor and the extent of your royal power [which] are otherwise well known throughout the whole empire of the Christian world, unless perhaps they ought to be there in the least where the most familiar, truly in this kingdom of England."[71]

Eden, however, had a different motivation for pointing out Mary and Philip's reputation throughout the Christian world. According to Jessica S. Hower, Eden "sought to use European activity overseas alongside ancient example and medieval precedents to simultaneously shame and cajole readers abroad."⁷² He therefore dedicated his text to both Mary and Philip so as to "trot out herculean Habsburg efforts toward colonizing, civilizing, and Christianizing the New World and ostensibly glorify their impressive feats, but also, by extension, press Tudor inadequacies in those very areas."⁷² Hower suggests that Eden used his text, and by extension, the dedication, to remind his fellow countrymen that Spain was reaping rewards from imperialist activities and that England must do the same, to both save souls and secure financial gains.⁷³

Eden argues that Mary could gain imperial power, while Cruser suggests that she already has it. Cruser points out Mary's imperial titles and influence to offer her a mirror by which to model her queenship after both her maternal ancestors and the ancient women in Plutarch's text so as to be an effective queen. By extension, he grants her significant authority and agency over England's political and dynastic place within Europe and the widening world. This is in stark contrast to the other dedications that Mary received in 1555, which, rather than acknowledging her place within imperial politics, were more interested in Mary's reign ushering in the return of Catholicism.⁷⁴ Most likely this is because, of the five dedications that Mary did receive in 1555, only Cruser's was in manuscript form; the other four were printed books. The printed books, even Eden's, were meant for a wide audience and to encourage admiration for Mary and the changes that came with her reign. Cruser's dedication, however, was written for Mary's personal readership, as it provided lessons and inspiration directly pertinent to her role as a pregnant regnant queen.

To conclude his dedication, Cruser justifies his translation and states why a compilation of the lives of heroic women from Plutarch is a suitable gift for Mary at this time. Cruser writes that he has dedicated his translation as a "monument" to her honor, for it contains the deeds of other women who are virtuous just as she is.⁷⁵ He undertook this task "eagerly" because of the great humanity that Mary was known to show her friends.⁷⁶ Cruser's dedication does not end with the typical praise and prayer for Mary's health and long reign. Rather, he tells her that "I commend your virtues to eternal memory by this writing."⁷⁷ According to Cruser, at least, only this text by Plutarch was sufficient to perform that task.

Conclusion

Herman Cruser's ambassadorial career greatly informed his dedications. He was well aware of current affairs as well as history, such as lineages and family connections, and he was able to deploy his personal knowledge of each individual monarch for whom he wrote a dedication. He dedicated his translation of Plutarch's *Virtues of Women* to Queen Mary I specifically as a manuscript and not a printed book because he meant it to be a personal gift to celebrate a new mother and queen who was able to put down rebellions and rule over vast dominions yet still perform her domestic duties. Cruser represented her as the epitome of brave womanhood for the early-modern era and as an important European and imperial queen. According to Cruser, this was a trait that ran in her family, with her mother, grandmother, and aunt. In this way, he was able to make his dedication to the queen very personal and meaningful.

Yet he also meant for his dedication and manuscript translation to serve as more than just a mirror for the queen. Since he gave it to Mary while on diplomatic mission to England, it served as a reminder of the relationship between England and Cleves. Ever since Henry VIII's marriage to Anne of Cleves in 1540 and Anne's decision to stay in England after their divorce, England and Cleves had maintained a special relationship based on mutual political and religious agreements. Now, with Mary's marriage to Philip and concurrent pregnancy, Cruser chose to reinforce that particular bond. With this manuscript Cruser reminded Mary not to break the alliance with Cleves, which was a possibility once Philip set about centralizing the territories under Habsburg rule. Throughout, Cruser treats Mary as a powerful queen, mother to the heir of a powerful blended dynasty, who must carefully balance the politics of her kingdom with that of its allies. His intimate manuscript to Mary conveys this idea of her power as a woman better than a printed book, which there was no guarantee she would see.

Independent Scholar

NOTES

1. Charles H. Herford, *Studies in the Literary Relations of England and Germany in the Sixteenth Century* (Cambridge, UK: Cambridge University Press, 1886).
2. George F. Warner and Julius P. Gilson, *Catalogue of Western Manuscripts in the Old Royal and King's Collections In the British Museum*, 4 vols. (London: British Museum, 1921), 2:158; Paul Oskar Kristeller, *Iter Italicum: Accedunt Alia Itinera: A Finding List of Uncatalogued or Incompletely Catalogued Humanistic Manuscripts of the Renaissance in Italian and Other Libraries*, 7 vols. (London: Warburg Institute; Leiden: Brill, 1963–1997), 4:203.
3. Günter Bers, *Die Schriften des niederländischen Humanisten Dr. Hermann Cruser* (Nieuwkoop, Netherlands: B. de Graff, 1971).
4. Marianne Pade, "Hermann Crusers Plutarchübersetzungen," in *Erudition and Eloquence: The Use of Latin in the Countries of the Baltic Sea (1500–1800)*, ed. O. Merisalo and R. Sarasti-Wilenius (Helsinki: Academia Scientiarum Fennica, 2003), 9–32.

5. Katherine M. MacDonald, "The Presence of Plutarch in the Preface to the Reader of Cruserius' Latin Translations of the Lives (1561)," *Bibliothèque d'Humanisme et Renaissance* 62.1 (2000):129–134.
6. Peter Ure, "Chapman's Use of North's Plutarch in *Caesar and Pompey*," *Review of English Studies* 9.35 (1958):281–284.
7. Studies on Plutarch in the early-modern period include Freyja Cox Jensen, "After Peter Burke: The Popularity of Ancient Historians, 1450–1600," *Historical Journal* 61 (2018):561–595; Cox Jensen, *Reading the Roman Republic in Early Modern England* (Leiden, Netherlands: Brill, 2012); Fred Schurink, *Plutarch in English, 1528–1603*, 2 vols. (Cambridge, UK: Modern Humanities Research Association, 2020).
8. Andrew Taylor, "How to Hold Your Tongue: John Christopherson's Plutarch and the Mid-Tudor Politics of Catholic Humanism," *Canadian Review of Comparative Literature/Revue Canadienne de Littérature Comparée* 41 (2014):411–431; Jeremy Maule, "What Did Morley Give When He Gave a 'Plutarch' Life?," in *"Triumphs of English": Henry Parker, Lord Morley, Translator to the Tudor Court*, ed. Marie Axton and James P. Carley (London: British Library, 2000), 107–130.
9. Fred Schurink, "Print, Patronage, and Occasion: Translations of Plutarch's *Moralia* in Tudor England," *Yearbook of English Studies* (2008):86–101. See also David R. Carlson, "Morley's Translations from Roman Philosophers and English Courtier Literature," in *"Triumphs of English": Henry Parker, Lord Morley, Translator to the Tudor Court*, ed. Marie Axton and James P. Carley (London: British Library, 2000), 131–151.
10. Schurink, "Print," 101.
11. Maule, "What Did Morley Give," 108–111.
12. Schurink, *Plutarch*, 1:11.
13. Ibid., 1:10.
14. Cruser is not specifically listed as escorting Anne on her progress from Cleves to England in 1539. However, the extant lists of Anne's attendants name only the most important members of Anne's train and quantify the rest as various gentlemen, gentlewomen, and servants. Cruser could have been one such gentleman. The National Archives (TNA) SP 1/155, fols. 85–88, 86r, Letter from Wotton to Cromwell, dated December 4, 1539. A list of members of Anne's train can be found in British Library, Harleian MS 296, fol. 169–170. Parts of this list are excerpted in Henry Ellis, ed., *Original Letters, Illustrative of English History*, third series (London: Richard Bentley, 1846), 3:251–252. BL, Cotton Vitellius MS C XI, fols. 220–224, is a copy of the information in BL, Harleian MS 296 in a later hand. *The Chronicle of Calais* reprints fols. 169 and 171 of BL, Harleian MS 296, as well as BL, Harleian 295,

fol. 152b, a list of how Anne would be received from Calais to Greenwich. John Gough Nichols, ed., *The Chronicle of Calais, in the Reigns of Henry VII and Henry VIII. To the Year 1540* (London: J.B. Nichols and Son, 1846), 167–179.
15. TNA, SP 1/160, fols. 161–164; *State Papers Published under the Authority of His Majesty's Commission: King Henry the Eighth, 1830–1852*, vol. 8, Part V, Foreign correspondence, 1537–1542 (London: Her Majesty's Commission for State Papers, 1849), 362–364, King Henry VIII to Wallop, dated June 22, 1540.
16. For details of Anne's finances after her divorce, see Retha Warnicke, *The Marrying of Anne of Cleves* (Cambridge, UK: Cambridge University Press, 2000), 252–255; and Mary Saaler, *Anne of Cleves: Fourth Wife of Henry VIII* (London: Rubicon Press, 1995), 103–111.
17. Martin A.S. Hume and Royall Tyler, eds., *Calendar of State Papers, Spain, Volume 9, 1547–1549* (London: Her Majesty's Stationery Office, 1912), 490, Letter from Van der Delft to the Emperor, dated December 19, 1549.
18. Warnicke, *Marrying of Anne of Cleves*, 253.
19. TNA, PC 2/3, fol. 63; *Acts of the Privy Council of England: A.D. 1542–June 1631*, vol. 2: *1547–1550*, 372, Meeting Tewisday, the xxviij of January 1549/1550.
20. TNA, SP 68/6, fol. 121, Letter from William Duke of Cleves to Edward VI, dated March 30, 1551. William B. Turnbull, ed., *Calendar of State Papers, Foreign, Edward, 1547–1553* (London: Her Majesty's Stationery Office, 1861), 81.
21. Royall Tyler, ed., *Calendar of State Papers, Spain, Volume 10, 1550–1552* (London: Her Majesty's Stationery Office, 1914), 282, Advices sent by Jehan Scheyfve, dated April 21, 1551.
22. TNA, SP 68/7, fol. 88, Letter from King Edward VI to William Duke of Cleves, 2 June 1551. Turnbull, *Calendar, Foreign, Edward*, 117.
23. Tyler, *Calendar, Spain*, 10:323, Advices sent by Jehan Scheyfve, dated 6 July 1551.
24. Royall Tyler, ed., *Calendar of State Papers, Spain, Volume 11, 1553* (London: Her Majesty's Stationery Office, 1916), 315.
25. "Oratori dicti domini et mariti nostri." TNA, SP 69/1 fol. 81; William B. Turnbull, ed., *Calendar of State Papers, Foreign Series, Queen Mary 1553–1558* (London: Her Majesty's Stationery Office, 1861), entry 39, Letter from Maria, Duchess of Cleves to Queen Mary, dated September 19, 1553.
26. A.W. Bouterwek, "Anna von Cleve," *Zeitschrift des Bergischen Geschichtsvereins* 6 (1869):150.

27. Ibid., 150. "*Maria war der verlassenen Anna immer freundlich entgegengettommen.*"
28. TNA, SP 69/3 fol. 119; Turnbull, *Calendar, Foreign, Mary*, entry 167, Letter from William Duke of Cleves to Queen Mary, dated March 14, 1554. See also Royall Tyler, ed., *Calendar of State Papers, Spain, Volume 12, 1554* (London: Her Majesty's Stationery Office, 1949), 203, Letter from Simon Renard to the Emperor, dated April 3, 1554.
29. TNA, SP 69/5, fol. 28; Turnbull, *Calendar, Foreign, Mary*, entry 258, Letter from William Duke of Cleves to Queen Mary, dated September 5, 1554. Bouterwek, "Anna," 151.
30. TNA, SP 69/6, fol. 77; Turnbull, *Calendar, Foreign, Mary*, entry 349, Letter from William Duke of Cleves to Queen Mary, dated April 28, 1555.
31. Bouterwek, "Anna," 151.
32. Plutarch, *Vitae comparatae illustrium Virorum, Graecorum & Romanorum, ita digestae ut temporum ordo series que constet*, trans. Herman Cruser (Basel: Thomas Guarin, 1564), fol. a3r, 190.
33. Richard Eden, trans., *The Decades of the Newe Worlde or West India* (London: William Powell, 1555).
34. Eden, *Decades*, fol. 4r:
    idem hic repetere superuacaneum sit, minimeque necessarium, quandoquidem Anglica lingua tibi Serenissima Regina vernacula est, idemque illustissimo Regi [quod] tibi scriptum aut dictum existimen, non solum que diuino vinculo vnum sitis in carne vna, sed etiam [quod] eadem animi lenitate, humanitiate, affabilitate, caeterissque virtutibus, non minus animi moribus quam carnis vinculo vnum sitis.
35. BL, Royal MS 15 B XIII, fol. 1a.
36. Ibid., fol. 7a.
37. Ibid., fol. 2a.
38. I would like to thank Jess Hower for providing me with these descriptions.
39. BL, Royal MS 15 B XIII, fol. 2a, "*Domina MARIAE regina Angliae. Francie. Neapolis, Hierusalem, et Hyberniae, fidei defensori. Principi Hispaniae. ac Siciliae, Archiduci Austriae, Duci Mediolani, Burgundiae, & Brabantiae: comiti Habsburgi, Flandriae, et Tirollis.*"
40. For details of how Mary and Philip prepared for the birth of their first child, see John Edwards, *Mary I: England's Catholic Queen* (New Haven, CT: Yale University Press, 2011), 266–268.
41. Johann Slotan, *De retinenda fide orthodoxa & Catholica aduersus haereses & sectas, & praccipue Lutheranam* (Cologne: Ioannes Nouesianus, 1555).
42. BL, Royal MS 15 B XIII, fol. 2a, "*consiliarius & legatus.*"

43. Ibid., fol. 2a–2b, "*imbecellicate tarditateque.*"
44. Ibid., fol. 2b, "*haud paribus vndequaque viribus aut indole fuerunt.*"
45. Maule, "What Did Morley Give," 109.
46. Ibid., 109–111.
47. James P. Carley, "The Writings of Henry Parker, Lord Morley: A Bibliographical Survey," in *"Triumphs of English": Henry Parker, Lord Morley, Translator to the Tudor Court*, ed. Maria Axton and James P. Carley (London: British Library, 2000), 28–29, 31.
48. BL, Royal MS 15 B XIII, fol. 3a, "*quis miretur*"; "*qui a prima etate et instituuntur diligenter.*"
49. BL, Royal MS 15 B XIII, fol. 3a.
50. Ibid., fol. 3b, "*easque ex vmbra in in lucem et solem, e domo extrahere in forum et publicum contendas, ne hic quidem foeminis quicquam ad.*"
51. Ibid., fol. 3b, "*Quid celebratuis Amazonibus?*"
52. Ibid., fol. 3b, "*Quid Semiramidis*"; "*ingenio, prudential, animo, promtitudine.*"
53. Susan L. Smith, *The Power of Women: A Topos in Medieval Art and Literature* (Philadelphia: University of Pennsylvania Press, 1995), 2.
54. Ibid., 2.
55. Ibid., 12.
56. Sarah Duncan, *Mary I: Gender, Power, and Ceremony in the Reign of England's First Queen* (New York: Palgrave Macmillan, 2012), 27–28; Sydney Anglo, *Spectacle, Pageantry, and Early Tudor Policy* (Oxford: Clarendon Press, 1969), 320–321.
57. BL, Royal MS 15 B XIII, fol. 4a, "*insignibus decorata virtutibus.*"
58. Ibid., fol. 4a, "*dum circumfideretur valida vrbs Granata, omnem illum longum et ancipitem laborem aestum, algoremque unacum eo in castris tolerabat.*"
59. Ibid., fol. 4a–4b, "*Ea emin, dum maritus bellum gereret Gallicum rex Henricus, Scotos, qui eius absentiam suam opportunitatem rati in acuam irrumpere Angliam moliebantur.*"
60. Ibid., fol. 4b, "*contracto exercitu repressit, atque eorum regem cesis legionibus interemit.*"
61. Ibid., fol. 4b, "*Ex eadem stirpe Regina Hungariae Maria est consobrian tua.*"
62. Valerie Schutte, *Mary I and the Art of Book Dedications: Royal Women, Power, and Persuasion* (New York: Palgrave Macmillan, 2015), 47.
63. Eden, *Decades*, fol. 3v.
64. Plutarch, Vitae comparatae, fol. a2v, "*prudentius.*"
65. Ibid., fol. a3v, "*inuitauit eo me splendor uirtutum insignium tum tuarum*"; "*non opus sit, posteri Maiestatis tuae foris ut quaerant lumina uirtutum, sed petere queante domo.*"

66. Ibid., fol. a3r, "*In imperatore Carolo patre Maiestatis tuae non una aut altera effulsit uirtus, sed tam multae, tamque sunt eius res praeclarae gestae, ut imperatoris post Carolum Magnum nullius.*"
67. BL, Royal MS 15 B XIII, fol. 5b, "*dum in erumnoso admodum salo nauigares.*" "*prudential multorum insidias versutissimorum declinaueris.*"
68. Ibid., fol. 5b, "*spem in posterum*"; "*locus mediussidius non est in orbe christiano, quin plenus sit tuorum praeconiurum.*"
69. Ibid., fol. 5b, "*Corona nobilissimi et connubium deinde, quo orbis totus maius non habuit nec illustrius. duplicemque. ex eo fructum cepisti.*"
70. Ibid., fol. 6a, "*simul in consortium vocata tot et tantorum sis regnorum, vt complexi viribus vestris fitis orbem pene vniuersum.*"
71. Eden, Decades, fol. 4r–4v, "*pertineat, Caeterum cum regiae vestre virtutes nominisque splendor ac regnorum amplitudo alias per vniuersa Christiani orbis imperia satis nota sint, nisi forte ibi miniem vbi maxime nota essa deberent, nempe in hoc Angliae regno.*"
72. Jessica S. Hower, *Tudor Empire: The Making of Early Modern Britain and the British Atlantic World, 1485–1603* (New York: Palgrave Macmillan, 2020), 210. See also Jessica S. Hower, "'Horrible and Bloudye' or 'Most Serene and Potent': Mary I and Empire," in *Mary I in Writing: Letters, Literature, and Representation*, ed. Valerie Schutte and Jessica S. Hower (New York: Palgrave Macmillan, 2022), 135–162.
73. Hower, *Tudor Empire*, 211–212.
74. John Angell, *The Agreement of the Holye Fathers, and Doctors of the Churche, vpon the Chiefest Articles of Christian Religioun as Appeareth on the Nexte Syde Folowinge, Very Necessary for All Curates* (London: William Harford, 1555); Slotan, *De retinenda fide*; Miles Hogarde, *A Mirrour of Loue, Which Such Light Doth Giue, That All Men May Learne, How to Loue and Liue* (London: Robert Caly, 1555).
75. BL, Royal MS 15 B XIII, fol. 6a, "*monumenta.*"
76. Ibid., fol. 6a, "*alacrius.*"
77. Ibid., fol. 6b, "*ego virtutes laudes que tuas eternae memorie hoc scripto commendem.*"

WORKS CITED

Primary Sources

British Library, Cotton Vitellius MS C XI.
British Library, Harleian MS 296.
British Library, Royal MS 15 B XIII.
The National Archives, PC 2/3.
The National Archives, SP 1/155.

The National Archives, SP 1/160.
The National Archives, SP 68/6.
The National Archives, SP 68/7.
The National Archives, SP 69/1.
The National Archives, SP 69/3.
The National Archives, SP 69/5.
The National Archives, SP 69/6.

Angell, John. *The Agreement of the Holye Fathers, and Doctors of the Churche, vpon the Chiefest Articles of Christian Religioun as Appeareth on the Nexte Syde Folowinge, Very Necessary for All Curates.* London: William Harford, 1555.
Eden, Richard, trans. *The Decades of the Newe Worlde or West India.* London: William Powell, 1555.
Ellis, Henry, ed. *Original Letters, Illustrative of English History.* Third series, vol. 3. London: Richard Bentley, 1846.
Hogarde, Miles. *A Mirrour of Loue, Which Such Light Doth Giue, That All Men May Learne, How to Loue and Liue.* London: Robert Caly, 1555.
Hume, Martin A.S., and Royall Tyler, eds. *Calendar of State Papers, Spain, Volume 9, 1547–1549.* London: Her Majesty's Stationery Office, 1912.
Nichols, John Gough, ed. *The Chronicle of Calais, in the Reigns of Henry VII and Henry VIII. To the Year 1540.* London: J.B. Nichols and Son, 1846.
Plutarch. *Vitae comparatae illustrium virorum, Graecorum & Romanorum, ita digestae ut temporum ordo series que constet,* trans. Herman Cruser. Basel: Thomas Guarin, 1564.
Slotan, Johann. *De retinenda fide orthodoxa & Catholica aduersus haereses & sectas, & praccipue Lutheranam.* Cologne: Ioannes Nouesianus, 1555.
State Papers Published under the Authority of His Majesty's Commission: King Henry the Eighth, 1830–1852. Vol. 8, Part V. Foreign correspondence, 1537–1542. London: Her Majesty's Commission for State Papers, 1849.
Turnbull, William B., ed. *Calendar of State Papers, Foreign, Edward, 1547–1553.* London: Her Majesty's Stationery Office, 1861.
———, ed. *Calendar of State Papers, Foreign Series, Queen Mary 1553–1558.* London: Her Majesty's Stationery Office, 1861.
Tyler, Royall, ed. *Calendar of State Papers, Spain, Volume 10, 1550–1552.* London: Her Majesty's Stationery Office, 1914.
———, ed. *Calendar of State Papers, Spain, Volume 11, 1553.* London: Her Majesty's Stationery Office, 1916.
———, ed. *Calendar of State Papers, Spain, Volume 12, 1554.* London: Her Majesty's Stationery Office, 1949.

Secondary Sources

Bers, Günter. *Die Schriften des niederländischen Humanisten Dr. Hermann Cruser*. Nieuwkoop, Netherlands: B. de Graff, 1971.

Bouterwek, A.W. "Anna von Cleve." *Zeitschrift des Bergischen Geschichtsvereins* 6 (1869):97–180.

Carley, James P. "The Writings of Henry Parker, Lord Morley: A Bibliographical Survey." In *"Triumphs of English': Henry Parker, Lord Morley, Translator to the Tudor Court*, ed. Maria Axton and James P. Carley, 27–68. London: British Library, 2000.

Carlson, David R. "Morley's Translations from Roman Philosophers and English Courtier Literature." In *"Triumphs of English": Henry Parker, Lord Morley, Translator to the Tudor Court*, ed. Marie Axton and James P. Carley, 131–151. London: British Library, 2000.

Cox Jensen, Freyja. "After Peter Burke: The Popularity of Ancient Historians, 1450–1600." *Historical Journal* 61 (2018):561–595.

———. *Reading the Roman Republic in Early Modern England*. Leiden, Netherlands: Brill, 2012.

Edwards, John. *Mary I: England's Catholic Queen*. New Haven, CT: Yale University Press, 2011.

Herford, Charles H. *Studies in the Literary Relations of England and Germany in the Sixteenth Century*. Cambridge, UK: Cambridge University Press, 1886.

Hower, Jessica S. "'Horrible and Bloudye' or 'Most Serene and Potent': Mary I and Empire." In *Mary I in Writing: Letters, Literature, and Representation*, ed. Valerie Schutte and Jessica S. Hower, 135–162. New York: Palgrave Macmillan, 2022.

———. *Tudor Empire: The Making of Early Modern Britain and the British Atlantic World, 1485–1603*. New York: Palgrave Macmillan, 2020.

Kristeller, Paul Oskar. *Iter Italicum: Accedunt Alia Itinera: A Finding List of Uncatalogued or Incompletely Catalogued Humanistic Manuscripts of the Renaissance in Italian and Other Libraries*. 7 vols. London: Warburg Institute; Leiden, Netherlands: Brill, 1963–1997.

MacDonald, Katherine M. "The Presence of Plutarch in the Preface to the Reader of Cruserius' Latin Translations of the Lives (1561)." *Bibliothèque d'Humanisme et Renaissance* 62.1 (2000):129–134.

Maule, Jeremy. "What Did Morley Give When He Gave a 'Plutarch' Life?" In *"Triumphs of English": Henry Parker, Lord Morley, Translator to the Tudor Court*, ed. Marie Axton and James P. Carley, 107–130. London: British Library, 2000.

Pade, Marianne. "Hermann Crusers Pluarchübersetzungen." in *Erudition and Eloquence: The Use of Latin in the Countries of the Baltic Sea (1500–*

1800), ed. O. Merisalo and R. Sarasti-Wilenius, 9–32. Helsinki: Academia Scientiarum Fennica, 2003.

Saaler, Mary. *Anne of Cleves: Fourth Wife of Henry VIII*. London: Rubicon Press, 1995.

Schurink, Fred. *Plutarch in English, 1528–1603*. 2 vols. Cambridge, UK: Modern Humanities Research Association, 2020.

———. "Print, Patronage, and Occasion: Translations of Plutarch's Moralia in Tudor England." *Yearbook of English Studies* (2008):86–101.

Schutte, Valerie. *Mary I and the Art of Book Dedications: Royal Women, Power, and Persuasion*. New York: Palgrave Macmillan, 2015.

Smith, Susan L. *The Power of Women: A Topos in Medieval Art and Literature*. Philadelphia: University of Pennsylvania Press, 1995.

Taylor, Andrew. "How to Hold Your Tongue: John Christopherson's Plutarch and the Mid-Tudor Politics of Catholic Humanism." *Canadian Review of Comparative Literature/Revue Canadienne de Littérature Comparée* 41 (2014):411–431.

Ure, Peter. "Chapman's Use of North's Plutarch in Caesar and Pompey." *Review of English Studies* 9.35 (1958):281–284.

Warner, George F., and Julius P. Gilson. *Catalogue of Western Manuscripts in the Old Royal and King's Collections In the British Museum*. 4 vols. London: British Museum, 1921.

Warnicke, Retha. *The Marrying of Anne of Cleves*. Cambridge, UK: Cambridge University Press, 2000.

Constructing Community in Late-Medieval French Lyric
LUCAS WOOD, ELIZAVETA STRAKHOV, S. C. KAPLAN

Poetry at the late-medieval Francophone court was a communal affair, created in and consumed by coteries whose literary activity was at once an amusing pastime, a means of cultivating, sustaining, and organizing politically valenced camaraderie, and a serious—sometimes, indeed, an ambitious and innovative—artistic endeavor.[1] The written records of fixed-form verse produced in social settings and thematizing exchange among writers accordingly blur the lines between historical lives and literary fictions, genuine and imagined relationships, conversation and authorship. Coterie manuscripts fashion and foreground intertextual networks in which the names and identities of contributors and their addressees or interlocutors become poetic signifiers, enriching dialogue on the page by positioning it both within and against real-world contexts of which modern scholarship can recover only the tantalizing trace. They also document diachronic dynamics of reception and composition, whereby mutual influence and response dissolve distinctions between author and audience, while flattening these processes' extensive temporality, enabling new patterns of synchronic reading and interpretation to emerge.

Courtly lyric co-creation frequently displays a playfully competitive dimension that partakes of the debating culture characteristic of fourteenth- and fifteenth-century French letters.[2] The members of poetic communities collaborate to grapple with erotological, ethical, and other questions, as well as to explore the possibilities of shared imagery and motifs, in ways that ultimately evince less individual ambition to win disputes or outdo companions than a collective desire to generate verse and foster fellowship. Polemical exchange that stages contrasting or complementary positions and personae thus refracts as much as it reflects the participants' authentic views: what appears to bespeak the *effet du réel*, the impact of extratextual reality on literary discourse, is often (also) an *effet de réel*, a simulacrum of the text's contiguity with the world.[3] The same paradigm applies to the affective as well as argumentative postures that writers assume. Late-medieval lyric is torn between the theoretical valorization of poetic utterance grounded in *sentement*—a feeling, fusing emotion and intellection, whose direct, spontaneous expression guarantees the sincerity and the excellence of verse—and delight in the self-conscious mastery and exhibition of literary artifice and technique.[4] In the poetry of community, not only declarations of love, but also expressions of friendly affection and social alliance linking lyric speakers, authors, and readers are suspended between these two poles. The resulting verse simultaneously performs, thematizes, and conflates virtuosity and intimacy—or fictions thereof.

Attending to these poems at once as free-standing texts and in manuscript and social context reveals how the material, conceptual, and rhetorical structures of the courtly lyric anthology and the compositions it contains shape, and are shaped by, interpersonal relations and literary sociability. This special cluster examines the imbrication of the textual, codicological, and social spaces in which literary coteries articulate their collective identities and aesthetic projects.[5] Elizaveta Strakhov considers the *Livre des Cent Ballades*, an influential fourteenth-century lyric sequence in the *débat amoureux* tradition, putatively co-authored by four poet-knights. By assessing the presentation and the plausibility of the text's claim to group authorship both within the *Cent Ballades* and in the contemporary *Livre des Fais de Boucicaut*, Strakhov uncovers its multiple layers of rhetoricity and literariness, problematizing its veracity so as to illuminate its poetic and cultural function. The *Cent Ballades*' mirage of collective composition underscores the value of homosociality and the role of literary activity in the performance of social class, which inform a particularly plastic understanding of authorship as an identity or vocation that could also, for certain late-medieval aristocrats, become a label to be adopted at will for the purposes of social advancement. Lucas Wood investigates related questions of homosocial community and sociopoetic self-fashioning in the famous personal manuscript of Charles d'Orléans (Paris, BnF fr. 25458), which bears witness to the rich literary dialogues nurtured at his ducal court at Blois. Through close readings of three of the many intertextual conversations between Charles and different partners—the otherwise unknown Fredet, fellow prince René d'Anjou, and the mixed group of courtiers who take up the trope of the *forest de Longue Actente*—orchestrated in this codex, Wood shows how the Blois coterie trades counsel and consolation and engages in agonistic play to frame intimacies that ambiguously straddle the public and private spheres. Turning to another mid-fifteenth-century courtly circle and to a celebration of women as subjects, addressees, and consumers of poetry, S.C. Kaplan appraises the occasional verse of Jean Régnier as it reflects (on) the social self-construction of his female aristocratic patrons in the orbit of the queen of France, Marie of Anjou, and the duchess of Burgundy, Isabella of Portugal. Kaplan unpacks Régnier's poems as both historical documents and textual spectacles of a female community (with the male poet at its margin) positioned on the threshold that separates and connects intimate experience, festive sociability, and the performative pursuit of cultural and political capital. Together, these three studies offer a multifaceted portrayal of poetry's privileged place and formative role in the life and the imaginary of courtly societies in the late Middle Ages.

NOTES

1. See, most notably, Jane H. M. Taylor, *The Making of Poetry: Late-Medieval French Poetic Anthologies* (Turnhout: Brepols, 2007); Adrian Armstrong, *The Virtuoso Circle: Competition, Collaboration, and Complexity in Late Medieval French Poetry* (Tempe, AZ: ACMRS, 2012); and, with a primary focus on English coterie dynamics, R. D. Perry, *Coterie Poetics and the Beginnings of the English Literary Tradition: From Chaucer to Spenser* (Philadelphia, PA: University of Pennsylvania Press, 2024).
2. Emma Cayley, *Debate and Dialogue: Alain Chartier in His Cultural Context* (Oxford: Clarendon, 2006).
3. See Nancy Freeman Regalado, "*Effet de réel, Effet du réel*: Representation and Reference in Villon's *Testament*," *Yale French Studies* 70 (1986): 63–77.
4. See Didier Lechat, "La place du *sentiment* dans l'expérience lyrique aux XIVe et XVe siècles," *Perspectives médiévales* 28 suppl. (2002): 193–207; Jacqueline Cerquiglini-Toulet, "Affect or Thought? *Sentiment* in Poetics at the End of the Middle Ages," in *Defining and Perceiving Feelings in the Late Middle Ages*, ed. Flocel Sabaté (Leiden: Brill, 2025), 35–44; and Jean-Claude Mühlethaler, *Charles d'Orléans, un lyrisme entre Moyen Âge et modernité* (Paris: Classiques Garnier, 2010), 157–74.

5. The essays in this cluster developed from papers presented together at the 2025 Sewanee Medieval Colloquium (University of the South, February 28–March 1, 2025). We are grateful for the questions and feedback of panel attendees, and especially of panel respondent R. D. Perry, on those early versions of this research.

Homosociality, Life-Writing, and the Claim to Coterie Authorship in the *Livre des Cent Ballades*

ELIZAVETA STRAKHOV

In her study of late medieval French coterie poetry, Jane H.M. Taylor suggests that poetry written in small intimate groups, or coteries, is a "passport" to high society in this period.[1] This feature of coterie poetry is visible not just from the social prominence of historical groups that co-composed poetry, such as the circle around Charles d'Orléans, but it is also felt in the way in which coterie poetry gets represented within literary texts. In the *Pastoralet* (ca. 1422–1425), for example, in which the main characters participate in an extensive display of coterie poetic exchange, Taylor notes that coterie poetry is portrayed "not as a saccharine, ornamental game, but rather as competitive and strategic, a way of expressing relationships in verse ... to consolidate an identity, or to mark a distinction. Poetry, here, is a highly sophisticated product ... a socially situated act of utterance."[2] Composing poetry with and alongside one's peers was not merely an ephemeral leisure pastime, but as meta-poetic discussions of it in contemporary literature reveal, an exercise in social self-definition and self-expression.

Composed a few decades before the *Pastoralet*, the once popular, now regrettably understudied *Livre des Cent Ballades* (1389) is a cycle of one hundred lyrics that situates itself curiously between the historical act of exchanging poetry within one's peer group and the dramatic staging of such exchanges in literary works.³ Specifically, the text proclaims itself to have been co-authored by four people: Jean de Saint-Père, Seneschal of Eu, often referred to by scholars as Jean le Seneschal, a name I will also adopt; Philippe d'Artois, Count of Eu; Jean II le Meingre, better known by his *nom de guerre* Boucicaut, who was Marshal of France and governor of Genoa; and the military commander Jean de Créseques.⁴ Oddly, however, while all the men are traceable within the historical record, none of them is known to have composed any other substantive poetry.⁵ Nevertheless, this claim is repeated in two other places. First, it is found in the thirteen responses to the text by other people, also traceable in the historical record, that circulate with all known complete manuscripts of the text. Second, the claim is partially repeated in the *Livre des Fais de Boucicaut*, a laudatory biography of Boucicaut completed twenty years later in 1409.

The *Cent Ballades*' main editor, Gaston Raynaud, did not question the fact of the text's co-authorship, given that all figures involved are, indeed, historical contemporaries orbiting the same social circles, as Raynaud's comprehensive gathering of known historical evidence for their interconnections helps show.⁶ But subsequent scholars have cast doubt on its veracity. Central to the issue is the vagueness and abruptness of the claim itself. Briefly summarized, the cycle relates how, while out riding, a young man meets a venerable older knight, Hutin, who earnestly counsels him that the good lover should remain faithful to his beloved. Six months later, the narrator rides out again and meets a mirthful young lady, La Guignarde, who offers him the opposite advice: faithfulness will only lead to heartbreak if met with refusal, and a young man might optimize his chances for success in love by courting multiple women at a time. At the very end of the work, the narrator takes his leave of the lady and announces his intention to discuss the debate he has heard with the Count of Eu. He then invites Boucicaut and Créseques to join them. In the final lines of Ballade XCIX, the narrator, heretofore using the first-person singular for the duration of the cycle, suddenly switches into first-person plural to proclaim that "ce livre" has been "par *nous* ... estruiz" [this book (has been) composed by us] (l. 34, emphasis added).⁷ The opening lines of Ballade C, inviting subsequent responses to the cycle, continue to speak in the collective voice: "Sy *prions* tous les amoureux / Que chascun seulz / Par une balade savoir / *Nous* face ..." [And so we pray all lovers, that each of them may let us know (their thoughts) in a ballade] (ll. 1–4, emphasis added).

Raynaud himself acknowledges that the stylistic integrity and formal complexity of the whole work belies its claim to four-person co-authorship. The text employs seven distinct ballade forms (comprising variations of stanza length, syllable count, and rhyme scheme) in clusters of twenty-eight ballades total; that is to say, every four lyrics the ballade form switches, going through seven different forms, only to restart again.[8] This virtuosity renders the claim to co-authorship far-fetched. Raynaud suggests that Jean le Seneschal, also the narrator of the whole cycle, is undoubtedly its main author and that it remains difficult to tell precisely what role the other co-authors historically played in the work's final shape.[9] Philip Knox draws attention to the cycle's uninterrupted quality, whereby it smoothly tells a coherent story from its first to its one hundredth ballade. In other texts, Knox observes, claims to co-authorship are formally substantiated by tangible changes in style, scope, and genre between parts of a text; by visual breaks, rubrics, or other codicological divisions; and/or by passages drawing attention to the break, e.g., "here the author died, and a new one took over." But no such break takes place in the *Cent Ballades*.[10]

Barbara K. Altmann notes the narrator's prominence in the miniatures accompanying the text in several of its manuscripts as well as his traditional presentation as both the inexperienced lover in need of advice and clerkly figure, relating his experiences to the reader, in line with other single-authored late-medieval French debate poetry. She argues that the claim to co-authorship is fully a poetic conceit where "the inclusion of names of illustrious contemporaries claims for the work a prestigious affiliation, whether fictitious or real. The participation of the men named, again whether fictitious or real, dignifies the subject matter and confers authority on the principal voice."[11] Where debate poetry might simply nod to an author's actual or would-be patrons to bolster its status and authority, this work is instead going further to present such illustrious noblemen as the narrator's close friends and peers.[12] The work's subsequent thirteen responses—by contrast, she argues, genuinely the products of a tight-knit coterie—participate within its collaborative fiction.[13] Similarly, Emma Cayley suggests that the text's "claim for collective authorship ... echoes the polyphony of the debate [between Hutin and La Guignarde] itself," becoming "part of the poem's deep fictional structure."[14]

In characterizing the claim to co-authorship as a conceit above, Altmann twice uses the phrase "whether fictitious or real" in an acknowledgment of the readiness in the *Cent Ballades* to position real people, who likely genuinely knew one another, within imagined literary situations and the ensuing complexity for our subsequent understanding of the dimensions of the conceit itself. Cayley, meanwhile, cogently suggests that, in naming its co-authors, the poem offers them as "textual identities [that] ... are *parallel with* but not assimilated to the historical identities of the poets."[15] Put otherwise, the vexed claim of the *Cent Ballades* to co-authorship depicts historical/real people as (also) literary/imagined.

In his study of late-medieval English coterie production, R.D. Perry argues that this very same tension—Perry terms its two poles as the "historical" and the "rhetorical"—is a feature of the coterie, rather than a bug.[16] The formal sign of coterie textuality, or the element that immediately makes us read works as coming out of a tight-knit group, is its internal self-referentiality: names, sobriquets, and diminutives jostle for space alongside references to shared texts, to other forms of cultural knowledge, and to mutual experiences, which are sometimes wholly illegible to outside readers.[17] For Perry, this hermeticism brings to the surface a key characteristic of coterie production, namely that:

> coteries are historical and social, that is they involve real individuals who are related to one another in specific historically and socially determined ways. But coteries are also rhetorical; writers perform the fact that they belong to a coterie through a variety of literary techniques ... Coteries never refer simply to some historical confluence of authors living in close social proximity. They instead are a *manifestation of audience that is incorporated formally into the work itself*.[18]

The late-medieval coterie is a self-consciously constructed micro-literary community offering an important intermediate step between individual authorial production and that production's eventual public reception. The coterie represents the author's initial, pointedly circumscribed audience that is anticipating, and in some ways, vetting a work for future reception in the broader literary sphere.[19] Thus, when writers incorporate names and references to the coterie in their work, they are not just naming their real-life friends. They are articulating the desired audience for their work, infusing real people with complex literary ideals and claims.

In agreement with Altmann and Cayley that the *Cent Ballades*' claim to co-authorship is a complex literary conceit, this article leans deeply into why the *Cent Ballades* reads to us as simultaneously "fictitious" and "real." I begin with the responses to the *Cent Ballades* because, in their formal heterogeneity and internal self-referentiality, they appear to be an instance of genuine and apparent coterie production, as appended to and contrasting with the main text's conceit of coterie production. And yet, as we will see, the responses only further problematize that conceit by directly playing into it. In this way, they articulate for us the challenge, noted by Perry for English coterie production above, of disentangling historicity from literariness in coterie thought. From here, I revisit the external corroboration for the claim to co-authorship found in the *Cent Ballades* that is provided in the *Livre des Fais de Boucicaut* and that has never been substantively analyzed. If the *Cent Ballades*' co-authorship is a conceit, then why and how does it recur two decades later in a biographical text? As we will see, the scenes in the *Fais* involving the *Cent Ballades* offer a sustained exercise in enmeshing historicity with literariness—in which the *Cent Ballades* itself plays a far greater role than heretofore recognized—to the point that the historical/ real and the literary/imagined fully collapse into one another until they become barely distinguishable. In the process, the *Cent Ballades* and the *Fais* help us see the ways in which, in the late Middle Ages, historical figures can sometimes function like literary characters, while literary characters can inspire, or be presented as inspiring, the actions of historical figures. By revealing how coterie texts inhabit *both* the fictitious *and* the real, the *Cent Ballades* and its adjacent texts put pressure on the idea of late-medieval authorship. In a period well documented for its rise of poets like Guillaume de Machaut and Christine de Pizan who collected their works into single-author codices, the *Cent Ballades* offers a different model of authorship as something surprisingly moveable and plastic, even ephemeral, even as it remains deeply socially significant.

The Claim to Coterie Production in the *Cent Ballades* and Its Responses

A key element of the *Cent Ballades*' claim to co-authorship is that it is subsequently corroborated by the responses that circulate, copied after the main text, in almost all its extant manuscripts.[20] As we recall, the *Cent Ballades* closes with a final ballade, in which the text's purported co-authors, referring to themselves as "nous" [we] (C, 4), request subsequent readers to append their own ballades weighing in on the text's broader debate between Hutin and La Guignarde. There are thirteen such contemporary responses, all attributed to different contemporary figures traceable within the historical record: namely, Regnaud de Trie; Jean de Chambrillac; Louis, Duke of Orléans; Lionnet de Coesmes; Jacquet d'Orléans; Guillaume de Tignonville; Jean, Duke of Berry; Jean de Mailly; Charles d'Ivry; François d'Aubercicourt; Guy VI de la Trémoïlle; Jean de Bucy; and Raoul, Bastard of Coucy. The initial response of Regnaud de Trie opens with an address to ".iiii. compagnons" [four comrades] (Response I, 2). Jean de Bucy similarly directs his response to the "seigneurs" [lords] (Response XII, 31) who have presented the debate. Guillaume de Tignonville opens his ballade with an address to "Philippe d'Artois, Seneschal, Bouciquaut / Et Creseques" (Response VI, 1–2), while Jean de Mailly opens by invoking the "doulx Seneschal" [gentle Seneschal] (Response VIII, 1).

Several theories have been proposed regarding the relationship between the *Cent Ballades* and its responses. Raynaud's synthesis of available chronicles and historical records reveals that all the men in question, *Cent Ballades* co-authors and respondents alike, belonged to the same extended social class and repeatedly crossed paths at various public events and in military campaigns.[21] Raynaud and, following him, Denis Lalande posit that the responses are the products of a courtly puy, a type of popular poetry competition originally organized by urban guilds and lay confraternities in a number of major northern French-speaking urban centers, such as Arras, Douai, and Amiens, from the late thirteenth century. They propose several possible dates at and circumstances in which all these men could have been present in one place.[22] Yet, given the difficulty of conclusively tracing all the historical figures involved to a single place and time, Craig Taylor suggests instead that the responses more likely represent an "imagined debate" between a historical coterie taking place via correspondence, rather than the product of an in-person poetic gathering.[23]

Altmann draws attention to an element of the responses missing from earlier scholarly analyses. Although their heterogeneity suggests them to be a posterior coterie production, they nevertheless function as a kind of appendix to the main text. They are copied immediately after the end of the text in each complete extant copy of the *Cent Ballades* in an integral bloc and largely stable order (though with variations consistent with the codicological mix-ups inherent to separable paratextual material), complete with illumination programs, mise-en-page, and decoration that visually consolidate them with the main text.[24] Altmann suggests that the responses are a genuine coterie production, but one whose illustrious co-authorship, made up of prominent members of the nobility, is set up to confer further authority to the *Cent Ballades* and its own claim to co-authorship.[25] Cayley pushes this line of questioning further. The highly popular genre of the late-medieval French debate, she demonstrates, perpetuates itself through continual additions and responses to earlier texts, such as the bevy of continuations spawned by the open-ended conclusion of Alain Chartier's *Belle dame sans mercy*. The *Cent Ballades* responses, she suggests, "bear traces of a coherent planning consistent with the notion of a larger fictional design" due to their heavy internal self-referentiality and adoption of a wide range of positions on the debate between loyalty and unfaithfulness espoused in the main text.[26]

So, were these responses written by a group of people after the conclusion of the original text, or are they part of that original work? Are they historical/real or literary/imagined? A good place to start disentangling this question might be to compare them to other instances of late-medieval French coterie production. Convening with members of one's social circle to write verse on shared themes and ideas is widely attested about two generations after the appearance of the *Cent Ballades*. The most famous example of this practice is collected within the monumental "poetry album" of Charles d'Orléans, now Paris, BnF fr. 25458, an unbound manuscript of Charles's own poetry, that appears to have been brought by him from England to his residence in Blois upon his release from captivity.[27] From ca. 1440 to his death in 1465, Charles added new quires of paper to the manuscript, which became filled, across the two decades, with over forty hands copying hundreds of lyrics.[28] Similar compilations featuring coterie productions emerge elsewhere, both linked to Charles's own court at Blois, and beyond, such as within the social circles of Charles's wife Marie of Cleves, of Arthur III, Duke of Brittany, and of Marguerite of Austria.[29]

These collections tend to make the coterie quality of the poetry visible through several distinct features. The works are almost always arranged into discrete, self-contained short groupings. These groupings then make visible the ways in which their authors signal their own interconnections by reusing prosodic features, such as refrains, incipits or key phraseological units; making overt allusions to each other's work; and/or, in line with Perry's comments above, deploying names and nicknames that draw attention to the lyrics' call-and-response status.[30] The so-called *concours de Blois* [Blois competition] offers a salient example: this is a cluster of lyrics by Charles d'Orléans and his guests and associates, all of which incorporate variations on the line "Je meurs de soif aupres de la fontaine" [I perish of thirst by the fountain] that vary widely in length and style.[31] Jane Taylor emphasizes that this formal reuse of recognizable elements offers late-medieval French coteries a distinct identity.[32] To Adrian Armstrong, that formal repetition of discrete elements turns coterie production into a kind of poetic "laboratory," where each poet can manifest their individuality while mutually experimenting with poetry.[33]

Interestingly, the responses to the *Cent Ballades* bear few similarities to these kinds of later coterie productions. Employing a total of eleven separate forms across thirteen responses, they are wholly heterogeneous.[34] Two (Response III by Louis, Duke of Orléans, and Response XII by Bucy) are not ballades at all but *chansons royaux*, despite the main text's requests for responses in ballade form. The thirteen responses argue both sides of the debate, and the split does not run down the middle: three stake out the position of the young woman, La Guignarde (Response I by Regnaud de Trie, Response II by Chambrillac, and Response VII by Jean, Duke of Berry); eight hold to that of the older knight Hutin (Response III by Louis, Duke of Orléans, Response IV by Lionnet, Response V by Jacquet d'Orléans, Response VI by Tignonville, Response IX by Charles d'Ivry, Response XI by Guy VI de la Trémoïlle, Response XII by Bucy, and Response XIII by Raoul, Bastard of Coucy); and two ambiguous responses, Response VIII by Mailly and Response X by François d'Aubercicourt, do not fall clearly on either side. The responses also contain none of the formal repetition characteristic of later coterie productions; they hardly even reuse similar imagery, let alone phraseology. In fact, paradoxically, the responses' formal heterogeneity, coupled with the uneven representation of the debate's two positions, lend them a sort of realism that formal regularity and a balanced exploration of the debate's opposing sides would have precluded: they read as genuinely unplanned individual responses to the *Cent Ballades*. The less they look like known examples of coterie productions, the more they read like genuine coterie productions.

And yet complexities continue to emerge. For example, although they are significantly formally less complex than the main text, they are also far from naïve or crude, often showcasing a deftness of stylistic touch and humor. Form marries content in Mailly's answer (Response VIII): he spends his first stanza outlining both sides of the debate, devoting an equal number of lines to each; the second stanza surveying Hutin's position; and the third surveying that of La Guignarde, before concluding in the envoy that he cannot reach a definitive opinion. In this way, the neutrality of his answer is mirrored by his meticulous structure. In his response, d'Aubercicourt advances his neutrality through abstruse syntax that avoids using indicative tense:

> Et non pour tant au fort je ne diroie
> Qu'estre leal ne feist plus a loer;
> Mais qu'on lui feust, autre bien ne volroye,
> Quant de ma part, querre, ne demander ...
>
> [And yet, in the end, I would not say
> That being loyal may not be most praiseworthy;
> But rather that, if one were loyal, I, for my part, would not want
> To seek nor ask for any other good ...] (Response X, 17–20)

Raoul's response (Response XIII), appears to be staunchly pro-Hutin in valorizing loyalty in love, as the author spends the first two stanzas conventionally declaring a lovesickness that has him at the point of death. But in the third stanza he inveighs against hypocritical lovers who profess to their beloveds to be upon the brink of death while secretly lying to them. Raoul's third stanza thus upends his preceding discourse, making the reader doubt the sincerity of the first two. The way in which the responses explore all possible sides of the debate, including, in these particularly ambitious installments above, the position of neutrality, brings us back to Cayley's suggestion that the responses are coherently planned, rather than *ad hoc*.

Further, as noted above, the responses are appended as a bloc to every full manuscript copy of the *Cent Ballades*, with none of the responses circulating independently, as if never, perhaps, intended to do so. They even run in largely the same order in almost all extant manuscripts.[35] The stability of the order is partly confirmed—though also partly challenged—by the responses' own internal references. Louis (Response III) addresses himself to Jean de Chambrillac and de Trie (l. 42), authors of the second and first responses, respectively. The order of the names in Louis's ballade is reversed, but the fact that de Trie's and Chambrillac's responses also occur codicologically before Louis, suggests that the standard manuscript order may at least partly reflect the original timeline of the responses themselves. Tignonville (Response VI) also notes the earlier contributions of Chambrillac and de Trie (l. 21), further underscoring their primacy to the debate. However, Tignonville's refrain also presents his ballade as responding to Charles d'Yvry (Response IX), even though d'Yvry appears after Tignonville in the manuscripts.

This discrepancy is not especially surprising: perhaps the original order of the short responses got scrambled early in the transmission process. Nevertheless, it highlights a gap between the responses' intradiegetic presentation of their co-authored status and the extradiegetic readerly experience of it, a mismatch suggesting that the responses may be telling us a *story* about the conversation surrounding the *Cent Ballades*, a story that does not fully line up with the available manuscript evidence. The mismatch resonates with Perry's point regarding the ways in which coteries meld the historical with the rhetorical. Jane Taylor similarly refers to the "fictions of intimacy" in which coterie production often traffics.[36] Likewise, for Cayley, debating communities coalesce around "collaborative fictions."[37]

But that sense of the *Cent Ballades* responses as "fictions" also emerges in the way they cursorily offer the reader key information left unsupplied by the main text, which offers no names for any of its main characters: narrator, knight, or lady. The narrator's identity is provided, we may recall, by Tignonville (Response VI) and Mailly (Response VIII), who both call him "Seneschal" with no other identifying details. On the one hand, this cursory reference reinforces the sense of intimate coterie. Tignonville and Mailly evidently feel no need to specify which of the numerous seneschals in France they are naming because their narrow audience already knows this particular one. Thus, calling him "Seneschal" makes the information appear casual, known, and incidental. And yet, hiding a protagonist's identity until a calculated later moment is a ubiquitous trope of medieval literature, especially medieval romance. Is keeping the narrator anonymous until the responses an accident of coterie production or a rhetorical effect? Is it a realistic rendering of how close friends talk, or is it a moment engineered to produce an illusion of realism?

Similarly, only the responses provide the names for the other two main characters in the *Cent Ballades*, left nameless in the main text. It is the very first response, by de Trie, that names the knight "Hutin" and the lady "La Guignarde." Here, the latter's name functions as a kind of shorthand for her half of the debate, when de Trie reiterates, in his refrain, "Je me tendray a la Guignarde" [I will hold to La Guignarde]. The sense of the names as stand-ins for the whole debate recurs especially prominently in the final response of Raoul, when he writes about hypocrites who "font serement / Que la Guignarde n'ensuyront nullement, / Hutin croyront ..." [swear oaths that they will never follow la Guignarde, they will trust in Hutin ...] (Response XIII, 20–22). Their nickname-like quality, and the names' transformation into metonymies for the key themes and ideas within the *Cent Ballades* itself, reinforce the sense of a coterie in-group. The knight and the lady, along with their argumentative positions, are so well known to this narrow audience that their names become a kind of topical argot.

But naming the beguiling female character, met in a *locus amoenus* and flirtatiously counseling unfaithfulness towards women, "La Guignarde" [the Coquette] aligns her with allegorical female figures such as the *Roman de la Rose*'s Oiseuse [Idleness]. By contrast, Hutin is a real name, rather than a descriptive sobriquet, and it has invited Raynaud, building off the work of earlier scholars, to identify the knight with the prominent military leader and crusader Hutin de Vermeilles who had particularly distinguished himself in the Hundred Years War against Edward the Black Prince, received royal favor throughout his life, and conducted numerous embassies to Avignon and other major European courts.[38] Significantly, Hutin de Vermeilles is also highlighted twice in Christine de Pizan's œuvre: in the *Epistre au dieu d'amours* (1399), where she devotes eight lines to praising him, and in the *Debat des deux amans* (1400).[39] The presence of references to the same historical figure in three closely contemporary literary texts highlights the porous boundary between history and its representation in literature: Hutin de Vermeilles is a real person, but he also seems to have functioned as a kind of trope, or well-known exemplum, for the idea of nobility, rendering him an apt literary figure for a discourse on faithfulness and knighthood within the *Cent Ballades*.

Furthermore, it is telling that the responses assign a realistic name associated with a well-known nobleman to the male character, openly favored by the narrator as the voice of reason (XCV, 1–10), whereas the female character, openly dismissed by the narrator (XCIV, 1–10), gets an allegorizing or moralizing nickname. In this way, the binary of male and female, already misogynistically mapped onto the distinction between fidelity and infidelity, deepens into a division between the historical/real and the literary/imagined. Sally Tartline Carden similarly notes that the pro-Hutin responses are especially self-referential, affirming the idea of a homosocial tight-knit group of men, firmly aligned in their mutual support of Hutin's position. The responses that uphold La Guignarde's position are, by contrast, intertextual, relying on literary references to other texts, rather than other members of the coterie, for support.[40] Thus, the casual use of naming within the responses makes them read like genuine coterie productions, but it also does some heavy rhetorical lifting for the *Cent Ballades*' main text. It helps us see the ways in which the historical actions of real people, like Hutin, can make them into literary characters or literary exempla. It also helps us understand that this poem is really about men bonding with other men, rather than its ostensible subject of the relationships between men and women. This feature invites us to wonder whether these responses are really the product of friends arguing over a fashionable set of poems or, rather, a calibrated extension of the original work, crafted to read as historical/real.

Literariness and Homosociality in the *Cent Ballades* and the *Livre des Fais de Boucicaut*

As noted above, Raynaud suggests that Jean le Seneschal is clearly the main author of the work, while the rest of the co-authors have some kind of less discernible influence on the cycle.[41] Knox goes further, casting doubt on the very idea of the cycle's co-authorship: "the *Cent Ballades* never identifies definite ligatures between discrete sections; instead it suggests an impossible unity, a communal identity so strong that the four voices who contributed to it are barely extricable, and the mechanisms of its composition remain ambiguous ... a lyric community whose coherence is absolute, even to the point where their voices merge into one."[42] And yet neither scholar goes so far as to say that the claim to co-authorship is completely fictional because, as both note, there is external historical corroboration of the *Cent Ballades*' co-authored status provided to us by a wholly separate work finished twenty years after the *Cent Ballades* in 1409: the *Livre des Fais de Boucicaut*. This anonymous biography, likely written by a French clerk working for Boucicaut in Genoa and written while its subject, who died in 1421, was still alive, is divided into four parts detailing Boucicaut's early military career, his governorship of Genoa, and his involvement with Italian politics and the Papal Schism; it culminates with a laudatory portrait of his virtues.[43] Altmann and Cayley, who do read the *Cent Ballades*' claim to co-authorship as fictional, do not address the *Fais* and how its external corroboration might interface with the fictionality of the *Cent Ballades*. My aim, accordingly, is to revisit the two texts' intriguing relationship to one another. As we are about to see, not only is this relationship as vexed as that between the main text and its responses in the *Cent Ballades*, but it helps us further understand what the *Cent Ballades*' claim to co-authorship is attempting to do.

In an early chapter on Boucicaut's youth, we learn that Boucicaut enjoys composing love poetry, specifically "balades" and other popular lyric forms of the period, "si comme il appert par le *Livre de Cent Balades*, duquel faire lui et le seneschal d'Eu furent compaignons ou voyage d'oultre mer" [as it appears from the *Livre de Cent Ballades*, which he and the Seneschal of Eu composed as companions while on an overseas voyage] (I, ix, 12–19).[44] A later chapter describes how in 1388, while in his early twenties, Boucicaut travels to the "oultre mer" (I, xvi, 7) where he learns that Philippe d'Artois, Count of Eu, the same person visited by the Seneschal at the end of the *Cent Ballades*, has been captured by the Mamluk Sultanate. Boucicaut ends up in prison alongside him. To Raynaud, the Middle Eastern setting and the involvement of Philippe suggests that this is the very voyage during which the *Cent Ballades* must have been composed. He therefore takes this story on good faith, painting a rich picture of Boucicaut and his friends who "devaient tenir à l'honneur, même sous la tente du désert ou dans les caravansérails primitifs de la Palestine, même dans les prisons du Caire, de continuer à rimer, comme ils l'auraient fait dans les salles les mieux closes et les plus richement tapissées de leurs demeures seigneuriales" [must have been determined, even in a desert tent or the primitive caravanserais of Palestine, even in the prisons of Cairo, to continue to make rhymes, as they would have in the most intimate and richly tapestried halls of their lordly domains].[45] Robert Cottrell, Lalande, and Craig Taylor uncritically repeat this assumption.[46] Knox remains less sanguine about Raynaud's conclusion, cautioning that "although it is by no means impossible that four men imprisoned far from home would compose a work set in the geographical and cultural bosom of French court culture, we should be suspicious of Raynaud's profoundly orientalist vision of how this work came into being."[47]

In fact, the *Fais*'s context for and presentation of these passages only further problematizes the idea of the coterie creation of the *Cent Ballades* and further pulls on that ongoing tension between the historical/real and the literary/imagined. Going back to the *Fais*'s clearest statement regarding the *Cent Ballades*' co-authorship—that Boucicaut and Jean le Seneschal wrote it on an overseas voyage—we immediately note two features. First, Philippe and Créseques are not listed as additional co-authors. Raynaud suggests that this omission has to do with the death of all three men at Nicopolis, Jean le Seneschal's role as protagonist justifying his retention while the other two fall out of the story by 1409.[48] This omission could indeed be historically conditioned by the men's real-life deaths. But it also mirrors the casual quality with which the original *Cent Ballades* treats the involvement of its purported co-authors. In Ballade XCIX, the narrator finishes his conversation with La Guignarde and then "ma conseilliere conduiz; / Et depuis / Enquestay de cest afaire / Au conte d'Eu, que je truiz / Prestz et duiz / A toute loiauté faire" [I escorted my counsel-giver to her home; and then I discussed this affair with the Count of Eu, whom I find ready and able to be fully faithful] (ll. 7–12). The change in setting between the park with La Guignarde and wherever this conversation with Philippe is taking place is not clearly indicated, though an earlier line notes that it is getting dark (l. 6), implying the narrator has gone back to some residence. But there is no mention of riding back nor gaining audience with the count: Philippe's name simply appears in the text. After the narrator ruminates some more on what he has heard from Hutin and La Guignarde, Boucicaut and Créseques enter the story just as abruptly when the narrator says: "Puis volz Bouciquaut *atraire* / Pour parfaire, / Et Cresequez *racon-duiz* ..." [then I wanted to bring in Boucicaut to complete this and brought over Créseques] (XCIX, 25–27, emphasis added). Where were Boucicaut and Créseques that they were able to join the narrator and Philippe so immediately and where is this whole scene taking place? To borrow a modern parlance from social media, the narrator has effectively not so much included Boucicaut and Créseques as characters as he has simply tagged them, as one might do today on Instagram. The same performance—authorship as a flexible means of grouping people together—appears to be going on in the *Fais*.

Further, the composition of the *Cent Ballades* is said by the *Fais* to take place "ou voyage d'oultre mer," a term literally meaning *overseas voyage* but also a term used in the High Middle Ages to specifically designate the crusader states of the Middle East.[49] That sense of "oultre mer" as toponym for a dreamy place of old-time derring-do becomes especially felt later on in the *Fais*. As a young man, the *Fais* tells us, Boucicaut "grant desir avoit de visiter la terre d'oultre mer" (I, xvi, 6–7), a sentence that can be translated as "had a great desire to go overseas" or, I would argue, more specifically, "had a great desire to visit the Outremer," thus linking a romanticized "East" with the idea of longing and adventure-seeking. In 1388, he and a companion take off for the Near East. They show up to the court of Ottoman Sultan Murad I, who lavishly hosts them, whereupon "ilz lui presenterent leur service en cas que il feroit guerre a aucuns Sarrasins" [they offered their service to him in the event that he was going to wage war on any Saracens] (I, xvi, 18–20). The eagerness of Boucicaut and his friend to join the Ottoman Turks in fighting literally any other unspecified pagan enemy paints Boucicaut as a young and fearless knight errant. Seeing no action in Turkey, Boucicaut and his companion briefly head over to Hungary. Thereafter, Boucicaut quickly experiences his overwhelming desire again: specifically, he "desiroit, comme dit est, visiter la Terre Sainte" [desired, as it is said, to visit the Holy Land] (I, xvi, 39–40). This repeated emphasis on Boucicaut's emotional pull towards Eastern wandering lends all his actions a kind of thoughtless quality, strengthening the text's portrayal of him as a romance hero.

The explanation of how and why Boucicaut subsequently winds up in prison alongside Philippe is worth quoting in its entirety:

> Si tost que Bouciquaut ot ce [= l'arrêt du Conte d'Eu] entendu, adont, non obstant que il eust laissié toute sa robe en une nave sus la mer en entencion d'aler en Prusse a la rese d'yver, par sa tres grant franchise et pour l'onneur du roy de France a qui le dit conte [Philippe] estoit parent, non obstant n'eust il oncques en lui gaires d'acointance, ala devers lui a Damas, dont le conte ot grant joye quant il le vit ... [L]e tresbon gentil chevalier franc et liberal Bouciquaut, qui s'en fust alé se il eust voulu, ne le voult laissier la estre prisonnier sanz lui, ains pour lui faire compaignie ... se mist en la prison avecques lui, et la demoura de sa voulenté et sanz contrainte, a ses propres despens, par l'espace de .IIII. mois que le dit conte fu es prisons du souldan qui aprés l'en laissa aler.

> As soon as Boucicaut heard about this [= Philippe's arrest], even though he had left all his possessions in a ship on the sea with the intention of going to Prussia for the winter Reise, acting out of his great generosity of spirit and for the honor of the king of France, of whom the said count [Philippe] was a relation, though Boucicaut was but barely acquainted with him, Boucicaut set out for Damascus, which caused the count great joy when he saw him ... The most good and noble knight Boucicaut, generous and unstinting, who could have left if he had so wished, did not want to abandon him in prison, and so, to keep him company ... he joined him in prison, and there remained out of his own free will and without being forced, at his own expense, for the length of the four months that the said count was the Sultan's prisoner, who later released him. (I, xvi, 47–71)

The only source for this account of Boucicaut's voyage to the Middle East is none other than the *Fais* itself.[50] Craig Taylor notes that Froissart's *Chroniques* has Boucicaut on a pilgrimage to the Holy Land in 1386, rather than 1388, and with a wholly different set of companions.[51] There is historical evidence of Philippe's capture and release from prison by the Mamluk Sultanate in Cairo, but that record does not mention any other prisoners besides Philippe himself.[52] And, as we can see, this part of the text continues to swim in romance tropes. Boucicaut generously gives up a chance at military glory for nativist solidarity. He magnanimously throws in his lot with a fellow French nobleman, whom he barely knows, fallen into the snare of a dreaded "souldan de Babiloine" [sultan of Babylon] (I, xvi, 47), a common exoticizing term for Cairo's ruler in this period taken from the *Book of John Mandeville*.[53] He stays in prison, paying for his own upkeep while being free to go at any time. Notably, this scene never actually puts Philippe, Boucicaut, Jean le Seneschal, and Créseques in one place, the latter two simply missing from the story, just like Philippe and Créseques went missing from the *Fais de Boucicaut*'s earlier account of the *Cent Ballades*' creation.[54] It also does not offer any discussion of Boucicaut's and Philippe's purported collaborative versification. In fact, the only actual link between the two episodes is that both take place in the Middle East while Boucicaut is a young man.

The link between the episodes emerges instead conceptually through both episodes' emphasis on adventure, knightly prowess, and homosocial companionship. Composing verse in prison is historically attested for several fifteenth-century poets, including, most famously, Charles d'Orléans, as well as James I of Scotland, George Ashby, and Jean Régnier, the latter also a subject of this essay cluster.[55] But the idea of prison writing also invokes the monumental literary influence of Boethius, especially widespread in the late Middle Ages, who famously encounters Lady Philosophy in the *Consolation of Philosophy* (523 CE) while awaiting execution in his prison cell.[56] Furthermore, in the case of Charles d'Orléans, in particular, that poet's historical captivity seems to have influenced the way in which he was represented by his contemporaries in other literary contexts. In the prologue to his compilation and facing-page Latin translation of Charles's poetry, the Italian humanist Antonio d'Astesano, a member of Charles's own household, explicitly compares Charles's poetry to Ovid's *Epistulae ex Ponto*, written by the great Latin poet while in political exile. As Astesano writes:

> Admiratus eram Nasonis sepe libellos,
> Quos in Pontana scripserat exul humo;
> At tantum vatem mirari desino quando
> Carmina captivi principis ista lego.
> In versus igitur librum hunc transferre latinos
> Institui [...] (fol. 9r, ll. 19–24)

> Often I had admired Ovid's book of verse that he had written as an exile in Pontus. But I cease to marvel at so great a poet when I read those songs of the imprisoned prince. I have taken it upon myself, therefore, to translate this book into Latin verses.[57]

While obviously vaunting Charles as the better poet, Astesano also declares the similarity between Ovid's and Charles's status as exiles as his motivation for rendering the French poet into Latin. This prologue is notably written by Astesano in the 1450s, at least a decade since the end of Charles's captivity, testifying to the hold Charles's imprisonment continued to exert over Astesano's conceptualization of the poet to whom he renders household service[58].

We see something similar in René I, Duke of Anjou, himself a prominent nobleman and poet, whose coterie poetry appears in Charles's poetic album, as well as owner of a lavish *Cent Ballades* manuscript.[59] His *Livre du cuer d'amours espris* features a lengthy sequence describing René's socially prominent friends and contemporaries. René presents Charles as saying:

> ... Prins fuz des Anglois et mené en servaige.
> Et tant y demouray qu'en aprins le langaige
> Par lequel fus acoint de dame belle et saige
> Et d'elle si espris qu'a Amours fis hommaige,
> Dont mains beaux dits dictié bien prisez davantaige.[60]

> I was taken by the English and led into bondage.
> And I spent so long there that I learned the language,
> By means of which I grew close to a beautiful and virtuous lady
> And was so taken with her that I pledged fealty to Love,
> About which I composed beautiful dits that were all the more praised.

René's laudatory portrait attributes Charles's entire poetic career to his experience of captivity in England, where Charles has, as per René, met the woman to whom he would consecrate all of his subsequent lyrics and even learned English for her.[61] Charles's historical experience of captivity forms part of his literary portrait decades after it ended.[62]

The very fact of imprisonment itself, sans attendant poetic activity, appears to be significant enough to warrant literary mention. In the same work, René discusses the aforementioned Jean, Duke of Berry—familiar to us as a *Cent Ballades* respondent—in terms oddly similar to Charles. In his sole reference to Jean, René describes him as having gone to England as a hostage in exchange for his father, where he met an Englishwoman and fell in love.[63] In 1360, as per the terms of the Treaty of Brétigny, Jean was indeed exchanged as a prisoner of war for his father, Jean II of France, who had been a prisoner of the English since being captured on the battlefield at the fall of Poitiers in 1356.[64] That René, writing a whole century later, has chosen to highlight this particular episode in the Duke of Berry's lengthy and illustrious career as a French royal and literary patron underscores the contemporary cultural significance of captivity to the literary treatment of a person's historical biography.

But René's stress on Jean's imprisonment is also an allusion to Machaut's monumentally popular *Fonteinne amoureuse* (1360).[65] Here, the narrator Guillaume—an avatar of the author himself, like in the *Cent Ballades*—strikes up an instant friendship with a nobleman he meets at a roadside inn. The text ends with Guillaume accompanying the nobleman to a thinly disguised Calais.[66] After extending an offer of patronage to Guillaume, the duke unhappily boards a ship bound for England, where he is doomed to reside in captivity. The nobleman's identity is never overtly stated, but Guillaume reveals that it has been encoded into the very beginning of the text as an anagram with an inserted solution. When solved, the anagram reveals the noble to be none other than Jean, Duke of Berry (ll. 40–51).[67] In this way, Jean's real-life imprisonment becomes a central aspect of his literary representation by two French poets separated by one hundred years.

But we might also read the *Fonteinne* as intertext for not just the *Fais* but for the *Cent Ballades* itself. Unlike any other major late-medieval lyric cycle, the main text of the *Cent Ballades* mixes lyric utterance and narrative elements to relate a cohesive, uninterrupted narrative from its first to its hundredth ballade in an unprecedented technique for which Knox has coined the term "narrative enjambment."[68] That is to say, the story of the narrator riding out twice through the countryside and conversing with characters is told across one hundred ballades, with narrative interludes occurring within and carrying across the ballades. Thus, Ballades LII to LVI relate how the narrator takes leave of the older knight; contemplates his advice; goes out riding again; comes across a company of young men and women in a park; sits apart from them on the riverbank; overhears them discussing his self-imposed isolation from the group; and is approached by a chatty lady who then repeatedly ignores his unwillingness to engage in conversation. This continuous narrative, interspersed with brief dialogue, runs, uninterrupted, across both stanza and ballade breaks. The *Cent Ballades*' length and narrative structure, along with its claim of being co-written by amateur poets belonging to the nobility, suggest that it is, at its core, a *dit amoureux* written in the style of those popularized by Machaut.

Machaut's *Fonteinne* is the paradigmatic text emphasizing the extent to which the ideal relationship between a poet and the illustrious nobleman who is his real-life patron is one of deep homosocial intimacy. Within a day of meeting, the rapport between Guillaume and the nobleman becomes so powerful that they fall asleep in each other's arms at the eponymous Fountain of Love to dream a shared dream. Altmann perceptively suggests that Jean le Seneschal manipulates his textual authority by presenting elite nobility as his "companions" and "social peers," borrowing his moves from those of contemporary debate poetry.[69] I suggest, however, that the Machauldian *dit amoureux* may be another significant textual source for the playful aims of the *Cent Ballades* and the texts within its orbit. The *Fonteinne* too blurs the line between the historical/real and the literary/imagined—

mixing the real Jean and his historical imprisonment with fanciful dreams at carved fountains—to present vertical social relationships between men as horizontal, deeply intimate. Jean treats the nobility as his peers not just to boost his authority but, more specifically, in order to conjure a romantic ideal of homosociality that is central to the themes of his poem and that the *Fais* is subsequently running with.

Thus, we discover that the *Fais* does not and cannot confirm the historical circumstances of the *Cent Ballades*' coterie production. The only statement repeated by both works is that Boucicaut and Jean le Seneschal co-wrote the *Cent Ballades*, and the only sources for that statement are the *Cent Ballades* and the *Fais* themselves, creating a closed circuit. Meanwhile, the *Fais* links Boucicaut's co-authorship of the *Cent Ballades* but circumstantially at best to his historically unverified imprisonment with Philippe, and the whole imprisonment episode itself reads like a chivalric romance subplot. Nevertheless, investigating this circumstantial link offers us purchase on the contemporary cultural connection between imprisonment and poetic creation and the ideal of homosociality that hovers over the idea of being imprisoned, or commenting on the imprisonment, of one's lord. It also helps us see the ways in which late-medieval French literature repeatedly fictionalizes the historical lives of real people, so that some, like the Duke of Berry, or Hutin, become ingrained in the contemporary cultural imaginary as both historical men and literary characters.

This collapse of historical people into literary characters, I posit, helps to elucidate the *Fais*'s allusive corroboration of Boucicaut's co-authorship of the *Cent ballades*. As we recall, the Outremer episode of Boucicaut's early life recounts his travels with a companion to Ottoman Turkey in search of "Saracens" to fight, followed by a hunt for military engagement through Hungary, before heading out on pilgrimage to the Levant and Egypt where he voluntarily joins Philippe in prison. Startlingly, this entire episode bears close similarities to a specific section of Hutin's advice to the narrator within the *Cent Ballades*.

As we remember, the narrator meets Hutin immediately in Ballade I, and the older knight's discourse continues all the way to Ballade L. Within this sequence, Ballades V to XVII specifically treat Hutin's relation of precepts given to him by the God of Love. The first two ballades spell out various advice regarding having grace, courtesy, fine dress, etc, familiar to readers of the *Rose*.[70] But fully half of Hutin's ventriloquization of the God of Love, Ballades VIII–XV, concerns the central importance of prowess in war to fulfilling the ideal of the faithful lover. The ideal lover should hold his own amid other brave knights on the battlefield and never hesitate to launch himself into the fray (VII, 27–35). If there is no war going on in his region, he must immediately set out to find one with a retinue of dependable men whom he treats well (VIII, 1–2, 13–36). He must be the best on the battlefield (IX, 1–7) and always fight in the vanguard (ll. 21–23). As soon as the military action hits a détente, he must immediately set off for new horizons with the very first person initiating a new military action he meets (ll. 25–28). This advice fully resonates with the *Fais*'s account of how Boucicaut's search for a decent skirmish, with a good companion, takes him from Turkey to Hungary with plans to keep going north: just like the ideal lover of the *Cent Ballades*, Boucicaut is always seeking to prove himself militarily. In Ballade X, Hutin discusses the importance of having good men around when fighting on the borders (*frontieres*) (l. 2), a specification that speaks to Boucicaut's thirst for adventure, alongside a close friend, in Ottoman Turkey against "aucuns Sarrasins" [any Saracens] (I, xvi, 20) and positions the Ottoman Empire, itself on the borders of Christian Byzantium, as a transitional zone between Europe and the rest of an undefined pagan East. Boucicaut's brief sojourn in Hungary in between stints in Turkey and the Levant similarly establishes it as a kind of European borderland.

From here, in Ballade XIII, the God of Love's precepts enjoin yet another significant action set up as corollary to all this fighting. Namely, having sought out wars everywhere possible, the ideal lover must then go on pilgrimage "en Surie, / Par navie, / Au sepulcre ou Dieu fu miz" [to Syria by ship to the sepulchre where God was placed] (ll. 13–15), that is, to the Church of the Holy Sepulchre in Jerusalem. Thereafter, he is to go "par les desers arrabiz, / Droit ou fu ensevelie … / Celle a qui Dieu fu amis / Et maris, / Katherine …" [by the Arabian deserts straight to where she, to whom God was a beloved and husband, Katherine, is buried] (ll. 27–33), that is, to the Monastery of St. Catherine on the Sinai Peninsula. In the *Fais*, our eponymous hero goes from Hungary to Venice, where he "prist son passage oultre mer. Si ala en Jherusalem ou pelerinage du Saint Sepulchre" [booked passage across the sea/to the Outremer. Thus he went to Jerusalem on pilgrimage to the Holy Sepulchre] (I, xvi, 40–42). It is immediately upon leaving this site that Boucicaut learns of Philippe's imprisonment in Damascus and goes there (I, xvi, 43–56). On their release, Boucicaut and Philippe return to Damascus and then head first to the Monastery of Saint Paul the Anchorite, southeast of Cairo, and then to none other but St. Catherine's Monastery in Sinai, before again returning to the Church of the Holy Sepulchre in Jerusalem (I, xvi, 72–77). Read against the *Cent Ballades* effectively a detour within the specific pilgrimage route laid out by Hutin.

Ballade XIV in Hutin's sequence has the ideal lover, having completed his pilgrimage, continue holding his ear to the ground for tales of any new military enterprises (ll. 7–10). The last stanza concludes with this recommendation:

Et s'au retraire [de Turquie] en galée,

> Empressée
> Vois la gent qui t'amena
> Par Sarrazins, qui l'entrée
>   Destournée
> Leur aient, or y parra
> Qui leur effort soustenra,
>   Et sera
> Le plus preux de l'assemblée;
> Pour voir, cil qui ce fera
>   Acquerra
> Proesce bien renommée.
>
> If upon returning [from Turkey] in a galley ship,
> You see the people
> Who brought you there
> Being beset
> By Saracens, who may have impeded
> Their passage, then it will grow clear
> Who is to support [those people] in their efforts
> And become
> The most courageous of the group;
> In truth, he who does this
> Will acquire
> Greatly renowned prowess. (ll. 25–36)

The ultimate task for the ideal lover, when journeying through the Near and Middle East, is to lend aid to anyone attacked by non-Christian ethnic groups of the region. This final precept dovetails remarkably closely with Boucicaut's impetuous decision to abandon all other plans in order to render support to Philippe as he languishes in Mamluk prison.

The close parallels between both texts, and their overt link, suggest the likelihood of some direct influence from the *Cent Ballades* onto the *Fais*. At the same time, it is also not beyond the realm of possibility that Boucicaut did really undertake such a voyage. Young noblemen in the fifteenth century did seek out multiple military engagements in areas of sustained political conflict, including the Near and Middle East, and pilgrimage to the Holy Land was a well-oiled machine by this time.[71] Boucicaut may have very well written, or taken some part in the creation of, the *Cent Ballades*, as both that text and the *Fais* allege.

But these texts also assert that Boucicaut has co-written the *Cent ballades*, I suggest, in a kind of intensification of the life-writing practiced by Machaut and others in the dits amoureux. In his discussion of coterie poetics cited above, Perry notes that coteries meld the historical with the rhetorical because they "are a manifestation of audience that is incorporated formally into the work itself."⁷² The *Fonteinne* offers the clearest articulation of this phenomenon, whereby Machaut flatters his real-life patron, the ideal audience for his work, by rendering him a character composing beautiful poetry within the text itself. The *Cent Ballades* and the *Fais* sharpen the same conceit, though with a key difference. If Machaut's real-life Jean remains firmly inscribed within the text's diegetic structure, the *Cent Ballades* and *Fais* break the fourth wall, as it were, so that Boucicaut is extradiegetically claimed as the co-author of the *Cent Ballades* in scenes purporting to relate his actual historical life, even as he functions within them as the idealized lover described by the plot of the *Cent Ballades*. In effect, in these works the boundary between Boucicaut as historical person and as literary character has all but collapsed. As a passport to high society in the late Middle Ages, poetry obviously reflects contemporary cultural expectations. But, less obviously, I suggest, the role of Boucicaut as both historical figure and literary character within the *Cent Ballades* and the *Fais* helps us see how contemporary cultural expectations can also in turn reflect poetic ideals, that is to say, how literature might shape historical action and the representation of historical action in ostensibly non-literary genres.

Conclusion

In a document dated from ca. the 1440s, we learn that in 1400 Philippe le Hardi, Duke of Burgundy, and Louis II, Duke of Bourbon, asked King Charles VI to establish a new institution dedicated to praising women that would function as an extensive *puy* to be based in Paris.⁷³ As per the document, which calls itself in its opening rubric a "chartre" [charter], this puy, known to scholarship as the "*Cour amoureuse*," would hold no less than fifteen costly individual poetry competitions, complete with special masses, splendid feasts, detailed formal prescriptions for each separate competition, and elaborate prizes cast from gold, all to take place annually at the Hôtel d'Artois, Philippe le Hardi's official residence in Paris.⁷⁴ Five lavishly illustrated armorials, ranging in date from the early fifteenth to early sixteenth centuries, list an astonishing 950 people total as being involved with this extensive institution.⁷⁵ Among them, we find several familiar names: Louis, Duke of Orléans; Jean, Duke of Berry; Boucicaut; de Trie; Chambrillac; Jacquet d'Orléans; Tignonville; d'Aubercicourt, and Ivry.⁷⁶ In particular, Tignonville is identified as one of the *Cour's* twenty-five "ministres" [ministers], the Cour's highest honorary ranking, as is Jean le Seneschal's son.⁷⁷ Finally, Amédée Hellot suggests that Hutin may be not the aforementioned Hutin de Vermeilles but, rather, Pierre d'Aumont, nicknamed Hutin, royal chamberlain and also a member of the *Cour*.⁷⁸ That some of the *Cent Bal-*

lades' co-authors and respondents are also members of the *Cour amoureuse* suggests yet another potential external corroboration of the text's claim to coterie production.

And yet, strangely, just like with the *Cent Ballades*, the historicity of the *Cour amoureuse* is challenging to pin down. It is in and of itself difficult to imagine that hundreds of people would gather at the Burgundian residence in Paris fifteen times a year in order to declaim amateur poetry. Theodor Straub and Tracy Adams have marshalled evidence suggesting that at least some of the nobles, listed in the charter as present for its original organizational meeting, are confirmed to have gathered at the residence of Isabeau of Bavaria in Melun in 1400, at which the planning of the *Cour* described by the charter could have taken place.[79] Nevertheless, there is only one historical record faintly suggesting that the proposed competitions subsequently occurred: a single entry in the mayoral account of Amiens of payment to a herald for bearing letters from Paris announcing a puy to be held in 1410.[80] We seem again to be dealing with the mythos of coterie production, rather than its historic reality. As Carla Bozzolo, Hélène Loyau, and Monique Ornato have shown, extant armorials listing alleged members of the *Cour* demonstrate noticeable Parisian and Burgundian slants in their make-up, suggesting that the *Cour*, in whatever form it existed, was a political organization trafficking, yet again, in the idea, rather than the practice, of coterie poetic production.[81]

Late-medieval French literature repeatedly testifies to the rise and development of the idea of the author, particularly within courtly culture. The work of poets such as Machaut, Eustache Deschamps, and Christine gets gathered into extensive collected works and/or large-scale compilations, often carefully rubricated and indexed to prominently display their names and sometimes even overseen by the poets themselves.[82] The rise of authorship as a definable category, to be prominently displayed, paves the way for our modern concept of the author's centrality to literary production, around which much of our contemporary scholarship continues to be based. But the *Livre des Cent Ballades* and its surrounding contexts productively problematize these late-medieval understandings and representations of authorship. We have teased out the supplementary role of the *Cent Ballades'* responses to the main text's claim of co-authorship and their ambiguous use of formal elements that testify alternately to realistic coterie production and to more planned design. The external corroboration of co-authorship promised by the biographical *Livre des Fais de Boucicaut* reveals itself to be heavily freighted with lacunae in its presentation of facts, engagement with late-medieval literary tropes about poetic productivity, and narrative details that transform its historical subject into a literary character straight from the *Cent Ballades* itself. Further external corroboration of *Cent Ballades* coterie members engaging in other kinds of poetic production within the institution of the *Cour amoureuse* yields only another tangle where insufficient historical evidence demonstrates not that coterie production took place but instead that the *idea* of coterie production seems to have been somehow socially expedient.

Taken together, the multiple elements surrounding the creation of the *Cent Ballades* yield an opposite vision of authorship from the model suggested by the contemporary rise of major single-author collected works manuscripts. In and around the *Cent Ballades*, authorship is a cultural label to be assumed and discarded by men whose success as contemporary poets may remain vague but whose elite social status is, by contrast, extremely visible. Authorship lends color, even flair, to the primary roles of lord, household member, or military man, by means of which men of influence negotiate their positions within a hierarchical social order. Coterie poetry is not just a passport to high society, as per Taylor above. It is a kind of safe conduct to bring along on a journey to forge some specific set of homosocial relationships, around which late-medieval courtly culture is constructed. This conception of poetic authorship—malleable, temporarily put on and quickly cast off again—might seem to stand in counterpoint to the weightiness of Machaut's or Christine's emphases on their authorial status, as underscored by the sheer size of their collected-works codices. Yet I will close by suggesting that the *Cent Ballades* helps us further understand these late-medieval projects of authorial self-fashioning by revealing to us the immense plasticity of claims to authorship, showing, in effect, the raw material out of which poets like Machaut and Christine could construct their literary authority.

Marquette University

NOTES

1. Jane H.M. Taylor, *The Making of Poetry: Late-Medieval French Poetic Anthologies* (Turnhout: Brepols, 2007), 35.
2. Taylor, *Making of Poetry*, 27.
3. The *Cent Ballades* is extant in nine late-medieval manuscripts (Brussels, KBR, MS 11218–11219 and its eighteenth-century copy Hague, Koninklijke Bibliotheek, MS KW 71 G 73; Chantilly, Bibliothèque et Archives du Château [Musee Condé] MS 491 (1680) and its eighteenth-century copy Paris, Bibliothèque nationale de France [hereafter BnF], nouvelles acquisitions françaises [hereafter naf.] MS 759; Copenhagen, Kongelige Bibliotek MS NKS 62 2; Lausanne, Bibliothèque cantonale et universitaire MS 350; Paris, BnF, fonds français [hereafter fr.] MS 826; Paris, BnF, fr. 2201; Paris, BnF, fr. 2360; Paris, BnF, naf. 1664; and Torino, Archivio di Stato, Jb.IX.10). It directly influences

late-medieval debate poetry, including Alain Chartier's *Belle dame sans mercy* and, in both form and title, Christine de Pizan's *Cent Ballades* (1394–1399) and *Cent ballades d'amant et de dame* (1402–1410), and John Gower's *Cinkante Ballades* (after 1390); see further Emma Cayley, *Debate and Dialogue: Alain Chartier in His Cultural Context* (Oxford: Oxford University Press, 2006), 13–15; R.F. Yeager, "John Gower's Audience: The Ballades," *Chaucer Review* 40.1 (2005), 81–105 (at 83–90). For the limited bibliography on the text, see "Livre des Cent Ballades, Collectif," *Jonas-IRHT/CNRS*, http://jonas.irht.cnrs.fr/oeuvre/7255 (accessed August 10, 2025).

4. Gaston Raynaud, ed., *Les Cent Ballades, poème du XVe siècle composé par Jean le Seneschal* (Paris: Firmin-Didot, 1905) gives the Seneschal's name as Jean de Saint-Pierre, reproduced in subsequent scholarship; I am following the orthography used in more recent scholarship on this family: see Carla Bozzolo and Hélène Loyau, eds., *La Cour amoureuse, dite de Charles VI*, 3 vols (Paris: Lion d'Or, 1982–1992), 1: 60–61.

5. On Jean le Seneschal, to whom Raynaud attributes another short work, see Raynaud, *Cent Ballades*, xliii–xlvi, li–liii; on Créseques, lv–lvi. On Philippe d'Artois, see Anselme de Sainte-Marie, *Histoire généalogique et chronologique de la Maison Royale de France* ... (Paris: La Compaignie des Libraires, 1726), 1: 389–390. On Boucicaut, see, for an overview, Craig Taylor, *A Virtuous Knight: Defending Marshal Boucicaut (Jean II le Meingre, 1366–1421)* (York: York Medieval Press, 2019), 11–47, and in depth, Denis Lalande, *Jean II le Meingre, dit Boucicaut (1366–1421): étude d'une biographie héroïque* (Geneva: Librairie Droz, 1988). Torino, Archivio di Stato, Jb.X.10 attributes additional ballades to Boucicaut, Philippe d'Artois, and Créseques, placed after the *Cent Ballades* itself; manuscript edited in Alessandro Vitale-Brovarone, ed., *Recueil de galanteries (Torino, Archivio di Stato, Jb.IX.10)*, *Le moyen français* 6 (1980). This unique situation is, I suspect, playing off the broader conceit of co-authorship surrounding the whole text and is fodder for an additional essay: cf. a similar suggestion in Philip Knox, "Circularity and Linearity: The Idea of the Lyric and the Idea of the Book in the *Cent Ballades* of Jean le Seneschal," *New Medieval Literatures* 16 (2016), 213–249 (at 246–248).

6. Raynaud, *Cent Ballades*, xliii–lvi.

7. Text from Raynaud, *Cent Ballades*; translations my own. The numbering of the ballades follows Raynaud's edition, with "Response" added to distinguish the numbering of the two sections. In his numbering, Raynaud follows the standard ordering for the main text and responses given in most manuscripts, see note 35 below. On the difficulties of translating *estruire*, see Barbara K. Altmann, "Notions of Collaborative

Authorship: *Les Cent Ballades* Attributed to Jean le Seneschal," *JEBS* 8 (2005), 71–96 (on 55–56).
8. See further Raynaud, *Cent Ballades*, xxv–xxvii.
9. Raynaud, *Cent Ballades*, xliii.
10. Knox, "Circularity and Linearity," 243–244.
11. Altmann, "Notions," 58.
12. Altmann, "Notions," 58–59.
13. Altmann, "Notions," 63–64.
14. Cayley, *Debate and Dialogue*, 43.
15. Cayley, *Debate and Dialogue*, 43 (emphasis added).
16. R.D. Perry, *Coterie Poetics and the Beginnings of the English Literary Tradition: From Chaucer to Spenser* (Philadelphia, PA: University of Pennsylvania Press, 2024), 4.
17. Perry, *Coterie Poetics*, 10–11.
18. Perry, *Coterie Poetics*, 12, emphasis original.
19. Perry, *Coterie Poetics*, 26–27.
20. The only manuscript missing the responses is Copenhagen, where the text breaks off at Ballade XCVII.
21. See Raynaud, *Cent Ballades*, xl–lxx. Notably, all four purported co-authors of the *Cent Ballades* ended up on the Crusade of Nicopolis, which only Boucicaut survived. For a brief but detailed overview of the crusade, see Philip Vaughan, *Philip the Bold: The Formation of the Burgundian State*, 2nd ed (Woodbridge: Boydell Press, 2002), 59–78.
22. Raynaud, *Cent Ballades*, xlviii–li; Lalande, *Jean II le Meingre*, 29–31.
23. Taylor, *Virtuous Knight*, 125.
24. Altmann, "Notions," 62–64.
25. Altmann, "Notions," 64.
26. Cayley, *Debate and Dialogue*, 43.
27. Mary-Jo Arn, *The Poet's Notebook: The Personal Manuscript of Charles d'Orléans (Paris BnF MS fr. 25458)* (Turnhout: Brepols, 2008), 56.
28. The manuscript is fully edited in John Fox and Mary-Jo Arn, eds., *The Poetry of Charles d'Orléans and his Circle: A Critical Edition of BnF MS fr. 25458, Charles d'Orléans's Personal Manuscript*, trans. R. Barton Palmer (Turnhout: Brepols, 2010); on its composite production, see Arn, *Poet's Notebook*.
29. On these and similar coterie productions, see Taylor, *Making of Poetry*; Adrian Armstrong, *The Virtuoso Circle: Competition, Collaboration, and Complexity in Late-Medieval French Poetry* (Tempe, AZ: ACRMS, 2012).
30. See esp. Taylor, *Making of Poetry*, 186–187.
31. For a thorough discussion, see Armstrong, *Virtuoso Circle*, 73–91.
32. Taylor, *Making of Poetry*, 211–212.

33. Armstrong, *Virtuoso Circle*, 75–77 (on 76).
34. See further Raynaud, *Cent Ballades*, xxvii–xxviii.
35. In Brussels; Chantilly; Lausanne; Paris, BnF fr. 826; BnF fr. 2001; and BnF fr. 1664, the order runs: de Trie, Chambrillac, Louis, Coismes, Jacquet, Tignonville, Berry, Mailly, Yvri, d'Aubercicourt, Trémoïlle, Bucy, Coucy. BnF fr. 2360 moves Berry after Coismes; notably, this manuscript bears the arms of Jean le Seneschal himself. See further Raynaud, *Cent Ballades*, xiii; Altmann, "Notions," 62. Torino, as noted in note 5 above, treats the responses differently from other manuscripts by interpolating other works, attributed to the *Cent Ballades* co-authors.
36. Taylor, *Making of Poetry*, 186–187.
37. Cayley, *Debate and Dialogue*, 53.
38. Raynaud, *Cent Ballades*, xxxvi–xxxix. Cf., on this pointed choice of names, Sally Tartline Carden, "Poetic Justice: The Revenge of La Guignarde in the *Livre des Cent Ballades*," in *Reassessing the Heroine in Medieval French Literature*, ed. Kathy M. Krause (Gainesville, FL: University Press of Florida, 2001), 133–151 (at 136).
39. Maurice Roy, ed. *Œuvres poétiques de Christine de Pisan*, 3 vols (Paris: Firmin-Didot, 1886–1896), II, 8 (*Epistre*: ll. 223–232), 97 (*Debat de deux amans*: ll. 1619–1621). In both instances, Hutin's name is placed immediately next to that of Oton de Granson, a notable collocation given that the *Cent Ballades* occurs with substantial collections of Granson's poetry in Lausanne, Torino, and BnF MS fr. 2201. The *Cent Ballades* also occurs with an incomplete copy of Pizan's *Livre de la cité des dames* in BnF fr. 826.
40. Carden, "Poetic Justice," 149–150.
41. Raynaud, *Cent Ballades*, xliii. Cf. Lalande, *Jean II le Meingre*, 28; Taylor, *Virtuous Knight*, 124.
42. Knox, "Circularity and Linearity," 243–244.
43. Denis Lalande, ed. *Le livre des Fais du bon messire Jehan le Maingre, dit Bouciquaut* (Geneva: Librairie Droz, 1985), xliii–lvii; on its authorship, Denis Lalande, "Nicolas de Gonesse est-il l'auteur du *Livre des Fais du Mareschal Bouciquaut?*," in *Miscellania Mediaevalia: Mélanges offerts à Philippe Ménard*, ed. J.-C. Faucon, A. Labbé and D. Quéruel, 2 vols (Paris: Honoré Champion, 1998) 2: 827–837; Hélène Millet, "Qui a écrit *Le livre des faits du bon messire Jehan Le Maingre dit Bouciquaut?*" in *Pratiques de la culture écrite en France au XVe siècle. Actes du Colloque international du CNRS, Paris, 16–18 mai 1992, organisé en l'honneur de Gilbert Ouy par l'unité de recherche "Culture écrite du Moyen Âge tardif,"* ed. Monique Ornato and Nicole Pons (Paris: CNRS, 1995), 135–149; and Craig Taylor and Jane H.M. Taylor, eds., *The Chivalric Biography of Boucicaut, Jean II Le Meingre* (Woodbridge, UK: Boydell & Brewer, 2016), 13–18. On the complexities of the work's portrait of Boucicaut,

see Lalande, *Jean II le Meingre*; Taylor, *Virtuous Knight*.
44. Text from Lalande, *Fais de Boucicaut*; translation my own.
45. Raynaud, *Cent Ballades*, xlvii–xlviii.
46. Robert Cottrell, "Le conflit de générations dans les *Cent Ballades*," *French Review* 37.5 (1964), 517–23 (at 517–518); Lalande, *Jean II le Meingre*, 28; Taylor, *Virtuous Knight*, 123.
47. Knox, "Circularity and Linearity," 242.
48. Raynaud, *Cent Ballades*, xlii–xliii.
49. See essays in *The French of Outremer: Communities and Communications in the Crusading Mediterranean*, ed. Laura Morreale and Nicholas L. Paul (New York, NY: Fordham University Press, 2018).
50. J. Delaville Le Roulx, *La France en Orient au XIVe siècle: Expéditions du Maréchal Boucicaut* (Paris: Librairie des Écoles françaises, 1868), 162–165; Raynaud, *Cent Ballades*, xlvi; Lalande, *Jean II Le Meingre*, 27.
51. Taylor, *Virtuous Knight*, 16, n29. Meanwhile, Anselme de Saint-Marie (*Histoire généalogique*, 1: 389) recounts that Philippe d'Artois, en route to the Holy Land, was captured by the Ottoman Turks, rather than the Mamluk Sultanate, with Boucicaut helping to negotiate his release, but in 1390, rather than 1388.
52. Delaville Le Roulx (*France en Orient*, 165, n1) and, following him, Raynaud (*Cent Ballades*, xlvii, n1), Lalande (*Jean II le Meingre*, 28, n79), and Taylor and Taylor (*Chivalric Biography*, 47, n67) all cite the following record as historical corroboration of the *Fais de Boucicaut*'s account: Venice, Archivio di Stato, Senato, MS 40 (Deliberazioni. Misti. Registro [03 ago 1385–27 apr 1389]), fol. 169r–v (viewable here: https://asve.arianna4.cloud/patrimonio/05a52338-dcb9-490e-91bc-367f1e8cd-3d9/40-deliberazioni-misti-registro-03-ago-1385-27-apr-1389, accessed September 15, 2025). However, this record concerns negotiations for the release of only Philippe d'Artois from captivity by the Mamluk Sultanate in Cairo and does not give the names of any fellow prisoners. I thank Bard Swallow and Jack McCart for helping me parse and transcribe this record.
53. Ilan Shoval, "'All the Way to the British Isles': Ayyūbid-English Diplomatic Networks in an Early Thirteenth-Century Exchange," *Speculum* 93.3 (2018), 638–668 (at 652, n56). I thank Jack McCart for this reference.
54. In support of his assertion that Jean le Seneschal is in prison with Philippe in Cairo, Raynaud (*Cent Ballades*, xlvi, n5) supplies a reference to Amedée Hellot (*Les Sénéchaux d'Eu, du XIIe au XVIe siècle, d'après les documents originaux. Le Livre des Cent Ballades* [Paris, 1899], 20), a source I have been unable to locate, who cites a 1394 record noting an undated earlier voyage "outre mer" undertaken by Philippe and Jean le Seneschal.
55. See Mary-Jo Arn and Linne Mooney, "Introduction," in *The Kingis*

Quair and Other Prison Poems, ed. Mary-Jo Arn and Linne Mooney (Kalamazoo, MI: Medieval Institute Publications, 2005); Julia Boffey, "Chaucerian Prisoners: The Context of the *Kingis Quair*," in *Chaucer and Fifteenth-Century Poetry*, ed. Julia Boffey and Janet Cowen (London: Centre for Late Antique and Medieval Studies, 1991), 84–102; Robert Epstein, "Prisoners of Reflection: The Fifteenth-Century Poetry of Exile and Imprisonment," *Exemplaria* 15.1 (2003), 159–198.

56. On the spread and translation of Boethius into vernacular writing, see esp. Alastair J. Minnis, ed., *The Medieval Boethius: Studies in the Vernacular Translations* of De Consolatione (Woodbridge, UK: D.S. Brewer, 1987).
57. Text from Grenoble, Bibliothèque municipale, MS 873; translation after A.E.B. Coldiron, *Canon, Period, and the Poetry of Charles of Orleans: Found in Translation* (Ann Arbor, MI: University of Michigan Press, 2000), 118.
58. See further Elizaveta Strakhov, "Opening Pandora's Box: Charles d'Orléans's Reception and the Work of Critical Bibliography," *Publications of the Bibliographical Society of America* 116.4 (2022), 1–37.
59. See Arn and Fox, *Poetry of Charles d'Orléans*, 839. René owned the Chantilly copy; see further Raynaud, *Cent Ballades*, x–xii.
60. Text from René d'Anjou, *Le Livre du cœur d'amour épris*, ed. and trans. Florence Bouchet (Paris: Librairie française générale, 2003), 338–340, ll. 1465–1469; translation my own.
61. For an overview of Charles's historical acquisition of English and composition of his English works, see Charles d'Orléans, *Fortunes Stabilnes: Charles of Orleans's English Book of Love*, ed. Mary-Jo Arn (Binghamton, NY: SUNY Binghamton Press, 1994), 12–39.
62. In an ironic twist of fate, Boucicaut and Charles, both taken prisoner at Agincourt, were imprisoned together for some time in Pontefract Castle in England, and Boucicaut died in 1421 without ever returning to his native soil.
63. "Jehan, duc de Berry suis … Qui en tenant prison et pour mon pere ostaige, / Le roy Jehan, qui estoit es mains des Anglois pris, / Je fu si ardaument d'estre amoureux espris / D'une dame englaische, servante au dieu d'Amours, / Que vaincu me senty …": René d'Anjou, *Cœur d'amour*, ed. Bouchet, 330, ll. 1423–1428.
64. For background, see Jonathan Sumption, *The Hundred Years War II: Trial by Fire* (Philadelphia, PA: University of Pennsylvania Press, 1999), 2: 445–454, 493–500.
65. For several classic studies, see Kevin Brownlee, *Poetic Identity in Guillaume de Machaut* (Madison, WI: University of Wisconsin, 1984); William Calin, *A Poet at the Fountain: Essays on the Narrative Verse of*

Guillaume de Machaut, 2nd ed. (Lexington, KY: University Press of Kentucky, 2014); Jacqueline Cerquiglini-Toulet,"*Un engin si soutil*": *Guillaume de Machaut et l'écriture au XIVe siècle* (Paris: Honoré Champion, 1985); and Deborah McGrady, *Controlling Readers: Guillaume de Machaut and His Late-Medieval Audience* (Toronto: University of Toronto Press, 2012).

66. James Wimsatt, *Chaucer and His French Contemporaries: Natural Music in the Fourteenth Century* (Toronto: University of Toronto Press, 1991), 82–83; Ardis Butterfield, *The Familiar Enemy: Chaucer, Language, and Nation in the Hundred Years War* (Oxford: Oxford University Press, 2009), 175.
67. See Guillaume de Machaut, *Œuvres de Guillaume de Machaut*, ed. Ernest Hoepffner (Paris, Firmin Didot, 1908–1921), 3: xxvi–xxvii; Laurence de Looze, "'Mon nom trouveras': A New Look at the Anagrams of Guillaume de Machaut, the Enigmas, Responses, and Solutions," *Romanic Review* 79 (1988), 537–557.
68. Knox, "Circularity and Linearity," 240.
69. Altmann, "Notions," 59.
70. On this text's reinscription of *Rose* themes, see Jane H.M. Taylor, "Inescapable Rose: Jean le Seneschal's *Cent Ballades* and the Art of the Cheerful Paradox," *Medium Ævum* 67 (1998), 60–84.
71. Cf. Cottrell ("Conflit des générations") who suggests that a greater number of the *Cent Ballades*' responses are pro-Hutin's position in the debate because his advice generally matches the real-life enthusiasm for war and crusade acted on by young members of the contemporary nobility, who are reading the text.
72. Perry, *Coterie Poetics*, 12.
73. See further Bozzolo and Loyau, *Cour amoureuse*, 1: 15–19.
74. Text edited in Bozzolo and Loyau, *Cour amoureuse*, 1: 35–45.
75. See further Bozzolo and Loyau, *Cour amoureuse*, 1: 7–30
76. See in Bozzolo and Loyau, *Cour amoureuse*, 1: 50–51 (Louis d'Orléans; Jean, Duke of Berry); 98-99 (Ivry); 128–129 (Boucicaut); 130–131 (Chambrillac); 138–139 (d'Aubercicourt); 2: 98–99 (Jacquet d'Orléans); 164–165 (de Trie).
77. See in Bozzolo and Loyau, *Cour amoureuse*, 1: 60–61 (Jean le Seneschal's son Jean; Tignonville).
78. Hellot, *Seneschaux d'Eu*, 35, quoted after Raynaud, *Cent Ballades*, xxxvi, n1. On Pierre d'Aumont, see Bozzolo and Loyau, *Cour amoureuse*, 1: 86–87.
79. Theodor Straub, "Die Grundung des Pariser Minnhofs von 1400," *Zeitschrift für Romanische Philologie* 77 (1961), 1–14; Tracy Adams, *The Life and Afterlife of Isabeau of Bavaria* (Baltimore: Johns Hopkins

University Press, 2010), 149–165.
80. Arthur Piaget, "Un manuscrit de la Cour amoureuse de Charles VI," *Romania* 31/124 (1902), 597–603 (on 603).
81. Carla Bozzolo and Hélène Loyau, "L'histoire de la ville de Tournai à travers les armoriaux de la Cour amoureuse dite de Charles VI," in *Congrés de Nivelles: 23–26. VIII. 1984, Actes*. 4 vols (Nivelles: Université des Nivelles, 1984), 4: 253–264; Carla Bozzolo, Hélène Loyau, and Monique Ornato, "Hommes de culture and hommes du pouvoir parisiens à la Cour amoureuse," in *Pratique de la culture écrite en France au XVe siècle: actes du colloque international du CNRS, Paris, 16–18 mai, 1992*, ed. Gilbert Ouy, Monique Ornato, and Nicole Grévy-Pons (Louvain-la-Neuve: Université de Louvain-la-Neuve, 1995), 245–278; Adams, *Life and Afterlife*, 157–165. For an argument as to the *Cour*'s being an elaborate social fiction, see Elizaveta Strakhov, "Building Identity through Heraldry and Poetry in the *Cour amoureuse*," *New Medieval Literatures* 26 (2026), forthcoming.
82. See esp. Lawrence Earp, "Machaut's Role in the Production of Manuscripts of His Work," *Journal of the American Musicological Society* 42.3 (1989), 461–503; Sarah Jane Williams, "An Author's Role in Fourteenth Century Book Production: Guillaume de Machaut's 'Livre ou je met toutes mes choses,'" *Romania* 90 (1969), 433–454; Clotilde Dauphant, "L'organisation du manuscrit des *Œuvres complètes* d'Eustache Deschamps par Raoul Tainguy," *Babel* 16 (2007), 155–184; James C. Laidlaw, "Christine de Pizan—A Publisher's Progress," *Modern Language Review* 82 (1987), 35–75; Sandra Hindman, "The Composition of the Manuscript of Christine de Pizan's Collected Works in the British Library: A Reassessment," *The British Library Journal* 9 (1983), 93–123.

WORKS CITED

Adams, Tracy. *The Life and Afterlife of Isabeau of Bavaria*. Baltimore, MD: Johns Hopkins University Press, 2010.

d'Anjou, René. *Le Livre du cœur d'amour épris*. Ed. and trans. Florence Bouchet. Paris: Librairie française générale, 2003.

Altmann, Barbara K. "Notions of Collaborative Authorship: *Les Cent Ballades* Attributed to Jean le Seneschal." *JEBS* 8 (2005), 71–96.

Armstrong, Adrian. *The Virtuoso Circle: Competition, Collaboration, and Complexity in Late-Medieval French Poetry*. Tempe, AZ: ACRMS, 2012.

Arn, Mary-Jo. *The Poet's Notebook: The Personal Manuscript of Charles d'Orléans (Paris BnF MS fr. 25458)*. Turnhout: Brepols, 2008.

Arn, Mary-Jo, ed. *Fortunes Stabilnes: Charles of Orleans's English Book of*

Love. Binghamton, NY: SUNY Binghamton Press, 1994.
Arn, Mary-Jo and John Fox, eds. *The Poetry of Charles d'Orléans and his Circle: A Critical Edition of BnF MS fr. 25458, Charles d'Orléans's Personal Manuscript.* Trans. R. Barton Palmer. Turnhout: Brepols, 2010.
Arn, Mary-Jo and Linne Mooney. *The Kingis Quair and Other Prison Poems.* Kalamazoo, MI: Medieval Institute Publications, 2005. https://metseditions.org/read/EQbkdkXHrE78u2YqFqNlLuZABGyVjqQ. Accessed May 19, 2025.
Boffey, Julia. "Chaucerian Prisoners: The Context of the *Kingis Quair.*" In *Chaucer and Fifteenth-Century Poetry,* ed. Julia Boffey and Janet Cowen. London: Centre for Late Antique and Medieval Studies, 1991. 84–102.
Bozzolo, Carla and Hélène Loyau. "L'histoire de la ville de Tournai à travers les armoriaux de la Cour amoureuse dite de Charles VI." *Congrés de Nivelles: 23–26. VIII. 1984, Actes.* 4 vols. Nivelles, 1984. 4: 253–264.
Bozzolo, Carla and Hélène Loyau, eds. *La Cour amoureuse, dite de Charles VI,* 3 vols. Paris: Lion d'Or, 1982–1992.
Bozzolo, Carla, Hélène Loyau, and Monique Ornato. "Hommes de culture and hommes du pouvoir parisiens à la Cour amoureuse." *Pratique de la culture écrite en France au XVe siècle: actes du colloque internationale du CNRS, Paris, 16–18 mai, 1992,* ed. Gilbert Ouy, Monique Ornato, and Nicole Grévy-Pons. Louvain-la-Neuve: Université de Louvain-la-Neuve, 1995. 245–278.
Brownlee, Kevin. *Poetic Identity in Guillaume de Machaut.* Madison, WI: University of Wisconsin, 1984.
Butterfield, Ardis. *The Familiar Enemy: Chaucer, Language, and Nation in the Hundred Years War.* Oxford: Oxford University Press, 2009.
Calin, William. *A Poet at the Fountain: Essays on the Narrative Verse of Guillaume de Machaut.* Lawrenceville, KY: University Press of Kentucky, 2014.
Carden, Sally Tartline. "Poetic Justice: The Revenge of La Guignarde in the *Livre des Cent Ballades.*" In *Reassessing the Heroine in Medieval French Literature,* ed. Kathy M. Krause. Gainesville, FL: University Press of Florida, 2001. 133–151.
Cayley, Emma. *Debate and Dialogue: Alain Chartier in His Cultural Context.* Oxford: Oxford University Press, 2006.
Cerquiglini-Toulet, Jacqueline, *"Un engin si soutil": Guillaume de Machaut et l'écriture au XIVe siècle.* Paris: Honoré Champion, 1985.
Coldiron, A.E.B. *Canon, Period, and the Poetry of Charles of Orleans: Found in Translation.* Ann Arbor, MI: University of Michigan Press, 2000.
Cottrell, Robert D. "Le conflit de générations dans les *Cent Ballades.*" *The French Review* 37.5 (1964), 517–523.
Dauphant, Clotilde. "L'organisation du manuscrit des *Œuvres complètes*

d'Eustache Deschamps par Raoul Tainguy." *Babel* 16 (2007), 155–184.
Delaville Le Roulx, J. *La France en Orient au XIVe siècle: Expéditions du Maréchal Boucicaut*. Paris: Librairie des Écoles françaises, 1868.
Earp, Lawrence. "Machaut's Role in the Production of Manuscripts of His Work." *Journal of the American Musicological Society* 42.3 (1989), 461–503.
Epstein, Robert. "Prisoners of Reflection: The Fifteenth-Century Poetry of Exile and Imprisonment." *Exemplaria* 15.1 (2003), 159–198.
Hellot, Amédée. *Les Sénéchaux d'Eu, du XIIe au XVIe siècle, d'après les documents originaux. Le Livre des Cent Ballades*. Paris, 1899.
Hindman, Sandra. "The Composition of the Manuscript of Christine de Pizan's Collected Works in the British Library: A Reassessment." *The British Library Journal* 9 (1983), 93–123.
Hoepffner, Ernest, ed. *Œuvres de Guillaume de Machaut*. Paris, Firmin Didot, 1908–1921.
Knox, Philip. "Circularity and Linearity: The Idea of the Lyric and the Idea of the Book in the *Cent Ballades* of Jean le Seneschal." *New Medieval Literatures* 16 (2016), 213–249.
Laidlaw, James C. "Christine de Pizan—A Publisher's Progress." *Modern Language Review* 82 (1987), 35–75.
Lalande, Denis. *Jean II le Meingre, dit Boucicaut (1366–1421): étude d'une biographie héroïque*. Geneva: Librairie Droz, 1988.
———. "Nicolas de Gonesse est-il l'auteur du *Livre des Fais du Mareschal Bouciquaut?*" In *Miscellania Mediaevalia: Mélanges offerts à Philippe Ménard*, ed. J.-C. Faucon, A. Labbé and D. Quéruel, 2 vols. Paris: Honoré Champion, 1998. 2: 827–837.
———, ed. *Le livre des fais du bon messire Jehan le Maingre, dit Bouciquaut*. Geneva: Librairie Droz, 1985.
Looze, Laurence de. "'Mon nom trouveras': A New Look at the Anagrams of Guillaume de Machaut, the Enigmas, Responses, and Solutions." *Romanic Review* 79 (1988), 537–557.
McGrady, Deborah L. *Controlling Readers: Guillaume de Machaut and His Late-Medieval Audience*. Toronto: University of Toronto Press, 2012.
Millet, Hélène. "Qui a écrit *Le livre des faits du bon messire Jehan Le Maingre dit Bouciquaut?*" In *Pratiques de la culture écrite en France au XVe siècle. Actes du Colloque international du CNRS, Paris, 16-18 mai 1992, organisé en l'honneur de Gilbert Ouy par l'unité de recherche "Culture écrite du Moyen Âge tardif,"* ed. Monique Ornato and Nicole Pons. Paris: CNRS, 1995. 135–149.
Minnis, Alastair J., ed. *The Medieval Boethius: Studies in the Vernacular Translations of De Consolatione*. Woodbridge, UK: D.S. Brewer, 1987.
Morreale, Laura and Nicholas L. Paul, eds. *The French of Outremer: Commu-*

nities and Communications in the Crusading Mediterranean. New York, NY: Fordham University Press, 2018.

Perry, R.D. *Coterie Poetics and the Beginnings of the English Literary Tradition: From Chaucer to Spenser.* Philadelphia, PA: University of Pennsylvania Press, 2024.

Piaget, Arthur. "Un manuscrit de la Cour amoureuse de Charles VI." *Romania* 31/124 (1902), 597–603.

Raynaud, Gaston, ed. *Les Cent Ballades, poème du XVe siècle composé par Jean le Seneschal.* Paris: Firmin-Didot, 1905.

Roy, Maurice, ed. *Œuvres poétiques de Christine de Pisan*, 3 vols. Paris: Firmin-Didot, 1886–1896.

"Livre des Cent Ballades, Collectif," *Jonas-IRHT/CNRS*, http://jonas.irht.cnrs.fr/oeuvre/7255. Accessed August 10, 2025.

Sainte-Marie, Anselme de. *Histoire généalogique et chronologique de la Maison Royale de France, des pairs, des grands officiers de la Couronne & de la Maison du Roy ... Tome Premier.* Paris: La Compaignie des Libraires, 1726.

Shoval, Ilan. "'All the Way to the British Isles': Ayyūbid-English Diplomatic Networks in an Early Thirteenth-Century Exchange." *Speculum* 93.3 (2018), 638–668.

Strakhov, Elizaveta. "Building Identity through Heraldry and Poetry in the *Cour amoureuse*," *New Medieval Literatures* 26 (2026), forthcoming.

———. "Opening Pandora's Box: Charles d'Orléans's Reception and the Work of Critical Bibliography." *Publications of the Bibliographical Society of America* 116.4 (2022), 1–37.

Straub, Theodor. "Die Grundung des Pariser Minnhofs von 1400." *Zeitschrift für Romanische Philologie* 77 (1961), 1–14.

Sumption, Jonathan. *The Hundred Years War II: Trial by Fire.* Philadelphia, PA: University of Pennsylvania Press, 1999.

Taylor, Craig. *A Virtuous Knight: Defending Marshal Boucicaut (Jean II le Meingre, 1366–1421).* York: York Medieval Press, 2019.

Taylor, Craig and Jane H.M. Taylor, eds. *The Chivalric Biography of Boucicaut, Jean II Le Meingre.* Woodbridge, UK: Boydell & Brewer, 2016.

Taylor, Jane H.M. "Inescapable Rose: Jean le Seneschal's *Cent Ballades* and the Art of the Cheerful Paradox." *Medium Ævum* 67 (1998), 60–84.

———. *The Making of Poetry: Late-Medieval French Poetic Anthologies.* Turnhout: Brepols, 2007.

Vaughan, Richard. *Philip the Bold: The Formation of the Burgundian State.* 2nd ed. Woodbridge: Boydell Press, 2002.

Vitale-Brovarone, Alessandro, ed. *Recueil de galanteries (Torino, Archivio di Stato, Jb.IX.10).* Montréal, CERES (*Le moyen français* 6) (1980).

Williams, Sarah Jane. "An Author's Role in Fourteenth Century Book Production: Guillaume de Machaut's 'Livre ou je met toutes mes choses.'" *Romania* 90 (1969), 433–454.

Wimsatt, James. *Chaucer and His French Contemporaries: Natural Music in the Fourteenth Century*. Toronto: University of Toronto Press, 1991.

Yeager, R.F. "John Gower's Audience: The Ballades." *Chaucer Review* 40.1 (2005), 81–105.

"*Oncques ne vy plus plaisant compaignie*": Jubilant Poetry as Record of Women's Puissance

S. C. KAPLAN

In high summer 1445, Jean Régnier (ca. 1390–ca. 1468), bailiff of Auxerre and also a poet, wrote a ballad dedicated to multiple noblewomen.[1] Although we have no manuscript copies, the ballad did survive in an early print edition.[2] In her edition of Régnier's poetic works, Eugénie Droz followed her early modern model's title in labelling it "*Balade que ledit prisonnier fist en l'an mil CCCCXXXIX, a la requeste de la royne de France, derniere trespassee, de madame la Daulphine et de madame de Calabre et de plusieurs autres, lesquelles dames estoient a Chaalons*" (Ballad which the said prisoner composed in the year 1439 [*sic*: 1445], at the request of the Queen of France most recently deceased, Madame the Dauphine, and Madame de Calabre and several others, which ladies were at Châlons).[3] This is quite the cortege of ladies gathered, according to the poem, for the pleasure of a joust. Was that all there was to this assembly, though?

In order to answer this question, I first read the poem as a historical document, investigating the truthfulness of its claims about the company of ladies that ostensibly commissioned it and their presence in this place at this time. Clarifying the relationship between this literary creation and capital-h History—recognizing the foundational truths hidden among the tropes—invites several more related questions: was this poem genuinely composed at the behest of the named women? What are its ties to other literature of the period? And what are its connections to and how did it function in the historical moment in which the women in question lived? In other words, to what degree can we trust this fictional text's presentation of biographical realities, and what are the implications for our reading of other, similar works of the period?

Guided by these inquiries, I consider this first poem alongside another two of Régnier's short verse works published in the same volume, the one composed a few months earlier for some of the same women and the other at his wife's request some fifteen years later. The intersections of women's literature, pleasure, and politics as evidenced by the differing subjects and divergent levels of intimacy in the three ballads allow me to conclude by speculating about the relationship between deliberately recorded moments of jubilation and the production and augmentation of female cultural and political capital in mid-fifteenth-century France and Burgundy.

Who Was There?

Régnier's first ballad reads:

	Qui est celluy qui se scauroit tenir	What man might know how to refrain
	D'estre joyeulx et de soy abstenir	From being joyous and to keep abstaining
	D'estre amoureux, sans joye et sans lyesse,	From being in love, without joy and jubilation,
4	Voyant roynes hault estat soustenir,	Seeing queens maintain their high estate,
	La daulphine plaisamment maintenir,	The dauphine pleasantly comport herself,
	De Bourgongne la trespuissant duchesse,	Of Burgundy the most powerful duchess,
	De Calabre la tresbelle princesse,	Of Calabria the most beautiful princess,
8	Avecques elles mainte chevaleresse,	With them much *chevaleresse*,[4]
	De damoiselles chascune bien garnie?	Each lady well adorned with damsels?
	Entre telz gens n'auroit jamais tristesse	Among such folk there would never be sadness,

	Car de doul[c]eur,⁵ de beaulté, de jeunesse	Because of sweetness, beauty, and youth,
12	Oncques ne vy plus plaisant compaignie.	Never have I seen more pleasant company.
	Qui a Chalons si eust voulu venir,	Whoever cared to come to Châlons
	Toutes ces choses on eust veu advenir,	Would have seen all of these things come to pass:
	De chevaliers, d'escuyers grant noblesse	Knights and squires of great nobility
16	Qui tous tendoient a honneur parvenir,	Who all strained to achieve honor,
	Les grans destriers bien faisoient soustenir	The great destriers helped them well to bear
	A la jouste pour monstrer leur proesse,	The joust in order to display their prowess,
	Chascun tendoit pour sa dame et maistresse	Each man striving for his lady and mistress
20	A rompre boys, lances par grant rudesse,	To break wooden lances with great force.
	A fort jouster chascun prenoit envye,	To joust strongly was each man's desire,
	Dont les aucuns cheoient a la renverse;	From which some were knocked over backwards;
	Quant ilz cheent tantost on les redresse.	When they fall, we immediately pull them back up.⁶
24	Oncques ne vy plus plaisant compaignie.	Never have I seen more pleasant company.
	Quant de ces belles je ay le souvenir,	When I remember these beauties,
	Le cueur, le corps me font rejouvenir,	They make my heart and body young again.
	Sans soucy suis, riens ne sens qui me blesse;	I am without worry, I feel nothing that hurts me.
28	Et leur servant leur plaist moy retenir,	If their servant it please them to keep me,
	Jamais autre je ne vueil devenir,	Never would I wish to become anything else,⁷
	Car nuyt et jour de penser je n'y cesse.	As night and day I do not cease thinking of it.

	Je leur fais veu et si leur fais promesse,	I make them a vow and make them a promise,
32	Maulgré dangier, vueille ou non vieillesse,⁸	Despite danger, whether old age wills it or no,
	A les servir tout le temps de ma vie;	To serve them for all the days of my life;
	Amours le veulent et mon cueur si m'en presse,	Love wishes it, and my heart presses me to it.
	Puis qu'ilz le veulent, fait sera sans paresse.	Because they want it, it will be done without sloth.
36	Oncques ne vis plus plaisant compaignie.	Never have I seen more pleasant company.
	Prince, le dieu d'amours ne la deesse	Prince, neither the god of love nor the goddess
	Si n'ont riens fait de plus grande haultesse,	Have ever made anything worthier,
	N'assemblee qui soit mieulx acomplie	Nor assembly which is fuller
40	De tout honneur et de toute richesse;	Of all honor and all riches;
	Heraulx crioient a haulte voix: "largesse";	Heralds cried out loud: "Largesse!"
	Oncques ne vy plus plaisant compaignie.	Never have I seen more pleasant company.

Between the rubric and the bulk of the first stanza, we have at least five important women gathered together: queens Marie of Anjou, of France (r. 1422–1461) and, as we shall see momentarily, Isabelle of Lorraine, titular queen of Sicily (r. 1431–1453); duchess of Burgundy Isabella of Portugal (r. 1431–1467); dauphine of France Margaret Stewart (d. 1445); and duchess of Calabria Marie of Bourbon (r. 1437–1448). According to the historical record, this much at least is true.

In her remarkable volume on Isabella of Portugal, Monique Sommé spends several pages discussing the negotiations between France and Burgundy that took place at Châlons from mid-May to July 1445.⁹ After years of rising tensions following France's failure to adhere to many of the stipulations of the 1435 Treaty of Arras and its inability to control the *écorcheurs* (armed mercenary bands) roaming and pillaging in Burgundian territory at the beginning of the 1440s, Charles VII had finally determined that he could not afford to continue alienating the duke of Burgundy if he also wished to revive the conflict with England.¹⁰ Among the women present at the negotiations were indeed the queen and her daughter-in-law, Isabella herself, and, according to Sommé, the countess of Étampes, Jacqueline d'Ailly (r. 1435–1470); Marie of Guelders, future queen consort of Scotland (r. 1449–1460 and as regent 1460–1463); and Isabella's ladies-in-waiting, whom Sommé names elsewhere in the book as Marguerite de Castro, lady of Montaigu; Isabelle de Sousa, lady of Arcis; Lienor Rodrigues; and Marguerite d'Aine, among others.[11] Marie of Bourbon's presence at Châlons can be independently supported, if not confirmed, by the fact that her husband, John II of Lorraine (r. 1453–1470), was among the men who had come to ratify the treaty that Isabella was negotiating with Charles VII (r. 1422–1461).[12]

Indeed, the presence of a great many of these women—Isabella of Portugal, Marie of Anjou, Margaret Stewart, Marie of Bourbon, Isabelle of Lorraine, Isabelle de Sousa—is recorded in Éléonore de Poitiers's *Honneurs de la cour*, composed in the 1480s and based on what Éléonore's mother Isabelle de Sousa recounted to her.[13] According to the *Book of the Deeds of Messire Jacques de Lalaing*, a text composed in the early 1470s about the events of the 1440s, there were also other women present, including the duchess of Orléans (Marie of Cleves, r. 1440–1465), specifically because they had come to town for the jousting.[14] The *Deeds* also claims that Marie of Cleves and Marie of Bourbon had each provided Jacques with a favor to wear at the jousting at Nancy a few weeks earlier. Olivier de La Marche, contemporary chronicler of the Burgundian court, confirms that *"joustes et grans festiemens"* (jousts and great festivals) followed at Châlons after everyone had gathered.[15] We may, then, safely take Régnier at his word regarding who was present.

In addition to the marked inclusion of female figures in each stanza of the ballad, two further points imply that Régnier was indeed writing for a female audience. In that first stanza, immediately after he has named the principal patrons of the ballad, Régnier notes that they are surrounded with *"mainte chevaleresse"* (l. 8). One possible way to interpret *Chevaleresse* is to render it as knights' (that is, *chevaliers'*) wives, respecting the joust context in which a great number of women of varying degrees of nobility find themselves together. However, this feminization of the word *chevalier* could instead be harkening back to Martin le Franc's use of *chevaleresse*, a female figure who fights like a knight, in his 1442 *Champion des dames*.[16] Although le Franc's text was ostensibly not well received by Philip the Good, Isabella's husband (to the point that le Franc wrote *La complainte du champion des dames a maistre Martin le Franc son acteur* very soon after), Régnier's allusion intimates that its subject matter—part of the *querelle des femmes*—might have been somewhat more appreciated by the duchess.[17]

Yet, as the second stanza is almost entirely focused on the joust rather than its audience, one could argue that the poem's narrator is speaking primarily to other men. And indeed, the use of the collective *on* in line 23 does group the speaker with his male fellows:

>   A fort jouster *chascun* prenoit envye, To joust strongly was *each man's* desire,
>   Dont les *aucuns* cheoient a la renverse; From which some [men] were knocked over backwards;
> 23   Quant *ilz* cheez tantost *on* les redresse. When they fall, we immediately pull them back up.

Each pronoun—*chascun, aucuns, ilz*—is masculine, making it clear via that *on* that the narrator is, too. However, the third stanza makes it evident that he is talking to women as well.

> 28   If their servant it please them to keep me,
>   Never would I wish to become anything else,
>   As night and day I do not cease thinking of it.
>   I make them a vow and make them a promise,
> 32   Despite danger, whether old age wills it or no,
>   To serve them for all the days of my life.

The speaking *I* does not directly address his oath to the ladies—there is no second-person plural *vous* in these verses, no use of the corresponding possessive *vostre*. Yet his use of the present tense, particularly in line 31, brings the declaration into the current moment. This is not a promise that he has already made, a record of times past that he is recounting to a nebulously defined audience, but one that he is making within the women's hearing even as he simultaneously tells the rest of his listeners about the act. His female patrons are an integral part of the social event and of courtly life more generally, even in those instances when the men's actions typically draw more attention.

Why a Joust?

According to Sébastien Nadot, jousts were often declared on short notice—when the usual suspects were all together anyway for other purposes (such as the negotiations just mentioned) and the dangers of having too many idle young men about loomed large.[18] Nadot also remarks that:

> literature's direct influence on *pas d'armes* is obvious. The décor, scenes, and roles played by knights testify to the tight ties to epics, romances, and poetry. However, literature likely played an even stronger role in the *pas d'armes* through the intermediary of the values it disseminated, particularly those related to the comportment which a good knight was required to adopt.[19]

All of these qualities appear in the second stanza of Régnier's ballad, which claims:

<pre>
     Whoever cared to come to
        Châlons
     Would have seen all of these
        things come to pass:
     Knights and squires of great
        nobility
16   Who all strained to achieve
        honor,
     The great destriers helped
        them well to bear
     The joust in order to display
        their prowess,
     Each man striving for his lady
        and mistress
20   To break wooden lances with
        great force.
     To joust strongly was each
        man's desire,
     From which some were
        knocked over backwards;
     When they fall, we immediately
        pull them back up.
</pre>

His description, comprised of vague, formulaic confrontations between valiant men who help each other up when they have been knocked down, and observed with presumed delight by high-born women, ties the physical reality of the day to the mythos of chivalry spanning from the twelfth-century works by Chrétien de Troyes through to fifteenth-century *romans*, painting everyone involved as its heirs.[20] These tropes would have been immediately recognizable to the female patrons of the poem. Philip had presented Isabella with a copy of a *Lancelot du lac* shortly after their wedding; Marie of Cleves also owned a copy of this text, BnF fr. 1430 (albeit some twenty years later), as well as more contemporary romances such as *Cleriadus et Meliadice* (BnF fr. 1439).[21] Courtly male behavior and *fin'amors* pervade the third stanza as well. The passion inspired by the mere sight of these women is such that Régnier can ignore the effects of his approximately fifty-five years and has the energy to continuously rededicate himself to their service.[22]

At no point are we privy to the women's point of view, and their agency in Régnier's love—isolated in the line "if their servant it please them to keep me"—can hardly be attributed to the women's impetus.[23] Yet this poem still clearly serves as a record of their social and political puissance, which was both based on and reinforced by their attendance at this joust and other events like it.[24] As Nadot reminds us, "it was the women who determined the value of the knights' prowess."[25] Without them, what reason would the men have for this play-fighting?[26] But, beyond that, as Bertrand Schnerb has remarked:

> The ritualized festival of the court was, thus, a spectacle appropriate to male/female relations within the heart of the aristocratic elite, but it was also, like at the Banquet of the Pheasant in 1454, the occasion to honor certain female members of the duke and duchess's entourage: the women of the ducal family, including the duke's illegitimate daughters, the ladies and girls of the house, and finally, within the framework of a politics of integration in which the court and its ceremonies played an important role, the ladies and young women of the regional nobility.[27]

Schnerb mentions many different groups of women—the high aristocracy, of course, but also those women's familial relations of closer and further degree, their ladies-in-waiting, and the upper echelon's deliberate attempts to strengthen ties to the lesser nobility by including them in these events. The jousts and festivities were not just spaces where women could meet men but where women could spend time with each other.

Women's being in each other's company is, among other things, a manifestation of the active sharing and inheritance of power over time. The four important women named in the ballad itself—the queen of France, the dauphine, the duchess of Burgundy, and the duchess of Calabria—were of two different generations, with Marie of Anjou and Isabella born toward the beginning of the fifteenth century, while Margaret and Marie de Bourbon were born in the 1420s. The older women shaped their younger counterparts through many means: providing them with explicit instruction on how to fulfill their roles as nobles but also acting as examples on which the newer generation could and should model their own behavior.[28]

These ladies also, as individuals, embody multiple different points of political contact across Western Europe. Marie of Anjou was born near the Alps and through her mother had ties to Aragon; her marriage to Charles VII brought her into the heart of the French court.[29] Isabella's mother was from England, her father was king of Portugal, and her husband was the powerful duke of Burgundy, sometimes rival to France.[30] Margaret was a Scottish princess but also had English roots through her mother and, as her title indicates, had married the French crown prince.[31] Marie of Bourbon, Isabella's niece, was part of another powerful ducal family and had married the oldest son of René of Anjou, another important cultural patron—and, of course, brother to the queen.[32] Adding in Marie of Guelders, Isabelle of Lorraine, and Marie of Cleves, to say nothing of each woman's ladies-in-waiting, makes this web of (inter)connections even more complicated.[33] Marie of Guelders spent several years at the Burgundian court under Isabella of Portugal's tutelage, as had her aunt Marie of Cleves in the decade before her; indeed, it was through the influence of the Burgundian duchess and duke that both Maries' marriages to important men manifested.[34] Isabelle of Lorraine, René of Anjou's first wife, was Marie of Bourbon's mother-in-law; she also had connections to Germany through her mother, Margaret of the Palatinate, extending this web of women further to the east.[35]

This group of nobles is representative of the multifaceted political familial networks typical of late-medieval aristocratic women and so often obscured by the historical record's focus on their male relatives.[36] They were not simply members of their families, hangers-on while their menfolk made the decisions. The women's time together provided the opportunity for conversation (and probably strategizing) of their own. Although La Marche dismisses Isabelle and the queen as nothing more than old women indulging in jealous gossip, their important role in the negotiations that preceded the joust in question strongly implies that, jealous or no, the women had worthwhile things to discuss.[37] Moreover, Marie of Anjou's daughter Catherine of France had been married to Isabella's son Charles for about five years—a match in which both women more than likely had a hand.[38]

There is also, finally, the fact that Régnier as poet was likely recommended to the queen by the duchess of Burgundy—he had, after all, been part of the Burgundian court for decades by that point—a clear example of women's cooperative role in facilitating the patronage and dissemination of literature.[39]

The politics of the author-patron relationship work in two directions in this ballad, as in medieval literature more generally. Régnier's valorizing of these women serves their egos as well as his own need for continued favor within the Burgundian court, being in the service of Isabella's husband, all of which contributed to his financial well-being. Too, this poem and the momentary relationship with the queen that it documents might have helped Régnier carve out a place for himself with the royal court in Paris. Régnier was well aware of the dangers of partisan affiliation, having been taken prisoner and held for ransom by Philip the Good's political adversaries in 1432, and so might have appreciated having potential patrons elsewhere.[40] The line "if their servant it please them to keep me" is a very deliberate prompt to his listeners, as is the herald's cry, "largesse," in the envoy of the poem. These sly addresses write Régnier into his own lyric as poet-performer rather than simply a member of the audience, blurring the line between fictionalized history and the *now* of "real life" through his stylized testimony about the joust—and doing the same for the historical women named within his text.[41]

The Work of Reins

Régnier's second ballade, written at most a few months previously, during an earlier stage of the negotiations, is quite different.[42] Its primary commonality with the first is the rubric, "*Autre balade que ledit prisonnier fit en la ville de Reims en l'an devantdit a la requeste de madame de Bourgongne et de toutes ses dames et damoiselles*" (Other ballad which the said prisoner composed in the city of Reims in the said year at the request of Madame de Bourgogne and all her ladies and damsels), wherein Régnier (or the text's early modern editor) specifies a place, a time, and the poem's patrons, some but not all of whom are the same as those of the Châlons ballade.[43] This earlier composition consists of a twenty-four-line debate between three washerwomen, followed by a four-line envoy inviting judgment by the listeners.

The poet plays on the homonymy between the branch (*rains*) on which the shirt has been laid, the city's name (*Reims*) and the word for kidneys and/or the lower back (*reins*). The latter two are spelled the same in the 1526 edition and, as the third woman implies in her question to Denise in the third stanza, pronounced the same as well. In his brief comments comparing the two poems, Jacques Paviot also clarifies that that "*l'ouvrage des reins*" is a euphemism for the sexual act, a somewhat scandalous phrase to find in the mouth of a young woman.[47]

	Je vis l'autrier sur ung rivage	I saw, the other day, on the riverbank,
	Entre trois femmes grant devise	A great discussion among three women,
	Qui lavoyent linge de parage.⁴⁴	Who were washing fancy laundry.⁴⁵
4	L'oeuvre devisoient a leur guise.	They were dividing up the work in their way.
	La plus jeune une chemise Mectoit seicher dessus des rains	The youngest a shirt Was putting to dry on some branches,
	Et dist aux autres, sans faintise,	And said to the others, without hesitation,
8	Qu'il n'est ouvrage que de reins.	That there's no work like that of reins.
	La seconde par grant courage Luy dist: "Vous parlez par maistrise,	The second, with great firmness, Said to her: "Are you speaking from mastery?
	Vous blasmez l'oeuvre et l'ouvrage	You criticize the activity and the production
12	De Damas, de Troyes, de Venise	Of Damascus, Troyes, Venice,
	Et de Paris la bien assise.	And Paris the well situated.
	Vous ont ce apris voz parrains"	Have your godparents taught you this?"
	La jeune dist, "Riens ne les prise	The young one said: "I deem them worthless,
16	Qu'il n'est ouvrage que de reins.	For there's no work like that of reins."
	La tierce qui fut caulte et sage	The third, who was subtle and wise,
	Luy va disant, "Ores, Denise,	Went toward her saying: "Now, Denise,
	Je n'entens point vostre langage,	I don't know what you're saying at all.
20	Reins est cité tresbien comprise,	Reims is a city, very well-known,
	Mais aussi bien qui bien l'advise,	But also, if one realizes it,
	Partie du corps sont les reins;	Kidneys are part of the body;

Declaration par vous soit mise.⁴⁶	A declaration has been made by you
24 Qu'il n'est ouvrage que de reins."	That there's no work like that of *reins.*"
Dames, ouyé avez l'emprise.	Ladies, you have heard the debate.
Jugez qui mieulx a dit ou moins.	Judge who said it better or worse.
La jeune se tient a sa prise	The young one held her ground,
28 Qu'il n'est ouvrage que de reins.	That there's no work like that of reins.

The joust ballad was written following the successful treaty negotiations between the duchess of Burgundy and the king of France after several years of rising tensions. This truly was a celebratory moment, the culmination of months, if not years, of work. The debate ballad, by contrast, was composed during a preliminary phase of that round of negotiations, during which the duchess and the king's ambassadors discussed those grievances deemed less important.⁴⁸ Not only was the king not there in person, but presumably whatever was decided in Reims needed to be ratified before it could take effect. We might therefore read the debate poem as both a necessary diversion during potentially stressful, unsatisfying times—sexual encounters and the laughter they often provoke both being notable stress relievers— and also a mocking nod to the lawyerly habit of picking apart every possible interpretation of every word in every clause in every sentence.⁴⁹

Unlike the ballad written in Châlons, there is no obvious moment of triumph or memorializing of the female patrons, nor any heterosocial interaction, no explicitly eroticizing male gaze, no legacy of chivalric literature. It testifies to women's sociality nevertheless: internally, in the form of the three women working together, and externally, in that it commands the female listeners ("*Dames*") to judge the debate. This latter is not only an invitation to discussion of a piece of literature that exists for their benefit and at their command but an invitation to analysis, to critical thinking, and to the pleasure of teasing out various meanings of the poet's wordplay in so doing. Moreover, whereas the rubric differentiates between categories of women, separating Isabella, *madame de Bourgongne*, from her older ladies, *dames*, who are in turn separated from the younger or less important, *damoiselles*, that final command to judge the debate brings them all back together and puts them on equal footing, naming them simply "*Dames.*" Like the joust, which provided an opportunity for sociability among the different degrees of nobility, this poem offers all of the female listeners a chance to occupy the same space and creates the fiction, if not the reality, of social cohesion.

The Intimacy of Old Age

In order to better appreciate how the first two ballads speak to their specific political audience, I now compare them to a third ballad by Régnier, also written for a woman: his wife, Ysabeau Chrestienne.[50] Composed in 1460, it is enclosed by a brief preface, which gives the date, and a briefer conclusion; Régnier uses these spaces to explain that Ysabeau requested that he write her a song or poem like he used to when they were both young (and that she was not impressed by what he came up with). The full text of the poem is as follows:

	Puis que je sens que vieillesse a moy vient[51]	Because I feel age coming upon me
	Et jeunesse me laisse et si m'oublie,	And youth leaving and forgetting me,
	Prendre congé des armes me convient;	It is fitting for me to say farewell to arms;
4	Car ma puissance si m'est du tout faillie,	As my force has entirely failed me,
	Mon fait ne vault desormais une oublie.	My deeds are henceforth not worth even forgetting.[52]
	Tel desjeuner ne quiert que le polet;	Only a chicken seeks such a breakfast;[53]
	Mieulx me vauldroit manger ung euf molet	It would be better for me to eat a soft-boiled egg
8	Pour soustenir mon corps en bon propos.	To keep my body in good shape.
	Je suis maistre, j'estoye meilleur varlet;	I am the master, I was better as a valet;
	Je ne quiers plus que l'aise et le repos.	I no longer seek anything but ease and rest.
	Quant du bon temps passé il me souvient,	When I remember the good times past,
12	Que nous allions chasser a l'acropie,	When we went hunting in a crouch,
	Et ou printemps, que chascun en avien[t],[54]	And when each spring came around,
	Que nous allions querans les nidz de pie,	When we would go looking for magpie nests . . .
	Et maintenant j'ay au nez la roupie,	And now I have a drippy nose,
16	Nulles dens n'ay, je mangeue soupes en laict.[55]	I have no teeth, I eat bread soaked in milk.

Fourré je suis et si ay mantelet.	I am layered with furs and wear a short coat,
Emprès le feu, vin et eaue en deux potz,	Near the fire, wine and water in two pots;
20 Les mains me tremblent et bois au gobelet;	My hands tremble as I drink from a goblet.
Je ne quiers plus que l'aise et le repos.	I no longer seek anything but ease and rest.
A m'amye! se temps la plus ne revient.⁵⁶	Ah, my dear! That time will never come again;
Se l'attendons, c'est a nous grant folye.	If we wait for it, it is our great folly.
Aller s'en fault sans scavoir qu'on devient,	We must go without knowing what we will become,
24 Crier nous fault: "oublye, oublye, oublye!"	We must cry out, "Forget, forget, forget!"
Mon desjeuner si sera de boulye.	My breakfast then will be porridge.
Des jeux sainct mort j'ay prins le chapelet.	Of the games of saint Death I have taken the crown.
Je scay trop bien que ce jeu vous est lait.	I know too well that this game is ugly to you.
28 Adieu, Amours, et a tous les suppos;	Goodbye, Love, and to all his subjects;
Ne m'amenez Margot ne Ysabelet;	Do not bring me Margot nor Ysabelet;
Je ne quiers plus que l'aise et le repos.⁵⁸	I no longer seek anything but ease and rest.
32 Prince, l'aage en ce point si me mect,	Prince, age has brought me to this point:
Je estudie kalendriers et compost,	I study calendars and *computus*,
Medecine de mon fait s'entremet.	Medicine takes on my case.
Je ne quiers plus que l'aise et le repos.	I no longer seek anything but ease and rest.

The first few verses make us think that we are to be treated to the speaker's recollections of his participation in chivalric culture while in his prime, while the line *"mon fait ne vault desormais une oublie"* can be read as part of the medieval modesty topos. Each of the first three stanzas offers a reflection on the passage of time before turning at least for a few lines to the question of food and its relationship to the narrator's aging body, and specifically, how he ingests it. This abrupt shift to the extremely quotidian, even domestic, matters of eating and staying in shape would be jarring were it not for the preface that informed us of the intimate nature of this poem's intended audience. We see this, too, in the details of the narrator's physical state: his runny nose, toothless mouth, and trembling hands paint a clear picture of a rheumy old man stuck by the fire because he cannot keep warm. Although these symptoms are quite similar to those depicted by Eustache Deschamps (ca. 1340–1404/05) in *"Les Signes de la mort en vieille personne"* (The Signs of Death in an Old Person), Deschamps does not ever explicitly address his audience as does Régnier in line 21.[59] Deschamps seems to be complaining for the sake of complaining, while Régnier plays with our expectations and his wife's request as he vacillates between recollections of how good the past was and the caricature of old age that he now embodies.

By contrast, in the joust ballad, Régnier glosses over the (im)practicalities of senescence, saying only that he is made young again by the memory of the noble ladies. This elision of the body is entirely consistent with the courtly nature of his audience and the subject matter; for example, Pontus, the protagonist of a French romance written in the first quarter of the fifteenth century, is described only as handsome, while the king of Brittany in that same romance is simply old.[60] Interestingly, the same does not hold true for the debate ballad despite its aristocratic audience, as we saw in the *"ouvrage de reins"* sexual subtext. There again, however, we can identify a connection between the lower subject matter (common washerwomen) and the lower tone used to talk about the body.

Love likewise gets much shorter shrift in this third poem, where Régnier says only: *"Adieu, Amours, et a tous ses suppos; / Ne m'amenez ne Margot ne Ysabelet"* (l. 28–29). In bidding farewell to Love and his supporters, Régnier withdraws from the field. However, his command that Love not bring Margot or Ysabelet (a diminutive of Ysabeau/Ysabel) to Régnier takes us out of the courtly register by implying carnal relations. That is, by naming specific women rather than referring to his inability to continue playing love's rather more generic games, Régnier concretizes the relationship between love and (potentially adulterous) sex. Such language stands in stark opposition to the *fin'amors* of the joust ballad, where Régnier talks about the invincibility which love of the noble ladies bestowed upon him, his desire to serve them and keep his promises to them—essentially, love from afar. The joke (is it a joke?) that he is too old and tired even to satisfy his wife anymore once again reminds us of the proclaimed intimate nature of the poem's intended audience, very different from the political and personal aspirations that appear in his discussion of the joust. This self-portrait, so at odds with the determined, rejuvenated man of that first ballad, also draws attention to the performative nature of social life even through the lens of the poetic fiction—to the varied characters one might (must) play depending on what company one is keeping.

Most medievalists would say that we must be extremely cautious about biographical and historiographic interpretations of fictional works, and I do not disagree.[61] However, in the absence of other evidence, I think that we can and should speculate. These ballads remind us that while consequential events were happening—negotiations and actions in which important, well-documented individuals played a decisive role—other people of many different statuses were also there, were also implicated at another level. And, too, the poems prove that there were moments of levity centered around the production and sociable consumption of literature to break up the difficult days—moments that nevertheless reinforced women's participation in the many social activities that sustained (or undermined) relationships. These particular records of female leisure (and presumably enjoyment), which imply a somewhat gender-segregated social scene, partially obscure the complex reality of the heterosocial network, both political and personal, in which everyone operated.[62] Yet Régnier's demarcation of the different ranks and types of women involved—queens, princesses, duchesses, ladies, damsels, washerwomen—also lays out for us some of the actualities of the hierarchically integrated nature of the creation of cultural capital and women's participation in the jubilation that undergirded it.

Louisiana Tech University

NOTES

1. For the poet's biography, see Jean Régnier, *Les fortunes et adversitez*, ed. E. Droz (Paris: Société des anciens textes français, 1923), xii–xxiv, https://babel.hathitrust.org/cgi/pt?id=mdp.39015030087087
2. The digitization of the edition held at the Bibliothèque nationale de France, Rés. Ye-1400, can be consulted at https://gallica.bnf.fr/ark:/12148/bpt6k71324g, and the poem in question begins on 135[v]. I was also able to consult the 1526 edition at Versailles's Bibliothèque Centrale, Goujet in-8 45, which for the poems treated in this article differs only in that *oeuvre* in l. 11 is spelled *euvre* instead. Despite this, both are clustered under USTC 10373, https://www.ustc.ac.uk/editions/10373.
3. Régnier, *Fortunes et adversitez*, 209. The correction to the date in the title is provided by Droz. Based on the inclusion of "*derniere trespassee*," the rubric must have been appended to the poem after December 1463 (death of Marie of Anjou) and before December 1, 1483 (death of Charlotte of Savoy, Marie's successor). After confirming the text in the 1526 edition (as explained below, no manuscript copies are known

to still exist), I have followed Droz's punctuation (which included resolving i/j and u/v but not adding the cedilla to soft *c* preceding *a*, *o*, or *u*) for ease of reading. All translations my own unless otherwise specified. I wish to thank Lucas Wood and Elizaveta Strakhov for their thoughtful comments on earlier drafts of the translations of the poems in particular.
4. I have deliberately left this word untranslated; see the discussion on it below. In addition to Droz's edition, the full poem is published in Jacques Paviot, "Les honneures de la cour d'Éléonore de Poitiers," in *Autour de Marguerite d'Écosse: Reines, princesses et dames du XVe siècle*, ed. Geneviève Contamine and Philippe Contamine (Paris, France: Champion, 1999), 175–176; I include it again here for ease of access.
5. *Douleur* (pain, hurt, sadness), as printed in the 1526 edition, does not make sense in this context, whereas *doulceur* (sweetness) does.
6. *On* as a third-person singular personal pronoun meaning "we" is not the most common usage, but is attested beginning in the second quarter of the fourteenth century. See Robert Martin, "ON, pron. pers.," *Dictionnaire du Moyen Français* (DMF) 2023, http://www.atilf.fr/dmf/definition/on.
7. Or perhaps, "Never would I wish to become anyone else's," if a *d'* has dropped off from in front of *autre*.
8. Although Droz capitalizes Dangier and Vieillesse in her edition, implying their role as personifications, I have opted to follow the 1526 capitalization here.
9. Monique Sommé, *Isabelle de Portugal, duchesse de Bourgogne: Une femme au pouvoir au XVe siècle* (Lille, France: Presses Universitaires du Septentrion, 1998), 404–409. Her conclusions are drawn from financial records, contemporary chronicles, and earlier research. See also Paviot, "Honneurs de la cour," 168.
10. Sommé, *Femme au pouvoir*, 404.
11. Ibid., 264–272.
12. Ibid., 407; Jacques Bénet, *Jean d'Anjou, duc de Calabre et de Lorraine (1426–1470)* (Nancy, France: Société Thierry Alix, 1997), 25–26. John's father, René d'Anjou, was husband to Isabelle of Lorraine.
13. Éléonore de Poitiers and Jacques Paviot, "Les états de France (Les honneurs de la cour)," *Annuaire Bulletin de la Société d'Histoire de France* (1996):89–91, https://www.jstor.org./stable/23407720?seq=1.
14. Rosalind Brown-Grant and Mario Damen, eds. and trans., *A Chivalric Life: The Book of the Deeds of Messire Jacques de Lalaing* (Woodbridge: Boydell, 2022), 121–122, and 36 for the dating of the text.
15. Olivier de la Marche, *Mémoires d'Olivier de la Marche, maître d'hôtel et capitaine des gardes de Charles le Téméraire*, ed. Henri Beaune and J. d'Arbaumont, 4 vols. (Paris: Librairie Renouard, Henri Loones, successeur, 1883), 2:56.

16. Martin le Franc, *Champion des dames*, ed. Robert Deschaux, 5 vols. (Paris: Champion, 1999).
17. Ibid., 1:ix. Jacques Paviot's exploration of *querelle* literature at the Burgundian court supports this conclusion; Jacques Paviot, "L'image de la femme à la cour de Bourgogne," in *Dame, draghi e cavalieri: Medioevo al femminile. Atti del Convegno Internazionale (Casale Monferrato Salone S. Bartolomeo—4–6 ottobre 1996)*, ed. Francesco de Caria and Donatella Taverna (Turin: Istituto per i beni musicali in Piemonte, 1997), 19–29. It is difficult to take the author's claims about his text's poor reception at face value, given that we still have at least ten manuscript copies and a 1488 edition extant today; see the lists of manuscript copies at "Champion des dames, Martin le Franc," Jonas-IRHT/CNRS, last modified Jan. 7, 2013, see 14.13]] https://jonas.irht.cnrs.fr/consulter/oeuvre/detail_oeuvre.php?oeuvre=2386, and Laurent Brun, "Le champion des dames," Archives de Littérature du Moyen Âge (ARLIMA), https://www.arlima.net/mp/martin_le_franc/le_champion_des_dames.html.
18. Sébastien Nadot, *Le spectacle des joutes: Sport et courtoisie à la fin du Moyen Âge* (Rennes: Presses universitaires de Rennes, 2012), 154.
19. *L'influence directe de la littérature sur les pas d'armes est évidente. Les décors, scénarios et rôles joués par les chevaliers témoignent du lien étroit avec les épopées, les romans et la poésie. Cependant, la littérature joue probablement un rôle encore plus fort sur les pas d'armes par l'intermédiaire des valeurs qu'elle véhicule, en particulier celles relatives au comportement que doit adapter un bon chevalier.*
Ibid., 179. On the *pas d'armes*, see also the recently published Rosalind Brown-Grant and Mario Damen, eds., *Pas d'armes and Late Medieval Chivalry: A Casebook* (Liverpool: Liverpool University Press, 2025).
20. Sarah Carpenter, "Chivalric Entertainment at the Court of Henry IV: The Jousting Letters of 1401," *Medieval English Theatre* 43, (2022): 39–107.
21. Hanno Wijsman, *Luxury Bound: Illustrated Manuscript Production and Noble and Princely Book Ownership in the Burgundian Netherlands (1400–1550)* (Turnhout: Brepols, 2010), 185. This manuscript, presumed no longer extant, has been assigned the shelfmark NE 139 in the Books of Duchesses: Mapping Women Book Owners, 1350–1550 project (hereafter Books of Duchesses); see S.C. Kaplan and Sarah Wilma Watson, "Book: NE 139 (Lancelot du Lac)," Books of Duchesses, https://booksofduchesses.com/books/NE%20139. For the current list of Marie of Cleves's books and associated bibliography, see Kaplan and Watson, "Book Owner: Marie of Cleves, duchess of Orleans," Books of Duchesses, https://booksofduchesses.com/owners/Marie%20of%20Cleves,%20duchess%20of%20Orleans/.

While we do not have proof that Marie of Anjou, Marie of Bourbon, and Margaret Stewart owned romances themselves, scholars have convincingly argued for the importance of social circles on an individual woman's access to and knowledge of literature that she might have not possessed. See, e.g., Emily Wingfield, *Scotland's Royal Women and European Literary Culture, 1424–1587* (Turnhout, Belgium: Brepols, 2023); S.C. Kaplan, *Women's Libraries in Late Medieval Bourbonnais, Burgundy, and France: A Family Affair* (Liverpool, UK: Liverpool University Press, 2022); Cynthia J. Brown, "Anne de Bretagne and Anne de France: French Female Networks at the Dawn of the Renaissance," in *Founding Feminisms in Medieval Studies: Essays in Honor of E. Jane Burns*, ed. Laine E. Doggett and Daniel E. O'Sullivan (Cambridge, UK: D.S. Brewer, 2016), 171–186.
22. On his age, and his aging body, in his corpus, see Gérard Gros, "Le 'gros bailli d'Auxerre': Autoportrait de Jean Régnier à l'automne et l'hiver de sa vie (1433–1463)," in *L'autoportrait dans la littérature française: Du Moyen Âge au XVIIe siècle* (Rennes: Presses universitaires de Rennes, 2013), 117–132.
23. Or, as Rosalind Brown-Grant asks, "do the narrative accounts of these events reveal how women could make themselves heard as desiring subjects who were in dialogue with, or even resistant to, the homosocial concerns that characterised the *pas d'armes*?" Rosalind Brown-Grant, "*Pas d'armes* and the Construction of Chivalric Masculinity: Ethics and Erotics of Knightly Combat," in *Pas d'armes and Late Medieval Chivalry: A Casebook*, ed. Rosalind Brown-Grant and Mario Damen (Liverpool: Liverpool University Press, 2025), 492.
24. E. Jane Burns, "Performing Courtliness," in *The Oxford Handbook of Women and Gender in Medieval Europe*, ed. Judith Bennett and Ruth Mazo Karras (Oxford: Oxford University Press, 2013), 396–412, esp. 398. The arrival of Philip's younger sister Agnes of Burgundy, dowager duchess of Bourbon, and her daughters in Burgundy in 1462, as documented by the archives, was celebrated with "*plusieurs joustes et esbattements*" (several jousts and amusements); Mario Damen and Michelle Szkilnik, "The Social and Literary Environment of a Chivalric Event: The Case of the *Pas du Perron Fée*, Bruges, 1463," in *Pas d'armes and Late Medieval Chivalry: A Casebook*, ed. Rosalind Brown-Grant and Mario Damen (Liverpool: Liverpool University Press, 2025), 410, their translation.
25. "*Ce sont elles qui attribuent de la valeur aux prouesses des chevaliers*"; Nadot, *Spectacle des joutes*, 185. Unfortunately, Nadot's discussion of the politics surrounding jousts focuses entirely on the men involved; ibid., esp. 297–303.

26. Bertrand Schnerb has likewise commented, "*Les exploits physiques des nobles, dans les joutes et les pas d'armes, ne pouvaient se concevoir sans un public de dames et de demoiselles admiratives et/ou effrayées*" (The noble[men]'s physical exploits in the jousts and *pas d'armes* could not be conceived of without a public of admiring and/or frightened ladies and damsels). Bertrand Schnerb, "Présence et influence des femmes à la cour de Bourgogne: Quelques réflexions historiographiques," in *Women at the Burgundian Court: Presence and Influence*, ed. Dagmar Eichberger, Anne-Marie Legaré, and Wim Hüsken (Turnhout: Brepols, 2010), 5. However, Ruth Mazo Karas has argued that the men were more interested in impressing each other; see Ruth Mazo Karras, *From Boys to Men: Formations of Masculinity in Late Medieval Europe* (Philadelphia, PA: University of Pennsylvania Press, 2003).
27. *La fête de cour ritualisée était donc un spectacle convenu des rapports hommes/femmes au sein de l'élite aristocratique, mais elle était aussi, comme lors du Banquet du Faisan de 1454, l'occasion de mettre à l'honneur certaines composantes de l'entourage féminin du duc et de la duchesse: les femmes qui appartenaient à la famille ducale, y compris les filles bâtardes du prince, les dames et demoiselles de l'hôtel et enfin, éventuellement, dans le cadre d'une politique d'intégration dans laquelle la cour et ses cérémonies jouaient un grand rôle, les dames et les demoiselles de la noblesse régionale.*
Schnerb, "Présence et influence," 5.
28. S.C. Kaplan, "Transmission of Knowledge to and between Women in 15th-Century France: Agnès de Bourgogne's Education and Library" (PhD diss., University of California, Santa Barbara, 2016), available on ProQuest Dissertations & Theses A&I, especially ch. 2. For the intellectual aspects of this modeling, see Kaplan, *Women's Libraries*, ch. 2.
29. Bernard Chevalier, "Marie d'Anjou, une reine sans gloire, 1404–1463," in *Autour de Marguerite d'Écosse: Reines, princesses et dames du XVe siècle. Actes du colloque de Thouars (23 et 24 mai 1997)*, ed. Geneviève Contamine and Philippe Contamine (Paris: Champion, 1999), 81–98.
30. Sommé, *Femme au pouvoir*, 21. See also Monique Sommé, "La correspondance d'Isabelle de Portugal, reflect du pouvoir d'une duchesse de Bourgogne au XVe siècle," in *Women at the Burgundian Court: Presence and Influence*, ed. Dagmar Eichberger, Anne-Marie Legaré, and Wim Hüsken (Turnhout, Belgium: Brepols, 2010), 28, which lists many of the important people with whom Isabella corresponded.
31. Wingfield, *Scotland's Royal Women*, 61–64.
32. Kaplan, *Women's Libraries*, 64. I know of no secondary source focused exclusively on Marie. The scholarship on René is extensive; see the bibliography in Marc-Édouard Gautier and François Avril, *Splendeur de l'enluminure: Le roi René et les livres*, ed. Ville d'Angers; Centre de monuments nationaux (Angers: Actes Sud, 2009).

33. Wingfield, *Scotland's Royal Women*, 139–142; Anne-Marie Legaré, "Princesses et duchesses bibliophiles à la cour de René d'Anjou," *Cuadernos del CEMYR* 20 (2012):42–43; Jacqueline d'Ailly, by contrast, is poorly documented, as are her parents Raoul d'Ailly and Jeanne de Béthune. See Ferdinand Van de Putte, "Biographie de Jean de Bourgogne, comte d'Étampes, seigneur d'Ingelmunster, Vive-Saint-Éloi, Rousbrugge etc.," *Annales de la Société d'Émulation de Bruges* 2nd ser., 3 (1845): 111–115, at 113–114, https://www.digitale-sammlungen.de/de/view/bsb10272621?page=134,135; Brown-Grant and Damen, *Chivalric Life*, 206, n. 399.
34. On Marie of Guelders's time with the Burgundian court, see Gerard Nijsten, *In the Shadow of Burgundy: The Court of Guelders in the Late Middle Ages*, trans. Tanis Guest (Cambridge: Cambridge University Press, 2004), 135, n. 90, as well as Olivier de La Marche, *Mémoires*, 2:52. On Marie of Cleves, see Catherine M. Müller, "Marie de Clèves, poétesse et mécène du XVe siècle," *Le Moyen français* 48 (2001):57–76.
35. She was not unusual in this respect. Marriages between German- and French-speaking nobles were a regular occurrence—think of Isabeau of Bavaria, queen of France (r. 1385–1422), for instance.
36. In addition to the already cited references, see Elizabeth L'Estrange, *Anne de Graville and Women's Literary Networks in Early Modern France* (Cambridge, UK: D.S. Brewer, 2023); S.C. Kaplan and Sarah Wilma Watson, "Books of Duchesses: Mapping Women Book Owners, 1350–1550: Five-Year Report," *Journal of the Early Book Society* 27 (2024):99–122; Elizaveta Strakhov and Sarah Wilma Watson, "Behind Every Man(uscript) Is a Woman: Social Networks, Christine de Pizan, and Westminster Abbey Library, MS 21," *Studies in the Age of Chaucer* 43 (2021):151–80; Christine Wand-Wittkowski, "Pfalzgräfin Mechtild und ihr literarischer Zirkel. Ein Irrtum der Mediävistik," *Internationales Archiv für Sozialgeschichte der deutschen Literatur* 30.1 (2005):1–27.
37. Olivier de La Marche, *Mémoires*, 2:54–55.
38. Sommé, *Femme au pouvoir*, 56 (for Isabella's role).
39. It is possible that Régnier had dealt directly with the royal couple during his sojourns in Paris on Philip's business; Régnier, *Fortunes et adversitez*, xv.
40. Ibid., xv–xvii. Indeed, by 1454, his oldest son Jean was a guard of the king's seal in the district of Auxerre; ibid., xxii.
41. My thanks to Lucas Wood for this observation.
42. Nancy Freeman Regalado, "Effet de réel, effet du réel: Representation and Reference in Villon's *Testament*," *Yale French Studies* 70 (1986):63–77; Régnier, *Fortunes et adversitez*, 211–212.

43. This is consistent with the rubrication of the other shorter compositions in the volume of collected works and is perhaps indicative of the desire to have patrons at many different courts.
44. I have made some adjustments to Droz's punctuation and diacritics.
45. *De parage* more literally means ornamental and/or related to lineage.
46. An anonymous reviewer pointed out that this subjunctive could also be, "Let you make the declaration" = "You should make." This does make sense in terms of the language, but I am not sure if it that is also true contextually, since Denise made her assertion several verses ago. Or perhaps the comedy lies in the unnecessary repetition.
47. Paviot, "*Honneurs de la cour*," 177.
48. Sommé does not specify what exactly these lesser complaints were; Sommé, *Femme au pouvoir*, 404.
49. On the complexity of legal French, see Anne-Hélène Miller, *The Invention of Frenchness: Negotiating Cultural Boundaries in the Literary Languages of Medieval France* (Liverpool: Liverpool University Press, forthcoming), esp. the section "Rethinking Literary Engagement: Diplomacy and Peace-Making in French" in ch. 5.
50. Régnier, *Fortunes et adversitez*, 222–223.
51. Again I have chosen to modify some of Droz's punctuation and capitalization.
52. *Oublie* was also the term for an unconsecrated Host and a sort of thin wafer (gaufre), per the *DMF*; see Robert Martin, "Oublie, subst. fém.," DMF 2023, http://www.atilf.fr/dmf/definition/oublie, which ties into the food-related discussion on the following two lines; however, Old French offers some support for understanding it as the nominalization of the verb *oublier*. F. Godefroy offers a couple of examples for *oublie* and *oubliee* that invoke "forgetting" as the most likely meaning, the first of which is "*J'ay aprins jusques a tout oublie*"; *Dictionnaire de l'ancienne langue française et de tous ses dialectes du IXe aux XVe siècle*, 10 vols. (1881–1902; repr. New York: Kraus Reprint Co., 1961), 5:664. It is entirely probable that Régnier is deliberately invoking both meanings.
53. In the figurative sense, *desjeuner* can also mean "little, a little thing, an hors-d'oeuvre," which aligns with Régnier's claims to lack significance at this point in his life. Pierre Cromer, "Desjeuner, verbe," DMF 2023, http://www.atilf.fr/dmf/definition/déjeuner.
54. BnF Rés. Ye-1400 reads *aviens*, which does not grammatically accord with the third-person singular subject *chascun*. The final *s* versus *t* would not have affected the rhyme, as those final consonants were not pronounced by this point. For discussion of this shift over the course of the thirteenth century and afterward, see E. Einhorn, *Old French: A Concise Handbook* (Cambridge, UK: Cambridge University Press,

1975); and Georges Straka, *L'évolution phonétique du latin au français* (Strasbourg, France: Klincksieck, 1964). My thanks to Annie Doucet and Christopher Callahan for these references.
55. Sic—read *mange*.
56. The edition offers *se* for *ce*, a still-common orthographical choice at this point in time. The *Se* opening the following line is equivalent to the modern *si*.
57. The French should perhaps read *Des jeux saincts*, in which case the English would be, "Of the holy games, I, dead, have taken the crown."
58. Droz silently changed *les* [the] in l. 28 to *ses* [his]. I am not sure why.
59. Eustache Deschamps, *Eustache Deschamps, ca 1340–1404: Anthologie thématique*, ed. James C. Laidlaw and Christine Scollen-Jimack (Paris: Classiques Garnier, 2017), 468–469, °241.
60. BnF n.a.f. 11676, fols. 2v–3r for Pontus, and fol. 5v for the king of Brittany. Jacques de Lalaing was called a *"nouvel Pontus"* (new Pontus) following the *pas d'armes* at Chalon-sur-Saône; Brown-Grant, "Ethics and Erotics," 496. We seem to get precise details only when the person being described deviates from the norm. Melusine's son Urien, for instance, is *"grant et droit et long et fort a demesure, mais il a le visaige court et large au travers, et l'un oeil rouge et l'autre perse et les oreilles grans a merveilles. Et sachiéz que de corps et de membres, c'est un des beaulx bacheliers que je veisse oncques"* (big, upright, tall, and outrageously strong, but his face is short and wide, with one red eye and the other green, and marvelously big ears. But know that in body and limb, he is one of the most handsome young men I have ever seen). Jean d'Arras, *Mélusine, ou la noble histoire de Lusignan. Nouvelle édition critique d'après le manuscrit de la bibliothèque de l'Arsenal avec les variantes de tous les manuscrits*, ed. and trans. Jean-Jacques Vincensini (Paris: Le Livre de Poche, 2003), 332.
61. See, e.g., the first few pages of Rory G. Critten, "The Political Valence of Charles d'Orléans English Poetry," *Modern Philology* 111.3 (2014):339–364; Marilynn Desmond, "Christine de Pizan: Gender, Authorship, and Life-Writing," in *The Cambridge Companion to Medieval French Literature*, ed. Simon Gaunt and Sarah Kay (Cambridge: Cambridge University Press, 2008), 123–135; Laurence De Looze, *Pseudo-Autobiography in the Fourteenth Century: Juan Ruiz, Guillaume de Machaut, Jean Froissart, and Geoffrey Chaucer* (Gainesville: University of Florida Press, 1997).
62. See the nuanced discussion of gender-based segregation of medieval spaces in Kim M. Phillips, "Public and Private: Women in the Home, Women in the Streets," in *A Cultural History of Women in the Middle Ages*, ed. Kim M. Phillips (London: Bloomsbury, 2013), 105–126, 246–253.

WORKS CITED

Bénet, Jacques. *Jean d'Anjou, duc de Calabre et de Lorraine (1426–1470)*. Nancy, France: Société Thierry Alix, 1997.

Brown, Cynthia J. "Anne de Bretagne and Anne de France: French Female Networks at the Dawn of the Renaissance." In *Founding Feminisms in Medieval Studies: Essays in Honor of E. Jane Burns*, ed. Laine E. Doggett and Daniel E. O'Sullivan. Cambridge: D.S. Brewer, 2016. 171–186.

Brown-Grant, Rosalind. "*Pas d'armes* and the Construction of Chivalric Masculinity: Ethics and Erotics of Knightly Combat." In *Pas d'armes and Late Medieval Chivalry: A Casebook*, ed. Rosalind Brown-Grant and Mario Damen. Liverpool: Liverpool University Press, 2025. 475–501.

Brown-Grant, Rosalind, and Mario Damen, eds. *Pas d'armes and Late Medieval Chivalry: A Casebook*. Liverpool: Liverpool University Press, 2025.

———, eds. and trans. *A Chivalric Life: The Book of the Deeds of Messire Jacques de Lalaing*. Woodbridge: Boydell Press, 2022.

Burns, E. Jane. "Performing Courtliness." In *The Oxford Handbook of Women and Gender in Medieval Europe*, ed. Judith Bennett and Ruth Mazo Karras. Oxford: Oxford University Press, 2013. 396–412.

Carpenter, Sarah, Meg Twycross, and Philip E. Bennett. "Chivalric Entertainment at the Court of Henry IV: The Jousting Letters of 1401." *Medieval English Theatre* 43 (2022):39–107.

Chevalier, Bernard. "Marie d'Anjou, une reine sans gloire, 1404–1463." In *Autour de Marguerite d'Écosse: Reines, princesses et dames du XVe siècle. Actes du colloque de Thouars (23 et 24 mai 1997)*, ed. Geneviève Contamine and Philippe Contamine. Paris: Champion, 1999. 81–98.

Critten, Rory G. "The Political Valence of Charles d'Orléans English Poetry." *Modern Philology* 111.3 (2014):339–364.

Damen, Mario, and Michelle Szkilnik. "The Social and Literary Environment of a Chivalric Event: The Case of the *Pas du Perron Fée*, Bruges, 1463." In *Pas d'armes and Late Medieval Chivalry: A Casebook*, ed. Rosalind Brown-Grant and Mario Damen. Liverpool: Liverpool University Press, 2025. 401–430.

d'Arras, Jean. *Mélusine, ou la noble histoire de Lusignan. Nouvelle édition critique d'après le manuscrit de la bibliothèque de l'Arsenal avec les variantes de tous les manuscrits*. Ed. and trans. Jean-Jacques Vincensini. Paris: Le Livre de Poche, 2003.

de La Marche, Olivier. *Mémoires d'Olivier de La Marche, maître d'hôtel et capitaine des gardes de Charles le Téméraire*. Ed. Henri Beaune and J. d'Arbaumont. 4 vols. Paris: Librairie Renouard, Henri Loones, successeur, 1883.

De Looze, Laurence. *Pseudo-Autobiography in the Fourteenth Century: Juan Ruiz, Guillaume de Machaut, Jean Froissart, and Geoffrey Chaucer.* Gainesville, FL: University of Florida Press, 1997.
de Poitiers, Éléonore, and Jacques Paviot. "Les états de France (*Les honneurs de la cour*)." *Annuaire Bulletin de la Société d'Histoire de France* (1996):75–118. https://www.jstor.org./stable/23407720?seq=1.
Deschamps, Eustache. *Eustache Deschamps, ca 1340–1404: Anthologie thématique.* Ed. James C. Laidlaw and Christine Scollen-Jimack. Paris: Classiques Garnier, 2017.
Desmond, Marilynn. "Christine de Pizan: Gender, Authorship, and Life-Writing." In *The Cambridge Companion to Medieval French Literature*, ed. Simon Gaunt and Sarah Kay. Cambridge: Cambridge University Press, 2008. 123–135.
Einhorn, E. *Old French: A Concise Handbook.* Cambridge: Cambridge University Press, 1975.
Gautier, Marc-Édouard, and François Avril. *Splendeur de l'enluminure: Le roi René et les livres.* Edited by Ville d'Angers; Centre de monuments nationaux. Angers: Actes Sud, 2009.
Gros, Gérard. "Le 'gros bailli d'Auxerre': Autoportrait de Jean Régnier à l'automne et l'hiver de sa vie (1433–1463)." In *L'autoportrait dans la littérature française: Du Moyen Âge au XVIIe siècle.* Rennes: Presses universitaires de Rennes, 2013. 117–132.
Kaplan, S.C. "Transmission of Knowledge to and between Women in 15th-Century France: Agnès de Bourgogne's Education and Library." PhD diss., University of California, Santa Barbara, 2016.
———. *Women's Libraries in Late Medieval Bourbonnais, Burgundy, and France: A Family Affair.* Liverpool: Liverpool University Press, 2022.
———, and Sarah Wilma Watson. "Books of Duchesses: Mapping Women Book Owners, 1350–1550: Five-Year Report." *Journal of the Early Book Society* 27 (2024):99–122.
Karras, Ruth Mazo. *From Boys to Men: Formations of Masculinity in Late Medieval Europe.* Philadelphia, PA: University of Pennsylvania Press, 2003.
L'Estrange, Elizabeth. *Anne de Graville and Women's Literary Networks in Early Modern France.* Cambridge: D.S. Brewer, 2023.
le Franc, Martin. *Champion des dames.* Ed. Robert Deschaux. 5 vols. Paris, France: Champion, 1999.
Legaré, Anne-Marie. "Princesses et duchesses bibliophiles à la cour de René d'Anjou." *Cuadernos del CEMYR* 20 (2012):37–54.
Miller, Anne-Hélène. *The Invention of Frenchness: Negotiating Cultural Boundaries in the Literary Languages of Medieval France.* Liverpool: Liverpool University Press, forthcoming.

Müller, Catherine M. "Marie de Clèves, poétesse et mécène du XVe siècle." *Le Moyen français* 48 (2001):57–76.
Nadot, Sébastien. *Le spectacle des joutes: Sport et courtoisie à la fin du Moyen Âge*. Rennes: Presses universitaires de Rennes, 2012.
Nijsten, Gerard. *In the Shadow of Burgundy: The Court of Guelders in the Late Middle Ages*. Trans. Tanis Guest. Cambridge: Cambridge University Press, 2004.
Paviot, Jacques. "Les honneures de la cour d'Éléonore de Poitiers." In *Autour de Marguerite d'Écosse: Reines, princesses et dames du XVe siècle*, ed. Geneviève Contamine and Philippe Contamine. Paris: Champion, 1999. 163–179.
———. "L'image de la femme à la cour de Bourgogne." In *Dame, draghi e cavalieri: Medioevo al femminile. Atti del Convegno Internazionale: Casale Monferrato, Salone S. Bartolomeo, 4–6 ottobre 1996*, ed. Francesco De Caria and Donatella Taverna. Turin: Istituto per i beni musicali in Piemonte, 1997. 19–29.
Phillips, Kim M. "Public and Private: Women in the Home, Women in the Streets." In *A Cultural History of Women in the Middle Ages*, ed. Kim M. Phillips. London: Bloomsbury, 2013. 105–126, 246–253.
Regalado, Nancy Freeman. "Effet de réel, effet du réel: Representation and Reference in Villon's *Testament*." *Yale French Studies* 70 (1986):63–77.
Régnier, Jean. *Les fortunes et adversitez*. Ed. E. Droz. Paris: Société des anciens textes français, 1923. https://babel.hathitrust.org/cgi/pt?id=mdp.39015030087087
Schnerb, Bertrand. "Présence et influence des femmes à la cour de Bourgogne: Quelques réflexions historiographiques." In *Women at the Burgundian Court: Presence and Influence*, ed. Dagmar Eichberger, Anne-Marie Legaré, and Wim Hüsken. Turnhout: Brepols, 2010. 3–9.
Sommé, Monique. "La correspondance d'Isabelle de Portugal, reflect du pouvoir d'une duchesse de Bourgogne au XVe siècle." In *Women at the Burgundian Court: Presence and Influence*, ed. Dagmar Eichberger, Anne-Marie Legaré, and Wim Hüsken. Turnhout: Brepols, 2010. 27–36.
———. *Isabelle de Portugal, duchesse de Bourgogne: Une femme au pouvoir au XVe siècle*. Lille, France: Presses Universitaires du Septentrion, 1998.
Straka, Georges. *L'évolution phonétique du latin au français*. Strasbourg: Klincksieck, 1964.
Strakhov, Elizaveta, and Sarah Wilma Watson. "Behind Every Man(uscript) Is a Woman: Social Networks, Christine de Pizan, and Westminster Abbey Library, MS 21." *Studies in the Age of Chaucer* 43 (2021):151–180.
van de Putte, Ferdinand. "Biographie de Jean de Bourgogne, comte d'Étampes, seigneur d'Ingelmunster, Vive-Saint-Éloi, Rousbrugge etc." *Annales de la Société d'Émulation de Bruges* 2nd ser., 3 (1845):111–115. https://www.digitale-sammlungen.de/de/view/bsb10272621?page=134,135.

Wand-Wittkowski, Christine. "Pfalzgräfin Mechtild und ihr literarischer Zirkel. Ein Irrtum der Mediävistik." *Internationales Archiv für Sozialgeschichte der deutschen Literatur* 30.1 (2005):1–27.

Wijsman, Hanno. *Luxury Bound: Illustrated Manuscript Production and Noble and Princely Book Ownership in the Burgundian Netherlands (1400–1550)*. Turnhout, Belgium: Brepols, 2010.

Wingfield, Emily. *Scotland's Royal Women and European Literary Culture, 1424–1587*. Turnhout: Brepols, 2023.

Inscribing Poetic Fellowship in the Personal Manuscript of Charles d'Orléans

LUCAS WOOD

A major strand of the Middle French lyric output of the Valois poet-prince Charles d'Orléans (1394–1465) after his release from English captivity in 1440 paints an aging introvert withdrawing, partly by choice and partly by necessity, from a social world and a model of amorous identity into which he struggles to fit. The duke's poetry of *nonchaloir* (detachment or indifference) voices a subject situated at a simultaneously wistful and jaded distance from its environment and given to peopling its solitude with allegorical personifications of its own emotions and partite self.[1] While writing this verse, however, the historical Charles presided over the flourishing cultural life of his court at Blois and recorded rich literary exchanges with a diverse circle of fellow poets in his personal manuscript, Paris, BnF fr. 25458.[2] Making room for work by numerous named authors who respond directly to the duke and to each other, this manuscript evolved from an orderly self-anthologizing compendium into a "journal poétique" (poetic diary) that is also "un journal de la poésie" (a diary of poetry) and "l'album d'une conversation courtoise" (the album of a courtly conversation).[3] As such, it has become a touchstone for scholars investigating the social and textual dynamics of the late-medieval literary coterie.

For Jane H. M. Taylor, the personal manuscript as coterie anthology is "a means of communication and dialogue" that both documents and facilitates "forms of sociability" articulated through verse with a predominantly "metacommunicative" function, that is, textual transactions wherein the main (though tacit) "subject of discourse is the relationship between the speakers" that poetic utterance foregrounds and affirms.[4] Placing a complementary emphasis on the seriousness of metacommunicative play, which fosters technical virtuosity as much as courtly recreation and camaraderie through "the twin mechanisms of collaboration and competition," Adrian Armstrong views the dialogues between Charles and his interlocutors as "contributions to the collaborative, social production of knowledge ... of the possibilities of language ... as poets collectively explore key metaphors and test the limits of established forms."[5] Both of these critics illuminate how literary sociability fuels creativity and demonstrate that intertextual reading in manuscript context is required to reveal or activate the system of "rhetorical acts in which authors signal their association with one another" and elaborate what R. D. Perry calls "a manifestation of audience that is incorporated formally into the work itself," constituting the coterie as a "public that retain[s] a sense of the private."[6] But in various places throughout MS fr. 25458, interpersonal relationships are not only implicitly encoded or performed in poetic practice, as Taylor and Armstrong demonstrate; they are also presented as an explicit theme of socially embedded composition. How, then, does the Blois circle's construction and celebration of poetic readership and fellowship intersect with the kind of introspective, often melancholic self-fashioning that is thematically central to Charles d'Orléans's lyric corpus?

The duke's literary project is by no means straightforwardly autobiographical, and the historical Charles must be distinguished from the postures assumed by his textual persona, even where cues within the poems themselves encourage the conflation of author and speaker. Nevertheless, the work gathered in MS fr. 25458 reflects a sustained concern with the articulation, examination, and management of the speaking subject's emotional life, at specific moments and over time. Eschewing any overt interest in Christian morality or the regiminal discourse of "princely virtue" in favor of a modest and often wry brand of quotidian wisdom, the lyric *je* labors to overcome despondency, anxiety, and vexation and cultivate equanimous well-being by limiting exposure to or investment in what is painful and grotesque in human experience.[7] Although rhetorical refinement often trumps spontaneous, intense affectivity and "le lecteur est non seulement confronté à une fragmentation du *moi* en une multiplicité de *moi* partiels, mais le *je* n'est pas toujours identique au *je*" (not only is the reader faced with a fragmentation of the self into a multiplicity of partial selves, the "I" is not always identical to the "I"),[8] the resulting verse thus partakes both of "self-care" and of something like a Foucauldian "care of the self" or "art of existence": an ongoing, conscious shaping of individual life and subjectivity bound up with the production of the person(a) as a stylized aesthetic work.[9] The present essay considers several clusters of poems in which the members of Charles's coterie collaborate on this enterprise. In their intertextual conversations, the lyric representation of private distress—a conventional topos that also gestures nebulously toward authentic emotional experience (which may be cast in poetry's mold) and the network of relationships conditioning it—seeks and finds both sympathetic response and bracing ludic agonism. The Blois poets frame poetic dialogue as a source of counsel and consolation while turning the performance of anguish into an occasion, and the manuscript page into a space, for the enjoyment of virtuosic collective composition and the community it nourishes. In so doing, they experiment with the unspoken rules and probe the practical advantages and constraints of thematized sociability in a coterie context.

I. *"Vouloir m'est pris de vous escripre"*

The consolatory power of literary friendship takes center stage in an epistolary (or pseudo-epistolary[10]) exchange in *complainte* form between Charles and one Fredet, which appears on pages 175–189 of the present MS fr. 25458 but is dated by Mary-Jo Arn to the "third stint" (mid-1440s to mid-1450s) of copying into the codex (or the unbound quires that would become it).[11] Fredet initiates contact to ask for the duke's help in overcoming the indifference of the beloved lady he calls "ma maistresse / Et ma terrienne deesse" (my mistress and my earthly goddess, Co5.25–26). Charles's supportive response encourages the frantic suitor to bear up under the great suffering that precedes greater joy in affairs of the heart, then appeals for Fredet's reciprocal advice on his own emotional and psychological predicament: not a cold mistress, but a cruel allegorical master, Soussy (Care), has contested soothing Nonchaloir's sway over his life, and Charles does not know how to satisfy them both. After obliging Charles with lengthy descriptions of Soussy and Nonchaloir that culminate in a commendation of the latter and an exhortation to banish the former, Fredet attempts to keep the conversation alive by soliciting "for a friend" the duke's opinion on whether it is preferable to continue the hopeless pursuit of an adored lady or to strategically transfer one's affections to another, more amenable object, but no reply from Charles survives.

Armstrong reads this lyric triptych as "marked by an uneasy balance between complicity and competition: each poet overtly ascribes authority to the other, while covertly claiming it for himself" through a display of technical skill, Fredet by deploying increasingly diverse and difficult stanzaick forms, Charles by using rich rhymes, seamlessly incorporating proverbial or idiomatic expressions into his original composition, and developing one of his characteristically graphic and sophisticated allegorical schemata.[12] Both poets also couch their requests for advice as "poetic challenge[s]"[13] that set a topic and identify the terms in which the interlocutor is prompted to address it. But these challenges double as invitations to deepen a homosocial bond forged in the act of writing, as the *captatio benevolentiae* built into Fredet's salutation already indicates:

Monseigneur, pource que sçay bien	My lord, because I well know
Que vous avez de vostre bien	That you have, in your goodness,
Autresfois pris plaisir a lire	Previously taken pleasure in reading
De mes fais qui ne vallent rien,	About my worthless affairs,
Dont trop a vous tenu me tien,	For which I am much obliged to you,
Vouloir m'est pris de vous escripre	The desire came over me to write to you
Et mon aventure vous dire,	And tell you about what has befallen me,
Laquelle conter vous desire,	Which I want to relate to you,
Car c'est raison que je le face,	As is only right,
Esperant que de mon martire,	Hoping that, regarding my suffering,
Tel conseil, qui devra suffire,	You will generously give me such
Me donnerez de vostre grace.	Counsel as may meet my needs.

(Co5.1–12)

This opening gambit deferentially reflects the two correspondents' asymmetrical positions in the sociopolitical hierarchy while at the same time rearticulating their relationship as a literary one with the potential to place them on a more equal footing. "Acknowledging Charles's preeminence in both poetic taste and amatory ethics"[14] allows a social inferior to ingratiate himself with a princely patron, but what could be cloyingly servile flattery mixed with self-promotion is mitigated by the evocation of a shared pleasure (as well as the shared tastes vital to coterie formation) at once textual and social. Charles has previously enjoyed Fredet's work—the latter's *fais*, constituted as the subject of writing and the object of reading, stand in for the verse fashioned of or about them[15]—and Fredet's savoring of the poet-prince's remembered appreciation sustains into the present a personal connection that grows out of an exchange of texts and produces new texts to be exchanged. Although Fredet ostensibly craves counsel on handling unrequited desire for the lady, the first and primary *vouloir* that he expresses is for written communication with Charles premised on the writer's candid, trusting self-exposure to his reader, which accentuates the intimacy between them. This function of Fredet's emotional self-portrait and plea for help is all the more salient because even if his thoroughly conventional erotic quandary is not a fiction, it readily lends itself to interpretation as such,[16] suggesting that the pretense of vulnerable self-exhibition is a pretext for the production of poetry (as it so often is in the lyric tradition) and, here, of the friendship it undergirds.

Indeed, while Fredet insists that he is solely fixated on the lady and bemoans the near-fatal "maulx et . . . ennuys" (woes and . . . afflictions, Co5.40) that torment him constantly because of her callous disregard, Charles d'Orléans supplants the female beloved as the focal point of the *complainte*. Forestalling questions about why his frustration in love should be the duke's concern, Fredet concludes by staging a self-justificatory allegorical encounter with personified Love himself. When entreated to alleviate the distress incurred for his sake, Love declares that he is helpless to intervene and forwards the petition to Charles,

Que fors lui n'en a la puissance.	For he alone has the necessary power.
Fay donc qu'ayes son accointance	Therefore, try to get to know him
Et te metz en sa bienveillance,	And commend yourself to his goodwill,
Car, si tu le puis faire ainsi,	For if you can achieve this,
Tu ne doibs faire doubtance	You need not fear
Que de ta dure desplaisance	That on your deep unhappiness
Il n'en ait voulentiers merci.	He will not readily take pity.

(Co5.102–108)

This prompts Fredet to tell Charles that "A vous doncques me fault venir / Et vostre du tout devenir" (I must therefore come to you and become entirely yours, Co5.109–110) because Charles alone holds the key to his happiness. If, Fredet asserts, "mes tant desirez souhais . . . par vous ne sont parfais, / User ma vie me fauldra / En languissant desoresmais" (my most cherished hopes . . . are not fulfilled by you, I will have to spend my life languishing forevermore, Co5.90–94); but

[S]e vous y faictes devoir	If you do your duty in this matter
Et voulez a mon fait entendre	And attend to my affairs
Tellement que je puisse avoir	So well that I can obtain
Celle qui tant me plaist a voir,	Her whom I so delight in seeing,
Vostre a tousjours je m'iray rendre.	I will go and surrender myself to you forever. (Co5.116–120)

Love's rather bizarre delegation of his traditional intercessory role to an unwitting human proxy inserts Charles into Fredet's intimate life as far more than a source of friendly advice about coping with the pain of rejection. Fredet's conceit establishes an equivalency between succeeding in love and cultivating Charles as both confidant and liege lord that is especially remarkable given that neither this poem nor Charles's reply suggests that the duke knows, or even knows the identity of, Fredet's unnamed mistress, let alone that he exerts any influence over her in matters of the heart that could materially further Fredet's suit.

Fredet's unorthodox twist on the familiar motif of the disconsolate lover's interview with and plea for help from personified Love may be a pointed intertextual gesture. In an early *balade* addressed to the prominent nobleman Jean de Garencières (ca. 1371–1415), Charles dons the mask of the "Dieu des amoureux" (God of lovers, B116.1) to teasingly upbraid the older poet-knight for presumptuously flouting Love's authority and faking lovesickness as a seduction strategy. Garencières's riposte proclaims his fealty to "Cupido" and redirects the god's ire toward "un enfant malicïeux" (a sly youth), obviously the young Charles himself, who is the real licentious liar and has been usurping "Le droit de vostre seigneurie" (Your rights of lordship, B117.11–20). This pair of poems must have been written before the likely death of Garencières at Agincourt and was copied, during the core "first stint" (ca. 1440 to mid-1440s) of scribal work on MS fr. 25458, in a conspicuous position at the beginning of a section entitled "Balades de plusieurs propos" (*Balades* on Various Subjects). If Fredet knew these texts, as seems possible, then his *complainte* might be placed in complex dialogue with them. On the one hand, Fredet correctively rewrites both *balades* by transposing their negative values into positive ones that are a credit to him and his burgeoning relationship with Charles:[17] Fredet's honest expression of heartfelt, agonizing adoration replaces Charles's and Garencières's mutual accusations of questionable loyalty to and sincerity in Love, while Charles's "usurpation" of Love's identity and prerogatives becomes a fully authorized service rendered to a comrade in need. On the other hand, the evocation of the earlier poetic exchange as a transformed model betrays Fredet's aspiration to participate in the kind of co-constructed poetic scenario and convivial badinage that Charles shared with Garencières.

Alternatively, Fredet could be making a broader intertextual reference to the first section of MS fr. 25458, which, presenting itself as a carefully structured erotic pseudo-autobiography in verse, memorably enframes Charles's early poetry between two allegorical narratives in which "Charles" first enters Love's service and then leaves it amicably in reaction to the death of his lady and the fading of his own youth.[18] In this case, Fredet's referral to Charles by impotent Love might be a nod to the duke's self-positioning on the margin of the courtly lyric world that Fredet's poetic persona fully inhabits. The post-erotic "Charles" frequently represents his half-voluntary, half-imposed renunciation of love as an exchange of intense experience for objective understanding, as in a rondel declaring that he has withdrawn from the lists of love to act as "herault" (herald, R4.2) and judge others' performance from the stands. Adding critical distance to both theoretical and firsthand knowledge of love as an affective, ethical, and poetic paradigm, "Charles" acquires a certain authority to assess the pros and (mostly) cons of the amorous "mestier" (occupation, *Songe en complainte* 137) and to adopt a detached, though not necessarily cynical, stance toward lovers' emotional paroxysms and their hyperbolic expression. This is essentially the spirit in which Charles interprets and answers Fredet's request for help in his own epistolary *complainte*. Rather than accepting the mantle of a "secular love deity"[19] capable of handing out erotic fulfilment or failure at his discretion, Charles assumes a kind of mentorship role. He refers to an emphatically past personal experience of the distress currently consuming Fredet—"De pieça je fuz en ce point," he says, "Encores pis, loing d'allegence" (Long ago I was in your shoes, and worse, far from relief, Co6.43–44)—to legitimize clear-eyed counsel in place of a magic seduction formula. The pangs of unrequited passion, the duke contends, are not so crippling as Fredet claims, and the lover can and should endure them manfully, avoiding working himself up into pointless "dueil et courrouz" (grief and chagrin, Co6.22) and keeping in mind that "Grant bien ne vient jamais sans paine" (No great good comes without effort, Co6.35).[20]

In this respect, Charles does not give Fredet quite the easy solution to his problems that the suitor claimed to want. Professing himself to be definitively "en repos / D'Amours" (untroubled by Love, Co6.66–67), declining to expand on Fredet's proposition that Charles has the *puissance* to actively intervene in his favor, and insisting that serving Love is a choice (not an inevitability) that entails opting into hardship can all be read as strategies of resistance to the pressure exerted by Fredet's poetic invitation or challenge on Charles's consistently crafted post-erotic persona. This persona's attitude toward courtly love as a way of life, a literary topos, and a poetic mode is generally ironic and often dismissive: "Ce n'est fors que plaisant folie" (It is nothing but amusing madness, B134.8)! Deigning to take courtly love discourse at least superficially seriously at Fredet's behest (while still interjecting his own eccentric perspective into its treatment) might therefore be understood as a concession made by the duke to Fredet as a member of his coterie, an act of generosity that lubricates the mechanisms of literary sociability and mitigates the creative tensions inherent in any process of poetic co-creation.[21] And such favors are routinely returned by the coterie in pairs or clusters of texts that take up Charles's original images or phrases and his preferred themes. This kind of literary conversation can survive only if it is supported by a foundation of receptivity, flexibility, and goodwill.

Thus, while pushing back in a limited way against Fredet's attempt to cast him as an empowered agent of Love, the duke does formally accept the more fundamental premise underlying Fredet's allegory and welcomes the invitation to intimacy that it transparently encodes:

Et pource que la lectre dit	And since the letter says
Qu'Amours veult que vers moy tirez,	That Love wants you to come my way,
De moy ne serez escondit	You shall not be denied by me
S'aucune chose desirez	If you desire anything that might
A vostre bien, quant l'escriprez.	Profit you, if you write about it.

(Co6.50–54)

Even as an intertextual reference to Charles's poetic catalogue, Fredet's recommendation to Charles by Love would ultimately draw attention to the literary relationship between the two men, signaling that Fredet has read and cared about the duke's textualized *fais* as well as vice versa. In terms of the poem's larger strategy, as Charles's assurance of open-hearted and open-handed comradeship seems to register, Love's explicit routing of Fredet's amorous ambitions through Charles facilitates the recentering of Fredet's desire on his correspondent himself, to whom the poet rhetorically transfers many of the affective attachments and scripts that would normally bind him to his lady. It is Charles who must grant Fredet's ardent *souhais* or else condemn him to die languishing; Charles to whom Fredet swears absolute and perpetually faithful devotion; Charles whom Fredet implores, exactly like a reluctant mistress, to hear his mournful cries, believe in their sincerity, and graciously, tenderly put an end to their cause:

Or n'oubliez pas, Monseigneur,	Now, my lord, do not forget
Vostre treshumble serviteur,	Your most humble servant,
Mais escoutez mes dolans plains	But listen to my doleful plaints,
Desquieulx je vous fais la clameur,	Which I loudly address to you,
Et vueillez par vostre doulceur	And, in your graciousness, grant
Que par vous ilz soient estains,	That they should be stilled by you,
Car croiez qu'ilz ne sont pas fains.	For, believe me, they are unfeigned.

(Co5.121–127)

The passion animating Fredet's *complainte* does not become queer, though, so much as the sexual yearning underpinning the courtly scenario that Fredet initially describes lends its language and transmits its force to an at least equally powerful, and much more easily actionable, desire for textual intercourse with his fellow poet. By causing the suffering that generates Fredet's lyric outpouring of misery, the lady's unresponsive silence affords him the opportunity to solicit a compensatory—or perhaps preferable—conversation and communion with Charles, whose anticipated sympathetic reply is imagined in the *complainte*'s final lines as a climactically euphoria-inducing speech act akin to, and substituting for, the beloved's promise of erotic requital: "Tel responce qui soirs et mains / Tout mon vivant joyeux me face" (An answer fit to make me rejoice evening and morning for the rest of my life, Co5.131–132).[22]

It is Fredet's appetite for epistolary intimacy that Charles clearly understands as the real message of the other man's *complainte*, for his own poem pairs banal and minimally useful counsel on seductive strategy (Fredet is advised essentially to wait and hope) with a vehement affirmation of friendship that offers the duke's permanent and palpable textually mediated proximity as a salve for the wounds dealt by the lady's emotional distance. The conceit of epistolarity, highlighted by rubrics identifying the poems as *lectres en complaintes* dispatched by their authors, emphasizes the opposition between spatial and sentimental togetherness and separation. Wretchedly one-sided erotic obsession is unfavorably compared to the plenitude of homosocial textual congress, which allows the correspondents to remain in figuratively physical touch just as their verbal effusions of fellow-feeling become contiguous on the manuscript page:[23]

Fredet, j'ay receu vostre lectre,	Fredet, I have received your letter,
Dont vous mercie chierement,	For which I thank you warmly,
Ou dedens avez voulu mectre	In which you have described
Vostre fait bien entierement.	Your current state exhaustively.
Fïer vous povez seurement	You can put your trust in me
En moy, tout, non pas a demi.	Entirely, not just halfway:
Au besoing congnoist on l'ami. . . .	A friend in need's a friend indeed. . . .
De ne vous oublier me lie,	I pledge not to forget you,
Autant[,] en ce que puis et doy,	Insofar as I can and should,
Que se me teniez par le doy.	Just as if you held me by the finger.

(Co6.1–7, 61–63)

The absoluteness of Charles's commitment mirrors the completeness of Fredet's affective self-portrait, which gives the duke access to his absent friend's interiority and to whose importance he returns five stanzas later:

Mais de voz doleurs raconter	But you do well, I think,
Faictes bien, ainsi qu'il me semble,	To recount your miseries
Et les assommer et compter	And sum up and enumerate them
Devant Amours, car il ressemble	Before Love, for he is like
A l'ostellier qui met ensemble	The innkeeper who gathers and sets
Et tout dedens son papier couche :	Everything down on his paper:
Pour parler est faicte la bouche.	The mouth is made for talking.

(Co6.36–[42])

Although Fredet is commended for having orally inventoried his woes for Love during their allegorical audience, the refiguration of Love as an innkeeper who meticulously itemizes his guests' consumption evokes not only Charles's other representations of erotic life as an account of emotional credits and debits that can be retrospectively audited,[24] but also Fredet's own detailed written description of his "dure merencolie" (cruel melancholy, Co6.58) in his verse letter to Charles. Writing one's inner self for the other is what enables and obligates him to respond as a friend; Charles vowed, after all, to deny Fredet nothing *quant l'escriprez*.

This is why, after nine stanzas, Charles abruptly forecloses further discussion of Fredet's problem—"Or retournons a mon propos," he says, "Et ne parlons plus de cecy" (Now let us turn back to my situation and speak no more of this, Co6.64–65)—in order to complain about his own struggle to maintain Nonchaloir in the face of Soussy's onslaught. This aggressively signposted turning point marks the duke's seizure of control over the conversation, reasserting the affective posture, thematic concerns, and allegorical style characteristic of Charles's post-erotic persona. His principle purpose, however, is less to dismiss Fredet's troubles or his thematic and stylistic choices than to reciprocate the gesture of intimate self-revelation, establishing an analogy between the two poets' distinct psychic impasses and offering Fredet, in his turn, the chance to extend counsel as a token of comradeship. "[J]e vous vueil aussy," the duke says, "De me conseillier travaillier : / L'amy doit pour l'autre veiller" (I wish to task you, too, with advising me: friends must look out for one another, Co6.68–70).[25]

For this chance, Fredet is inestimably grateful. His second *lectre en complainte* announces that the personal "bon vouloir" (goodwill) infusing Charles's reply, which he has pored over "de mot a mot" (word for word), has "tout mon dueil . . . deffait" (obliterated . . . all my grief, Co7.2–8). As Fredet anticipated at the end of his first missive, the balm of a congenial *responce* effaces the misery that necessitated it, and empathetic verbal exchange itself provides all the "allegence" (relief, Co5.99) that is required even without realizing any of the lover's erotic *souhais*. Fredet goes on to thank Charles for having "voulu que j'aye sceu[,] / De quoy il ne m'a point despleu, / Ce qui tant vous griefve ou refait" (allowed me to know—which by no means displeased me—what so greatly troubles and heartens you, Co7.10–12); the anxiety that deprives Charles of Plaisance (Enjoyment) gives Fredet the only slightly perverse pleasure of knowing and sharing it, and the unadulterated joy of reacting to it in a new poem. His eagerness to write "Pour faire vostre vouloir" (To comply with your wishes, Co7.91) is manifest in the formal exuberance and immoderate scale—194 lines, nearly double the length of Charles's text—of his ultimately nugatory *conseil*, which does little more than reiterate in an abstract, didactic vein the duke's original observations about the ill effects of Soussy and the preferability of Nonchaloir without answering Charles's real question about how, not whether, he should rid himself of Soussy.

In fairness, though, Charles's poem similarly tendered little more than a compassionate mirror of his correspondent's plight. It is telling that each writer avoids instructing the other what to *do* and instead advises him on how to *feel*, suggesting a change of subjective perspective rather than a concrete plan of action. If the resulting counsel is conceptually quite banal, it is also true to the affective dynamics of conversation between affectionate confidants. Who has not encouraged a despairing, sorrowful friend to foster positivity, even for no objectively valid reason, or urged an anxious comrade simply to let demoralizing troubles go? In such interpersonal communication, as in Charles's and Fredet's epistolary poems, the vacuity of the advice almost enhances its efficacy by affirming the emotional rather than intellectual nature of the supportive connection that it phatically foregrounds, positing the mere touch of the other's words as consolation enough.

Any attempt to explain why the exchange of *lectres en complaintes* breaks off after Fredet's second poem must remain speculative. Perhaps, as Armstrong suggests, Charles was uninspired by Fredet's "profoundly unoriginal" question about amatory ethics, on which the tradition of erotological treatises, debates, and *demandes d'amour* gave "ready-made guidance."[26] Perhaps, at least as plausibly, it was the passage from intimate discussion of the two writers' personal psychological affairs to the treatment of an purely theoretical problem that the duke found off-putting. Despite Fredet's best efforts to expand the circle of mutual care to include "un mien amy tres en malaise" (a very wretched friend of mine, Co7.163) and present working together on this friend's case as a bonding opportunity—"Vostre conseil avoir m'en fault" (I need your advice on it), he insists, because "L'adviz de deux mieulx que d'un vault" (Two heads are better than one, Co7.165–166)—the nameless *amy* and his stale dilemma seem suspiciously like inventions designed to artificially prolong the exchange of counsel poems beyond its natural end. But then, Fredet's own unluckiness in love was a courtly cliché, and even the tug-of-war between Nonchaloir and Soussy in Charles's psyche is a stock trope within the duke's more idiosyncratic oeuvre. Perhaps, in other words, the two writers' emotive self-fashioning as sufferers and concerned counselors was primarily, though not only, an ironic game that has been played out once each man has had a chance to assume both roles.

If so, though, it was a game that could bear replaying in multiple formats and with amusingly various outcomes. Much later in the duke's manuscript, on pages 362–363 and 432–433, the poets return in two separate pairs of rondels to the basic framework of Fredet's desperate plea for aid and Charles's response. The first condenses the gist of the *lectres en complaintes*, with Fredet humbly begging Charles to help him "mectre a fin la grant doleur / Que par trop amer je reçoy" (end the great suffering caused me by excessive love, R143.1–2) and Charles urging Fredet to share his woes and declaring himself "Prest de vous ayder a toute heure ... Quant vous tenez mon serviteur, / Et vostre doleur apparçoy" (Ready to help you any time ... since you declare yourself my servant and I perceive your suffering, R144.8–13). In the second rondel pair, however, Fredet's histrionic account of always almost fatal pain that Charles is rather imperiously enjoined to end elicits an unexpectedly tart and practical reaction that modulates the duke's image of bookkeeping Love into an entirely literal concern for the resources he has personally squandered on his friend's endless problems:

Se regrettez voz dolens jours,	You may mourn your dismal days,
Et je regrette mon argent	But I mourn my money,
Que j'ay delivré franchement,	Which I freely furnished,
Cuidant de vous donner secours.	Thinking I was helping you. (R216.1–4)

Is Charles genuinely frustrated with Fredet's importunate requests for succor that never seems to take lasting effect, or is he simply exploring the literary potential of a less unconditionally solicitous rejoinder in piquant contrast to the *lectres* and the first pair of rondels? The indiscernibility of the extent to which the two writers' formalized poetic outpourings of distress, compassion, and undying amity reflect, refract, or produce genuine fellow-feeling that ramifies into real social relations is the mystery that lingers to tantalize the modern reader of late-medieval coterie verse.

II. "*C'est beau debat que de deux bons*"

The pleasures of amicable agonism rather than mutual consolation dominate a six-poem series, located on pages 323–326 of MS fr. 25458 and assigned by Arn to the "second stint" (also mid-1440s to mid-1450s) of copying, in which Charles d'Orléans trades rondels and measures miseries with his fellow poet-prince René d'Anjou (1409–1480), identified in the rubrics as "Secile" in recognition of his titular kingship of Sicily. The sequence's point of departure voices Charles's speaker's criticism of his neglectful former lord, Love, by whom he has been unjustly abandoned after years of loyal service. "Du plaisir qu'il m'avoit donné / Sans cause m'a tost desservy" (Of the pleasure he had given me, he suddenly deprived me without cause), the plaintiff complains of Love, wherefore his heart "Plus ne lui sera asservy" (Will no longer be subject to him, R9.3–8). Although rubricated attributions keep the two dukes' authorship firmly in view, none of the texts in the series includes a name or any other concrete detail identifying either speaking *je* with the historical Charles or René. However, these lines presumably refer obliquely to the poetic (auto)biography of Charles's lyric persona outlined earlier in the manuscript: robbed both suddenly and too soon of love's delights by the death of his lady, the speaker opts to make virtue of necessity and cut his losses by embracing a somewhat bitter liberty, expanding his dissatisfaction with love into a larger sense of existential victimhood with the ironic remark that "Je croy que suis a ce don né / D'avoir mal pour bien desservy" (I think I was born to this gift, to receive ill in place of deserved good, R9.10–11). Unlike Fredet's *lectre en complainte*, this self-contained rondel, rubricated only as such, makes no request, nor indeed any obvious space, for a reply. Beginning with a rhetorical question—"Ne suis je pas mal guerdonné ?" (Am I not badly recompensed?, R9.2)—that the speaker answers in the affirmative through a solipsistic combination of introspection and retrospection, the poem ends with two categorical statements, the first definitively severing his ties with Love, the second enshrining undeserved ill-luck and consequent emotional destitution as his general condition and inevitable fate.

René's response, therefore, acts transformatively upon Charles's text in a way that exemplifies the fecundity of writing and reading in manuscript context. He replies informally, without salutation or preamble, and as though spontaneously, opening with a conjunctive adverb that establishes a seamless, conversational transition from one poem to the next:

Pour tant se vous plaignez d'Amours,	Although you complain of Love,
Il n'est pas temps de vous retraire,	It is not yet time for you to withdraw,
Car encor il vous pourra faire	For he may still do you
Tel bien que perdrez voz dolours.	Such good as will relieve your sufferings.

(R10.1–4)

René's counterargument turns the disgruntled rhetorical question inaugurating Charles's poem into a genuine one whose answer is up for debate. His intervention destabilizes the doleful equilibrium established in Charles's final cinquain and perforates its fatalistic closure. René disputes his kinsman's conclusions by reorienting the exclusively retrospective perspective on which they are based, finding in futurity the promise of a radical reversal that could yet overwrite what Charles calls elsewhere "La vraye histoire de douleur" (The true story of suffering, R46.3) with a satisfaction sufficient to wipe clean the slate of sorrow. René thus attempts to do for the dispirited ex-lover what his text does for the manuscript reader of rondel 9 who turns the page to discover René's reply overleaf: reactivate relinquished or foreclosed potential for intellectual and emotional evolution as well as for a productively (inter)active mode of literary reception.

Of course, Charles's poem might make its case against Love as absolutely as it does precisely in anticipation of René's challenge, as the social situation from which these works emerged may well have linked them from the beginning. Only two pages earlier in MS fr. 25458, a St. Valentine's Day rondel (R5) attributed to René is bracketed by three of Charles's poems on the same occasional topic, suggesting their shared origin in literary activity associated with holiday celebrations at Blois. Charles's disparagement of love and René's pro-erotic rejoinder could be the fruit of a similar bout of poetic recreation, with or without a larger audience, or even of the same one. For Taylor, these rondels show how "René d'Anjou pursues the conversation with Charles which started . . . with the Valentine's Day exchange,"[27] although the sequence beginning with rondel 9 is separated from the preceding cluster by several seemingly unrelated poems and, more importantly, is at once distinguished and unified by the way in which the individual lyrics (after the first) directly index and react to each other, as the St. Valentine's Day pieces do not.

On the other hand, it is equally possible that the visiting René somehow encountered Charles's preexisting and originally freestanding poem, found it provocative, and chose to initiate a dialogue where only lyric monologue had been foreseen. The desire to extenuate a certain well-meaning presumption is audible in the second half of René's rondel, which stresses that if he contradicts Charles, "Je ne dy pas pour vous desplaire" (I do not say it to vex you), and purports to give imperative instructions to keep serving fickle but powerful Love—"Ayez fiance en lui tousjours / Et mectez paine de lui plaire" (Maintain your trust in him and make an effort to please him)—only reluctantly, "Combien que mieulx me voulsist taire, / Car vous pensez tout le rebours" (Although I would rather stay silent, for you think just the opposite, R10.6–11). René's tone, however, is not deferential (he acknowledges that his input may be unwelcome, but not that it might be misguided or that he ought not to impart it) so much as politely placating, as one might carefully address unsolicited advice to a stubborn or touchy family member. The overall effect is nevertheless reminiscent of the exchange of counsel between Charles and Fredet in that a friendly outside observer claims to offer objective analysis and counsel to a speaker too invested in and overwhelmed by his unhappiness to understand it clearly. In fact, René exhorts Charles to continue putting his trust in Love much as Charles instructed Fredet "Que souffrez qu'Amours vous demaine" (That you should let Love guide you, Co6.34).

This paradigm changes drastically when René follows his initial response poem with a second one comparing Charles's circumstances to his own.[28] In his *lectre en complainte*, Charles differentiates his perspective as an enlightened ex-lover from Fredet's view of love from in *medias res*, but positions his personal problem within a domain of affective experience completely separate from the amorous life: "Vray est que je suis en repos / D'Amours, mais non pas de Soussy" (It is true that I am untroubled by Love, but not by Care, Co6.66–67). By framing his psychological condition in terms of the princely, but also universally human, struggle with anxious Soussy rather than developing on the aftereffects of a traumatically unrewarding career in Love's service, as he does in rondel 9, Charles pointedly avoids directly opposing his situation to Fredet's in a way that could encourage evaluative comparison between them. On the contrary, Charles keeps his and his correspondent's predicaments fundamentally distinct so that they remain equal in perceived significance or emotional weight, foregrounding the act of reciprocal advice-giving that establishes parity and mutually supportive intimacy between the poets. By contrast, René d'Anjou's second rondel introduces the erstwhile confidant-counselor's own troubles in an explicitly competitive spirit:

Se vous estiez comme moy,	If you were like me,
Las ! vous vous devriez bien plaindre,	Alas, you would be right to complain,
Car de tous mes maulx le meindre	For the least of all my woes
Est plus grant que vostre ennoy.	Is greater than what you suffer.
Bien vous pourriez, sur ma foy,	Then, by my faith, you could really
D'Amours alors vous complaindre,	Lament your treatment by Love,
Se vous estiez comme moy.	If you were like me.
Car si tresdolent me voy,	For I am so deeply disconsolate
Que plus la mort ne vueil craindre.	That I no longer shrink from death.
Toutesfoiz, il me fault faindre.	Nevertheless, I must dissemble.
Aussi feriez vous, se croy,	You would do the same, I think,
Se vous estiez comme moy.	If you were like me. (R11.1–12)

As an active lover (René was some fifteen years Charles's junior), the speaker contends—gesturing toward the conventional courtly erotic scenario described in more detail by Fredet—that he alone has a rightful case against Love, for the other man's distanced disaffection cannot hold a candle to the immediacy and intensity of hopeful desire still striving agonizingly toward its requital.[29] Here, the preceding rondel's altruistically comforting move to downplay the gravity of Charles's plight becomes a self-aggrandizing gambit that trivializes a rival's heartache and delegitimizes his grievance. Where Fredet and Charles constructed lyric self-exhibition as a textual technology enabling mutual understanding and empathy, René juxtaposes his own affective self-portrait with Charles's in order to accentuate irreducible difference and incomprehension. The refrain "Se vous estiez comme moy" centers the poem on the counterfactuality of their resemblance, while the dismissive claim that Charles's suffering pales in comparison to the most minor of René's many *maulx* paints the two poets' experiences as radically incommensurable. Even the expression "*me voy*" (literally, "I see myself"), although semantically equivalent to "*suis*" (I am), lexically makes the speaker and not his audience the ideal spectator of his misery's most powerful paroxysm in the closing cinquain. The only overt indication of intimacy between the two dukes' personae is René's reference to his obligation to *faindre*, that is, to conceal his amorous affliction in public so as to protect the secret (and the female object) of his passion.[30] Since René's speaker is clearly willing to drop his guard in conversation with Charles's, they must share at least some measure of comradely trust.

The poem as a whole, though, is so patently hyperbolic and aggressively competitive that its condescension and self-promotion turn over into ironic play. Charles's answering rondel follows suit, taking up René's gauntlet with a caustic proverb—"Chascune vielle son dueil plaint" (Every old woman bemoans her woes, R12.1)[31] —that clashes comically with the high courtly register in which the younger writer evokes love-born suffering, using incongruous inversions of gender, age, and class to make light of René's bombastic claims and gently mock his speaker's self-absorbed belief that his "mal passe / Tout aultre" (pain surpasses all others, R12.2–3). Without falling into the same trap, Charles goes on to vindicate his initial complaint and elaborate on the emotional drawbacks of post-erotic life, which becomes conflated with a pessimistic view of the human condition more generally:

[J]a ne parlasse	I would not speak
Du mien, se n'y feusse contraint.	Of mine if I were not forced to do so.
Saichez, de voir, qu'il n'est pas faint	Know that, truly, it is not feigned,
Le torment que mon cuer enlasse.	The torment that ensnares my heart.
Chascune vielle son dueil plaint.	Every old woman bemoans her woes.
Ma paine pers, comme fait maint,	I waste my effort, as many do,
Et contre Fortune je chasse.	And strive against Fortune's will.
Desespoir de pis me menasse,	Despair threatens me with worse;
Je sens ou mon pourpoint m'estraint.	I feel where my doublet pinches.
Chascune vielle son dueil plaint.	Every old woman bemoans her woes.

(R12.3–12)

The first half of this passage constitutes a subtle response to René's remark that he is forced to *faindre* (although he should be supremely entitled to *se plaindre*) and that Charles would do the same in his shoes. The implication is that Charles's willingness to speak openly about his unhappiness unintentionally demonstrates its triviality. Charles counters that, on the contrary, giving vent to his feelings is an involuntary symptom of their power and sincerity. Not being, like René, a whiner given to exaggeration, he translates his pain into words only because he is forced to do so, *contraint* by a distress too authentically profound (*pas faint*) to be dissimulated (*faint*). In this context, the rondel's refrain seems to underscore Charles's claim to endure irrepressible torment: old women (and certain young men) indulge in hollow jeremiads, but the mature poet laments sincerely against his will. In the poem's final couplet, however, a typically self-deprecating Charles turns his ironic gaze back on himself. Another prosaic proverb analogizes the psychological straits of the subject hemmed in by misfortune and despair to the body's uncomfortable confinement in a too-tight doublet, setting up the closing iteration of the refrain to position the speaker among, not against, the chorus of *vielles*—now figures of a universal humanity genuinely beleaguered by the hardships of existence but also prone to dwell on and magnify its troubles—for whom each private sorrow is the worst of all.

With each poet having made his case for the significance of his own tribulations and the dubious substance of the other's groans, the sequence ends on a conciliatory note with a pair of rondels that make explicit the ludic nature of the whole exchange and spell out its metacommunicative function. "Bien deffendu, bien assailly" (Nice defense, nice attack, R13.1), René congratulates himself and his sparring partner; "Bien assailly, bien deffendu" (Nice attack, nice defense, R14.1), Charles replies, echoing his opponent's satisfaction and reciprocating his gesture of mutual respect. The fencing metaphor captures not only the poets' mischievous mock aggression but also the quick rhythm and symmetry of the verbal blows they trade, which reflect the constraints and affordances of the rondel form. Charles goes on to affirm that "Tresfort vous avez combatu, / Et j'ay mon billart bien tenu" (You have put up a good fight, and I have wielded my stick well, R14.6–7), mixing the image of swordplay with that of the more peaceful pastime of *billes* or *boules* to stress the lightheartedness of the encounter.[32] Neither party shows any interest in declaring victory or otherwise ranking their performances, for this recreational combat is less a zero-sum contest than an exercise in technique that, like an exhibition duel, produces the flourish of rhetorical thrust, parry, and riposte as both invigorating sport and aesthetically pleasing spectacle: "C'est beau debat que de deux bons" (Two worthy adversaries make for a fine debate, R14.8).[33]

Charles cleverly uses the term "*debat*," which can mean either an armed confrontation or a verbal dispute or clash of opposing ideas, to articulate the metaphor of combat with an understanding of the "debat nouvel advenu" (debate that just occurred, R14.5) as an intellectual struggle that concludes cordially with an agreement to disagree. "Quant assez aurons debatu," he says, "Il fault assembler noz raisons" (When we have debated enough, we must sum up our arguments, R14.2–3), but the lines that bring the whole sequence to a close do not really restate the poets' polemical positions so much as highlight the gulf separating their life stages and emotional circumstances, acknowledging that their disaccord stems from subjective biases that cannot and need not be either reconciled or impartially decided between:

Vray est qu'estes d'Amour feru	It is true that you are Love-struck
Et en ses fers estroit tenu,	And bound tightly in his fetters,
Mais moy non[,] ainsi l'entendons.	But I am not; that is how we see things.
Il a passé maintes saisons	It has been many seasons
Que me suis aux armes rendu.	Since I surrendered my weapons.

(R14.10–14)

Charles's conciliatory stance mirrors René's readiness to admit that "Chascun dit qu'il a grant dolours" (Each of us says he suffers greatly, R13.2), shelving the question of whose suffering is greater while avowing as a personal ideological commitment his unshaken intention to "croire Amours / Par qui le debat est sailly" (believe in Love, who gave rise to the debate, R13.3–4). Whether characterized as a duel, a game, or a debate, the conversation between René and Charles renounces the goal of judgment or resolution and instead derives its purpose from the eloquent expression of contrasting points of view, forming a harmonious literary whole for whose success the two poets willingly share credit.[34]

Following a verbal skirmish that emphasizes the dissimilarity between the two participants and seeks to situate them in a hierarchy of suffering, Charles's reference to himself and René as *deux bons* effaces their differences and renders them equal and virtually interchangeable. Beyond asserting that the dukes are well matched in terms of wit and poetic ability, the phrase locates them within what Emma Cayley calls a "collaborative debating community" whose members "assume debating positions, and adopt complex personae," in order to animate compelling "collaborative fictions" in and across texts that anticipate and perform responsive readership.[35] Interpreting the rondel sequence in this light emphasizes that the speakers of the poems should not be confused with, and the emotions they depict cannot be ascribed to, the historical *Orlians* and *Secile* to whom the rubrics attribute the poems. But the *debat* that pits "René" against "Charles" also concerns the extratextual Charles and René. It reaffirms their status as friends who "respond to each other with a literary language that they share, and which seals the social (and artistic) bond between them[,] . . . mobilizing certain literary and behavioural idioms as signs of cultural sophistication and rhetorical mastery—and personal affection and respect."[36] And even if the distress voiced in Charles's opening rondel was fabricated to produce the first move in a literary game, the thematic arc of the ensuing dialogue offers an object lesson in the power of poetic competition and companionable raillery, as much as the softer form of succor exchanged by Charles and Fredet, to transmute helpless private misery into a celebration of artistic fraternity and collective achievement.

III. "*En la forest de Longue Actente*"

A more expansively polyphonic configuration of lyric conversation and community takes shape across the twelve poems by nine different authors that exploit the motif of the *forest de Longue Actente*. The "forest of Long Waiting" is one of the best-known of the allegorical formulae, coupling a concrete noun to an abstract one by means of the preposition "*de*" to produce a compact unit of nonsystematic figurative meaning, that constitute "un véritable 'indicatif poétique' de Charles d'Orléans, un trait caractéristique de son style" (a true "poetic signature" of Charles d'Orléans, a characteristic feature of his style).[37] Like other clusters of variations on a particular metaphor—the *trucheman de ma pensee* (interpreter of my thought), for instance, or the *amoureux de l'observance* (lovers of the Observant order)—or line, such as the fruitfully paradoxical "Je meurs de soif auprés de la fontaine" (I die of thirst beside the spring) famously taken up by the participants in the so-called *concours de Blois*, the forest poems exemplify how "the dynamics of quotation and cross-reference foster Charles' creative process" and that of his interlocutors as they recontextualize, repurpose, extend, and vary elements of the texts to which they respond.[38]

As in the *concours*, whose traditional critical designation belies the fact that there is no evidence of any attempt to rank *balades* or crown one poet as the victor in a poetic "contest," the operative model of literary and intellectual production is cumulative and collaborative rather than competitive; "some poets' reputations may suffer in comparison with the achievements of others in Charles's coterie, but the amassed capital of poetic understanding outweighs any fluctuations in the cultural capital enjoyed by individuals."[39] The forest group thus employs some of the same intertextual composition techniques used in the *debat* between Charles and René d'Anjou while eschewing its initially agonistic dimension as well as its linear structure. Loosely constellated, the poems are held together, as a rule in the absence of explicit commentary or direct address making one text referentially dependent upon or sequentially posterior to another, by the allegorical image and the material manuscript space they share. The forest poems also converge, however, around diversely framed and focused expressions of individual dysphoria and frustration that both display and test the plaintive isolation of the lyric sufferer, negotiating the speaker's relationship to a fictional peer group while performing, in parallel, the lyric poet's self-insertion into a literary community through the act of collaborative writing.

The figure of the *forest de Longue Actente* first appears in MS fr. 25458 in the incipit of a *balade* by Charles d'Orléans copied onto page 131 during the "third stint" of its production. It marries the temporal duration, confusing complexity, and emotionally arduous character of the speaker's journey through earthly life:

En la forest de Longue Actente,[40]	In the forest of Long Waiting,
Chevauchant par divers sentiers	Riding along various paths,
M'en voys, ceste annee presente,	I am going this year
Ou voyage de Desiriers.	On the journey of Desire.
Devant sont allez mes fourriers	My quartermasters have gone ahead
Pour appareiller mon logeis	To prepare my lodgings
En la cité de Destinee,	In the city of Destiny,
Et pour mon cueur et moy ont pris	And have booked for my heart and me
L'ostellerie de Pensee.	The inn of Thought. (B81.1–9)

Maintaining an intriguing tension between extreme concreteness and metaphorical expression, Charles devotes the second stanza to the logistical challenges of accommodating his sizeable retinue while on the road, then returns to the high allegorical mode, exchanging the first stanza's static "reifications"[41] for agential personifications to describe the daily round of "maintz travaulx avanturiers" (many risky efforts, B81.20) in which the speaker is opposed by Fortune and Dangier[42] but reinforced by an army of Espoirs (Hopes). Although the precise nature and object of the desire driving these peregrinations are left undefined in a way that makes the poem's structuring conceit at once profoundly personal and readily universalizable, the "inn of Thought" in the "city of Destiny" is clearly the endpoint of an existential rather than an erotic quest. The trek through the forest of Long Waiting is a kind of secularized *pelerinage de vie humaine*—the "Prince" traditionally apostrophized in the *envoy* becomes God, for whose grace the speaker prays, but the *ostellerie de Pensee* remains a this-worldly refuge— that aspires to exchange the vagaries of capricious Fortune, a recurring antagonist in Charles's verse who is similarly denounced in the duke's *lectre en complainte* to Fredet (Co6.80–84), for the stability of a realized Destiny and a complementary inner state of reflective quietude.[43]

In this respect, the poem revises and correctively updates a much earlier *balade*, positioned toward the end of the "autobiographical" first section of MS fr. 25458, that situates Charles's speaker "en la forest d'Ennuyeuse Tristesse" (in the forest of Woeful Sorrow, B63.1) following his lady's death. Here, too, Fortune is to blame for the poet's plight, as he explains to the Goddess of Love when she appears to inquire about his affairs. This poem's refrain, "L'omme esgaré qui ne scet ou il va" (The lost man who knows not where he goes, B63.8), emphasizes the link between the forest's somber, mournful atmosphere—the objective correlative of the bereaved lover's grief—and its bewilderingly labyrinthine structure, which reflects his self-image as an exiled, directionless wanderer whose personal identity and purpose have withered along with the object of his desire. Within the paradigms of erotic subjectivity and courtly poetics, there is no way out of the impasse facing the lyric lover robbed of the lady on whom he is still fixated. Only by stepping back from the amorous life to achieve a more panoramic perspective can Charles refigure *Ennuyeuse Tristesse* as *Longue Actente* and exchange miserable deadlock for renewed hope and revived desire.

In this sense, the *forest de Longue Actente* is initially a relatively positive image of patiently expectant orientation toward an imagined futurity. Five manuscript pages later, however, it is made to signify rather differently in a *balade* attributed to "Jacques, bastart de la Tremoille" that appropriates Charles's incipit as its formally and thematically central refrain. La Trémoïlle, for whom "Long Waiting" evidently evoked the endless-seeming torment of the unrequited courtly suitor, makes the forest "a kind of purgatory for all lovers, who must perform arduous service for their god in order to earn rewards."[44] Like the young Charles's *forest d'Ennuyeuse Tristesse*, this allegorical landscape is home to martyrs for love, but here, the hardships they endure are more conventionally represented as a key to eventual escape rather than the consequence of its impossibility. La Trémoïlle's poem retains the teleological aspect of goal-oriented *actente* even as the semantic field of suffering, barely suggested in Charles's *balade*, is substantially developed at the expense of the concept of the journey, which persists only vestigially in the idea that Love ultimately helps his sufficiently mortified servants to sidestep the "brigandages / De Dangiers par petiz boucages, / Puis les duit en la droicte sente" (of Dangier among the copses, then leads them onto the right path, B86.20–22) out of the woods.

Both Charles's existential and La Trémoïlle's courtly erotic visions of the forest are reflected in the rondels built around the same refrain. Five occupy the upper halves of pages 413 through 417, with unrelated rondels copied beneath; four more are packed onto a single leaf on pages 447 and 448. Only one author, the highborn page Philippe Pot, explicitly identifies his speaker's sylvan wanderings as a (so far painfully fruitless) quest for "Ce qui tous amoureux contente" (What satisfies all lovers, R244.5). The others, including La Trémoïlle in a rondel diverging from the imagery of his *balade*, either enunciate unhappiness in pointedly general terms that neither preclude nor invite interpretation within an erotic frame, or else clearly signal their participation in a different discourse. One of Charles's two contributions most elaborately bemoans his emotional bankrupting by stingy Vieillesse (Old Age), compounded by the "vent de Fortune Dolente" (wind of Bitter Fortune, R194.2) that has caused him to lose his bearings amidst a chaos of fallen branches. His third duchess, Marie de Clèves (1426–1487), and Philippe's father Guiot Pot, count of Saint-Pol and an important member of the ducal household, also present themselves in vaguer terms as victims of "Fortune qui me tourmente" (Fortune, who torments me, R195.5; cf. R246.7), while Fredet blames the Soussy of which Charles complained to him in their epistolary exchange. All of the writers, however, build on the conception of the *forest de Longue Actente* as an inhospitable allegorical locus or landscape of distress, disorientation, and helpless stagnation in which, as Philippe le Bon's cousin Charles de Nevers puts it, "La demeure est trop ennuyeuse" (Sojourning is most unpleasant, R193.6).

Like René d'Anjou's rejoinder to Charles d'Orléans's remonstration against Love, the poems that borrow and embroider on the figure of the *forest de Longue Actente* act on the duke's original *balade* by drawing it into a conversation that nothing within the text seems to solicit. However, where the *debat* between noble kinsmen foregrounded the two participants' individualized voices, if not necessarily their historical identities, and the personal relationship between them, ultimately making direct dialogue both the principal form and the thematized content of both writers' lyric expression, the poetic colloquy enacted by the forest suite occurs (with the exception of Charles's second rondel, which answers Fredet) solely on the intertextual level. In the absence of a narrative frame or order either constituted or referenced by the poems, they are iterative and conceptually simultaneous. As compossible perspectives on or permutations of a complex psychological and aesthetic problem explored by functionally indistinguishable speaking subjects, the rondels could be mistaken for the traces of a single artist's experimentation with variant affective postures and imagistic programs were it not for the manuscript paratext offering "le plaisir des noms propres retrouvés dans les rubriques qui révèlent l'identité de l'individu, alors que les thèmes communs (qui refusent l'anecdote) confirment la collaboration lyrique" (the pleasure of proper names discovered in the rubrics that reveal individual identity, while common themes, which resist the anecdotal mode, confirm lyric collaboration) on a relatively large scale.[45] This literary polylogue therefore highlights aspects of coterie poetics and dynamics less salient in Charles's intimate textual tête-à-têtes with Fredet or René d'Anjou. In particular, it brings into focus the duke's role as *primus inter pares* of the Blois circle.

As Nancy Freeman Regalado observes, poetic sociability in Charles's milieu "est fondée sur une fiction d'égalité communautaire, d'une communion lyrique autour du cœur, d'échanges sans hiérarchie de rang ou de classe, bien qu'en fait tous les échanges lyriques partent du duc ou se dirigent vers lui" (is founded on the fiction of communal equality, of lyric communion around the heart, of exchanges free of hierarchies of rank or class, although in fact all of the lyric exchanges originate from the duke or are directed toward him).[46] While collective creativity "thrives on the encounter of multiple voices, none of which, at least in the context of the manuscript, is obviously privileged over the other,"[47] in the forest suite, Charles is the only writer to contribute more than one rondel or to respond directly to another poet, as well as being the source of the refrain used by the whole group. But his position of primacy is not one of authority, at least not in the sense of a power exercised prescriptively or restrictively to limit invention or fix meaning. If the duke clearly presides at the center of his collaborative network and serves as its informal arbiter of taste, he never assumes the status of a "destinataire privilégié placé en position de juge" (privileged addressee instated as a judge) over poems or poets, any more than he chooses to "organiser les poèmes de son recueil afin de leur imprimer un ordre déterminé" (organize the poems in his anthology so as to impose a determinate order upon them), perpetually opting instead to "relancer le débat ou le jeu poétique auquel l'invitent à son tour les différentes pièces qui s'y trouvent ajoutées" (reinitiate the poetic debate or game in which the various pieces added to it invite him to join in his turn).[48] Charles—the man and the textual corpus—furnishes the group with a shared vocabulary and a common model (from which deviation is nevertheless permitted), serving as a resource, an inspiration, and an ongoing impetus for the communal literary activity in which he is also a participant.

The duke thus fulfills in an unusual manner the function normally reserved for "tradition" in the life of the literary coterie. Perry argues that

> Traditions form coteries as artists seek out other artists with whom they share the same response to that tradition .... Likewise, coteries form traditions as that shared artistic response exerts its own influence on the very tradition that created it, revealing new aspects of the tradition and shaping it ... in response to the predilections of the coterie.[49]

Although the Blois group is deeply influenced by other literary-historical formations, especially the literary ideologies and canons of courtliness and *fine amour* and their attendant allegorical poetics, it is above all to Charles himself that his circle responds. By imitating and quoting but at the same time appropriating, elaborating on, and reworking his signature imagery and style, the coterie members put pressure on—that is, creatively reread—Charles's original verse *qua* "traditional" source while also continuously conditioning the duke's ongoing poetic production and contributing to his personal manuscript, the repository and workshop of a living tradition.⁵⁰ The forest cluster exemplifies these patterns of mutual influence very locally, where Charles seems to revise the affective charge associated with his metaphorical environment to match its (re)interpretation by his interlocutors, and at the larger level on which the serially reimagined forest motif evinces the push and pull of thematic and ideological preferences. The duke leads most of his companions into versions of his favorite disillusioned existential musings, but a few resisters draw Charles's image—as Fredet's *complainte* dragged Charles—back into the courtly erotic sphere that is probably their own poetic comfort zone.

The constructive contestation of other writers' lyric postures and stylistic conceits inherent in parallel, mutually aware variation on a common motif or theme differs from the playfully overt agonism of Charles's *debat* with René d'Anjou, but it generates a similarly provocative friction that is fertile ground for literary and human community. It is therefore fitting that the texts of the forest poems play on the tension between individual, private emotion and collective experience that also informs their composition and reception. In the early *balade* set in the *forest d'Ennuyeuse Tristesse*, Charles makes paradoxical use of allegorical personification to simultaneously emphasize and temporarily assuage his speaker's solitude. "Un jour m'avint qu'a par moy cheminoye," he recounts, when "Si rencontray l'Amoureuse Deesse" (One day it happened that, while traveling alone, I encountered the Goddess of Love, B63.2–3), with whom he goes on to discuss his troubles: the artifice of conversation with the benevolent deity endows isolated, self-pitying introspection with dialogic form. With the substitution of *Longue Actente* for *Ennuyeuse Tristesse*, "la *forest* aurélienne connaît un changement notable, puisqu'elle devient, . . . non plus un espace propice au discours, mais . . . le théâtre d'une expédition qui conduit . . . à *l'ostellerie de Pensee*, image même d'un repli dans le silence" (the Aurelian *forest* undergoes a significant change, becoming, . . . rather than a space conducive to discourse, . . . the theater of an expedition leading . . . to the *ostellerie de Pensee*, the very image of withdrawal into silence).⁵¹ Although the *balade* enumerates the scores of retainers and horses escorting the speaker on his journey, the depersonalized mass of "officiers" (officers, B81.11) is part of the allegorical furniture that fleshes out the analogy between Charles's emotional or existential odyssey and real-world aristocratic travel without rupturing the inward-looking subject's sublime self-containment.

La Trémoïlle's *balade* rewrites the forest as a figure of the standard fate reserved for "les vaillans hommes et sages . . . qui Amours servent" (the valiant and wise men . . . who serve Love, B86.2–17), but if the suitors' travails seem to be endured together, the absence of a speaking *je* who might identify with and put a singular face on their misery maintains the text's focus on abstract erotological doctrine, not interpersonal relationships. Nevers's rondel, the first in order of appearance, draws even more attention to the theoretically general, if not necessarily communal, quality of sylvan suffering in a similarly objective tone:

En la forest de Longue Actente,	In the forest of Long Waiting,
Mainte personne bien joyeuse	Many very joyful people
S'est trouvee moult doloreuse....	Have found themselves most doleful...
D'y estre nul ne s'en talente....	Nobody desires to be there...
Chascun qui pourra s'en abscente....	Everyone avoids it who can...
Pas de cent ung ne se contente	Not one among a hundred is satisfied
En la forest de Longue Actente.	In the forest of Long Waiting. |//
(R193.1–12)

Other rondels, however, introduce first-person speakers who compare and contrast their own plights with those of fellow forest-dwellers imagined, unlike the entourage evoked in Charles's *balade*, as subjects in their own right. Philippe Pot counts himself among the "mainte personne" (many people, R244.2) treading the greenwood's dolorous paths; Guiot Pot concludes by translating the story of his heart's miserable meanderings into an exemplary lesson for others in the same situation, "Car chascun se doit tenir seur / Que l'on fault bien a son entente / En la forest de Longue Actente" (For everyone can be assured that one's aspirations come to naught in the forest of Long Waiting, R246.13–15). Marie de Clèves complains that "Souvent Espoir chascun contente, / Excepté moy, povre dolente" (Hope often satisfies everyone except me, poor wretch that I am, R195.6–7). The cupbearer Anthoyne de Lussay likewise presents the forest as a place where "les contentés Dieu contente" (God satisfies those who find satisfaction, R245.2), but he himself has thus far received not a whit of divinely apportioned joy.

Marie also opens her third stanza with a rhetorical question—"Ay je donc tort se me garmente / Plus que nulle qui soit vivente ?" (Am I wrong, then, to lament more than any other woman living?, R195.10–11)—that is promptly resolved in the negative, but not before creating the impression of addressing her self-portrait "en grant langueur" (in great enervation, R195.4) to a known audience and opening it to the possibility of a response. Lussay submits the boundaries of the lyric soliloquy to further stress, repeatedly inscribing his discourse's unidentified but individuated addressee by means of personal pronouns and imperative verbs—"Je vous asseure sur ma foy ... Pensez se ma vie est dolente" (I assure you, by my faith ... Consider whether my life is sorrowful, R245.3–6)—and even the conversational interjection "savez vous quoy ?" (do you know what?,

R245.13) that interrupts the final sestet's single sentence. Pressing on in the same vein, Fredet appeals to an unnamed *vous* not only to contemplate his tribulations, but to intervene actively in the affairs of his hapless heart, which has been taken captive and is now being tortured by a gang of allegorical bandits:

En la forest de Longue Actente,	In the forest of Long Waiting
Des brigans de Soussy bien trente	Thirty brigands of Care's band,
Helas ! ont pris mon povre cueur,	Alas, have taken my poor heart prisoner,
Et Dieu scet se c'est grant orreur	And God knows it is horrible
De veoir commant on le tourmente.	To see how he is tormented.
Priant vostre ayde, lamente	Begging for your help, he laments
Pource que chascun d'eulx se vente	Because every one of them boasts
Qu'ilz le merront a leur seigneur	That they will take him to their lord
En la forest de Longue Actente[.]	In the forest of Long Waiting.
Et pource, a vous il s'en garmente,	And therefore, he bewails this to you,
Car il voit bien qu'ilz ont entente	Seeing clearly that they intend
De lui faire tant de rigueur	To treat him so harshly
Qu'il ne sera mal ne doleur,	That there is no pain or suffering
Se n'y pourvoyez, qu'il ne sente	That he will be spared unless you see to it,
En la forest de Longue Actente.	In the forest of Long Waiting.

(R196.1–15)

And this time, someone answers. In the only poem in the forest cluster that internally marks its explicit dialogical relationship with another text in the group, Charles d'Orléans registers Fredet's cry for help and promises that it will not go ignored:

En la forest de Longue Actente,	In the forest of Long Waiting,
Forvoyé de joyeuse sente	Misdirected off the path of joy
Par la guide Dure Rigueur,	By the guide Severe Harshness,
A esté robbé vostre cueur,	Your heart has been abducted,
Comme j'entens, dont se lamente.	As I understand, wherefore he laments.
Par Dieu ! j'en cognois plus de trente	By God, I know more than thirty men
Qui, chascun d'eulx, sans que s'en vente,	Each of whom, without boasting of it,
Est vestu de vostre couleur	Wears the same color as you
En la forest de Longue Actente.	In the forest of Long Waiting.

Et en briefz motz, sans que vous mente,	And, in short, with no word of a lie,
Soiez seur que je me contente,	You may be sure that I will be glad,
Pour allegier vostre doleur,	In order to alleviate your suffering,
De traictier avec le seigneur	To treat with the lord
Qui les brigans soustient et hente	Who supports and frequents the brigands
En la forest de Longue Actente.	In the forest of Long Waiting.

(R197.1–15)

Was Charles the original and only intended addressee of Fredet's rondel, perhaps in a specific social context of composition or performance that obviated the need to name him, or did the duke simply seize an opportunity afforded by the text's inviting openness to conversation with all comers? The former hypothesis might be supported by the intriguing correspondences between this pair of poems and the same authors' exchange of *lectres en complaintes*. As in that series, Fredet deploys an allegorical conceit that magnifies the intensity of his distress (although here, the introduction of the heart as protagonist makes Fredet the onlooker rather than the subject of the pain that Charles nevertheless recognizes as his), then uses it to supplicate for Charles's intercession, which alone can alleviate the speaker's torment; Charles's reply summarizes and acknowledges receipt of Fredet's message, creatively extends the initial conceit, and finally confirms his sympathetic support and pledges his assistance. In the rondels, however, Fredet sets for the poetic duet a thematic and metaphorical key doubly indebted to Charles for the framing metaphor of the forest and for the choice of personified Soussy—the bugbear whom Charles claimed to "tant redoubter" (so greatly fear, Co6.96) in his *lectre*, and on whose pernicious effects he prompted Fredet to expatiate—as fearsome principal antagonist, as well as (probably) to La Trémoïlle's *balade* for the motif of emotional *brigandage*. Accordingly, although Charles is still the one to answer Fredet's plea for aid, he now offers to negotiate with the very foe that left him paralyzed, powerless, and in need of Fredet's counsel in the *complainte*. With the writers' intellectual and artistic contributions thus imbricated, the accepted challenge and the generous concession (as well as the idea of unidirectional "influence") as paradigms for their textual cue-giving and -taking are lost in a circular flow of collaboratively generated, refined, and modulated poetic material.

In the rondels as in the *lectres en complaintes*, Fredet and Charles affirm their intimate rapport by reading and responding to each other, but the forest poems occlude the mediating role of writing that the epistolary verse celebrated, instead founding friendship on the inscription of the two poetic personae within a shared allegorical world. From deep in the woods of hopeless alienation, Fredet's speaker calls out to Charles's and is heard by another (lyric) subject who evidently inhabits the same emotional and spatial environment. And the duke revises Fredet's imagery to underscore that they are not alone, turning Soussy's thirty henchmen—personifications of the speaker's multitudinous cares and not human individuals—into thirty miserable fellow travelers through the *forest de Longue Actente*, decked out, like Fredet and Charles himself, in the unenviable livery that figuratively externalizes a common interior state. In manuscript context, it seems very plausible to interpret Charles's *trente* as a numerically exaggerated reference to the authors of the other forest poems, each wandering a separate circuitous *sente* in sorrowful solitude but aware, as only Charles and Fredet say but most of the others suggest, that they are all alone together. Even La Trémoïlle, whose rondel (the last in order of appearance) depicts him "Tout seul, presque desesperé" (All alone and almost despairing, R251.13) after a frightening and fruitless hunt gone awry, takes his place within an intersubjective conversation and a literary fellowship elaborated not within the texts, but between them.[52]

The poetry of Charles d'Orléans often beats a defensive retreat into loci of introspective enclosure like the *ostellerie de Pensee* that his *balade* anticipates on the far side of *Longue Actente*.[53] In this group of rondels, however, the *forest de Longue Actente* comes to feel rather like a destination in its own right, a place where the melancholic lyric self can venture to live and write with others and, in so doing, discover a different kind of solace. Although described as a *locus horribilis*, the forest thus functions as a "véritable *locus amoenus* de la poésie aurélienne" (true *locus amoenus* of Aurelian poetry).[54] Indeed, if the forest cluster, and by extension the duke's personal manuscript and the Blois court as a whole, are laboratories for literary experimentation—"a space in which poets test their products, varying and refining the ways in which they deploy the fundamental elements of courtly poetry"[55]—then both the *forest de Longue Actente* as an allegorical environment and the textual constellations and manuscript pages in and on which Charles's coterie co-develops, shapes, and reshapes it are collectively imagined and inhabited spaces for representing, negotiating, and perhaps alleviating unhappiness while (and by) constructing and performing community and reveling in collaborative virtuosity. In this sense, the poetic dialogues between Charles and Fredet and between Charles and René d'Anjou can also be situated within the figurative forest. And although this sphere's textual and social parameters are provisionally outlined by the confines of MS fr. 25458 and the relationships reflected and constructed in the codex's anthologized poems, it offers other engaged readers and writers the possibility of donning the Blois circle's *couleur* and inserting themselves into spatiotemporally extensive "virtual coteries,"[56] as in MSS Paris, BnF fr. 9223 and nouv. acq. fr. 15771 and Carpentras, Bibliothèque inguimbertine 375,[57]

where adding new poems on the same theme to versions of the original group allows latecomers to the *forest de Longue Actente* to partake of the pleasures of eloquent lamentation and the consolations of poetry among friends.
Texas Tech University

NOTES

1. On Charles's *nonchaloir*, see Alice Planche, *Charles d'Orléans ou la Recherche d'un langage* (Paris: Champion, 1975), 612–626; Shigemi Sasaki, *Sur le thème de Nonchaloir dans la poésie de Charles d'Orléans* (Paris: Nizet, 1974); and Costanza Pasquali, "Charles d'Orléans e il suo 'Nonchaloir,'" in *Studi in onore di Angelo Monteverdi*, 2 vols. (Modena: Società tipografica, 1959), 2:549–570.
2. Texts in this manuscript will be quoted from John Fox and Mary-Jo Arn, eds., *Poetry of Charles d'Orléans and His Circle: A Critical Edition of BnF MS. fr. 25458, Charles d'Orléans's Personal Manuscript*, trans. R. Barton Palmer (Tempe, AZ, and Turnhout: ACMRS and Brepols, 2010). The numbering of poems in this edition, which reflects a codicological study of the order in which groups of poems were copied into the manuscript (and thus, in many cases, the periodization of their probable composition), is used throughout the present essay. All translations are my own. Different numbering is used in the other two available editions—Charles d'Orléans, *Le Livre d'Amis: Poésies à la cour de Blois (1440–1465)*, ed. and trans. Virginie Minet-Mahy and Jean-Claude Mühlethaler (Paris: Champion, 2010), and Charles d'Orléans, *Poésies*, ed. Pierre Champion, 2 vols. (Paris: Champion, 1923–1927)—but poems can be located by page number in the manuscript, which all three editions provide.
3. Gérard Gros, "Écrire et lire au *Livre de Pensée*: Étude sur le manuscrit personnel des poésies de Charles d'Orléans (Paris, B.N.F., FR. 25458)," *Travaux de littérature* 11 (1998): 63. The successive stages of the manuscript's production are reconstructed in Mary-Jo Arn, *The Poet's Notebook: The Personal Manuscript of Charles d'Orléans (Paris, BnF, MS fr. 25458)* (Turnhout: Brepols, 2008), which supersedes Pierre Champion, *Le Manuscrit autographe des poésies de Charles d'Orléans* (Paris: Champion, 1907). On the anthology's structure as it impacts on interpretive reading, see also Daniel Poirion, "Création poétique et composition romanesque dans les premiers poèmes de Charles d'Orléans," *Revue des sciences humaines* 90 (1958): 185–211; Christopher Lucken, "Le poème délivré: Le désœuvrement de Fortune et le passe-temps de l'écriture dans le manuscrit personnel de Charles d'Orléans," in *Mou-*

vances et Jointures: Du manuscrit au texte médiéval, ed. Milena Mikhaïlova (Orléans: Paradigme, 2005), 283–313; and Virginie Minet-Mahy, "Polyphonie et problèmes de langage dans l'album poétique de Charles d'Orléans (Paris, BnF, fr. 25458)," in Le Recueil au Moyen Âge: La fin du Moyen Âge, ed. Tania Van Hemelryck and Stefania Marzano (Turnhout: Brepols, 2010), 213–232.

4. Jane H. M. Taylor, *The Making of Poetry: Late-Medieval French Poetic Anthologies* (Turnhout: Brepols, 2007), 112, 114, 8. See also Jane H. M. Taylor, "Courtly Gatherings and Poetic Games: 'Coterie' Anthologies in the Late Middle Ages in France," in Book and Text in France, 1400–1600: Poetry on the Page, ed. Adrian Armstrong and Malcolm Quainton (Aldershot: Ashgate, 2007), 13–29.

5. Adrian Armstrong, *The Virtuoso Circle: Competition, Collaboration, and Complexity in Late Medieval French Poetry* (Tempe: ACMRS, 2012), xvi, 73.

6. R. D. Perry, *Coterie Poetics and the Beginnings of the English Literary Tradition: From Chaucer to Spenser* (Philadelphia, PA: University of Pennsylvania Press, 2024), 4, 12, 6.

7. See, e.g., Daniel Poirion, *Le Poète et le Prince: L'évolution du lyrisme courtois de Guillaume de Machaut à Charles d'Orléans* (Paris: Presses universitaires de France, 1965), 571–572; Jacques Lemaire, "L'humanisme de Charles d'Orléans: Une conception originale de la vie de cour," *Fifteenth-Century Studies* 10 (1984): 111–112; Gérard Defaux, "Charles d'Orléans ou la poétique du secret: À propos du rondeau XXXIII de l'édition Champion," *Romania* 93.2 (1972): 195; Florence Bouchet, "Charles d'Orléans, le penseur dans le labyrinthe," in *Être poète au temps de Charles d'Orléans (XVe siècle)*, ed. Hélène Basso and Michèle Gally (Avignon: Éditions universitaires d'Avignon, 2012), 137–143; Florence Bouchet, "Les ballades de Charles d'Orléans, une quête de sagesse?," *Le Moyen Français* 70 (2012): 21–33; and Florence Bouchet, "La joie dans la peine au XVe siècle: Du paradoxe à la sublimation," *Le Moyen Français* 62 (2008): 7–26.

8. Jean-Claude Mühlethaler, *Charles d'Orléans, un lyrisme entre Moyen Âge et modernité* (Paris: Classiques Garnier, 2010), 61. See also ibid., 157–174, and Jean-Claude Mühlethaler, "Ouvrir le recueil, prendre la parole: Postures lyriques entre effusion affective et maîtrise de soi chez Charles d'Orléans," in *Être poète au temps de Charles d'Orléans (XVe siècle)*, ed. Hélène Basso and Michèle Gally (Avignon: Éditions universitaires d'Avignon, 2012), 18–44.

9. See, e.g., Michel Foucault, *Histoire de la sexualité 2: L'usage des plaisirs* (Paris: Gallimard, 1984), 16–17, and Michel Foucault, *Histoire de la sexualité 3: Le souci de soi* (Paris, France: Gallimard, 1984), 57–85. See also Hélène Basso, "Les mots comme monde: Le lyrisme de Charles

d'Orléans entre art d'écrire et manière de vivre," in *Être poète au temps de Charles d'Orléans (XV*[e] *siècle)*, ed. Hélène Basso and Michèle Gally (Avignon, France: Éditions universitaires d'Avignon, 2012), 152–189.

10. Mathias Sieffert, "'Vouloir m'est pris de vous escripre': L'échange lyrique de Fredet et Charles d'Orléans dans le manuscrit de Blois," in *Relier, délier les langues: Formes et défis linguistiques de l'écriture épistolaire (Moyen Âge–XVIII*[e] *siècle)*, ed. Elvezio Canonica, Maria Cristina Panzera, and Agathe Sultan (Paris: Hermann, 2019), 313–331. See also Yvonne LeBlanc, *"Va Lettre Va": The French Verse Epistle (1400–1550)* (Birmingham, AL: Summa, 1995), 76–77.

11. The estimated dating of all poems in MS fr. 25458 is tabulated in Arn, *Poet's Notebook*, 196–197. Virtually nothing is definitively known about Fredet (or Fradet) beyond what can be gleaned from the poems he contributed to Charles d'Orléans's manuscript after 1444. Available biographical information about Fredet and the other contributors to MS fr. 25458 is furnished in an appendix to Fox and Arn, eds., *Poetry of Charles d'Orléans*, 829–841.

12. Armstrong, *Virtuoso Circle*, 92; see 91–99.

13. Ibid., 95.

14. Ibid., 94.

15. In fact, the term *"fais"* might ambiguously denote either Fredet's activities or his texts. Charles refers to composers of poetry as "faiseurs" (makers, R264.2), and the Burgundian chronicler Olivier de La Marche (ca. 1425–1502) attributes his own gratifyingly warm reception by Charles to the fact that the duke "estoit moult bon rethoricien, et se delectoit tant en ses faictz comme en faictz d'aultruy" (was an excellent rhetorician, and delighted both in his own compositions and in those of others): Olivier de La Marche, *Mémoires*, ed. Henri Beaune and J. d'Arbaumont, 4 vols. (Paris: Renouard, 1883–1888), 2:115.

16. Not only is Fredet's situation entirely formulaic, his passion is said to have originated "comme par destinee" (as though it were fated, Co5.22) from a St. Valentine's Day ritual of ludic courtship and coupling—including the aleatory allocation to each participant of a "per par destinee" (partner as fate decrees, R223.2), that is, by lottery—of the sort whose artificiality is apparent in many of the St. Valentine's Day poems featured in MS fr. 25458 (see R3, R5–6, R74, R128, R264–265, R270–271).

17. Sieffert, "'Vouloir m'est pris de vous escripre,'" 321, conjectures that the placement of the epistolary poems earlier in the manuscript than Charles's other, seemingly roughly contemporary poetic exchanges with Fredet could serve to construct them as the inauguration of sustained literary relations between the two men.

18. Ibid., 325, notes that the metrical variations in which Fredet will indulge in his second letter "font écho à une pièce antérieure: la requête adressée par Charles d'Orléans au Dieu d'Amour" (echo an earlier piece: the request addressed by Charles d'Orléans to the God of Love), although nowhere in Fredet's *complainte* is either the metrical structure or the rhyme scheme of Charles's *Requeste* reproduced exactly.
19. Armstrong, *Virtuoso Circle*, 95.
20. Compare B71.
21. Compare R200, in which Charles petitions on the lovesick Fredet's behalf for him to receive "l'aumosne de Doulceur" (the alms of Sweetness, R200.2) that Fredet depicts himself awaiting in R199.
22. Compare B36, in which the young "Charles" expresses intense gratitude for a letter of consolation from his absent lady.
23. This is an interesting inversion of the praise of epistolary writing as a means of transparent communication between lovers voiced by the young "Charles" in B21.
24. On this motif, see Christopher Lucken, "*Mirlifiques oberliques*: Charles d'Orléans marchand de chansons," in *L'Offrande lyrique*, ed. Jean-Nicolas Illouz (Paris: Hermann, 2009), 125–128, and Lucas Wood, "Charles d'Orléans's Heart and Its Books," *Medium Ævum* 87.2 (2018): 357–359.
25. *Pace* Sieffert, "'Vouloir m'est pris de vous escripre,'" 325, for whom the role reversal that turns the consoler into the consoled is a "procédé parodique" (parodic device). The proverbial line "Car un amy doit pour l'autre veillier" (For friends must look out for one another, B123.18) also features—along with the claim that "Mon fait vous vueil descouvrir et chargier / Du tout en tout" (I wish to reveal and entrust to you the state I'm in entirely, B.123.5–6) and a request "Que me faittes . . . De vostre estat aucunement sentir" (To give me . . . some idea how you are, B124.3–4)—in a trio of *balades* addressed by Charles to Jean I de Bourbon (1381–1434) that is clearly epistolary in character, although the texts are rubricated and internally referred to as poems rather than letters. On these *balades* and a neighboring set (B127–131) exchanged with Philippe le Bon of Burgundy (1396–1467) that traffics slightly differently in politicized *amicitia*, see Estelle Doudet, "Orléans, Bourbon et Bourgogne, politique de l'échange dans les *Ballades* de Charles d'Orléans," in *Lectures de Charles d'Orléans: "Les Ballades*," ed. Denis Hüe (Rennes: Presses universitaires de Rennes, 2010), 125–140.
26. Armstrong, *Virtuoso Circle*, 98.
27. Taylor, *Making of Poetry*, 131.
28. Although R11 bears no authorial attribution in the manuscript and unattributed poems are normally assumed to be Charles's by default, this

one must logically be René's. The name "Secile" penned in the upper margin of page 324 is probably intended to apply to both rondels on the page. This view is supported by Sylvie Lefèvre, "L'auteur Charles d'Orléans dans les éditions manuscrites et imprimées," in *L'Auteur dans ses livres: Autorité et matérialité dans les littératures romanes du Moyen Âge*, ed. Luca Barbieri, Yasmina Foehr-Janssens, Roberto Leporatti, Caterina Menichetti, and Marion Uhlig (Wiesbaden: Reichert, 2024), 143.

29. A different reading, according to which this "première phase du débat met en scène une rivalité où chacun cherche à prouver la perfection de son amour en affirmant l'intensité, voire l'indicibilité de sa douleur" (first phase of the debate stages a rivalry in which each man tries to prove the perfection of his love by affirming the intensity and even the ineffability of his pain), is proposed by Mühlethaler, *Charles d'Orléans*, 45.

30. Compare B26.9–15.

31. *Contra* Minet-Mahy and Mühlethaler (Charles d'Orléans, *Le Livre d'Amis*, ed. Minet-Mahy and Mühlethaler, 647), who read *"vielle"* as denoting the stringed instrument in the context of a metaphorical expression, I understand it as a variant spelling (attested elsewhere in the manuscript) of *"vieille."* This view is supported by Fox and Arn, eds., *Poetry of Charles d'Orléans*, 889, and Giuseppe Di Stefano, *Nouveau Dictionnaire historique des locutions: Ancien Français—Moyen Français—Renaissance*, 2 vols. (Turnhout: Brepols, 2015), s.v. "Vieux, vieille, vieillesse."

32. "Il semble bien clair qu'en dépit de cette symphonie de lamentations, aucun ne croit aux douleurs de l'autre, et qu'il s'agit d'un jeu poétique" (It seems clear that despite this symphony of lamentations, neither man believes in the other's sufferings, and that it is all a poetic game): Gabriel Bianciotto, "Le roi René, la fête, l'amour et la poésie: Lecture contradictoire de quelques textes," in *Les Arts et les lettres en Provence au temps du roi René*, ed. Chantal Connochie-Bourgne and Valérie Gontero-Lauze (Aix-en-Provence: Presses universitaires de Provence, 2013), 274. The *billart* is a phallic symbol that introduces a note of sexual innuendo into R14 according to Mühlethaler, *Charles d'Orléans*, 45, and Claudio Galderisi, *Le Lexique de Charles d'Orléans dans les "Rondeaux"* (Geneva: Droz, 1993), 158, both following Champion's suggestion in Charles d'Orléans, *Poésies*, ed. Champion, 2:648. This is certainly conceivable in the context of the dukes' homosocial banter, although it would seem extraneous to the exchange's thematic concerns, and a ribald boast of virile potency would run counter to Charles's reiteration, in the following stanza, that he has not been an active lover for many years.

33. A case for the dramatic performability and marked "orientation vers le public" (orientation toward the public) of "cet échange où seul compte l'habileté rhétorique à trouver la parade en jouant les cartes de la surenchère et de l'ironie, ceci pour le plus grand plaisir de l'auditoire" (this exchange in which all that counts is rhetorical dexterity in parrying blows by playing the cards of escalation and irony to heighten the audience's enjoyment) is made in Virginie Minet-Mahy and Jean-Claude Mühlethaler, "De la lecture à la performance: Le 'Livre d'Amis' de Charles d'Orléans," in *Les Manuscrits médiévaux témoins de lectures*, ed. Catherine Croizy-Naquet, Laurence Harf-Lancner, and Michelle Szkilnik (Paris: Presses Sorbonne Nouvelle, 2015), 182–183. Palmer translates *"bons"* as "proofs"; Fox and Arn, eds., *Poetry of Charles d'Orléans*, 889, cite Godefroy's medieval French lexicon in support of this reading and note that the term might secondarily suggest sexual pleasure, building on the *billart*'s possible erotic connotations. However, it seems more logical to take the word simply as a nominalization of the adjective "good" that praises the debaters' personal qualities.
34. The absence of a decisive verdict, synthesis, or closure and a corresponding focus on the conflictual juxtaposition of opposing perspectives—usually articulated by one author's multiple characters rather than by two different authors, as in Charles's own Co4, a dialogical argument in *complainte* form between Love and an aggrieved Lover—is typical of the late-medieval stanzaic debate poems to which Charles and René implicitly compare their exchange. See Pierre-Yves Badel, "Le débat," in *Grundriss der romanischen Literaturen des Mittelalters*, vol. 8.1, *La Littérature française aux XIVe et XVe siècles: Partie historique*, ed. Daniel Poirion (Heidelberg: Winter, 1988), 104, and Emma Cayley, *Debate and Dialogue: Alain Chartier in His Cultural Context* (Oxford: Clarendon, 2006), 12–51.
35. Cayley, *Debate and Dialogue*, 2–5.
36. Taylor, *Making of Poetry*, 133.
37. Armand Strubel, "'En la forêt de longue actente': Réflexions sur le style allégorique de Charles d'Orléans," in *Styles et Valeurs: Pour une histoire de l'art littéraire au Moyen Âge*, ed. Daniel Poirion (Paris, France: SEDES, 1990), 168. See also Paul Zumthor, "Charles d'Orléans et le langage de l'allégorie," in *Mélanges offerts à Rita Lejeune*, 2 vols. (Gembloux, Belgium: Duculot, 1969), 2:1481–1502, and Claudio Galderisi, *En regardant vers le païs de France: Charles d'Orléans, une poésie des présents* (Orléans, France: Paradigme, 2007), 127–161. For overviews of the poetic values associated with Charles's figurative forests, see Planche, *Charles d'Orléans*, 201–210; Shigemi Sasaki, "Fontaine et forest," *Études de langue et littérature françaises* 22 (1973): 11–35; Jacqueline Cerquiglini-Toulet, "*Espèces d'espaces*: Espace physique et es-

pace mental dans la poésie de Charles d'Orléans," *Le Moyen Français* 70 (2012): 12–17; Carole Bauguion, "L'écriture introspective de Charles d'Orléans ou la recherche d'une nouvelle poétique de l'image '*En la forest de Longue Actente*,'" *Dalhousie French Studies* 111 (2018): 17–33; and Olivia Robinson, "In the Forest of Long Waiting: Charles d'Orléans and the *Querelle de la Belle Dame sans mercy*," *Medium Ævum* 87.1 (2018): 81–105, which also reflects on the relationship between the forests of MS fr. 25458 and the "gaste forest de Longue Actente" mentioned in the *Requeste faicte et baillee aux dames contre Maistre Alain* that forms part of the cycle of literary responses to Alain Chartier's *La Belle Dame sans mercy*.

38. Taylor, *Making of Poetry*, 123. See also Armstrong, *Virtuoso Circle*, 73–91; Jane H. M. Taylor, *The Poetry of François Villon: Text and Context* (Cambridge: Cambridge University Press, 2001), 58–68; Minet-Mahy and Mühlethaler, "De la lecture à la performance," 186–196; Galderisi, *En regardant vers le païs de France*, 98–112, 181–189; Poirion, *Poète et le Prince*, 182–185; and the editors' introduction to Charles d'Orléans, *Le Livre d'Amis*, ed. Minet-Mahy and Mühlethaler, 41–44.
39. Armstrong, *Virtuoso Circle*, 91.
40. Fox and Arn capitalize "*Forest*" in this poem and the others discussed here, but I prefer to leave it uncapitalized, like the concrete terms in all of the other "reifications" featured in these texts.
41. See Strubel, "'En la forêt de longue actente.'"
42. "Dangier" is more difficult to define and translate than Charles's other personifications because it appears in various contexts "signifying any factor that comes between the poet and his desires": John Fox, *The Lyric Poetry of Charles d'Orléans* (Oxford, U.K.: Clarendon, 1969), 82. See also Planche, *Charles d'Orléans*, 443–449; Daniel Poirion, *Le Lexique de Charles d'Orléans dans les "Ballades"* (Geneva, Switzerland: Droz, 1967), 63; and Galderisi, *Lexique de Charles d'Orléans dans les "Rondeaux*," 173.
43. See Poirion, *Poète et le Prince*, 612–613. On the *ostellerie de Pensee* in the context of Charles's other figurations of Thought, see Planche, *Charles d'Orléans*, 641–655.
44. Armstrong, *Virtuoso Circle*, 76.
45. Nancy Freeman Regalado, "*En ce saint livre*: Mise en page et identité lyrique dans les poèmes autographes de Villon dans l'album de Blois (Bibl. Nat. ms. fr. 25458)," in *L'Hostellerie de pensée: Études sur l'art littéraire au Moyen Âge offertes à Daniel Poirion par ses anciens élèves*, ed. Michel Zink, Danielle Bohler, Eric Hicks, and Manuela Python (Paris: Presses de l'Université de Paris–Sorbonne, 1995), 361. See also Taylor, *Making of Poetry*, 186, 198. These paratextual attributions at once

resist and reinforce the impression that, as "refrains et incipit circulent d'une poésie à l'autre, l'individuel se fond dans le collectif, de sorte que la subjectivité lyrique tient bien plus du jeu de société que d'un cri du cœur" (refrains and incipits circulate from one poem to another, the individual merges with the collective, making lyric subjectivity more like a parlor game than a spontaneous effusion): Mühlethaler, *Charles d'Orléans*, 12.

46. Regalado, "*En ce saint livre*," 361. See also Taylor, *Making of Poetry*, 135, and Poirion, *Poète et le Prince*, 190.
47. Taylor, *Making of Poetry*, 128. See also Armstrong, *Virtuoso Circle*, 94.
48. Christopher Lucken, "De la cour au livre: La communauté poétique de Louis à Charles d'Orléans," in *Être poète au temps de Charles d'Orléans (XVe siècle)*, ed. Hélène Basso and Michèle Gally (Avignon: Éditions universitaires d'Avignon, 2012), 84–85.
49. Perry, *Coterie Poetics*, 3.
50. See Taylor, *Making of Poetry*, 112; Lucken, "De la cour au livre," 83; and Gros, "Écrire et lire au *Livre de Pensée*," 66.
51. Mathias Sieffert, "*Loingtain* et *profond*: L'espace lyrique chez Othon de Grandson, Jean de Garencières et Charles d'Orléans," in *Un territoire à géographie variable: La communication littéraire au temps de Charles VI*, ed. Jean-Claude Mühlethaler and Delphine Burghgraeve (Paris: Classiques Garnier, 2017), 281. The adjective "*aurélien(ne)*" (from the Latin name of Orléans) is commonly used in French scholarly discourse about Charles.
52. Philippe Frieden, "Deux poètes au chevet de leur livre: François Pétrarque et Charles d'Orléans," in *Être poète au temps de Charles d'Orléans (XVe siècle)*, ed. Hélène Basso and Michèle Gally (Avignon: Éditions universitaires d'Avignon, 2012), 107, notes that while in its "premières apparitions, la forêt semble isoler le moi du poète, dans sa reprise au cœur des rondeaux, elle réunit dans une écriture plurielle" (first appearances, the forest seems to isolate the poet's self, when it is taken up again in the midst of the rondeaux, it brings together in a kind of plural writing) the various authors who rework the motif.
53. See Poirion, *Poète et le Prince*, 304, 569–570; Planche, *Charles d'Orléans*, 228–256; Cerquiglini-Toulet, "*Espèces d'espaces*," 8–12; Bouchet, "Charles d'Orléans," 134–136; Karen Newman, "The Mind's Castle: Containment in the Poetry of Charles d'Orléans," *Romance Philology* 33.2 (1979): 317–328; and Friedrich Wolfzettel, "Le cœur de Charles d'Orléans: Un univers meublé," in *"Li premerains vers": Essays in Honor of Keith Busby*, ed. Catherine M. Jones and Logan E. Whalen (Amsterdam: Rodopi, 2011), 545–555.
54. Galderisi, *En regardant vers le païs de France*, 144.

55. Armstrong, *Virtuoso Circle*, 77.
56. Perry, *Coterie Poetics*, 13–14.
57. See Taylor, *Making of Poetry*, 147–212; Jean-Claude Mühlethaler, "Le poète en ses réseaux: Du recueil manuscrit à l'anthologie imprimée (Le cas Blosseville)," in *L'Auteur dans ses livres: Autorité et matérialité dans les littératures romanes du Moyen Âge*, ed. Luca Barbieri, Yasmina Foehr-Janssens, Roberto Leporatti, Caterina Menichetti, and Marion Uhlig (Wiesbaden: Reichert, 2024), 39–65; and Poirion, *Poète et le Prince*, 185–189. The BnF manuscripts are edited in Gaston Raynaud, ed., *Rondeaux et autres poésies du XVe siècle* (Paris: Didot, 1889), and Barbara L. S. Inglis, ed., *Le Manuscrit B.N. nouv. acq. fr. 15771: Une nouvelle collection de poésies lyriques et courtoises du XVe siècle* (Geneva: Slatkine, 1985).

WORKS CITED

Armstrong, Adrian. *The Virtuoso Circle: Competition, Collaboration, and Complexity in Late Medieval French Poetry*. Tempe, AZ: ACMRS, 2012.

Arn, Mary-Jo. *The Poet's Notebook: The Personal Manuscript of Charles d'Orléans (Paris, BnF, MS fr. 25458)*. Turnhout: Brepols, 2008.

Badel, Pierre-Yves. "Le débat." In *Grundriss der romanischen Literaturen des Mittelalters*, vol. 8.1, *La Littérature française aux XIVe et XVe siècles: Partie historique*, ed. Daniel Poirion, 95–110. Heidelberg: Winter, 1988.

Barbieri, Luca, Yasmina Foehr-Janssens, Roberto Leporatti, Caterina Menichetti, and Marion Uhlig, eds. *L'Auteur dans ses livres: Autorité et matérialité dans les littératures romanes du Moyen Âge*. Wiesbaden: Reichert, 2024.

Basso, Hélène. "Les mots comme monde: Le lyrisme de Charles d'Orléans entre art d'écrire et manière de vivre." In *Être poète au temps de Charles d'Orléans (XVe siècle)*, ed. Hélène Basso and Michèle Gally, 152–189. Avignon: Éditions universitaires d'Avignon, 2012.

———, and Michèle Gally, eds. *Être poète au temps de Charles d'Orléans (XVe siècle)*. Avignon: Éditions universitaires d'Avignon, 2012.

Bauguion, Carole. "L'écriture introspective de Charles d'Orléans ou la recherche d'une nouvelle poétique de l'image 'En la forest de Longue Actente.'" *Dalhousie French Studies* 111 (2018): 17–33.

Bianciotto, Gabriel. "Le roi René, la fête, l'amour et la poésie: Lecture contradictoire de quelques textes." In *Les Arts et les lettres en Provence au temps du roi René*, ed. Chantal Connochie-Bourgne and Valérie Gontero-Lauze, 261–276. Aix-en-Provence: Presses universitaires de Provence, 2013.

Bouchet, Florence. "Les ballades de Charles d'Orléans, une quête de sagesse?" *Le Moyen Français* 70 (2012): 21–33.
———. "Charles d'Orléans, le penseur dans le labyrinthe." In *Être poète au temps de Charles d'Orléans (XVe siècle)*, ed. Hélène Basso and Michèle Gally, 132–150. Avignon: Éditions universitaires d'Avignon, 2012.
———. "La joie dans la peine au XVe siècle: Du paradoxe à la sublimation." *Le Moyen Français* 62 (2008): 7–26.
Cayley, Emma. *Debate and Dialogue: Alain Chartier in His Cultural Context*. Oxford: Clarendon, 2006.
Cerquiglini-Toulet, Jacqueline. "*Espèces d'espaces*: Espace physique et espace mental dans la poésie de Charles d'Orléans." *Le Moyen Français* 70 (2012): 7–20.
Champion, Pierre. *Le Manuscrit autographe des poésies de Charles d'Orléans*. Paris: Champion, 1907.
Charles d'Orléans. *Le Livre d'Amis: Poésies à la cour de Blois (1440–1465)*. Ed. and trans. Virginie Minet-Mahy and Jean-Claude Mühlethaler. Paris: Champion, 2010.
———. *Poésies*. Ed. Pierre Champion. 2 vols. Paris: Champion, 1923–1927.
Defaux, Gérard. "Charles d'Orléans ou la poétique du secret: À propos du rondeau XXXIII de l'édition Champion." *Romania* 93.2 (1972): 194–243.
Di Stefano, Giuseppe. *Nouveau Dictionnaire historique des locutions: Ancien Français—Moyen Français—Renaissance*. 2 vols. Turnhout: Brepols, 2015.
Doudet, Estelle. "Orléans, Bourbon et Bourgogne, politique de l'échange dans les *Ballades* de Charles d'Orléans." In *Lectures de Charles d'Orléans: "Les Ballades,"* ed. Denis Hüe, 125–140. Rennes: Presses universitaires de Rennes, 2010.
Foucault, Michel. *Histoire de la sexualité 2: L'usage des plaisirs*. Paris: Gallimard, 1984.
———. *Histoire de la sexualité 3: Le souci de soi*. Paris: Gallimard, 1984.
Fox, John. *The Lyric Poetry of Charles d'Orléans*. Oxford: Clarendon, 1969.
———, and Mary-Jo Arn, eds. *Poetry of Charles d'Orléans and His Circle: A Critical Edition of BnF MS. fr. 25458, Charles d'Orléans's Personal Manuscript*. Trans. R. Barton Palmer. Tempe, AZ, and Turnhout: ACMRS and Brepols, 2010.
Frieden, Philippe. "Deux poètes au chevet de leur livre: François Pétrarque et Charles d'Orléans." In *Être poète au temps de Charles d'Orléans (XVe siècle)*, ed. Hélène Basso and Michèle Gally, 88–111. Avignon: Éditions universitaires d'Avignon, 2012.
Galderisi, Claudio. *En regardant vers le païs de France: Charles d'Orléans, une poésie des présents*. Orléans: Paradigme, 2007.

———. *Le Lexique de Charles d'Orléans dans les "Rondeaux."* Geneva: Droz, 1993.
Gros, Gérard. "Écrire et lire au *Livre de Pensée*: Étude sur le manuscrit personnel des poésies de Charles d'Orléans (Paris, B.N.F., FR. 25458)." *Travaux de littérature* 11 (1998): 55–74.
Inglis, Barbara L. S., ed. *Le Manuscrit B.N. nouv. acq. fr. 15771: Une nouvelle collection de poésies lyriques et courtoises du XVe siècle.* Geneva: Slatkine, 1985.
La Marche, Olivier de. *Mémoires.* Ed. Henri Beaune and J. d'Arbaumont. 4 vols. Paris: Renouard, 1883–1888.
LeBlanc, Yvonne. *"Va Lettre Va": The French Verse Epistle (1400–1550).* Birmingham, AL: Summa, 1995.
Lefèvre, Sylvie. "L'auteur Charles d'Orléans dans les éditions manuscrites et imprimées." In *L'Auteur dans ses livres: Autorité et matérialité dans les littératures romanes du Moyen Âge*, ed. Luca Barbieri, Yasmina Foehr-Janssens, Roberto Leporatti, Caterina Menichetti, and Marion Uhlig, 129–147. Wiesbaden: Reichert, 2024.
Lemaire, Jacques. "L'humanisme de Charles d'Orléans: Une conception originale de la vie de cour." *Fifteenth-Century Studies* 10 (1984): 107–119.
Lucken, Christopher. "De la cour au livre: La communauté poétique de Louis à Charles d'Orléans." In *Être poète au temps de Charles d'Orléans (XVe siècle)*, ed. Hélène Basso and Michèle Gally, 46–87. Avignon: Éditions universitaires d'Avignon, 2012.
———. "*Mirlifiques oberliques*: Charles d'Orléans marchand de chansons." In *L'Offrande lyrique*, ed. Jean-Nicolas Illouz, 109–140. Paris: Hermann, 2009.
———. "Le poème délivré: Le désœuvrement de Fortune et le passe-temps de l'écriture dans le manuscrit personnel de Charles d'Orléans." In *Mouvances et Jointures: Du manuscrit au texte médiéval*, ed. Milena Mikhaïlova, 283–313. Orléans: Paradigme, 2005.
Minet-Mahy, Virginie. "Polyphonie et problèmes de langage dans l'album poétique de Charles d'Orléans (Paris, BnF, fr. 25458)." In *Le Recueil au Moyen Âge: La fin du Moyen Âge*, ed. Tania Van Hemelryck and Stefania Marzano, 213–232. Turnhout: Brepols, 2010.
———, and Jean-Claude Mühlethaler. "De la lecture à la performance: Le 'Livre d'Amis' de Charles d'Orléans." In *Les Manuscrits médiévaux témoins de lectures*, ed. Catherine Croizy-Naquet, Laurence Harf-Lancner, and Michelle Szkilnik, 175–196. Paris: Presses Sorbonne Nouvelle, 2015.
Mühlethaler, Jean-Claude. *Charles d'Orléans, un lyrisme entre Moyen Âge et modernité.* Paris: Classiques Garnier, 2010.
———. "Ouvrir le recueil, prendre la parole: Postures lyriques entre effu-

sion affective et maîtrise de soi chez Charles d'Orléans." In *Être poète au temps de Charles d'Orléans (XVe siècle)*, ed. Hélène Basso and Michèle Gally, 18–44. Avignon: Éditions universitaires d'Avignon, 2012.
———. "Le poète en ses réseaux: Du recueil manuscrit à l'anthologie imprimée (Le cas Blosseville)." In *L'Auteur dans ses livres: Autorité et matérialité dans les littératures romanes du Moyen Âge*, ed. Luca Barbieri, Yasmina Foehr-Janssens, Roberto Leporatti, Caterina Menichetti, and Marion Uhlig, 39–65. Wiesbaden: Reichert, 2024.
Newman, Karen. "The Mind's Castle: Containment in the Poetry of Charles d'Orléans." *Romance Philology* 33.2 (1979): 317–328.
Pasquali, Costanza. "Charles d'Orléans e il suo 'Nonchaloir.'" In *Studi in onore di Angelo Monteverdi*. 2 vols., 2:549–570. Modena: Società tipografica, 1959.
Perry, R. D. *Coterie Poetics and the Beginnings of the English Literary Tradition: From Chaucer to Spenser*. Philadelphia, PA: University of Pennsylvania Press, 2024.
Planche, Alice. *Charles d'Orléans ou la Recherche d'un langage*. Paris: Champion, 1975.
Poirion, Daniel. "Création poétique et composition romanesque dans les premiers poèmes de Charles d'Orléans." *Revue des sciences humaines* 90 (1958): 185–211.
———. *Le Lexique de Charles d'Orléans dans les "Ballades."* Geneva: Droz, 1967.
———. *Le Poète et le Prince: L'évolution du lyrisme courtois de Guillaume de Machaut à Charles d'Orléans*. Paris: Presses universitaires de France, 1965.
Raynaud, Gaston, ed. *Rondeaux et autres poésies du XVe siècle*. Paris: Didot, 1889.
Regalado, Nancy Freeman. "*En ce saint livre*: Mise en page et identité lyrique dans les poèmes autographes de Villon dans l'album de Blois (Bibl. Nat. ms. fr. 25458)." In *L'Hostellerie de pensée: Études sur l'art littéraire au Moyen Âge offertes à Daniel Poirion par ses anciens élèves*, ed. Michel Zink, Danielle Bohler, Eric Hicks, and Manuela Python, 355–372. Paris: Presses de l'Université de Paris–Sorbonne, 1995.
Robinson, Olivia. "In the Forest of Long Waiting: Charles d'Orléans and the *Querelle de la Belle Dame sans mercy*." *Medium Ævum* 87.1 (2018): 81–105.
Sasaki, Shigemi. "Fontaine et forest." *Études de langue et littérature françaises* 22 (1973): 11–35.
———. *Sur le thème de Nonchaloir dans la poésie de Charles d'Orléans*. Paris: Nizet, 1974.
Sieffert, Mathias. "*Loingtain* et *profond*: L'espace lyrique chez Othon de Grandson, Jean de Garencières et Charles d'Orléans." In *Un territoire à géographie variable: La communication littéraire au temps de Charles*

VI, ed. Jean-Claude Mühlethaler and Delphine Burghgraeve, 273–295. Paris, France: Classiques Garnier, 2017.

———. "'Vouloir m'est pris de vous escripre': L'échange lyrique de Fredet et Charles d'Orléans dans le manuscrit de Blois." In *Relier, délier les langues: Formes et défis linguistiques de l'écriture épistolaire (Moyen Âge–XVIIIe siècle)*, ed. Elvezio Canonica, Maria Cristina Panzera, and Agathe Sultan, 313–331. Paris: Hermann, 2019.

Strubel, Armand. "'En la forêt de longue actente': Réflexions sur le style allégorique de Charles d'Orléans." In *Styles et Valeurs: Pour une histoire de l'art littéraire au Moyen Âge*, ed. Daniel Poirion, 167–186. Paris: SEDES, 1990.

Taylor, Jane H. M. "Courtly Gatherings and Poetic Games: 'Coterie' Anthologies in the Late Middle Ages in France." In *Book and Text in France, 1400–1600: Poetry on the Page*, ed. Adrian Armstrong and Malcolm Quainton, 13–29. Aldershot: Ashgate, 2007.

———. *The Making of Poetry: Late-Medieval French Poetic Anthologies*. Turnhout: Brepols, 2007.

———. *The Poetry of François Villon: Text and Context*. Cambridge: Cambridge University Press, 2001.

Wolfzettel, Friedrich. "Le cœur de Charles d'Orléans: Un univers meublé." In *"Li premerains vers": Essays in Honor of Keith Busby*, ed. Catherine M. Jones and Logan E. Whalen, 545–555. Amsterdam: Rodopi, 2011.

Wood, Lucas. "Charles d'Orléans's Heart and Its Books." *Medium Ævum* 87.2 (2018): 343–367.

Zumthor, Paul. "Charles d'Orléans et le langage de l'allégorie." In *Mélanges offerts à Rita Lejeune*, 2 vols., 2:1481–1502. Gembloux: Duculot, 1969.

Nota Bene: Brief Notes on Manuscripts and Early Printed Books

Highlighting Little-Known or Recently Uncovered Items or Related Issues

An Unrecorded Prayer of St. Edmund of Abingdon in Madrid, Biblioteca Nacional MS 6422[1]

R. F. YEAGER

Madrid, Biblioteca Nacional MS 6422 is a mid-to-late thirteenth-century psalter very likely copied in Norwich for the nuns of the Benedictine priory of St. Mary of Carrow, constructed a short distance beyond the then city limits, now the site of the Norwich City football club.[2] Founded in 1146 to 1147 by two sisters from the earlier priory of St. Mary and St. John, St. Mary of Carrow expanded rapidly with notable support from numerous aristocratic families.[3] By the end of the century, a large complex included a priory church, chapter house, cloister, dormitory, probably a separate house for guests, prioress's house, and other buildings unidentified by various archaeological digs undertaken in the late nineteenth century.[4] Initially St. Mary's included nine nuns, a prioress, priests to perform the holy offices, and their various servants. By 1400, three more nuns had been added for a maximum total of twelve.[5] As even this thumbnail sketch indicates, in the thirteenth century, Carrow priory was prosperous, and sufficiently well-endowed to house fine books for the use and pleasure of the noble sisters who could appreciate them.[6]

Madrid, Biblioteca Nacional MS 6422 (hereafter simply MS 6422) is such a book. Copied by two or three scribes in Gothic textura at sixteen lines to the page in a text block of 150 x 116 mm, with large, historiated capitals on folios 7r, 32v, 48v, 62v, 63v, 77v, 96v, 113v, 132r, it contains, in addition to a calendar and all the Psalms, a *Confiteor, Exultavit, Te Deum, Magnificat*, Athanasian Creed, assorted other prayers, and a number of litanies.[7] One of these litanies is for Edmund of Abingdon, Archbishop of Canterbury (d. 1240, canonized 1246). St. Edmund is named twice more in the manuscript: in celebration of his feast day (16 November), and in a note, in a fourteenth-century hand, on the verso of the first of two flyleaves. The note, in French, records a Latin prayer written by St. Edmund for "Alice de Rokelle":

> Ceste oreson fist ceint Esmon de ponntenye et la mannda a dame Alice de la Rokelle q'ant quelle la vorroit dire apres Agnus dei p[or] deux.[8]
> [This is the prayer written by saint Edmund of Pontigny and given to the lady Alice of Rokelle, so that she would say it before the *Agnus Dei* (at mass) for the both of them.]

Just who Alice was, or what her relationship might have been either to the saint or to Carrow Priory, cannot be determined precisely.[9] A strong possibility, however, is that she was a nun at Carrow. This would explain why, after a century and a half, someone chose to include the prayer and name the writer and the recipient in a Carrow psalter. If so, given that St. Edmund died in 1240, Alice would have served under the leadership of Carrow's second prioress, Agnes de Monte Kensi (on whom more below, note 3), roughly when MS 6422 was being copied. There is no record of Edmund visiting Carrow, or even Norwich, though his movements, particularly before becoming Archbishop, are difficult to trace.[10] The later date of inscription notwithstanding, the tone of the explanation for the prayer's writing suggests that a relationship of some tenderness was known to exist between the saint and Alice: "la vorroit dire apres Agnus dei p[our] deux."

The "oreson" of St. Edmund for Alice de Rokelle is as follows:

> Dulcissime domine ihesu criste in hanc verissima
> carne tua consolida nos ad amandum te [et]
> patiendum pro te & [et] laua nos & [et] debería in hoc
> verissimo sanguine tuo vt omnibus mundialibus
> pro te ad plenum spretis & [et] omnibus sordibus fusis;
> plenissime tibi vniamur et fac nos ex te dignos
> amore tuo & [et] ministerios tuo & [et] flagello tuo [et]

non fias nobis in alien[um?] parcens nobis in die malo.
Hic vre & [et] seca; & [et] in future misericordia glorifica—
Amen.

[Most sweet Lord Jesus Christ, in this truest flesh unite us firmly to love and suffer for you. Strengthen us and cleanse us from everything worldly in this most true blood of yours, make us scorn every sordid thing, and having shed all filth, we may be fully united with you, and worthy of your love, ministry, and beatings (i.e., those endured by Christ). Do not allow any of us to become separate from you, sparing us on the evil day. Burn and cut us here and mercifully glorify us in the future. Amen.]

Beyond its interest as a rare survival of a private act of open-heartedness from a saint to a person who, at this distance in time, is altogether unknown, the prayer has several things to tell us about Alice and Edmund both. Of the latter, it is further confirmation of a generosity for which the saint was justly celebrated.[11] Of Alice it suggests an affective, fervent piety, focused on the corporeal sufferings of Christ—hardly unique for a cloistered woman of the thirteenth century—and very likely her literacy. It seems not too far a stretch to suggest that initially the psalter belonged to Alice, whose presence at Carrow must have had enough of an impact for her prayer to be recorded long after her death, perhaps through the legacy of the psalter itself, which would either have been passed down from sister to sister, or—most probably—put into common use at Carrow, subsequent to Alice's time there.[12]

Most remarkable is that Edmund's "oreson" has existed unnoticed and unpublished, although to some degree the presence of the manuscript in the Biblioteca Nacional may serve to explain this lengthy obscurity. Purchased for Felipe V in England (undoubtedly by an agent) at the beginning of the eighteenth century, MS 6422 has remained in Madrid for three hundred years, off the beaten track for English-speaking medievalists who rarely explore Spanish collections but who might have special interest in a "new" work by Edmund of Abingdon.[13]

NOTES

1. Research for this article has been funded by the Spanish National Research Agency (Agencia Estatal de investigación) through the research project "Missions and Transmissions: Exchanges between Iberia and the British Isles in the early modern period" (ref: PID2020-113516GB-I00).

2. Nigel Morgan argues for a Norwich origin, partly on stylistic grounds, citing several contemporary manuscripts with firm Norwich connections similarly illustrated. See *Early Gothic Manuscripts, 1250–1285*, 2 vols. (London: Harvey Miller, 1988), II, 90–91. One of these, the sumptuously illuminated Baltimore, Walters Art Gallery MS W.34, another psalter, found its way to Carrow priory in the fifteenth century. For a full description of the manuscript, see R. F. Yeager, "English Manuscripts in Spanish Libraries: Madrid, Biblioteca Nacional MS 6422," forthcoming in *The Library*.

3. An unusual feature of MS 6422 is the presence of nine shields placed beside psalms through fol. 29. Presumably these are the arms of priory patrons. The blazons are those of de Clare, de Warenne, Bigod, Fitz-Roger, Marshall, de Mandeville, (probably) Peverel, Sully, and de Grey. Instead of the last, Morgan proposes a variant of the "Montchansey" blazon, a possibility since, among the obits (fol. 3) in BN 6422, is one for a "A. de Monte Kensi prioressa de Karhowe." An Agnes de Monte Canisio (or Gavisio) was the second prioress of Carrow, serving from 1221 to after 1237. See Francis Blomefield, *An Essay Towards a Topographical History of the County of Norfolk*, 11 vols. (London: William Miller, 1805–10), iv. 525; Walter Rye and E. A. Tillett, "Carrow Abbey," *Norfolk Antiquarian Miscellany* (1883), First Ser, II, pt. II, 465–508, at 475–76, and David M. Smith and Vera C. M. London, eds., *The Heads of Religious Houses: England and Wales*, vol. II, 1216–1377 (Cambridge: Cambridge University Press, 2001), 591, who list a variety of dates for her leadership of Carrow, drawn from various sources, including those cited previously in this note, and spanning the years 1230–1257.

4. The exact location of the original priory of St. Mary and St. John, on land provided by King Stephen, is not known. See Rye and Tillett, "Carrow Abbey," 466 and no. 3; and further, David Knowles and R. Neville Hadcock, *Medieval Religious Houses of England and Wales* (London: Longmans, Green, 1953), 254, 262. Archaeological campaigns beginning in 1880 were funded by J. J. Colman, who bought the property as a site for his mustard factory and housed his library of works "by Norfolk men or having a Norfolk subject" in the renovated prioress's house. See Frederick Dolman, "The Man and the Town: Mr. J. J. Colman, M.P., and Norwich," *The English Illustrated Magazine*, 141 (June, 1895), 196–201, at 201. On Colman's excavations, see E. P. L. Brock, "On the Excavation of the Site of Carrow Abbey, Norwich, by J. J. Colman, Esq. in 1880–1881," *Journal of the British Archaeological Association*, First series, 38 (1882), 165–77. Eric Fernie provides architectural drawings envisioning the church at its completion in the thirteenth century; see "Carrow Priory," *Archaeological Journal* 137 (1980), 290–91.

5. At the Dissolution, the commissioners reported eight nuns, two priests, and fifteen "others" in residence.
6. Rye and Tillet, "Carrow Abbey," 477–86, list lands and rectories providing income for St. Mary's. The taxation roll of 1291 sets the annual value of the priory at £69 2s. 1d., drawn from some seventy-five Norfolk parishes, and two in Suffolk. Carole Hill, *Women and Religion in Late Medieval Norwich* (Woodbridge: Boydell & Brewer for the Royal Historical Society, 2010), 156–57, has remarked that "It would appear that burial at Carrow was for the affluent minority, some of whom were already resident there."
7. There were two hands also applying the penwork, the first evident from the beginning through fol. 179v, the second from fol. 180r to the end. The second is more colorful and whimsical, filling endlines with spiney blocks in red and blue together, instead of simply alternating red and blue. On fol. 184 the first of a sequence of beaked heads fills the endlines, and at page-bottom is a delicate red wyvern.
8. "Esmon de ponnteneye" is Edmund [Rich] of Abingdon, Archbishop of Canterbury 1224–40, who died at Pontigny while travelling to Rome to protest a papal decision to grant English benefices to Roman clerics. He is buried at the Cistercian abbey there. N.B.: The description in the catalogue of the Biblioteca Nacional reads "de la Robelle" in error, following, probably, José Janini and José Serrano, *Manuscritos Liturgicos de la Biblioteca Nacional* (Madrid: Dirección General de Archivos y Bibliotecas, 1969), 87, and (possibly) Morgan, *Early Gothic Manuscripts*, 90.
9. The de Rokelle arms—*lozengy ermine and gules*—are not among the blazons depicted in the manuscript. There is a Norfolk presence for the family, however: a Richard de Rokelle held the manor of "Bekeham" (now West Beckham) in 1242, located approximately twenty-five miles from Norwich; Patent Rolls 26 H III, 289.
10. See J. C. Russell, "Notes on the Biography of Edmund of Abingdon," *Harvard Theological Review*, 54 (1961), 147–58; and, in particular, C. H. Lawrence, *St. Edmund of Abingdon: A Study of Hagiography and History* (Oxford: Oxford University Press, 1960), 141–42.
11. Matthew Paris, for example, lauds Edmund's selflessness. See *The Life of St. Edmund by Matthew Paris*, ed. and trans. C. H. Lawrence (Stroud, Glos.: Alan Sutton, 1996), 38–40.
12. For a Benedictine nun, restrictions against private ownership would have applied. Benedictine monks and nuns were permitted to keep books for private use only *ad terminum vitae*; thereafter, a volume should become common property. See David N. Bell, *What Nuns Read: Books and Libraries in English Medieval Nunneries* (Kalamazoo, MI: Cistercian Publications, 1995), 38–39, 51 note 38.

13. Many factors point to Felipe's obtaining the psalter in England early in the eighteenth century, including its Cambridge-style binding, with "Psalms of David MSS" in gold lettering in the space between the second and third cordings, and the name "Jo Pay" on the initial paper flyleaf, the latter portion of the surname torn away. For further discussion of the manuscript's journey from England to Spain, see Yeager, "English Manuscripts," forthcoming.

Aristotle in Pieces
LISA FAGIN DAVIS

The development of collections of European premodern manuscripts in North America was and is significantly different from that of European collections. Unlike most manuscripts in European collections, every manuscript in North America has had a value placed on it, by sale, gift, theft, or legacy, and none of them remain at their places of origin. Because all European manuscripts have traveled to reach their North American homes, it is not enough to explore the origins and content of a particular manuscript. The story of its journey must be investigated and told as well. Provenance research is therefore a critically important component of the study of premodern European manuscripts in North American collections. Such research may uncover surprising connections and important transformations. The following case study is an illuminating example.

Up until the 1200s, Aristotle was barely known in the Latin West, although his texts were widely circulated among Greek and Arabic readers. Over the course of the thirteenth century, Aristotle became increasingly popular, and by the late thirteenth century, nearly half of Aristotle's known works had been translated into Latin. The study of philosophy, specifically

Aristotle, had become a central component of the curricula in newly established universities throughout Europe. Nobles such as Manfred, King of Sicily, employed translators at court to make Greek, Arabic, and Hebrew texts accessible to a Latinate readership. The works of Aristotle and other ancient authors were being translated, copied, and circulated throughout Europe by the hundreds.

It is in this rich intellectual milieu that Huntington Library Manuscript 1035 (Huntington Library, San Marino, California) was produced. Huntington Manuscript 1035 (hereafter HM 1035) is a collection of three Aristotelian texts addressing the characteristics and properties of the animal kingdom: *De naturis animalium, De partibus animalium, and De generatione animalium*.[1] The manuscript begins with an historiated initial containing a lively depiction of translator Michael Scotus lecturing to an audience of men, women, and animals (Fig. 1).[2] This carefully written and beautifully decorated luxury manuscript is a perfect example of the late-medieval interest in the works of Aristotle.

Although the precise origin of the manuscript, and of others discussed below, is not the primary subject of this essay, it is important to investigate those origins to some extent in order to establish the beginning of the journey. Several clues on the very first page of HM 1035 help to pinpoint when and where the manuscript was written and for whom. At the bottom of the first page are three coats of arms, only one of which is now legible. This has been identified as the familial arms of Charles I of Anjou.[3] Charles was a thirteenth-century French prince, the youngest son of King Louis VIII. Unwilling to settle for the typical fate of a youngest son—the life of a cleric or monk—Charles took up the sword. With the Pope's blessing, he captured the kingdom of Sicily in 1266 and established the Angevin court in Naples, where he ruled as king until his death in 1285. His coat of arms was likely added to the Huntington manuscript sometime between those two dates, a range that is consistent with the stylistic evidence, as the style of the handwriting and decoration also place the manuscript in the second half of the thirteenth century. The presence of this coat of arms implies that the manuscript belonged to someone in Charles' family, if not to Charles himself, and that the manuscript was likely part of the library at the Angevin court in Naples.

But was the manuscript actually *written* in Naples? Not necessarily. The script appears Italian in origin, but the decoration uses a French palette and style. Experts, however, disagree on this point. In 1935, Seymour de Ricci described it as "possibly written in France," but more recently paleographer Consuelo Dutschke ascribes to the manuscript an origin in southern Italy.[4] In addition to the coat of arms, the manuscript has physical features (such as its parchment and quire structure) that support the case for Italy, so a

Figure 1: San Marino, Huntington Library, HM 1035, fol. 1r.

likely attribution might be "written in Italy and decorated by a French artist." It is not uncommon to see such international mixing of production and artisanship, especially in the later Middle Ages. In fact, writing about a different group of manuscripts produced at the Angevin court in Naples, the great manuscript scholar François Avril says, "The presence in Naples of a French illuminator is not surprising: the early fourteenth-century Neapolitan archives reveal that for some time during this period a large number of artists of French origin were employed by the Angevin court."[5]

Inside the fifteenth-century limp vellum cover is evidence of the modern portion of the manuscript's story. There are several modern pencil annotations inside the front cover, including a small, nondescript note in the lower left corner reading "A117" (Fig. 2). The placement and format of this number are distinctive; it is a stock number written by bookseller Wilfrid Voynich in the early twentieth century.

Voynich was a successful rare book dealer with shops in Florence, London, and New York City. The notation "A117" indicates that this was the 117th manuscript added to his American stock. Voynich is best-known as the purveyor of the Voynich Manuscript, the mysterious and infamous codex that is now MS 408 in Yale University's Beinecke Rare Book & Manuscript Library. HM 1035 also passed through Voynich's hands, and its journey to San Marino is, in fact, closely connected to the history of Beinecke MS 408.

Wilfrid Voynich purchased his eponymous manuscript in 1912 from a community of Jesuits in Rome, along with two dozen or so other manuscripts.[6] The Beinecke Library holds a significant amount of material related to Voynich and his mysterious manuscript, including a collection of slips of paper from the nineteenth century describing some of the other manuscripts that he purchased at the same time, all of which include the *ex libris* of Jesuit librarian Petrus Beckx, who died in 1897. The third slip in the sequence (Fig. 3) describes a Latin manuscript containing ten translated works of Aristotle.[7] Voynich's assistant Anne Nill, who took pains to annotate each slip with the respective manuscript's current location, if known, was uncertain about the disposition of the Aristotle, writing: "Now in Huntington Library? See Census of Mss I p. 82." This note refers to the entry for HM 1035 on page 82 of the 1935 *Census of Medieval and Renaissance Manuscripts in the United States and Canada* by Seymour de Ricci.[8] But there is a problem, which is why Anne added that question mark: the Huntington manuscript includes only the last three texts recorded by the Jesuit librarian: *De historiis animalium* (called *De naturis animalium* in the manuscript), *De partibus animalium*, and *De generatione animalium*. So, is it the same manuscript, or is it not? At first glance, it seems not.

ARISTOTLE IN PIECES

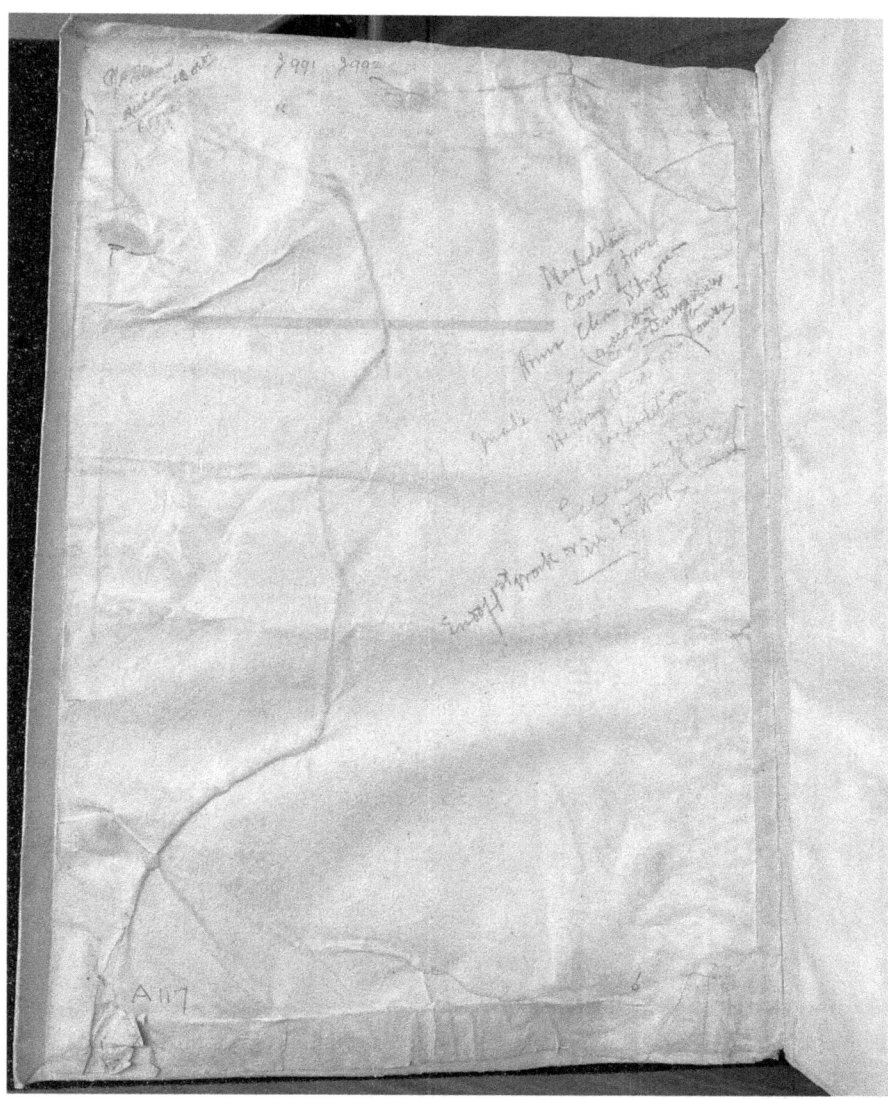

Figure 2: San Marino, Huntington Library, HM 1035, front pastedown.

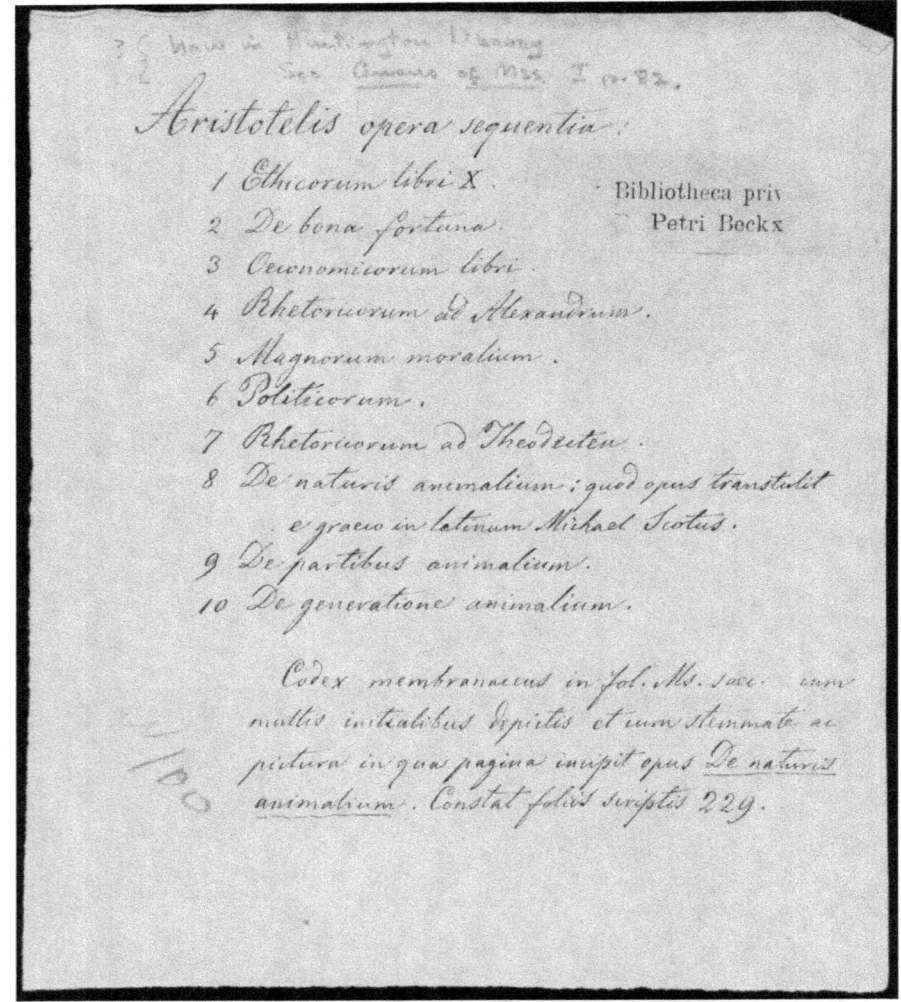

Figure 3: Yale University, Beinecke Rare Book & Manuscript Library MS 408A, Beckx Slip no. 3.

Returning to the opening page of HM 1035, we find a partially erased folio number on the first recto: 131. In addition, the last verso includes a note, "*Sono carte duecento trenta*" [There are 230 pages]. Yet the Huntington codex has only ninety-eight leaves, not 230. On the Beckx slip we find a note in his hand observing that his Aristotle comprised 229 written pages. Given this evidence, Voynich researcher René Zandbergen theorized on his Voynich website that HM 1035 was originally part of the Beckx codex. Seeking proof of this hypothesis, he reviewed all of the Aristotle manuscripts in the Census to try and identify the rest of the manuscript.[9] After completing his survey, Zandbergen had identified two manuscripts that seemed to record all of the missing texts. At the University of Illinois, Manuscript 8 (hereafter UI MS 8) comprises the first five texts recorded by Beckx: *Ethica, De bona fortuna, Oeconomica, Rhetorica ad Alexandrium,* and *Magna Moralia*.[10] At the Armour Institute of Technology in Chicago, Manuscript 3 records the two remaining texts: *Politica* and *Rhetorica*.[11] Because Zandbergen lives outside North America, he was not able to visit the manuscripts in person to ascertain whether his theory was correct or if these manuscripts just happened to contain the missing texts by coincidence. With his consent, the present author has reviewed the evidence on site. These in *situ* studies combined with historical evidence confirm the identification of these three manuscripts as once comprising the codex acquired by Voynich in 1912.

An examination of the manuscript at the University of Illinois reveals that it is foliated 1–66 by the same hand as the Huntington manuscript (Fig. 4). According to the 1962 *Supplement to the Census*, the Armour Institute manuscript was purchased in 1954 by the Newberry Library in Chicago, where it is now MS 23.1.[12] An examination of that codex shows the same foliation, numbered 67–130 (Fig. 5). For its part, HM 1035 is numbered 131 to 229. The three manuscripts do indeed appear to have once been bound together. Material evidence confirms the connection; offsets on the final verso of the University of Illinois manuscript align with the opening leaf of the Newberry codex, and offsets on the final verso of the Newberry codex (only visible under ultraviolet light) correspond with the opening leaf at the Huntington. For ease of reference, these codices will be referred to as Part 1, Part 2, and Part 3 for the remainder of this essay, as in Table 1:

Having established that these three manuscripts were once bound together as a single codex, later under the care of Petrus Beckx and purchased by Wilfrid Voynich in 1912, we must now ask when and under what circumstances that codex was later divided into three parts. Combining information from the *Census* and *Supplement* with annotations in the manuscripts themselves, we can reconstruct the timeline. The A117 note would have been added to Part 3, the Huntington manuscript, when Voynich brought the book to his American shop in New York around 1915. Part 3 has a sec-

Manuscript	Beckx text no.	Orig. foliation	Text
Part 1: UI MS 8	1	1–32	*Ethicorum libri X*
	2	32–33	*De bona fortuna*
	3	33–38	*Oeconomicorum libri*
	4	38–51	*Rhetoricum ad Alexandrium*
	5	51–65	*Magnorum moralium*
		65v–66v	[blank]
Part 2: Newberry MS 23.1	6	67–104	*Politicorum*
	7	104–129v	*Rhetoricorum ad Theodecten*
		130–130v	[blank]
Part 3: Huntington HM 1035	8	131–177	*De naturis animalium*
	9	178–199	*De partibus animalium*
	10	200–229v	*De generatione animalium*

ond Voynich stock number, this one in the upper right corner of the first page: a8665a. This is a number from his London shop, implying that he tried to sell the manuscript in London before bringing it to America. Part 1 has a similar number, also on the first page: a8665. Part 2 has no such annotation, even though it was part of the original codex. This evidence indicates that Voynich broke the codex into two parts while it was still in London: a8665, comprising Parts 1 and 2 together, and a8665a comprising Part 3 as a second volume.

How did the two codices then become three? The Census records that Voynich sold both books in 1915: a8665 (Parts 1 and 2) to a Chicago collector named Frank Gunsaulus and a8665a (Part 3) to New York bookseller George Smith.[13] Soon thereafter, Gunsaulus broke his book in two and had both parts rebound (this explains why there is no Voynich "a" stock number on Part 1; Voynich would have written it inside the front cover,

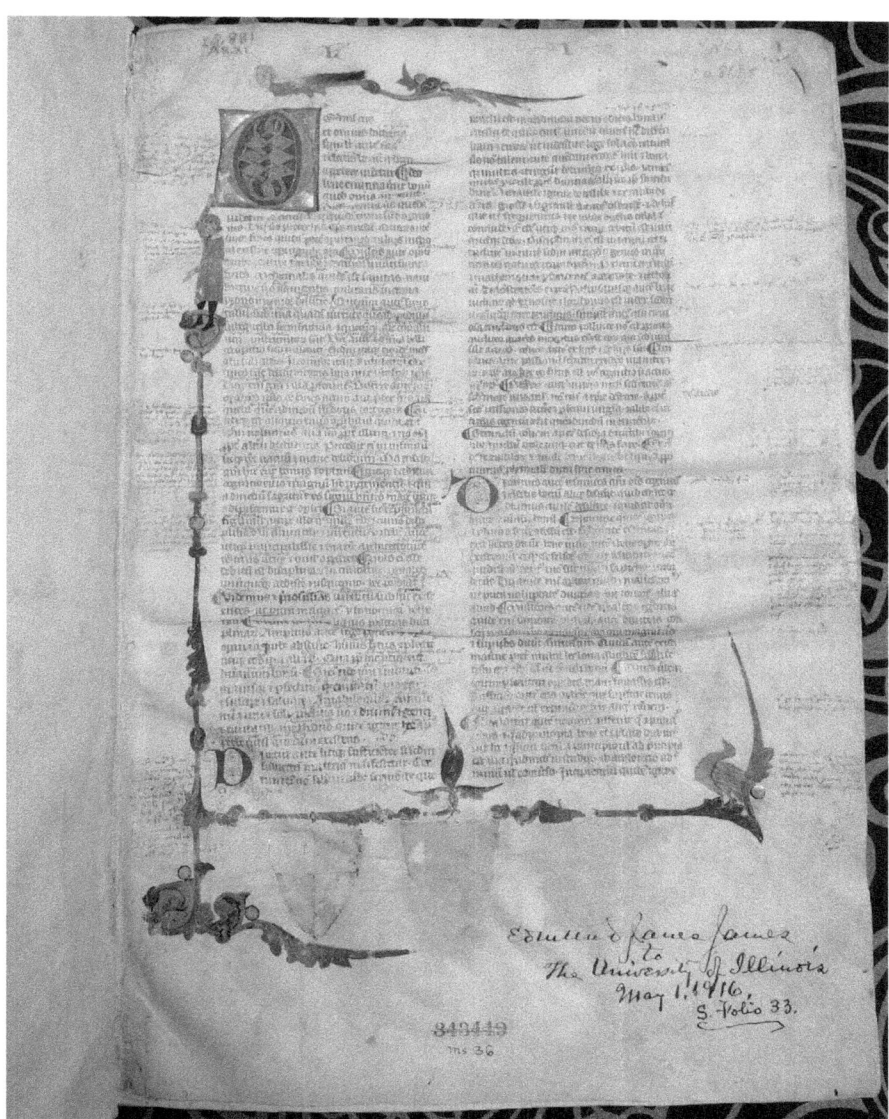

Figure 4: Urbana-Champaign, University of Illinois MS 8, fol. 1r.

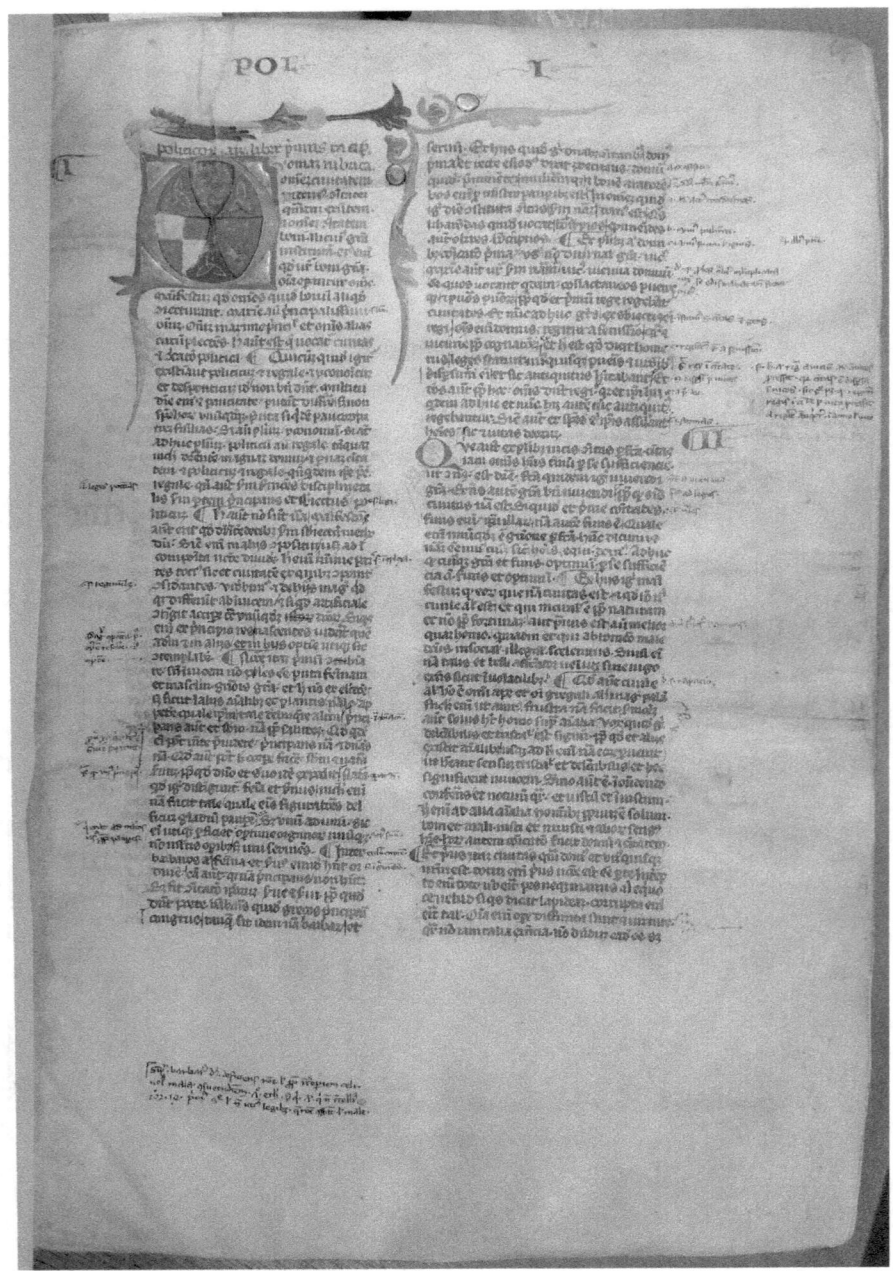

Figure 5: Chicago, Newberry Library MS 23.1, fol. 1r.

which Gunsaulus discarded when he broke the manuscript and rebound the two parts). After dividing his manuscript in two, Gunsaulus gave Part 1 to his friend Edmund James and Part 2 to the Armour Institute of Technology. James, who was the president of the University of Illinois at the time, left a lengthy inscription on folio 33 of Part 1, recording that he donated the manuscript to the University in 1916. Smith sold Part 3 to Henry E. Huntington 1918.[14] Finally, the Newberry Library acquired Part 2 from the Armour Institute in 1954 (see Fig. 6).[15]

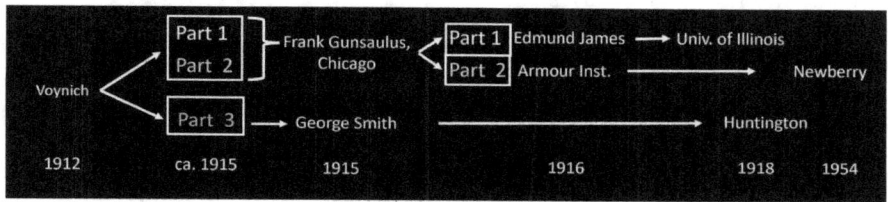

Figure 6: Timeline of post-Voynich history of Part 1, Part 2, and Part 3.

All three manuscripts contain evidence of their origins. The three parts were written by two or three different scribes, and not at the same time. Paleographical evidence suggests that Part 1 may have been written several decades later than Parts 2 and 3, and probably by a French scribe. Before we draw conclusions about the origins of each part, we also need to consider the material, or physical, evidence. In Part 1, the sheets are signed within each quire using a system of small red dots. Part 2 uses a system of letters to sign each nested sheet. In Part 3, the bifolia are sequenced using small Roman numerals. Significantly, each system starts over at the beginning of each part. The activity of different scribes using different signature systems strongly suggests that these were originally three separate manuscripts that had been bound together by Beckx's lifetime. So now we must ask a different question: how did three manuscripts become one?

Like the Huntington manuscript, Parts 1 (UI MS 8) and 2 (Newberry MS 23.1) were originally decorated with coats of arms on the first page, nearly all of which have been defaced, scraped away, or overpainted. This is a fairly common practice, generally perpetrated by later owners who wanted to disguise a manuscript's history or mark it as solely their own. We have already seen that one of the three coats of arms in Part 3 has been tentatively identified as belonging to Charles I of Anjou. The opening initial in Part 2 incorporates three escutcheons (Fig. 7). Under ultraviolet light, the upper arms appear to be a repeating white element on a blue background, possibly, although not definitively, those of Charles I himself. The arms in the lower right can be described as a lion rampant with a forked tail, probably in silver, on a red background, or, in heraldry parlance, "gules, a lion rampant double-queued argent."[16] The same arms appear in an Angevin manuscript that is closely associated with the court in Naples (Chantilly MS 726), where the arms have been been identified as belonging to Guy of Montfort, one of the key members of Charles I's army in his Sicilian campaign.[17] The Chantilly manuscript also includes fragmentary arms tentatively identified as those of Charles I.[18]

The final arms in the opening initial of Part 2 are quartered a *saltire*, that is, divided into four parts diagonally, with common arms on each diagonal. Quartered arms represent a marriage or parentage, with quarters 1 and 4 (upper left and lower right) representing the male, and 2 and 3 representing the female. In this case, quarters 2 and 3 are the silver lion on red, associating these arms with a daughter of the house of Montfort. Guy and his wife Margherita had two daughters; the elder, Anastasia, married into the important Orsini family in 1293, and it is quite possible that these arms represent that union.[19] The combined arms of Montfort and Orsini can be seen today in Sorano (in the province of Grosseto in southern Tuscany), on the gates of the fortress built by Margherita's family and renamed for the Orsinis after Anastasia's marriage.[20] Here, quarters 1 and 4 are Orsini, and quarters 2 and 3 are Montfort, the lion rampant. Knowing all of this, when we return to Part 1, we can hypothesize that the damaged left-hand escutcheon, saltire in red and white, may also be the Montfort/Orsini arms, and the one in the center, blue as it is, might even be Charles of Anjou, which would mean that all three manuscripts were likely found in the Kingdom of Sicily early on, if not actually at the Angevin court in Naples.

Figure 7: Chicago, Newberry Library MS 23.1, fol. 1r detail (under ultraviolet light, post-processing by Peter Kidd).

In her description of HM 1035, Dutschke writes that the manuscript previously:

> Belonged to Pier Leoni (d. 1492), physician to Lorenzo de' Medici [in Florence].... The inventory of Leoni's books was compiled in 1582, long after his death, and was published by Léon Dorez in 1897, where this manuscript has been identified with item 8, 'Aristoteles de natura animalium.'[21]

The evidence for Leoni's ownership is the spine, on which the contents are recorded in a style typical of his manuscripts.[22] The 1582 inventory records titles for each manuscript by referring to what is written on the spine. Dutschke continues: "The single title [that is, number 8 in the inventory], corresponding to HM 1035 as it stands today, suggests that the book had [once] been bound in [a] more complete state [and was] dismembered before 1582, when the inventory of Leoni's library was compiled."[23] However, as demonstrated above the manuscript was still bound with its sisters as late as 1912, when Voynich bought it. It was not yet divided in 1582, when the Leoni inventory was written. This means that the Huntington manuscript cannot be Leoni no. 8. There is another Aristotle in the Leoni inventory: no. 132, "*Aristotelis Ethica et Oeconomica*" (i.e., the first two texts of Part 1). This is almost certainly the combined codex, as the inventory records the first few texts in exactly the same way as does the annotation on the spine of HM 1035. Rather than breaking up the codex as Dutschke suggests, Leoni must have been the one who combined the three manuscripts in the first place.

Having investigated all of the evidence, we can now tell the full story of how these manuscripts were combined, separated, and made their way to their North American homes (Fig. 8). In the thirteenth century, the manuscripts were likely in southern Italy, presumably Naples. In the fifteenth century, Leoni brought them to Florence and combined them into a single codex. The codex was in the care of Petrus Beckx in nineteenth-century Rome, where Voynich acquired it in 1912. Voynich brought the manuscript to London, where he broke Leoni's codex into two manuscripts, both of which he brought to New York. One went to Chicago in 1915, where Frank Gunsaulus divided it into its two constituent manuscripts, one of which stayed in Chicago while the other made its way south to the University of Illinois in Urbana-Champaign. Voynich sold the other codex to George Smith, who sold it to Henry Huntington in 1918.

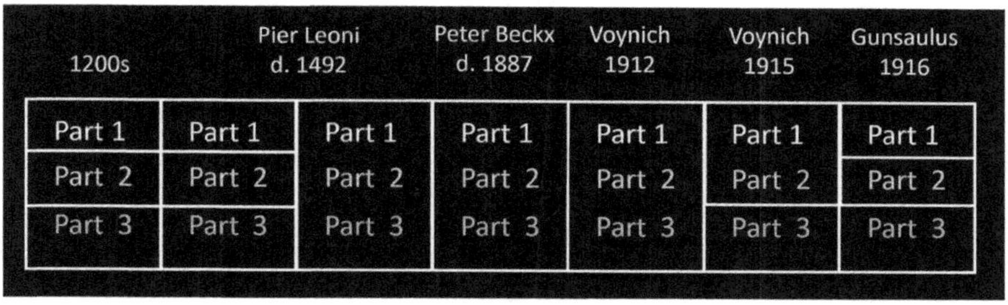

1200s	Pier Leoni d. 1492	Peter Beckx d. 1887	Voynich 1912	Voynich 1915	Gunsaulus 1916
Part 1	Part 1	Part 1	Part 1	Part 1	Part 1	Part 1	Part 1
Part 2	Part 2	Part 2	Part 2	Part 2	Part 2	Part 2	Part 2
Part 3	Part 3	Part 3	Part 3	Part 3	Part 3	Part 3	Part 3

Figure 8: Timeline of combining and dispersal of all three parts.

By investigating the evidence left by previous owners and readers, it becomes possible to recover otherwise-lost facets of the history of these three codices and to demonstrate how they are related to one another. According to the *Directory of Collections in the United States and Canada with pre-1600 Manuscript Holdings*, there are more than twenty thousand early European codices and twenty-five thousand single leaves in more than five hundred North American collections.[24] Every one of these manuscripts has a story to tell, if we know how to listen.

Medieval Academy of America and
Simmons University School of Library and Information Science

NOTES

1. Huntington Library Manuscript 1035, *De animalibus*, Huntington Library, San Marino, California, https://hdl.huntington.org/digital/collection/p15150coll7/id/52102.
2. George Lacombe, *Aristoteles Latinus, pars prior* (Rome: La Libreria dello stato, 1939), 245, no. 19.
3. Consuelo W. Dutschke, *Guide to Medieval and Renaissance Manuscripts in the Huntington Library*, vol. 1 (San Marino: Huntington Library, 1989), 299–301.
4. Seymour de Ricci, *Census of Medieval and Renaissance Manuscripts in the United States and Canada* (New York: American Council of Learned Societies, 1935), 1:82; Dutschke, *Guide*, 300.
5. François Avril, "Trois manuscrits napolitains des collections de Charles V et de Jean de Berry," in *Bibliothèque de l'École des chartes*, 127 (1969):291–328, at 296, https://www.persee.fr/doc/bec_0373-6237_1969_num_127_2_449834: "La présence à Naples d'un enlumineur français n'a rien qui doive surprendre: les archives napolitaines du début du xive siècle ont révélé depuis longtemps qu'un grand nombre d'artistes d'origine française étaient employés à cette époque par la cour Angevine."
6. Raymond Clemens, *The Voynich Manuscript* (New Haven: Yale University Press, 2016), 8.
7. Yale University, Beinecke Rare Book & Manuscript Library Digital Collections, Wilfred M. Voynich and Ethel Voynich Provenance and Research Files on the Cipher (Voynich) Manuscript (Beinecke MS 408A), Correspondance, https://collections.library.yale.edu/catalog/2041525.
8. De Ricci, Seymour, *Census of Medieval and Renaissance Manuscripts in the United States and Canada* (New York: Wilson, 1935), I:82.

9. Zandbergen, René, "An Aristotle MS Bought by W. Voynich from the Jesuits in 1912," December 31, 2024, https://www.voynich.nu/extra/aristotle.html.
10. *Aristoteles Latinus* no. 20; de Ricci, *Census*, 1:700; Illinois University Library, Manuscript: *Ethica Nicomachea*, https://i-share-uiu.primo.exlibrisgroup.com/permalink/01CARLI_UIU/gpjosq/alma99519250012205899.
11. *Aristoteles Latinus* no. 11; de Ricci, *Census*, 1:512.
12. C.U. Faye and W.H. Bond, *Supplement to the Census of Medieval and Renaissance Manuscripts in the United States and Canada* (New York: Bibliographical Society of America, 1962), 151–152; Newberry Library, Manuscript: *Politica et Rhetorica*, Aristotle https://i-share-nby.primo.exlibrisgroup.com/permalink/01CARLI_NBY/i5mcb2/alma992262888805867.
13. de Ricci, *Census*, 1:512 and 1:700.
14. Dutschke, *Guide*, 301.
15. Faye & Bond, *Supplement to the Census*, 151–152.
16. With thanks to Peter Kidd for postprocessing assistance.
17. https://portail.biblissima.fr/ark:/43093/mdatae75521071a-6c97a7bb24bd933d4d11f6f9bb4263, fol. 109.
18. Ella Williams, "Two Manuscripts of the *Faits des Romains* in Angevin Italy," *Italian Studies*, 72:2 (2017):157–176, at 160. https://www-tandfonline-com.ezproxy.simmons.edu/doi/epdf/10.1080/00751634.2017.1307554?needAccess=true.
19. Anthony Corbet, *Edward IV, England's Forgotten Warrior King* (iUniverse: Bloomington, 2015), 267.
20. The Maremma *Guide* to Tuscany's Secret Places, "The Fortezza Orsini di Sorano," https://www.maremmaguide.com/fortezza-orsini.html.
21. Dutschke, *Guide*, 300–301. See also L. Dorez, "Recherches sur la bibliothèque de Pier Leoni, médecin de Laurent de Médicis," *Revue des Bibliothèques* 7 (1897):81–106.
22. José Ruysschaert, "Nouvelles recherches au sujet de la bibliothèque de Pier Leoni médecin de Laurent le Magnifique," *Bulletin de la classe des lettres et des sciences morales et politiques de l'Académie royale de Belgique*, ser. 5, 46 (1960):37–65, pl. Ia.
23. Dutschke, *Guide*, 301.
24. Melissa Conway and Lisa Fagin Davis, "The Directory of Institutions in the United States and Canada with Pre-1600 Manuscript Holdings: From its Origins to the Present, and its Role in Tracking the Migration of Manuscripts in North American Repositories,"*Manuscripta* 57.2 (2013):165–181. See also Melissa Conway and Lisa Fagin Davis, "Directory of Collections in the United States and Canada with Pre-1600

Manuscript Holdings," *Papers of the Bibliographical Society of America*, 109.3 (2015):273–420, https://www.journals.uchicago.edu/doi/full/10.1086/682342.

Philological Missing Links: The "*-Manuscripts" in the Stemma of the German Translation of Lanfranc's *Chirurgia magna*

CHIARA BENATI

Although less widely circulated than the *Chirurgia parva*, Lanfranc of Milan's *Chirurgia magna* was also frequently translated into vernacular languages. In the High German linguistic area, only one East Upper German complete version of the work is known and preserved in three manuscript copies. However, philological analysis of the textual relationships between these manuscript witnesses suggests the existence of at least three additional copies that have since been lost. These hypothetical manuscripts have been incorporated into the *stemma codicum* and marked with an asterisk. This study focuses on these "asterisk-manuscripts," examining them through a philological comparison of the extant copies. By analyzing textual variations, it aims to shed light on how each of these lost manuscripts may have contributed to shaping the currently preserved German translation of Lanfranc's *Chirurgia magna*.

1. Lanfranc of Milan's *Chirurgia magna* and Its Fortune in the High German Language Area

Lanfranc's *Chirurgia magna* stands as his most significant work, completed in 1296 while he was in Paris following his political exile from Milan.[1] Dedicated to Philip the Fair, King of France (1285–1314), this comprehensive surgical treatise reflects both his extensive practical experience and the influence of academic medicine. The *Chirurgia magna* was written in a period when the Parisian faculty of medicine was striving to bring surgery under the authority of theoretical medicine.[2] In this context, Lanfranc's knowledge and approach gained recognition, securing him a place among the most respected surgeons of his time. Although less widely circulated than its shorter counterpart, the *Chirurgia parva*, Lanfranc of Milan's *Chirurgia magna* was also frequently translated into vernacular languages, further extending its influence beyond the Latin-speaking scholarly community.

In German, parts of Lanfranc of Milan's *Chirurgia magna* have been preserved in two distinct translations. The first is a complete translation of the entire text, which, along with a second German translation of the *Chirurgia parva*, has survived in two manuscripts: Kalocsa, Főszékesegyházi Könyvtár, Ms. 376, folios 1r–208v, and Erlangen, Universitätsbibliothek, Ms. B 32, folios. 1ra–193ra. An incomplete copy of this translation is also found in London, Wellcome Institute for the History of Medicine, Ms. 398, folios 17r–51v and 212r–480v.

A second, independent German version, which contains only the fifth treatise (the *antidotary*) of the Latin text, is preserved in a single manuscript: Budapest, Országos Széchényi Könyvtár, Cod. Germ. 59, fols. 274r–320v, thus witnessing an independent circulation of this part of the work, as already observed, for example, in the Middle English tradition of the text.[3]

In the present study, the manuscript tradition of the complete translation of the surgical handbook will be taken into consideration with respect to the hypothetical witnesses, whose existence can be postulated on the basis of a systematic comparison between the extant copies of the text.

2. The German Manuscripts and Their Relationships

2.1. Kalocsa, Főszékesegyházi Könyvtár, Ms. 376 (*K*)

Ms. 376 of the Cathedral Library in Kalocsa is a paper manuscript from the fifteenth century, bound in a thick wooden cover with light brown leather. It consists of 354 leaves (310 x 205 mm) arranged in 31 quires. At the bottom left of the last verso pages in each gathering, some of the quire marks are still visible, while others have been cut away. Folios 1–314 are numbered in ink in Arabic numerals by a seventeenth-century hand, which also wrote the index on folios 316r–340r.

The fifteenth-century text is written in a single column in a clear and regular bastarda script, attributed to the pharmacist Konrad Schreck of Aschaffenburg, as indicated by a scribe's note on folio 314v. A second, contemporaneous hand has made some corrections and added a pointing hand (*manicula*) either above the lines (e.g., fols. 33r, 94r) or in the margin (e.g., fol. 130v). Each section begins with simple red initials, two to five lines in height, whose shafts—as well as those of the letters of the first and last lines of each page—are often extended. Headings, majuscule dashes, and underlining of proper names are executed in red ink.[4]

In terms of content, the manuscript can be described as a medical collection or "surgical-pharmaceutical compendium,"[5] which includes:

1. folio Ir—a fragment of the preface to Lanfranc's *Chirurgia magna*, breaking off after eleven lines, accompanied by two partially erased lines from the sixteenth century, reading: "Vnd bin aüch In gütter G...üs Vnd bin auch In gutter hoffnung... alle...," and the name "Lanndtfranckus doctor parisiensis" in red ink;
2. folios 1r–208v—the German version of Lanfranc's *Chirurgia magna* of Milan;
3. folios 209v–234v—the German translation of Lanfranc's *Chirurgia parva*;[6]
4. folios 234v–247v—a collection of recipes, including Heinrich von Rees's *Die wunt meler zu uertreiben* (fol. 235r) and remedies for eye ailments;[7]
5. folios 247v–251v—the first part of the "Upper German" version of Guy de Chauliac's *Chirurgia parva*;[8]
6. folios 252r–256v—some indications and recipes for wound treatment, against apostema and cancer;
7. folios 256v–270r—the second part of the German version of Guy de Chauliac's *Chirurgia parva*;
8. folios 271r–284r—one of the German versions of Johannes de Rupescissa's *De consideratione Quintae essentiae*;[9]
9. folios 284r–285r—an *aqua vitae* recipe;
10. folios 286r–311v—a German anatomy in the form of questions and answers about the nature of human limbs, which belongs to the tradition of the so-called *Problemata Aristotelis*;[10]
11. folios 312r–314v—chapters I-IV from Konrad von Megenberg's *Von der Sel*;[11]
12. folios 314v—the scribe's note by Konrad Schreck and the dating of the manuscript (1472);
13. folios 316r–340r—an alphabetical index of the manuscript by a seventeenth-century hand.

As for the language of the manuscript, different authors have described it and its scribe in different ways: "High German,"[12] "Central German,"[13] from the "German southeast."[14] Additionally, Berg,[15] the editor of the vernacular version of Lanfranc's *Chirurgia parva* transmitted in *K*, pointed to an Alemannic substrate based on the presence of full vowels in unstressed syllables (see, e.g., *trucknost*, fol. 211v; *gesegnott*, fol. 221r; *rotlocht*, fol. 221v) and *-in*-abstract nouns (see, e.g., *grobin*, fol. 216v; *sterckin*, fol. 218r; *scherpffin*, fol. 225v), which he also postulates for both the *Chirurgia magna* and the *Chirurgia parva* of Guy de Chauliac. A cross-examination of the occurrence of these Alemannic forms in the German version of the *Chirurgia magna* has shown that several instances of full unstressed syllables in weak participles (e.g., *geoffenot*, fol. 51r; *gevestnot*, fol. 58v; *geordnott*, fol. 122v; *begegnott*, fol. 154r) as well as *-in*-abstract nouns (e.g., *lassin*, fol. 162r; *grobin*, fol. 137v; *scherpffin*, fol. 22v) also appear in this text, which supports Berg's hypothesis.

Apart from this Alemannic substrate, the language of manuscript *K* shows several features of the early modern Eastern Upper German linguistic landscape (Sonderegger 1979: 170; Wolf 2000: 1536), i.e., the New High German diphthongization, the initial hardening of the labial plosive,[16] the dissimilated form *darumb*, and the abstract suffix *-nus*.[17] On the other hand, the language of *K* also shows a feature of the Central German, namely monophthongization, which occurred only sporadically in the Upper German-speaking areas.[18] Nevertheless, the difference between monophthongizing and non-monophthongizing linguistic landscapes is reflected only to a limited extent in spelling (Paul 2007: 35) and the monophthongized spellings were also adopted into Upper German writing during the course of Early Modern High German (Reichmann and Wegera 1993: 67; Wolf 2000: 1534). For this reason, the presence of Central German monophthongization cannot be considered a valid criterion for the dialectal classification of the language used in the German translation of the *Chirurgia magna* in *K*.

2.2. Erlangen, Universitätsbibliothek, Ms. B 32 (*E*)

Erlangen, Universitätsbibliothek, Ms. B 32 is a paper manuscript consisting of 266 leaves (289x205 mm) and twenty-two quires and is bound in a flexible parchment cover made from a leaf of a fifteenth century liturgical manuscript, featuring red four-line notation. The third quire (fols. 25–36) has been misbound before the second (fols. 13–24), as indicated by a later annotation on folio Iv. The recto of each leaf bears an older foliation in the upper margin, possibly dating from the manuscript's original completion. This numbering ends with leaf 264 rather than 266.

The manuscript's leaves are divided into two columns, typically containing thirty-four to thirty-six lines each. The text was transcribed by two very different hands: Hand 1 (fols.1ra–63va) is characterized by irregular and inconsistent writing, while hand 2 (fols. 63va–266va) is clearer and more regular. An additional hand has made marginal interventions, expanding abbreviations, inserting corrections, glosses, or additions. On folio 1ra, yet another hand has noted a possible identification of the text: "Cyrurgia, an forsan sit Lanfrancj." Each section begins with simple three-line red initials and red headings.

The manuscript originates from the library of Heilsbronn Monastery, where it was catalogued under the shelfmark Libri med. 309.[20]

In terms of content, E largely overlaps with K and contains the following texts:

1. folios 1ra–193va—Lanfranc's *Chirurgia magna*;
2. folios 193va–251va—Lanfranc's *Chirurgia parva*;
3. folios 252ra–265va—The same German version of Johannes de Rupescissa's *De consideratione Quintae essentiae*, which is also preserved in K;[21]
4. folios 265va–266va—The *Aqua vitae* recipe.

On folio 266va we find the explicit "Laus deo" and, in red, the date "Anno *domini* 1484."

The language of the version of the *Chirurgia magna* in E has been described as "Upper German." However, it shows traces of an Alemannic substratum: apart from full unstressed syllables in weak participles and *in*-abstract nouns, it also exhibits, in some words, Alemannic diphthongized forms; and it is characterized by the New High German diphthongization, the shift to affricate of German */p/ in all positions, the initial hardening of the labial plosive, and the dissimilated form *darumb*. Occasionally, especially in the part written by Hand 1, it also displays Bavarian spellings <b> for /w/,[22] and <ai> for the Middle High German diphthong /ei/,[23] which support a Bavarian origin of the manuscript.

2.3. London, Wellcome Institute for the History of Medicine, Ms. 398 (*L*)

Ms. 398 from the Wellcome Institute for the History of Medicine in London was acquired by the Institute in 1911 as part of the collection of the medical historian and librarian of the Royal College of Physicians Joseph Frank Payne (1840–1910). This quarto paper manuscript (190 x 145 mm), comprising 481 leaves, is preserved in a modern wood and parchment binding.[24]

The text is written in a single column in a clear and regular bastard script by a single scribe, with eighteen to twenty lines per page. Initials and the letters in the first and last lines feature elongated decorative strokes. The headings of individual text sections, as well as the questions in the questionnaire on folios 53r–130r are centered on the page.

In terms of content, the manuscript is a surgical compendium that can be divided into the following sections:

1. folios 1r–15v—an epitome of surgery based on Lanfranc's work, whose beginning, "Offt vnnd dick hab ich pey mir selbs betracht die wundersammen werck des schoppfers der natüren Wie er an dem anbegynn der himel hat beschaffen die mayster der wunden ein erczney vnd zw painpruchen die alle nach iren gestaltten zehaillen," clearly reminds us of the incipit of the 1485 *Garten der Gesundheit*;[25]
2. folios 17r–51v—the complete fourth tractate of Lanfranc's *Chirurgia magna*;
3. folios 53r–139r—a catalogue of questions based on Lanfranc's work, which could possibly have been used to prepare surgical apprentices for the end point assessment;[26]
4. folios 141r–201r—a series of recipes for the preparation of plasters;
5. folios 212r–281r—a fragment of the first treatise of the *Chirurgia magna* (I.iii.1);
6. folios 281r–371v—the second treatise of the *Chirurgia magna*;
7. folios 371v–480r—the third treatise of the *Chirurgia magna*, which breaks off after the title of the eighth chapter of the second doctrine (III.ii.8).

On folio 479v, the following explicit can be read: "Iohannes weispurgensis anno Im 8 Iare in die epihanie scripsit," dating the completion of the manuscript to the year 1508.

The language of the London manuscript has up to now never been examined. In the course of my editorial work on the German translation of the *Chirurgia magna*, it was found to display several of the aforementioned features typical of the Early Modern Eastern Upper German and Bavarian linguistic area, such as the New High German diphthongization, the shift to affricate of germ. */p/, the initial hardening of the labial plosive, dissimilated forms *darumb, umb, siechtumb*, the abstract suffix -nus, the Bavarian spelling <ai> for the Middle High German diphthong /ei/. On the other hand, a few Alemannic forms also appear occasionally, which can, again, be attributed to an Alemannic substratum. The explicit (f. 479v), which identifies the scribe as "Iohannes weispurgensis" (from Weißenburg in Bavaria?), also seems to indicate a Bavarian origin for the scribe of *L*.

2.4. The Relationship Between the Manuscript Witnesses

The relationship between the manuscript witnesses of the complete German version of Lanfranc's *Chirurgia magna* has yet to be thoroughly investigated. However, the connection between K and E has been repeatedly observed in relation to other texts.

Keil[27] suggests that E may be an abbreviated and possibly direct copy of K. In contrast, Berg,[28] in his edition of the *Chirurgia parva*, proposes a stemma in which K and E descend from a common exemplar that is distinct from the original German translation. As a result, K and E would be considered "roughly equal to each other."

The connection between K and E, already observed in the transmission of other texts within these manuscripts, is likewise evident in the German version of Lanfranc's *Chirurgia magna*, as both manuscripts reproduce the text almost verbatim and can therefore be traced back to the same translation of the Latin original.

Apart from this generic connection between the two, the assumption of a genetic relationship is sustained by the presence in both of a series of innovations to the Latin original. The most significant of these is constituted by the addition of the remark of a scribe copying the text who is unsure about the correctness of the vernacular translation provided in the exemplar from which he is copying and suggests a correction.[29] Moreover, both K and E add material which is not present in the 1498 *editio princeps*[30] nor in a series of digitized manuscripts of the Latin text that I was able to consult.[31] A prescription is inserted at the end of the thirteenth chapter of the third section of the first book (I.iii.13; K: fols. 31r–v; E: fol. 16ra); an experiment to treat cold pain in the teeth is added at the end of chapter III.iii.4 (K: fol. 127v; E: 118vb); the haematoscopical part of the Latin bloodletting treatise *De phlebotomia* by John of St Amand is translated into German and interpolated at the end of chapter III.iii.16 on bloodletting (K: fols. 164r–165r; E: fols. 152va–153rb).

Theoretically, the similarities between the two textual witnesses can be explained in two ways: either they originate from Konrad Schreck, the scribe of K, and were directly adopted in E, or they can be traced back to a common antecedent in the tradition. The first scenario, which would align with Keil's opinion,[32] can be ruled out due to a series of errors present in K that are not reproduced in E. These errors mostly consist of words or sentences omitted in K (eye skips), but preserved in E. See, for example:

K: ob den musculos ist so den der siech (fol. 144r)
E: ob den musculos ist **oder darvnter, jst das die fistel ob den musculos ist**, so den der siech (fol. 143rb);

K: Vnd thutt cutellaria cauteria mit den sinbeln cauterio (fol. 172r)
E: Vnd tut man cutellare cauterium **tzwischen den vingeren in die hand gesucht. Man tut cauteria** mit den sinwelen cauterio (fol. 159va).

If a direct dependency of E on K can be ruled out, we must assume that the two manuscripts derive from a common exemplar, as already suggested by Berg[33] based on the German version of the *Chirurgia parva*.

As for the relation of L to the other two witnesses, systematic collation of the text across all three manuscripts has revealed a series of *loci critici* that may indicate the position of the London manuscript within the tradition of the German complete translation of Lanfranc's *Chirurgia magna*. Some of these suggest a closer connection between E and L, while others point to a link between K and L.

An attentive evaluation of these *loci critici* has allowed ruling out the first scenario, as the errors suggesting a dependence of L on E appear scarcely significant, as they are more likely to have been produced independently in the work of both copyists than those indicating a connection between K and L.

If K and L belong to the same branch of the tradition, two possible scenarios can be imagined: either L is directly dependent on K, or both manuscripts derive from a common exemplar. A direct dependence on K can be ruled out based on some errors present in K that are not reproduced in L. See, for example:

E: das du mit der hant **leichtlich darauff** greiffst (fol. 164rb)
K: das du mit der hant greiffest (fol. 177r)
L: das du mitt der hanntt **leichtligklich darauff** greyfft (fol. 26v)

As a result of these considerations, it is possible to formulate the following stemmatological hypothesis:

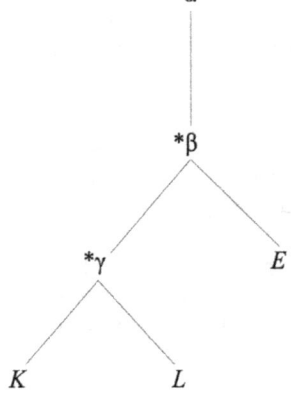

3. Tracing Back the Evolution of the German *Chirurgia magna* Through the *-Manuscripts

In the stemma, the existence of at least three now lost manuscript witnesses of the text has been postulated, each representing a different stage in the vernacular reception of the Latin surgical text. In the following discussion the essential traits of these key points in the transmission will be highlighted, based on a comparison of the three extant copies of the text. This analysis aims to shed light on how each of these lost manuscripts might have contributed to shaping the German version(s) of Lanfranc's *Chirurgia magna* that survive today.

3.1. *α: The Vernacular Archetype

Manuscript *α represents the vernacular archetype, that is, the original German translation of the Latin *Chirurgia magna*. This must have been completed at some point in the fourteenth century, a period when the demand for vernacular translations of surgical texts—including Lanfranc's works—grew increasingly intense across Europe.[34]

The presence—in all three extant copies of the text—of grapho-phonemic forms indicating an Alemannic substrate suggest this translation might originate from the South-Western part of the German-speaking area or was produced by an individual writing in this specific dialect. Given the geographical proximity of the Alemannic language area to France—the country where Lanfranc had gained recognition and popularity in both medical academia and the surgical community—this localization of the original translation of his major work appears particularly compelling.

The general structure of the Latin *Chirurgia magna*—divided into five books dealing with anatomy (wounds in general; the anatomy and the wounds of specific parts; other surgically treatable diseases; fractures and dislocations; medicines), and further divided into sections (*doctrinae*) and/or chapters (*capitula*)—is maintained by the German translator, who possibly also faithfully reproduced the order of the single chapters.

The Latin exemplar used for this translation is unknown, nor can be easily identified, since research on the tradition of the Latin text is incomplete. Not only is a critical edition lacking, but also a comprehensive *recensio* of all textual witnesses is still a desideratum. For this reason, even though a preliminary comparison based on the collation of six manuscript copies of the Latin *Chirurgia magna* has made it possible to distinguish at least two branches in the transmission of the text and to identify the exemplar of the German translation as belonging to one of them, we cannot entirely rule out the possibility that some of the additions and interpolations to the Latin text were already present in the Latin archetype.

3.2. *β: The Copy Commented by the "Critical" Scribe

*β, the second *-manuscript postulated in the stemma above, represents a copy—direct or mediated by other copies—of the original German translation of the text. This copy is characterized by the presence of the above-mentioned comment, in which the scribe disagrees with the one specific choice of the German translator and suggests a different reading of the passage:

Man hat in dem teutschen Landfrancko lauch vorsche Ich glaub Es sol sein das puluer von Cicados die singent zu der zeit der hitz auff dem paummen...³⁵
[In the German Lanfranc we have *lauch vorsche* I believe it should be the powder of the Cicadas that sing on the trees when it is hot...]

The difficult interpretation of the two words *lauch vorsche* attributed to the exemplar from which the scribe is copying seems to indicate that this passage was already corrupted, possibly as a result of a relatively long chain of transmission between *α and *β.

The dialectal features of the three extant copies of the text, apart from the above-mentioned Alemannic substrate, can be situated within the East Upper German region, more specifically in Bavaria. Moreover, both *K* and *E* independently—i.e. in two different contexts—point to Bavaria: (*K*: *peyerischer wein*, f. 100v "Bavarian wine"; *E*: *peyrische maß*, f. 145ra "Bavarian measure"), which leads to the assumption that this copy originated in the Bavarian language area, which, in turn, suggests a shift in the German transmission of Lanfranc's *Chirurgia magna* from west to east.

As both *K* and *L* exhibit minor changes in the order of the chapters—for instance, they invert chapter III.iii.11 as well as III.iii.12 and V.6 and V.7—we can assume that these alterations to the sequence of the Latin original originated at this stage of the transmission. This discrepancy with the Latin text may have resulted from an erroneous ordering of the leaves in the exemplar from which *β was copied.

3.3. *γ: The Copy by the "Linguistically Uncertain" Scribe

From this commented-upon East Upper German / Bavarian intermediary stage originate *E*, which largely preserved the original wording and has allowed the emendation of several corrupt passages in *K*, and *γ, which represents the common antecedent of *K* and *L*.

This copy is still to be situated in the East Upper German / Bavarian region. Moreover, its scribe appears to have been extremely uncertain regarding the grapho-phonemic form of certain words found in his exemplar. This uncertainty is particularly evident in one of *γ's descendants, *K*, where the word *feuln* appears and is used to translate both Latin *corruptio* "corruption," *putredo / putrefactio* "putrefaction, rottenness," and *multitudo* "multitude" / *quantitas* "quantity," but also *plenitudo* "fullness, abundance." While in the first sense, the spelling *feuln* presents no issue—since it derives from the abstract *fäule* < MHG *viule* < OHG *fûli* "putrefaction, rottenness"—its use in the second meaning is problematic. Here, the word appears to conflate the abstract nouns *viele*, "quantity, abundance," and *fülle*, "fullness," rendering them with an unusual spelling that may stem from the scribe's confusion regarding the application of the Modern High German diphthongization. Less frequently, the same issue with the vernacular rendering of Latin *multitudo* can also be found in the other descendant of *γ, *L*, where the term is sometimes translated as fewlen or fullein. The presence of this linguistic confusion in both *K* and *L* suggests that it originated in their common ancestor.

In this regard, the very fact that the word fundamentally causing the confusion—the abstract *viele*—is mainly attested in the Swabian-Alemannic linguistic area is particularly significant.[37] It is possible that it remained unchanged in the exemplar copied by the scribe of *γ, who then attempted to adapt it to the linguistic conventions of his own region. However, in doing so, he introduced an anomalous spelling that not only altered the original meaning of the text but also led to misunderstandings.

The text of *γ is fully preserved in *K* and only partially in *L*. Moreover, the version transmitted in *L* is not only fragmented—beginning with the complete fourth book followed by an acephalous first book, the complete second book, the first doctrine, and the first seven chapters of the second doctrine of the third book—but it also appears to have undergone a deliberate process of revision and, in most cases, simplification. As part of this revision, many passages are reduced. See, for example:

> *K*: Ist es aber on hitz **vnd auch das glid hat kein hitz** so wasch es mit cochung...[38]
> [But if it is without heat and the limb also has no hat, then wash it with the decoction...]
> *L*: ist Es aber von hicz So wasch es mitt der kochüng...[39]
> [But if it is of heat, then wash it with the decoction...]

In some cases, however, *L* also includes additions to both the Latin original and the other vernacular witnesses. See, for example, the reference to the Biblical episode of Peter cutting off the ear of Malchus, the high priest's servant and Christ reattaching it in John 18:10, which is added to the chapter dealing with the wounds of the nose:

vnnd wen nü jr vil von der wuntten der nasen liegent Wen*n* sie sprechenn das etlich tragent die abgesnitten nasen jn der hant vnd darnach sey sie wider an jr stat geheilt Das doch ein grosse lugen ist Wen der leiplich geist wirt zuhant verlorn vnd auch der beweglich vnd vnd speißlich.[40]
[And many of them lie about wounds to the nose. For they say that someone carried the cut-off nose in the hand and this was later healed to its place. But this is a great falsehood, since the vital spirit is immediately lost and so are the mobile and the nourishing ones.]

So nün von der wunden der nasen liegen wan sy sprechen Sy trugen die abgeschnitten in der hanndt vnnd darnach wider hin an gehailtt doch erst ain grosse lüg ist Wan der leblich gaist wirtt zw hanndt da verloren vnd aüch der bewegklich vnnd der speißlich **vnnd mitt diser künnst Wer man geleich vnnserem heren ieshu cristo der dem malcho das ör widervmb annseczt das doch vmb armen sünderen vnmoglich ist**[41]
[And many of them lie about wounds to the nose. For they say that someone carried the cut-off nose in the hand and this was later healed onto its place. But this is a great falsehood, since the vital spirit is immediately lost and so are the mobile and the nourishing ones. And with this art one would be similar to our Lord Jesus Christ who reattached the ear to Malchus, which, however, is impossible among poor sinners.]

Expansively reformulated is also the passage explaining the genesis of old ulcers at the beginning of chapter I.iii.11:

K: Die geswer werden von schneydung der Aposteme*n* oder offenung durch sich selbs oder auß der wun*n*tte*n* In seiner heiln zeit[42]
[Ulcers results from the cutting of abscesses, their spontaneous opening, or from wounds during their healing process.]

L: Dye altten geschwer werden Offt auß den gemeinnen schweren die vbel gereigieret oder gereinigt werden als von jn ziechennden dingen die den fluß meren vnnd die feüchtten dar lawffen Oder es enthaltten oder durch sich selbs Oder auß der wündenn poßlich gehaylt dar auch anders werden mag als der krebs *etc.*
[Old ulcers often develop from common sores that are badly cleansed as by attractive substances that increase the discharge and cause humors to flow there, by retention, spontaneously, or by bad healing of the wound that may also take a different course, as cancer, etc.]

This effort to discuss a thesis—such as the impossibility of reattaching an amputated nose—by reinforcing the concept, with a Biblical reference,[43] or to describe a process in extremely detailed terms, as seen in the explanation of the genetic process of old ulcers, stands in clear contrast to a series of evident misunderstandings of the source found in L. Many of these errors reveal the copyist's ignorance, particularly regarding Latin loanwords. See, for example:

K: Ist das du die Anathomey dits buchs gantz hast[44]
[If you have the complete anatomy from this book]

L: Jst das du dy **astromey** dicz puecs ganncz hast
[If you have the complete astronomy from this book]

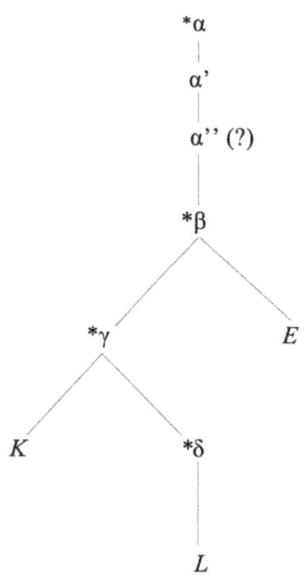

For this reason, it seems reasonable to assume that L is no direct copy of *γ, and that at least one additional text witness must have existed in the transmission chain between *γ and L. This intermediary could be *δ and represent the copy by the "attentive and verbose scribe striving for extreme clarity," which was later partially corrupted and partially misunderstood by the scribe of L, who inserted parts of it in the incomplete epitome of surgery in the form of questions and answers constituted by the manuscript London, Wellcome Institute for the History of Medicine, MS 398. Unfortunately, this assumption, as that of at least one intermediary between *α and *β, is not supported by strictly philological evidence and cannot, therefore, be incorporated into the evidence-based stemmatological hypothesis presented above. Nevertheless, a stemma modified in this sense (see to the right) remains extremely suggestive and likely provides insight into the detailed transmission path followed by Lanfranc's *Chirurgia magna* in the German vernacular.

4. Concluding Remarks

Based on a strictly philological reconstruction of the German tradition of Lanfranc of Milan's *Chirurgia magna*, which postulates the existence of three lost manuscript witnesses, this present study aims to reconstruct them through the philological and linguistic comparison of the three extant manuscripts of the complete translation of Lanfranc's work.

On the one hand, through linguistic reconstruction, it was possible to trace the transmission of the text from the southwestern to the southeastern German-speaking region and to identify some of the challenges this geographical shift posed to the manuscripts' scribes and, possibly, also to the readers and users of this translation of Lanfranc's *Chirurgia magna*.

On the other hand, the analysis of a series of errors, omissions, additions and revisions of the original text has made it possible to reconstruct how and why the original vernacular translation was modified from one copy to another. Part of this reconstruction remains speculative, as it lacks solid philological evidence. For example, in the absence of such evidence, the existence of intermediaries between two transmission stages can only be hypothesized. Nevertheless, this form of reasoning—essentially considering what is missing and lost by contrast of what is actually present and attested—allows for a plausible reconstruction of the circulation of knowledge and texts across space, time and dialects. It also offers deeper insight into the processes behind the genesis of textual variants which are crucial in philological and editorial work.

University of Genoa

NOTES

1. See also Christoph Weißer, Chirurgenlexikon. *2000 Persönlichkeiten aus der Geschichte der Chirurgie* (Berlin: Springer, 2019), 183; E. Gurlt, Geschichte der Chirurgie und ihrer Ausübung. *Volkschirurgie–Alterthum–Mittelalter–Renaissance*. Vol. 1 (Berlin: Verlag von August Hirschwald, 1898; 765–791; Roman Sosnowski, *Volgarizzamento della Chirurgia parva di Lanfranco da Milano nel manoscritto Ital. quart. 67 della collezione berlinese, conservato nella Biblioteca Jagellonica di Cracovia*. Collectio Fibulae, 8 (Kraków: Faculty of Philology, Jagellonian University of Kraków, 2014), 9–11.
2. Michael McVaugh, *The Rational Surgery of the Middle Ages*. Micrologus' Library, 15 (Florence: SISMEL/Edizioni del Galluzzo, 2006), 38.
3. On this, see also Marialuisa Caparrini, "The English Translations of Lanfranc of Milan's Surgical Works and Their Intended Audiences," in *The Vernacular Reception of Lanfranc of Milan's Surgical Works in Late Medieval Europe*, ed. Chiara Benati and Marialuisa Caparrini (Newcastle upon Tyne: Cambridge Scholars' Press, 2024), 106–131, at 107–109.
4. András Vizkelety, *Beschreibendes Verzeichnis der altdeutschen Handschriften in ungarischen Bibliotheken*. Vol. 2 (Wiesbaden: Harrassowitz, 1973), 211–214.
5. Gundolf Keil, "Schreck, Konrad, von Aschaffenburg," in *Die deutsche Literatur des Mittelalters. Verfasserlexikon*, ed. Kurt Ruh *et al*. Vol. 8 (Berlin and New York: de Gruyter, 1992), 846–848.

6. The text of the *Chirurgia parva* was edited by Armin Berg, "Lanfranks 'Chirurgia parva' in der Abschrift Konrad Schreck von Aschaffenburg. Altdeutsche Lanfrank-Übersetzungen III," PhD diss., University of Würzburg, 1975.
7. The text of the recipe is edited in Gerhard Eis, "Zu Heinrich von Rees," *Centaurus. International Magazine of the History of Mathematics, Science, and Technology* 13 (1969): 285–290, at 288–289.
8. Gisela Weber, "Eine altdeutsche Fassung der 'Kleinen Chirurgie' Guys de Chauliac in der Abschrift Konrad Schrecks von Aschaffenburg (1472)," PhD diss., University of Würzburg, 1982, 17; 21. On this, see also Karl Sudhoff, *Beiträge zur Geschichte der Chirurgie im Mittelalter. Graphische und textliche Untersuchungen in mittelalterlichen Handschriften. Zweiter Teil* (Leipzig: Verlag von Johann Ambrosius Barth, 1918), 474–479.
9. On the various German translations of the alchemical text, see Udo Benzenhöfer, *Johannes' de Rupescissa Liber de consideratione quintae essentiae omnium rerum Deutsch: Studien zur Alchemia medica des 15. bis 17. Jahrhunderts mit kritischer Edition des Textes* (Stuttgart: Franz Steiner Verlag, 1989), 50–54.
10. On this, see Volker Honemann "Aristoteles," *Die deutsche Literatur des Mittelalters. Verfasserlexikon*, ed. Kurt Ruh *et al.* Vol. 1 (Berlin and New York: de Gruyter, 1978), 436–450, at 440.
11. Walter Buckl, *Megenberg aus zweiter Hand. Überlieferungsgeschichtliche Studien zur Redaktion B des Buchs von den natürlichen Dingen* (Hildesheim, Zürich, New York: Olms-Weidmann,1993), 75.
12. Gerhard Eis, *Medizinische Fachprosa des späten Mittelalters und der frühen Neuzeit* (Amsterdam: Rodopi, 1982), 289.
13. Vizkelety, *Beschreibendes Verzeichnis*, 211.
14. Gundolf, Keil "Heinrich van Rees," *Deutsche Apotheker-Biographie* I, ed. Wolfgang-Hagen Hein, Holm-Dietmar Schwarz (Frankfurt am Main: Wissenschaftliche Verlags-Gesellschaft, 1975), 255–256, at 256.
15. Armin Berg, "Lanfranks 'Chirurgia parva' in der Abschrift Konrad Schreck von Anschaffenburg. Altdeutsche Lanfrank-Übersetzungen III," Ph.D. diss., University of Würzburg, 1975, 17–18.
16. See Hermann Paul, *Mittelhochdeutsche Grammatik*. 25. Auflage, neu bearbeitet von Thomas Klein, Hans-Joachim Solms and Klaus-Peter Wegera (Tübingen: Niemeyer, 2007), 36 and Oskar Reichmann and Klaus-Peter Wegera, *Frühneuhochdeutsche Grammatik. Von Robert Peter Ebert* (Tübingen: Niemeyer, 1993), 89.
17. Herbert Penzl, *Frühneuhochdeutsch* (Bern, Frankfurt am Main, Nancy, New York: Peter Lang, 1984), 19.
18. See Reichmann and Wegera, *Frühneuhochdeutsche Grammatik*, 67.

19. Otto Pültz, *Die deutschen Handschriften der Universitätsbibliothek Erlangen* (Wiesbaden: Harrasowitz, 1973), 44.
20. Johann Ludwig Hocker, *Bibliotheca Heilsbronnensis sive Catalogvs Librorum Omnium, tam manvscriptorvm, qvam impressorvm, qui in celeberrimi monasterii heilsbronnensis bibliotheca pvblica adservantvr* (Nürnberg: apud P.C. Monath, 1731), 229.
21. Benzenhöfer, *Johannes' de Rupescissa*, 29.
22. Paul, *Mittelhocheutsche* Grammatik, 147, 153.
23. Reichmann and Wegera, *Frühneuhochdeutsche Grammatik*, 58.
24. Samuel Arthur Joseph Moorat, *Catalogue of Western Manuscripts of Medicine and Science in the Wellcome Historical Medical Library I: Mss. written before 1650 A.D.* (London: Publications of the Wellcome Historical Medical Library, 1962), 268–269.
25. Johannes von Cuba, *Und nennen diß Buch zu latin Ortus sanitatis: uff teutsch ein Gart der Gesuntheit* (Mainz: Peter Schöffer, 1485) fol. 2r.
26. Similar questionnaires can also be found in Stuttgart, Landesbibliothek, Cod. med. et phys. 2o 5, Bl. 206r-212r (ca. 1482–1501) and Cod. med. et phys. 2° 8, Bl. 3r-10r (ca. 1550–1518). On this, see Manfred Gröber, *Das wundärztliche Manual des Meisters Hans Seyff von Göppingen (ca. 1440–1518). Der Cod. med. et phys. 2° 8 der Württembergischen Landesbibliothek Stuttgart*. Göppinger Arbeiten zur Germanistik, 656 (Göppingen: Kümmerle Verlag, 1998), 70–78; 274–276.
27. Keil, "Schreck, Konrad, von Aschaffenburg," 847.
28. Berg, "Lanfranks 'Chirurgia parva'," 116.
29. On this, see also Chiara Benati, "Latin Surgery in a New Skin: The German Translation of Lanfranc of Milan's *Chirurgia magna*," *Journal of the Early Book Society* 27 (2024): 73–98, at 79.
30. Lanfranc of Milan, "Chirurgia magna," *Cyrurgia Guidonis de cauliaco. Et Cyrurgia Bruni. Theodorici. Rogerij. Rolandi. Bertapalie. Lanfranci* (Venetijs: Impressarum mandato Octaviani Scoti Liuis Modoetiensis Cua et ante Boneti Locatelli Bergomiensis, 1498).
31. The following six manuscripts have been consulted: *GC*: Cambridge, Gonville and Caius, MS 159 (209) (https://cudl.lib.cam.ac.uk/mirador/MS-GONVILLE-AND-CAIUS-00159-00209/1); *Er*: Erfurt, Universitäts- und Forschungsbibliothek Erfurt/Gotha, Cod. Ampl. 4o 174 (https://dfg-viewer.de/show?tx_dlf%5Bdouble%5D=0&tx_dlf%5Bid%5D=https%3A%2F%2Fdhb.thulb.uni-jena.de%2Fservlets%2FMCRMETSServlet%2Fufb_derivate_00014407%3FXSL.Style%3Ddfg&tx_dlf%5Bpage%5D=184&cHash=0d09c5f0c81545e5e258ecfa84b8509d); *P*: Paris, Bibliothèque Nationale, MS Lat. 6992 (https://gallica.bnf.fr/ark:/12148/btv1b90670946/f195.item.zoom); *PL*: Città del Vaticano, Biblioteca Apostolica Vaticana, Pal. Lat. 1310 (https://digi.

vatlib.it/view/MSS_Pal.lat.1310 or https://dfg-viewer.de/show?tx_dlf%5Bdouble%5D=0&tx_dlf%5Bid%5D=https%3A%2F%2Fdigi.ub.uni-heidelberg.de%2Fdiglit%2Fbav_pal_lat_1310%2Fmets&tx_dlf%5Bpage%5D=9&cHash=e7e50cbd67e12be249153b267e2bd697); RL_1: Città del Vaticano, Biblioteca Apostolica Vaticana, Reg. Lat. 1345 (https://digi.vatlib.it/view/MSS_Reg.lat.1345); RL_2: Città del Vaticano, Biblioteca ApostolicaVaticana, Reg. Lat. 1963 (https://digi.vatlib.it/view/MSS_Reg.lat.1963). This analysis has highlighted how it is possible to identify at least two distinct branches within the Latin tradition: a first group of witnesses, consisting of the manuscripts *GC*, *Er*, and RL_1, which diverges in several passages from the *editio princeps*; and a second group of manuscripts, generally closer to the Venetian print of 1498, represented by *P*, *PL*, and RL_2. While, on the one hand, we can confidently rule out the possibility that any of the examined Latin manuscripts constitutes the direct exemplar of the German translation, on the other hand, the numerous correspondences between the vernacular text and the branch of the Latin tradition represented by *GC*, *Er*, and RL_1 suggest that the translator had access to a version of the text traceable to this branch of the tradition.
32. Keil, "Schreck, Konrad, von Aschaffenburg," 847.
33. Berg, "Lanfranks 'Chirurgia parva'," 116.
34. On this, see McVaugh, *The Rational Surgeons*, 241.
35. Kalocsa, Főszékesegyházi Könyvtár, MS 376, fol. 144r. The same comment is present in Erlangen, Universitätsbibliothek, MS B 32, fol. 134r.
36. Jakob and Wilhelm Grimm, *Deutsches Wörterbuch*, vol. 3 (Stuttgart: Hirzel Verlag, 1862), 1374.
37. See Jakob and Wilhelm Grimm, *Deutsches Wörterbuch*, vol. 12.2 (Stuttgart: Hirzel Verlag, 1951), 218.
38. Kalocsa, Főszékesegyházi Könyvtár, MS 376, fol. 26v.
39. London, Wellcome Institute for the History of Medicine, MS 398, fol. 356v.
40. Kalocsa, Főszékesegyházi Könyvtár, MS 376, fol. 45v.
41. London, Wellcome Institute for the History of Medicine, MS 398, fol. 314r.
42. Kalocsa, Főszékesegyházi Könyvtár, MS 376, fol. 25v.
43. On this see also, Chiara Benati and Marialuisa Caparrini, "Where Has God Gone in the Vernacular Renderings of Lanfranc's *Chirurgia magna*?," in *Miracles and Wonders in the Middle Ages and Early Modern Period: Experiencing Transcendence Between Reality and Imagination*, ed. Albrecht Classen (Berlin and Boston: de Gruyter, 2025), 477–504.
44. Kalocsa, Főszékesegyházi Könyvtár, MS 376, fol. 18v.
45. London, Wellcome Institute for the History of Medicine, MS 398, fol. 228v.

A New Middle English Fragment of John Arderne's *Extracta Hemorroidarum*: Evidence for the Surgical Readership of Translation T

CALEB PRUS

John Arderne (ca. 1307–1392) was one of the most influential English surgeons of the later Middle Ages, renowned for his innovative treatment of anal fistulas.[1] His principal work, the *Practica* on *fistula in ano* (1376), circulated widely in Latin and was often embedded within his larger surgical compendium, the *Liber medicinarium sive receptorum liber medicinalium*.[2] The *Practica*'s prominence is evident in its survival in over forty Latin manuscripts and four Middle English translations, distinguished by scholars as **E**, **P**, **T**, and **S**.[3] This article introduces a previously unrecognized Middle English fragment of Arderne's *Extracta Hemorroidarum*, a tract from his *Liber medicinalium*, preserved in London, British Library, Sloane MS 73. Though brief, this witness expands the known circulation of Arderne's Middle English translation **T** and demonstrates that **T** was excerpted for surgical use, despite its editorial differences from the Latin original.

Sloane 73 is a composite manuscript of several independent booklets, copied by different scribes and assembled in the sixteenth century by an owner who added foliation and marginal notes throughout. A previously unrecognized fragment of John Arderne's *Extracta Hemorroidarum* appears at the end of one such booklet, folios 57–97, written in a late fourteenth- or early fifteenth-century hand. The contents of this forty-leaf booklet are as follows:

1. A bilingual collection of remedies, alphabetically arranged and alternating between Latin and Middle English (fols. 57r–88r);
2. A Latin list of medical ingredients (fol. 88v);
3. *Anatomia Ricardi Anglici* (fols. 89r–95r);
4. A Middle English fragment of *Extracta Hemorroidarum* (fols. 96r–97r).

The Arderne text was added to the booklet's final leaves by a different scribe, whose hand is datable to the mid-fifteenth century.[4] This later hand filled the previously blank pages with a short but significant excerpt from the Middle English translation known as **T**, which until now has been attested only in Cambridge, Trinity College, MS O.9.37.[5] The Sloane fragment corresponds to TCC O.9.37, folios 24v–25v, beginning "Knowe þe weel whane þu puttist puluis siue pare or vitriol or ony oþir poudre corosif wiþinne þe ers" and ending "do hem on þe emeroudis or ficus or condolamata or on deed fleisch where euer it be ... afore ony þing of þe world."[6] As **T** has yet to be edited, an edition of the fragment appears in the appendix.

The Sloane fragment provides new evidence that challenges the existing view of **T** as a poorly transmitted and little used translation. In Sloane 73, several key variants appear in passages where the Trinity copy seems to suffer from scribal error, suggesting the Sloane text preserves a fuller version of **T** from a now lost exemplar. One striking example occurs at the beginning of the extract:

> Knowe þe weel whane þu puttist puluis siue pare or vitriol or ony oþir poudre corosif *wiþinne þe ers ouer þe corosyon or fretynge or ouer fissuris, thanne ouer þe poudre corosif* owiþ þe poudre of bole armoniak [emphasis added].[7]

By contrast, TCC O.9.37 reads:

> Know þu well when þu puttist puluis siue or vitriol or ony oþer pouder corosif owiþ þe poudre of bole armoniak to be doon...[8]

The Trinity version omits the critical warning against internal application of corrosive powders ("wiþinne þe ers"), likely due to a scribal eye skip triggered by the repetition of "poudre corosif." This omission is not merely a textual error but is potentially dangerous advice for a practicing surgeon.

A similar issue arises in a list of blood-staunching agents: Sloane 73 reads "vitreole *combuste* hareheer y breond & also brend henne feþeris *combuste* with þe whi3t of an ey," while the Trinity copy condenses this to "vitreole *combuste* with þe white of an egge" [emphasis added].[9] Such differences confirm that neither manuscript is copied from the other and that both descend from a more complete common source. The newly discovered fragment thus expands the known stemma of **T** to at least a family of three and suggests a broader circulation of the text than previously recognized.

Beyond its textual significance, Sloane 73 offers insight into how **T** was excerpted by readers engaged in surgical practice. While Sloane 73 shares no direct overlap with TCC O.9.37, its medical texts and annotations align it with the broader culture of surgical readers in fifteenth-century England. Most notably, it preserves the *Anatomia Ricardi Anglici*, a Latin anatomical treatise that presumes a level of formal education. Its Middle English recipe collection also draws on the learned surgical tradition: one recipe reproduces the *Unguentum viride cirurgicorum* from Lanfrank of Milan's *Chirurgia Magna*, while another explicitly contrasts the techniques of Henri de Mondeville and Theodoric of Cervia:

> Henry makiþ þis same plastir on þis wise ... but thederik doiþ not so / & as henry seiþ þis cure is good to alle maner woundes.[10]

Additional recipes cite "Johannam leche de chester," likely John Leche of Chester (fl. 1373–1410), royal surgeon to Edward III and Richard II, and "Magistrum Johannem M." or "M. J. M," which may identify Master John Malvern (fl. 1393–1422), physician to Henry IV.[11] Such attributions suggest either personal familiarity with or direct access to the medical networks in which these figures operated. Marginalia in English and Latin further reinforce the manuscript's practical orientation, including a fifteenth-century note summarizing the five essential ointments that "a surgian worching craftili scholde ber with him."[12] These features characterize Sloane 73 as a practical manuscript, in which the Arderne fragment has been added as a deliberate act of compilation, further tailoring the booklet for surgical use.

The surgical emphasis of Sloane 73 invites renewed scrutiny of the professional context in which the other witness of translation **T** (TCC O.9.37) was produced and read, particularly in light of its long-assumed association with the London barber-surgeon Richard Dod (fl. 1445–1468). Peter Murray Jones has twice suggested that Dod commissioned the Trinity manuscript, citing the ownership inscription *Iste liber constat Richardo Dod de London Barbor Surior*.[14] However, this inscription does not appear in TCC O.9.37 but in Sloane 5, a closely related codex.[15] Jones's misattribution likely stems from his reading of Faye Getz, who proposed that both manuscripts were copied by the same hand—later identified as Dod's servant, John Vynt.[16] Yet Getz's claim too warrants revision. A closer comparison reveals that TCC O.9.37 was copied by a different scribe, whose hand is distinguished by more secretary features and a more angular ductus than the one found in Sloane 5, complicating efforts to link Dod directly to the Trinity manuscript.

While TCC O.9.37 was not copied for Dod himself, its textual contents suggest that it may have been commissioned by a London surgeon operating within his professional milieu. The manuscript shares with Sloane 5, Dod's manuscript, an otherwise unattested cluster of Middle English medical texts, appearing in the same sequence and with the same incipits:

> *Age is mother of forgetilhed...* (TCC fols. 31r–32v, Sl 5 fols. 61r–63r)
> *Scotomy is such a sickness...* (TCC fols. 34v–122r, Sl 5 fols. 63v–151v)
> *Conception (id est) the conceiving...* (TCC fols. 122r–123r, Sl 5 fols. 152r-153r)
> *Lepra is a corruption...* (TCC fols. 123r–124r, Sl 5 fols. 153r-155r)
> *Raudeco (id est) hoarsehood...* (TCC fols. 125r–126r, Sl 5 fols. 155r–157r)
> *Soris we shall understand...* (TCC fols. 126r–129v, Sl 5 fols. 158r–172v)

Indeed, these two manuscripts constitute the only surviving witnesses of this distinct version of the Middle English *Compendium Medicinae*, which begins with *Scotomy*. They are also two of only three known copies of the Middle English *De Prognositics* of Bernard de Gordon and of the *Sekeness of Women* variant beginning with the word "sores."[17] This degree of textual overlap strongly suggests a shared exemplar—almost certainly one circulating in London. Against the inherited medical core, the inclusion of Arderne's *Practica* at the beginning of TCC O.9.37 (fols. 1r–25v), copied in the same hand as the rest of the manuscript, appears to have been an intentional choice to reframe the compilation for surgical use.[18]

Further evidence that the Trinity text was read by surgeons emerges from its marginal annotations. Though the original patron remains unknown, sixteenth-century notes indicate that TCC O.9.37 likely continued to circulate among London practitioners. One annotation declares, "yf a surgen thow wyllt be," revealing a reader's surgical aspirations—or perhaps even self-identification—as a "surgen."[19] Another note records a journey through the city: "As I walked by pols chaine? to polse wharf was buy gat ther did I see a prentice prend? a pareled on this rate," offering vivid, locative evidence for a London setting.[20] In this context, the signature of "Thomas Jhonsone," though a common name, may plausibly identify Thomas Johnson (fl. 1537–d. 1551), barber-surgeon and warden of the London guild in 1541 and again in 1550.[21] Such evidence reinforces the view that TCC

O.9.37 was not only produced for a metropolitan surgical audience but remained embedded in that professional community well into the sixteenth century.

Taken together, TCC O.9.37 and Sloane 73 reveal the varied material contexts in which translation **T** was copied, read, and adapted. The Trinity manuscript is professionally laid out: it combines parchment and paper, and it features rubrication and decorative initials which might suggest that **T** was made for private reference or educational study—not hands-on medical use. However, Sloane 73 demonstrates that **T** was also valued for its immediate, practical utility by working surgeons. The Arderne fragment appears in a utilitarian booklet tailored for everyday consultation—produced entirely on paper, lacking decorative elements, and organized for functional access with a concise table of contents and alphabetically arranged remedies. Likewise, marginal annotations throughout the booklet, many in the same fifteenth-century hand, include added recipes in both Latin and Middle English, witnessing active reader engagement and adaptation. Taken from the longer translation of the *Liber medicinalium*, the fragment from the *Extracta Hemorroidarum* extends the surgical function of the pamphlet, providing focused instruction on the treatment of hemorrhoids, a common condition that would have been frequently treated by medieval surgeons.

The discovery of Sloane 73 marks a significant addition to the vernacular corpus of John Arderne's writings, offering new evidence that translation **T** was valued for its surgical utility. For Peter Murray Jones, the connection between **T** and surgeons raises an "alarming" possibility: that surgeons were being "led astray by the manuscripts that were supposed to instruct them."[22] Jones describes **T** as a "shortened and edited version" of Arderne's text, marked by "wordy" and" literary" expansions that, in his view, compromise its medical accuracy.[23] Yet the survival of **T** in TCC O.9.37, and the deliberate excerption of the text in Sloane 73, attests that it was not only tolerated but actively used. Its enduring appeal reflects the pragmatic reading habits of late medieval surgeons, who may have prioritized access to remedies and operative instructions in the vernacular over strict fidelity to Latin sources. However imperfect, translation **T** remained a functional medium through which Arderne's surgical knowledge was transmitted, excerpted, and put to use by the practitioners it was designed to serve.

University of Rochester

Appendix: Middle English Fragment of
John Arderne's *Extracta Hemorroidarum*

The text is transcribed from London, British Library, Sloane MS 73, fols. 96r–97r, retaining the original spelling and letterforms. Light punctuation and paragraphing have been added for clarity. Abbreviations have been silently expanded (e.g., *i* to *id est*). Missing or uncertain readings are indicated in square brackets, and interlinear additions are noted with carets at the insertion point.[24]

[fol. 96r] Knowe þe weel whane þu puttist puluis siue, pare, or vitriol, or ony oþir poudre corosif wiþinne þe ers ouer þe corosyon or fretynge or ouer fissuris, thanne ouer þe poudre corosif owiþ þe poudre of bole armoniak to be doon for to difende þe poudre corosif, þat the moisture in þe ers enquenche and wasche awey þe poudre corosif. For bole bi his dryenes & his viscosite consumeþ þe moisture, wherfore þe poudre corosif þe more bettir may worchen and abiden. And þou haue no boole, þanne take sotil barly mele for it is myche driynge.

Also alle þese restreynen blood: a boiste, sett on with [s]carificacion on þat oþir side, & mirre, & grene iasper stoon þat hath on him blodi colouris naturel, safiris, reed corel, a swynes toord of þe feeld. Also alle þese staunchen blood of her owne propirtees, as þe iuys of walwort, þe iuys of þe reed nettil grounden wiþ al his substaunce with salt, or þe iuys of þe reed nettil y drunken in euery place of þe body it staunchiþ blood in man & in woman. But vndirstonde þat to a woman menstruat & to men hauynge emerowdis, þe rotis & þe croppis of nettil owen to be ȝeuen y grounden & i temperid wiþ rennynge watir or with reyny watir þat is bettere. Alle þese ben þa þat staunchen blood: *id est* mumme, bole armoniak, san dragon, encense, aloe, vitreole combuste, hareheer y breond, & also brend henne feþeris combuste with þe whiȝt of an ey, ben mele bounde with good communyng of þe wounde lippis on eiþir half & manye siche oþere. & if þese forseid failen not, þanne þe veyne must be cauterised & y brend, & it is on moost remedie. & aftir þe brennynge doon a poudre of bole, & sang dragon, aloes, mirre with þe whiȝt of an ey, & hare heer, & lete him be bounden ij or iij dayes [fol. 96v] or foure til he falle awey. & if it clene leie more of þe same medicyn more neische, & þat is sufficient.

& if þe pacient blede at þe nose, putte hise ballockis in vynegre or in cold watre & it sufficiþ. And summe ben staunchid of bledynge at þe nose with a good drauȝt of coold watir y drunken; and summe putte her ballokis in cley þat is temperid wiþ vynegre, or with watir, or with iuys of plaunteyn, & þat is good for hem þat bleden at þe nose, & ȝitt bettere if þe forheuyed were so emplastrid, & þe templis with þe same emplastre of cley, & also vndir þe arm hoolis. For siche emplastrynge ceessiþ & restreyneþ þe woundis of blood & drawith it aweyward & myche more strenger with þe poudris aforseid.

Now a litil afore þe whiche staunchiþ þe bledyng of emorowdis, & her akþe & her dolour, poudre of hare heer brend & temperid with þe whiȝt of an ey, & with delicat stupis y leid to or wiþ cotun. But se how comyn & aloes leid, y taken wiþ at mouþ, openeþ þe mouþis of the veynes in þe ers. & þe same leid to wiþoutforþ, þei restreyneþ bledynge of hem. & so doiþ þe leeues of moleyn y grounden & temperid wiþ þe whyȝt of an ey & y leyd on þe emeroidis þat bledith, it constreyneþ him fro bledyng. So doiþ þe wolle of a schep y wett in iuys of leekis y hett & leid on þe emeroudis þat ben swollen, & so ofte ^tymes^ remeued & heeliþ emerowdis of swellynge. & if poudre of comyn be þerwiþ it helpiþ bettere & sunner. If þe emerowdis ben for swollen & apperen as it were an henne tord, p take þerto moleyne grounden with blak sope & so do hem þerto ij daies & on þe þridde day þei schulen non appere. Oyle of violet grounden & medlid with þe whiȝt of an ey & leyd to, merueylously þei staunchen þe grete heet & þe dolour & þe brennyng of þe emeroudis.

[fol. 97r] Also aȝens þe grete bledynge of emeroudis & of menstrues þe beste restreynynge medicyn & moost desiccatif is to make on þis maner: in þe beste lumbardis enke, resolue a greet quantite of gumme arabik, þe which resolued put in poudre of bole armoniak, mastik, mummie, sunak, reed coral combuste, bdelly, gallis, psidie of pomegraynys iuys, of sloon dried, þe ȝeilke of roses dried, ipoquystieos anteros, sotilly poudrid and sarcid & do hem in þe iuys aforseid wiþ gumme arabik so þat þei may renne þoruȝ þe nastere nastare into þe ers be putt yn. Wiþ þis medicyn was heelid de demeit ^de^metrius kyng of pers of a cristen man þat was taken & putt into prison, bi þat same kyng was mad riȝt riche for þis aforeseid medicyn & to cristendom was sent hoom by þe commandementis of þe same king. & manye oþere prisoneris wiþ him were delyuerid freeli fro prisoun.

Panis cuculy, *id est* wodesour, alleluya, is aloon & growiþ on buyschis & in wodis in þe maner of þre leeues gras as it is peyntis here & beriþ white flouris. & it is a sour eerbe þat we calle alleluya panis cuculy. An handful or two in a lynen clooþ y wet i wrungen out from watir or in þe leeues of reed dockis y wrappid & leid vndir hoote emeries of fier, & so lete hem rosten þat þei drie not. & aftirward drawe hem out & do hem on þe emeroudis, or ficus, or condolamata, or on deed fleisch where euere it be. & ficus it bitiþ esily & it rememeneþ al þe forseid afore ony þing of þe world.

NOTES

1. John Arderne is also known as John of Arderne, John de Arderne, or John le Leche de Arderne. For biographies of John Arderne, see Peter Murray Jones, "John Arderne," in *Oxford Dictionary of National Biography*, (Oxford: Oxford University Press, September 2004); Theodore Beck, *The Cutting Edge: Early History of the Surgeons of London* (London: Lund Humphries, 1974), 49–51; and C.H. Talbot and E.A. Hammond, *The Medical Practitioners in Medieval England: A Biographical Register* (London: Wellcome Historical Medical Library, 1965), 111–112. While Jones suggests Arderne died ca. 1380, Beck presents convincing evidence for a death in 1392.

2. For an edition of Arderne's text, see D'Arcy Power, *Treatises of Fistula in Ano, Haemorrhoids, and Clysters by John Arderne*. EETS, o.s. 139 (London: Oxford University Press, 1910). Extracts from the *Liber medicinarum sive receptorum liber medicinalium* are also edited by Power in "The Lesser Writings of John Arderne," *XVIIth International Congress of Medicine: Section XXIII, History of Medicine* (London, 1914), 107–133.
3. Peter Murray Jones, "Four Middle English translations of John of Arderne," in *Latin and Vernacular Studies in Late Medieval Manuscripts*, ed. A.J. Minnis (Cambridge: D.S. Brewer, 1989), 65. See also "Fistula in Ano [252]" in *A Manual of Writings in Middle English, 1050–1500*, ed. George R. Keiser, vol. 10, *Science and Information* (New Haven, CT: Connecticut Academy of Arts and Sciences, 1998), 3832. Keiser designates the four translations as versions 1–4 respectively, with Translation **T** corresponding to Keiser's Version 3.
4. London, British Library, Sloane MS 73, fol. 95v. The hand is similar to the scribe who copied the *Book of Quintescense* on fols.10–27, but different enough to suggest a separate scribe.
5. Jones, "Four Middle English Translations," 61–89. For a description of Cambridge, Trinity College, MS O.9.37, see Clarck Drieshen, "Cambridge, Trinity College, MS O.9.37," *Cambridge University Digital Library*, accessed August 10, 2025, http://cudl.lib.cam.ac.uk/view/MS-TRINITY-COLLEGE-O-00009-00037/1.
6. BL, Sloane MS 73, fols. 96r–97r. Translation **T** has yet to be edited from TCC O.9.37, but the fragment of *Extracta Hemorroidum* in Sloane 73 represents the following lines in Power's edition (Translation **P**): p. 65, line 31 to p. 68, line 9.
7. BL, Sloane MS 73, fol. 96r.
8. TCC O.9.37, fol. 24v.
9. BL, Sloane MS 73, fol. 96r; TCC O.9.37, fol. 25v.
10. BL, Sloane MS 73, fol. 86v. For *Unguentum viride cirurgicorum*, see Robert von Fleischhacker. *Lanfrank's "Science of Cirurgie"*, EETS, o.s. 102 (London, 1894), 350, lines 11–20 (cf. Sloane 73, fol. 65r)
11. "Emplastrum mirabilitur secundum Johannem leche de chester" (fol. 66r). For John Leche of Chester's biography see Beck, *Cutting Edge*, 56–57, 73–74 and Talbot and Hammond, *Medical Practitioners*, 161–162. Other recipes include "emplastrum per stomache secundum Magistrum Johannem M." (fol. 52r) and "cerotum album secundum M. J. M" (fol. 58v). For more on John Malvern's biography, see Talbot and Hammond, *Medical Practitioners*, 166–167.
12. BL, Sloane MS 73, fol. 87r. This same hand also attributes an "alio mod pultem pestilenci" to "Sir William Jamis," possibly identifying William James (Jamys) (fl. 1376–1420), Lollard physician and fellow of Mer-

ton College, Oxford. For a biography of William James, see Faye Getz, "Archives and Sources: Medical Practitioners in Medieval England," *Social History of Medicine* 3, 2 (August 1990), 245–83 and A.B. Emden, ed., *A Biographical Register of the University of Oxford to A.D. 1500*, vol. 3 (Oxford: Clarendon Press, 1959), s.v. "William James (Jamys)," 1012–1013.

13. For the most recent biographical sketch of Richard Dod, see David Moreno Olalla, *Lelamour Herbal (MS Sloane 5, ff.13r–57r): An Annotated Critical Edition* (Bern: Peter Lang, 2018), 60–64.
14. Peter Murray Jones, "Language in Medieval Britain: Networks and Exchanges," in *Proceedings of the 2013 Harlaxton Symposium*, ed. Mary Curruthers (Donington: Shaun Tyas, 2015), 88; see also Jones, "Four Middle English Translations," 61–62.
15. Though Jones claims the ownership inscription is in TCC O.9.37, he cites the folio number in BL, Sloane MS 5: fol. 157r. TCC O.9.37 does not have a fol. 157r. This mistake is unfortunately perpetuated in Carole Rawcliffe, *Medicine & Society in Later Medieval England* (Stroud: Alan Sutton, 1995), 132.
16. Faye Marie Getz, *Healing and Society in Medieval England: A Middle English Translation of the Pharmaceutical Writings of Gilbertus Anglicus* (Madison: University of Wisconsin Press, 1991), lxx. Getz suggests a new hand begins the Middle English Gilbertus in TCC O.9.37, with the old hand resuming on fol. 40r. While there are some slight differences, I agree with Clarck Drieshen that the manuscript is the work of a single hand. For the argument that the scribe of Sloane 5 is John Vynt, see Olalla, *Lelamour Herbal*, 63–65, and David Moreno Olalla, "Spelling Practices in Late Middle English Medical Prose: A Quantitative Analysis" in *The Multilingual Origins of Standard English*, ed. Laura Wright (Berlin: De Gruyter, 2020), 143–144. This same hand appears in HM 505, a copy of Henry Daniel's *Liber Uricrisciarum*, which also bears Dod's ownership mark.
17. Monica Green reads the first word as "Sirs" in *Making Women's Medicine Masculine: The Rise of Male Authority in Pre-Modern Gynaecology* (Oxford: Oxford University Press, 2008), 191. She uses this male address to argue the text gave men 'permission' to read the text. However, the word in Sloane 5 is *sars* (sores), as seen in TCC O.9.37 where the text begins with soris and contains the heading: "Sores and greuance þat women haue" (fol. 126r). The third copy of this version is preserved in Longleat House 174.
18. Booklet I (fols. 1–30) is Quires 1^{12} (1st–3rd and 12th wanting), 2^{12}, and 3^{10} with leaf signatures A–C.

19. TCC O.9.37, fol. 75r. In his catalogue entry, Clarck Drieshen has mis-transcribed this as "Yf a bargen thow wyllt be..."
20. TCC O.9.37, fol. 40r.
21. Will of Thomas Johnson, 1551, PROB 11/34/23, The National Archives, Kew.
22. Jones, "Four Middle English Translations," 88–89.
23. Jones, "Four Middle English Translations," 73–74, 89. Carole Rawcliffe similarly laments that Arderne's treatise "suffered particular indignities" in the hands of **T**'s translator in *Medicine and Society*, 132.
24. For a helpful guide to Middle English medical terms, see Juhani Norri, *Dictionary of Medical Vocabulary in English, 1375–1550: Body Parts, Sicknesses, Instruments, and Medicinal Preparations* (London and New York: Routledge, 2016).

More Messing With Old Books: The Rewards of Bodleian Library, MS Laud Misc. 603

It is always shameful to know only what someone else says and
offer nothing of your own,
at line 9, where there are more good things.[1]

RALPH HANNA

I am a great believer in serendipity, or in following one's nose, pursuing what looks interesting, rather than some fixed programme on well-trodden subjects (like Middle English, even Chaucerian MSS, for example). Since it drags one outside one's comfort zone, venturing like this both improves one's reach and may lead to informative discoveries.[2] That is the way I came upon the subject of this essay, Bodleian Library, MS Laud Misc. 603. I was first attracted to this book several years ago because of its constellation of texts compiled by the Oxford-Paris Franciscan John Waleys, also known as John of Wales (d. 1285). A little research piqued my interest further because of the book's provenance: it is signed by a Durham monk whose name appears in eight or nine surviving books. And finally, quite independently, like those first two tweaks to my interest, I chanced on Graham Pollard's reference to part of the book as having texts lineated in fives.[3] That concatenation of rather random details was enough to stimulate me to investigate further, and as I hope the following pages will demonstrate, just examining medieval books will turn up topics of what I take to be of more than minor interest.

Because this book can scarcely be described as a familiar one, I introduce my account with an abbreviated formal description.

Oxford, Bodleian Library, MS Laud Misc. 603

s. xiv in. and med. or s. xiv². Folios ii + ii (fols. 1–2) + 112 (fols. 3–114) + ii (fols. 115-16). Overall, 305 mm x 210 mm. For further details, for separately produced segments, all on membrane, see below.

Manuscript I (or Ia) = folios 3–60

s. xiv in. Folios 58. Writing area 225–40 mm x 130–45 mm. Written in textura rotunda. 35 long lines to the side. The hand is a relatively anonymous one of s. xiv¹, and dating depends upon a number of marginal notes, in contemporary anglicanas; see, for example, folio 39 outer margin (not a fully looped anglicana 'a,' but a high transverse stroke, shoulderless anglicana 'r,' broad strokes or shading as conventional in hands of s. xiii ex.–xiv in.).

[1] Folios 3–59ᵛ: Martin of Troppau, *Chronicon summorum pontificum et imperatorum Romanorum*. Folio 60 is blank.[4]

Collation: 1–4¹² 5¹² (lacks 10 and 11, both excised stubs, and both blank). Neither formal signatures nor catchwords, but much faded brown ink notations '1 quaternus', etc., low on the feet of folios 14ᵛ, 26ᵛ, and 38ᵛ. The last two leaves of the first quire appear to have been pasted to their stubs, and the text does not appear to be continuous.

Manuscript II (or Ib) = folios 61–102

s. xiv in. Folios 42. Writing area 230 mm x 150–55 mm. Written in textura rotunda. 41 lines to the side in double columns. The hand is contemporary with, of the same general type as, but not identical with, what precedes.

However, the decoration suggests these segments are, if not related in scribal production, probably so in finishing. Here, although this segment of the manuscript lacks the profuse punctuational marking of text [1], there are striking similarities in the flourishing of initials, particularly the red floral infill on large initial capitals. This depicts leaves with multiple surrounding tendrils; see folios 3, 61, and 99. Likewise, the extended tails of marginal paraphs are at least similar.[5]

[2] Folios 61ʳᵃ–98ᵛᵇ: John of Wales, *Compendiloquium*. On most leaves (further details below), in the intercolumnar space, line numbering by fives, using Arabic numerals; a great many original notes, in informal early anglicana (here not simply the conventional shading, but occasional "hooked" or "split ascenders"), at the foot of the page. Since these notes are often set off with colored paraphs, they are part of the original formatting of the manuscript, although any index to which the notes might point does not apparently survive. For extensive further detail and discussion, see below.

[3] Folios 98vb–102vb: John of Wales, *Breviloquium de sapientia sanctorum*. There are only six written lines on folio 102vb, the remainder blank. Collation: 6–8^{12} 9^6. No signatures, but regular catchwords.

Manuscript III (or II) = folios 103–14

s. xiv med. or s. xiv^2. Folios 12. Writing area 220 mm x 150 mm. Written in rather squat anglicana formata. 44–46 lines to the side in double columns. The membrane here, while of book quality, is inferior to that used earlier, and the scribe wrote without ruling the pages.

[4] Folios 103ra–14va: John of Wales, *Breviloquium de virtutibus antiquorum principum et philosophorum*. The final column is blank. Sporadic marginalia, but none from the hands that had marked earlier portions of the book.

Collation: 10^{12}. No signatures.

Binding: s. xix, plain brown leather, with two associated paper flyleaves at each end (fols. i–ii, 115–16).

Provenance: Clearly a book from the library of Durham Cathedral priory (this collection hereafter referred to as DCL = Dean and Chapter Library). I introduce further detail below, since one can construct a continuous history from the fourteenth century, perhaps from production, to the present.

Previously described: H. O. Coxe, rev. R. W. Hunt, *Laudian Manuscripts, Quarto Catalogues* 2 (Oxford: The Bodleian Library, 1973), cols 429–430 and page 573.

Ordinarily, one would begin an examination by an attempt to locate the site in which the book had been produced. One would begin by seeking books with the same texts (and, hopefully, sequences of such) and attempting to find analogies for the textual presentations here. However, the expansive circulation of the texts here (the "rarest" texts, those of MS II/Ib, survive in more than twenty separate books), renders any such search fairly futile. Nothing about the transmission of any of the three relevant texts coheres, or points to any particular locale one might identify as central, beyond vague hints of a center, perhaps Oxonian.

However, one feature of Laud Misc. 603 does at least stimulate thought. As I have noted above (see text [2]), the manuscript's text of the *Compendiloquium* has been heavily annotated. This has involved numbering the lines on each side, by fives in Arabic numerals, between the book's two columns, and by adding notes, identified as referring to specific lines of each column, at the feet of many leaves. Two features demonstrate that this activity was not a late intrusion, but integral to the production:

(a) Most flamboyantly and demonstratively, the finishing of the volume involved the rubricator decorating the page-foot notes (that is, the notes in the lower margins) by affixing paraphs at their heads. These appear to be in the same form and ink as used throughout MS Iab. Obviously enough, they indicate that the annotations were already present when the book was still in production.

(b) Subordinately, and particularly interestingly, the hand responsible for line numeration and notes was parsimonious.[6] That is, line numbering through this segment of the book is not universal. It begins only belatedly, starting a full leaf into part 3 of John of Wales's text, at folio 69^v, a point that corresponds to edn 3.2.1, folio 181vb/499. The seventeen preceding sides have no numeration, nor do folios 72^v, 78–79, 81, and 95^v. Line-numbering is also incomplete at the end of the text; although the head of part 10, at the foot of folio 97rb, has been heavily annotated, numeration ceases at that point. Moreover, excepting three isolated notes, at folios 64ra, 66ra, and 97ra, no page lacking line numeration has any page-foot notes at all, suggesting that this feature has been provided selectively only to facilitate the page-foot references. Exceptionally, a clump of six relatively proximate sides, folios 75^{rv}, 79^v, and 81^v–82^v, have line numbering, but lack any notes, perhaps simply because within a sequence of leaves numbered and noted. However, on the whole, the annotator did only the bare necessity for his purposes, to provide a line-reference sequence to which he might affix annotations.[7]

Moreover, this work appears roughly coordinated with the finishing of the book. This activity includes, not only the rubricator providing chapter headings, usually in the margins, along with a set of notes in rubric identifying topics discussed, but also the provision of running titles. These, which identify the book and chapter (or distinction, since the text offers both) on the page, begin at folio 64 (= "uel diuiditur philosophia simplex modus uiuendi et rudis contenti"), a point that corresponds to the first appearance of a note by the page-foot annotator, on folio 64ra: <...> "dicuntur artes liberales 20" (= 1.2, fol. 172vb/481). The running titles continue on every leaf to folio 93, the head of John's part 7 (= 6.5, fol. 222ra/580); in contrast, marginal rubricated materials identifying topics discussed, although reduced in frequency, run to the end of the text. One should also note a further break in the rubricator's work: on folio 89vb (= 5.7, fol. 216va/569), although he had routinely done so previously, he ceased providing rubricated paraphs at the head of the annotator's page-foot notes. Thereafter only the annotator's punctuation, rather hasty paraphs in his text ink to mark heads of entries, survives.

There is a certain amount of sloppiness involved in this finishing. The scribe responsible for the original text had not always left space for decorative capitals at textual divisions; as a result, the rubricator's marginal materials frequently supply numeration and, where there is room, the headings. Unlike this person's frequent and more formal marginal indications of subject-matter, the running titles are a bit fitful and unspecific, frequently only the "pars," sometimes with the added "distinctio." But they are guides, as I shall show in a moment, corresponding to column numbers in related books, that enable narrow placement of the page-foot line-numbered notes in the context to which they refer and which would allow these references to be converted into an index or *tabula*. In this context, the (in)accuracy of the running titles does not matter, since any index will have been book specific, created to explain this rendition of the text and not readily transferable to any other copy. The running titles would remain useful in directing a user of an index to at least a short sequence of folios. Narrower specifications, e.g., the *distinctiones* within the parts, would make the index more useful, and, since the annotator could have derived references from the text signalled on the sides in question, might have been supplied in any formal index.

This hyper-annotation of the volume must reflect two different "authors," as it were. The rubricator's marginalia presumably reflect his exemplar. Thus, they represent a straightforward act of transfer, more or less routine copying. However, the lineated page-foot notes, a great deal more specific, reflect a complementary ongoing reading of the text. The author of these, presumably the book's "patron" or first designated user, must have known, at least roughly, the shape of the exemplar and of its marginal subject directions, which would facilitate continuous reading or scanning. He was providing a second and different form of access, not for scanning, but more selective consultation, the result of an original (and individual) detailed reading and textual marking.

As an example of the complementary quality of this work, consider the aids to readers provided on folio 76va: first, the marginal rubrication, which I have marked with the supplied lineations:

[2] Notice this (by "And this follows: Plato says that all philosophers should seek this death") (= 3.4.5, fol. 192vb/521)
[6] Chapter 6. Plato's contempt for all worldly things[8]
[15] On Plato's cleansing himself of emotion
[20] On the philosophers' opinion
[26] Chapter 7. On overcoming one's inner emotions. Notice this
[39] That when one is angry, one should put off punishment[9]

The page-foot notes for the same column offer:

Notice that the best cure for anger is delay described at line 30; there's an example below 35 (= 3.4.7, fol. 193rab/522)

No one can understand anything when they are upset, line 35 (= 3.4.7, fol. 193rb/522)
(cut off at the foot of the leaf:) Against pleasant attacks [1][10]

The first set, the rubricator's marginalia, represents conventional topic- or subject-marking, the "finding notes" typical in many manuscripts (and older Early English Text Society editions); the second offers what one might call detailed "soundbites" and references to specific anecdotal material.

There is a further conclusion to be drawn from the marking the text receives here. It is probable, I would think, that the rubricator had been just as parsimonious in providing running titles and paraphs at the page-foot as the indexer had been in providing line numbering. That is, he would only have marked those successive sides already equipped with notes and eschewed this punctuation where notes did not occur. The proposition receives some confirmation from details associated with the page-foot annotations; these imply that that indexer may have continued his work even after the rubricator's "finishing," presumably after the now decorated pages were returned to him.

Nearly (but not quite) all the page-foot annotator's notes appear in a reasonably fixed position. They regularly begin four or five line spaces below the ruled text columns. Yet there are some telling exceptions: first of all, unrubricated examples very low on the page, often toward the gutter. I have cited one example above. Others are frequently rather general, very unlike this hand's usual annotative regime, e.g., 'De Senech' 25' (fol. 86vb, in the gutter at page-foot = 4.17, fol. 211rb/558), or 'De Boetio 31' (fol. 87ra, in the gutter at page-foot = 4.18, 211vb/559). Seven further examples, all detached from the usual annotation, appear at folios 93vb–94rb to identify 'good' representatives of each of the seven liberal arts (punctuating 7.3–7.8, fols. 223ra-24^{rab}/582–84).

More emphatically, although generally the notes are sequential, follow the discussion down the page in the column above,[11] there are informative glitches. Most usually, the rubricator's paraph appears by the first note in a sequence—yet not always. For example, on folio 86vb, although the notes are in sequence, two entries precede the rubricator's paraph and appear in what is normally the blank space separating annotation and text. More striking are annotations presented out of order and in the usually blank space above the first note and paraph. For example, on folio 76rb, annotations to lines 17 and 29 appear above the rubricator's paraph, which introduces the ordered sequence 4, 14, 21, 34; similarly, on folio 86rb, annotation to line 33, which is related to the following entry, appears in blank space preceding the paraph and notes to lines 6 et infra, 17.

Signs like this, I would think, confirm the complementarity of rubricator's and annotator's work. But they also highlight a certain non-complementarity, its most blatant sign that the annotating hand keeps on indexing *after* the rubricator had ceased adorning the heads of his entries at folio 89vb *and after* that person had ceased providing running titles at folio 93. There would seem to be two runs at page-foot annotation here, the second of them occurring only after the rubricator had concluded his work and returned the book to the annotator.[12]

Before passing on to consider this annotation in detail, I would draw one further conclusion. The only sensible reading of this situation is that the annotating hand is in fact the book's 'patron' (if you will) or intended audience and that this individual was working in cooperation with the professional bookmen who had produced his volume. First of all, as the selectivity of what is annotated would suggest, notations like this are personal – 'what I found noteworthy and want to be easily directed to again'; they are only useful to the person who made them, although he probably assumes that he is what one might describe as a 'normative reader/user.' And they are, of course, with their line numbering, utterly copy-specific, of use in This Book alone. Second, this hand had to have worked, at least partly, midproduction: he needed the text in its fixed copied form for his line references; and he worked before the quires were given to the decorator. So, this was a sophisticated student seeking a volume for continued reference in a situation of sophisticated book arts.

These annotations must be guides for an index. They are not particularly useful in their current state for the continuous reader, who will be guided to general discussions by the rubricator's marginal indication of subjects. Moreover, their creator must have known this to be a mediate step in producing the book, which was to be returned to the rubricator and was awaiting more readily accessible and formal marking in the marginal rubrication for subjects. But it was also a mediate procedure in that it provided notes awaiting transformation into a formal index, presumably to be alphabetically arranged, rather than following text order.

Here one might consider one customary way one imagines making an index. One would probably copy desired annotations onto a sequence of individual *schedulae*. These would be small, probably waste bits of membrane or paper capable of shuffling into alphabetical order for formal recopying.[13] This indicates that production of a formal finished index is separable from that of the remainder of the manuscript and the text it describes. If it is preserved with the book, it will always be a separate fascicle, and because personalized, easy enough to discard by later users as unhelpful. Further, one must assume a considerable (and invisible) editorial transformation between what appears in MS Laud Misc. 603, which constitute what one might designate 'indexing notes,' and any prepared formal index. The notes take a form where the projected head entry in an index is far from always clear (as may be, for example, the Seneca and Boethius references I have cited above). But, for example, "Nota de X" or "Quod X" presumably are to be filed under "X" in an appropriate alphabetical sequence.

Tabulae, like the draft example in evidence here, are an unduly ignored feature of manuscript culture, although one hopefully coming into prominence.[14] They remain generally unexamined for two reasons. First of all, they are non-authorial, supratextual additions not necessarily written by the same hands as the texts they describe. They are further overshadowed in discussions by an absurd emphasis on so-called memory tools; many texts that have been treated under such a rubric come equipped with variously detailed *tabulae*. The presence of such extra-textual devices indicates an expectation of normal research procedures, consultative use of the volume in hand by topic, as these are identified in the *tabulae*. Moreover, memory tools are silent, but the selectivity involved in indexing (what is important here? and in what respect?) in fact raises the issue of a directed, if selective, reading strategy. It should be stressed, as is overtly the case here, that this device (and the associated strategy) generally is supplementary or complementary. That is, since rubrics and sidenotes, or simple textual familiarity, enable one to access an author's ongoing general argument, indexes always present only fine-grained detail, what one would not expect to find with ease in a consecutive reading experience. However, in order to assess what purpose any index might serve, one needs to undertake a detailed examination, to make an effort at using it and figuring out what textual features and subjects it highlights. Only such a study will direct one toward the reading strategy to which the text has been subjected.

MS Laud Misc. 603 includes roughly 300 such putative index entries, and clearly rebuffs detailed reproduction.[15] I simply offer a sample, here a sequence of entries, from folios 94vb–95ra, part of the annotation of *Compendiloquium* 8.2 (= edn fols. 225^{ra-va}/586–87). Here John of Wales is presenting Virgil, not as the consummate poet, but, as frequently in the Middle Ages, the consummate necromancer. He is explicitly recycling a report of Virgil's activities that he found described in Alexander Neckam:

> Concerning Virgil, line 18. That he was the best and most outstanding of the poets, line 27.
> That Virgil's name was derived from *virga* "a wand," and why, line 35.
> How Virgil freed Naples, infested with a plague of leeches, by throwing a golden leech into a well, line 1.
> How Virgil preserved raw flesh for fifty years, line 10.
> How Virgil defended his garden with unmoveable air like a wall, line 13.

How Virgil built a palace in Rome with a statue representing every province and holding a bell in its hand, and however often that region dared plot against Roman rule, line 17 (see further below).

When Virgil was asked how long a palace he had built would last, he answered that it will stand until a virgin should give birth, line 28.[16]

The great majority of page-foot entries in Laud Misc. 603 resemble these. They represent brief yet direct textual citations, here essentially Neckam's topic sentences introducing various incidents. While many examples, like these, simply cite, a very large number are introduced by markers such as "Nota," "Quod," or "Quomodo." A fair-sized minority might be described as "soundbites" or "punchlines" lifted from anecdotal accounts, e.g., "you've got a mouth" (os habere), folio 70va = 3.2.6, folio 183rb/502 [= Seneca, *De ira* 3.38.1]; or "nothing in excess" (ne quid nimis), folio 88va = 5.5, folio 214va/565 [= Jerome, epistola 130, PL 22:1116]. Here, although the on-the-page-entries emphasize "Virgil," or maybe "magician," that is unlikely to have been the entry in any constructed index. From a list of chapters or parts, or from textual knowledge, it is possible to predict and find John's general discussion. These notes are more apt to signal headings like "virga," "sanguissuga," or "palacium" (or "campana").

A substantial number of entries, perhaps fifteen in all, resemble the motto I have affixed to the head of this essay, marked "ubi bona" (where there are many good things). These draw attention to strings of provocative citations (with the philosophers, where it occurs frequently, these always accompany examples of their conduct as illustrative) or of brief exemplary narratives, for example:

> There is no place of exile where a good man is, where there are many things [to notice], with a brief story, line 39 (fol. 91rb = 5.12, 219ra/574).[17]

The annotation draws attention to these textual materials:

> And it says there of such people [= Cicero, *Tusculanae disputationes* 5.36.106–9 passim], "They carried their own goods with them, that is, their virtues; therefore, no exile was onerous for them." For this reason, Seneca tells Helvia [= *Dialogi* 12.9.3–7 passim]:
> A lowly shack received their virtues; therefore, it was more beautiful than any temple when justice, continence, piety, prudence, and other virtues were spotted there. The place that takes up this great crowd of virtues is scarcely a narrow one, and it is no onerous exile, when someone is accompanied by such a following. Brutus said he had seen Marcellus exiled at Mytilene and living very happily, so far as that is possible for humans; and he was not more avid in his pursuit of beneficial knowledge than at that time. Brutus added that, when he left, he

thought that he was passing into exile, never to return to him, rather than leaving him in exile. And the Senate proclaimed on his behalf, lest they be exiles, as they would be, were they without him. For to lose one's homeland is not evil, since for a strong spirit, everywhere is a homeland.[18]

Informatively, the indexer appears not to have recognized the full extent of Seneca's discussion. He describes the passage as if he believed Seneca responsible for only the first two sentences ascribed him, and Brutus's statement an independent supporting anecdote, capped off by another maxim-like statement. The treatment accords with a number of the annotator's explicit markings, repeated a dozen times, of "exemplum," "fabula," or "narracio." He appears to have heeded—he certainly identified it as worth special attention—John of Wales's own statement, a citation from Seneca, *Epistulae morales* 6.5: "Abstract precepts construct a long journey, but examples a brief and effective one" (fol. 73va).[19] It is probably not an accident that the Oxford Dominican Robert Holcot repeats the Virgil anecdote I have cited above from Laud Misc. 603, folio 95ra, line 17, as a moralized exemplum at *Convertimini* 21 (the images with warning bells moralized as the soul's defences against sin), probably relying upon John's account.[20]

Here the double annotation of the *Compendiloquium* I have suggested above may throw up some interesting, if not predictable, topics for analysis. The belated inception and truncated conclusion to the annotator's first run at the text may suggest something of his interests. That is, he ignored nearly completely John's opening general arguments—What is philosophy? What is a philosopher? (the subjects of *Compendiloquium* parts one and two)—and concentrated on John's history of philosophy and the lives and opinions of eminent philosophers. These emphases are consonant with an historical interest, indeed a complement to the preceding text of the manuscript, Martin's chronicle. The narrative development of papal and imperial rule and activity is here supplemented by the analogous development of intellectual activity. Moreover, this interest might suggest why John's *Breviloquium de virtutibus* concerning rulers (and secondarily, philosophers) appears in MS Laud Misc. 603 only as an added text: it is a tract arranged to inculcate the classical cardinal virtues, and although its materials are historical, these are topically presented (although the *Compendiloquium*'s lives of philosophers often displays a similar technique). Within this segment of the book, annotation emphasizes both provocative actions and pregnant *sententiae*.

This initial interest appears to have broken off somewhere late in part five of John of Wales's text. At this point, the annotator showed no interest in parts six through nine: "de sectis philosophorum," "de artibus liberalibus," "de phisicis sive poetis," and "de octo modis abusionis philosophie." And, of course, he lost interest in the text once John began his discussion, at the head of part ten, of places where study flourished. He did annotate its opening, a conventional historical account of the *translatio studii* (which John of Wales eventually and originally extends from Greece-Rome-Paris to include England and Ireland), but was uninterested in the post-classical materials.

In extending his notations (here on the pages where running titles had not been provided), the annotator appears to have been attracted by two nodes of material. He particularly emphasizes a lengthy discussion of communicating philosophical materials in a situation, prominent in classical accounts yet apparently antithetical to philosophical meditation, the banquet or symposium (fol. 90^{rab} = 5.8–9, edn fols. 216vb–17va/569–71). This, of course, emphasizes the orality of instruction and the dynamic necessary in meeting and effectively addressing nonacademic audiences, disseminating sophisticated ideas to a varied cadre. This idea is inherent in John of Wales's designation of many works as *-loquia*, "chats," yet equally implies the annotator's interest in such outreach. This interest is further developed through the annotations of John's part nine, on "abuses" of philosophy, a primer for convincing self-presentation as responsible teacher. The other emphatically annotated portion of this extension concerns the marking "Nota exemplum" four times in *Compendiloquium* 8.6 (fols. 96^{ra-va} = edn fols. 227^{ra-vb}/590–91). In each instance, these markings highlight the usefulness of the Aesopian fables John cites there. Notations like these may well "bare the device" underlying all the annotator's procedures: that, as John of Wales had hoped, these notations direct readers to provocative classical "prooftexts" and exemplary materials of use in general oral instruction, not limited to formal sermons. They speak, not just to the monastic environment where this manuscript was preserved, but to the possible instructional interface between Cathedral and the surrounding *saeculum*.

I turn now to the manuscript's provenance, for this will allow a more detailed discussion of context and use. Here the main evidence is provided by inscriptions in the volume itself:

On fol. 2^v, the second of the two medieval front flyleaves: a contents table (for the whole, and more or less accurate, save for fusion of texts [2] and [3]), with the shelfmark '$2^a 7^i$ ff', both s. xv med.

Along the upper margin of fol. 3, the opening leaf of the manuscript proper: "Liber Roberti Brakenbery"; "Cronica martini cum aliis de communi libraria monachorum dunelm" (erased, but, as Hunt says, "sufficient traces remain"); the letter-mark 'I', and the added shelfmark "$1^a 7^{mi}$ ff" of s. xv med. 'I' indicates the book's placement, by 1395, in a Durham cloister *armorium*, where it had this designation among the "Libri historiales."[22]

The earliest record of the book is Robert Brackenbury's inscription, indicating his ownership of the volume, s. xiv². Brackenbury appears in Cathedral records for half a century; first, when he was probably around twenty years old, in 1342, when he was ordained acolyte. He advanced through orders to ordination as priest in 1347. He held various minor chapter offices from the late 1340s to the mid-1360s and was fairly regularly present in chapter in the early 1380s. Although he was thought mortally ill in 1383, he only died during summer 1391.[23]

The only details one can add to this account—its author, Alan Piper, spent a lifetime in the Durham muniments—concern Brackenbury's antecedents. He was a local lad. In the fourteenth century, his family were Cathedral tenants, holding the manor of Little Broom (in St. Oswald's parish, New Elvet, Durham, but roughly two miles west of both that church and the Cathedral). Piper also notes that on one occasion he was referred to as "Robert of Layton." This directs one to another contemporary family holding, Layton, a manor in "The Isle [of Bradbury]," Sedgefield, county Durham: "The manor of Layton appears to have been settled on Cecily widow of a Layton of Hetton who married as her second husband Peter de Brackenbury. She died in or about 1370."[24]

In addition to Piper's citation of a record indicating that he had given a volume now lost, with miracles of the Virgin and *St Patrick's Purgatory*, to the Cathedral's cell at Farne, Brackenbury left his name in nine Durham books, including this one. Only two of these might be thought halfway contemporary, i.e., produced during s. xiv. All the remainder were certainly from Cathedral stock; for these, Brackenbury had, it appears, lifetime use. Five of the volumes contain rather basic texts, in which one might imagine any intellectually stimulated monk to have an interest, e.g., Isidore's Etymologies (now DCL B.IV.15), a psalter with Peter Lombard's commentary (now DCL A.III.7), or the *Decretales* (now DCL C.II.3).

The remaining four books point to what might be specialized personal interests. First in medicine, where Brackenbury owned two books with comprehensive texts of Arabic medicine translated by Constantine the African (now DCL C.I.19 and C.IV.12). In the former, his signature may not be associable with the Constantine portions, but nonetheless appears attached to a medical text, Bernard of Gordon's *Lilium medicinae*. The other two books, including the volume discussed here, point in a different direction, toward history. Brackenbury owned one very famous volume, now British Library, MS Harley 491, a very early s. xii copy of William of Jumièges's history of Normandy; its copying had been directed by the great Durham historian, Simeon.[25] And then there is this volume, like the others, its production marked as too early for Brackenbury to have been concerned in any way with its creation. Like the remainder of his marked library and given that he does not seem to have had anything except what might be acquired locally, he can only have extracted it from the common stock out of some personal interest. But that does suggest something about the table I have been discussing.

These page-foot notes, keyed to an imposed lineation, involve an unconventional form of textual marking. Customarily, from the Carolingian revolution in book presentation to the end of the Middle Ages, textual marking takes two forms. On the one hand, usually associated with brief notes, narrowly speaking, "textual glosses," the provision of synonyms, often interlined, entries are keyed to the text though the use of "signes de renvoi," arbitrary marks that match the text with the proferred gloss. Longer explanations are connected with the appropriate textual loci by lemmata, brief repetitions, usually only the incipit of the passage commented, of the relevant text.[26]

The nature of this patron's endeavour probably identifies the locale in which one might situate the activity that has produced this book. The procedures the annotator is following are distinctive and with a limited sphere of use.[27] Annotating manuscripts with consecutive Arabic column-numbering and with lineation, usually by fives, is a distinctly localizable technique. The only example I have seen a reference to with an utterly comparable system providing clues for an index is Oxford, Merton College, MS 30, folios 1–132^v (Chrysostom on Matthew, s. xiii1, the text perhaps copied in France). This book features numbered columns, intercolumnar lineation by fives, and page-foot topic lists with line references. This has been a Merton College book since *ca*. 1300, donated by a Fellow active s. xiii ex., and the page-foot notations are contemporary with this provenance, i.e., s. xiii/xiv.[28]

This system of columns and lines numbered in Arabic was initially developed by mendicant scholars in Oxford around 1250 as a mechanism for indexing topical discussions in the commentaries on Peter Lombard's *Sentences* written by their theology students. The technique is unknown elsewhere, but it spread from strictly theological texts to works of pastoral theology, and it was often exported to large Benedictine monastic houses by those students whom houses were required to send to Oxford to study. In many cases, particularly hyperdivided texts, only lineation, not column numbering, appears. In such instances, the textual divisions, signalled by running titles at the heads of the leaves, offered sufficient signals for the purpose. Such is the case here, where, as I have indicated, something approximating John of Wales's divisions (the segments signalled in the titles do not always correspond to those of the text) have been provided by the rubricator. Although there are a few late outliers, such indexing procedures had a lifespan of only about seventy years, and had passed into desuetude by about 1320 (another reason for identifying the production here as 's.

xiv in.' or 's. xiv$^{1/4}$'). Given the general absence of book production from monastic locales for about a century and a half before Laud Misc. 603 was compiled, I do not think one should doubt that this is an Oxford produced book, although very likely one made under monastic auspices.[29]

If indexing of this sort is indeed Oxonian, there is a plausible, if not unproblematic, narrative to connect it with Durham and Brackenbury's ownership. That is, from late in the thirteenth century, the monastic house had a cell in Oxford. This was, for most of the fourteenth century, somewhat erratically stocked with Durham monks, and its foundation as a continuing residential College (now absorbed in Trinity College), with a fixed rota of monastic students, dates only from the 1380s. The difficulty concerns what we know of book acquisition and use in this Priory outpost. From Thomas of Westhoe's booklist (*ca.* 1300), recording what were very likely Priory-sponsored book purchases, the residents' interests appear to have been strictly theological. Neither of the texts in the core manuscript I–II (Iab) easily fits within that profile.[30]

Although the subject matter and methods used differ, there are provocative materials in Thomas's surviving books. First of all, among his acquisitions were *tabulae*, indexes that would provide ready access to discussions in complicated texts. Moreover, Thomas added marginal annotation to his books and, in one case, an index, although keyed for folio and column, not lineation. This appears to be the inception of what Piper describes as "a type of scholarly tool much favoured by the late medieval [Durham] community," the local construction of *tabulae*. Thomas certainly is not the annotating hand of the Laud MS, although that is of a similar script type and date—and surely suggestive of analogous behaviors.[31]

Whatever the differences from Thomas of Westhoe's work, at least two other contemporary Durham books with comparable indexing materials have appeared in past discussions. In both cases, these involve Arabic column-numbering, but not lineation. However, both include texts of a stripe that would have been most useful at the Oxford outpost: DCL A.III.13 (Nicholas Gorran on the psalter, s. xiv in., item 15 in Thomas's booklist), and DCL B.I.5 (Aquinas, *Sentence* commentary, s. xiv in.).[32]

Piper's account of Durham indexing, which I have mentioned above, centers around a single relevant manuscript. This lacks Oxonian numeration—it proceeds strictly by book and chapter—but involves a text particularly relevant in the context of Laud Misc. 603. DCL A.IV.8, fols 79–116^v, contains a *tabula* to Valerius Maximus, *Dicta et facta*, in this instance of alien manufacture (but English, s. xiv^1). However, this index has been extended, at folios 75–77^v, 117–38^v, in the house by the monk Peter of Kelloe, active for about thirty years before 1345 or 1346.[33] In this case, we have a finished index, absent the text—although there is no reason to provide an index to an absent text, and the Priory must have at this time possessed a copy. Moreover, that text is particularly relevant to the activities of John of Wales, since it is one source from which he pillaged much of his classical lore. In the full *Breviloquium de virtutibus*, for example (although a late addition to the Laud MS), there are about fifty citations from this text alone.

Here, a little library history might be telling. Our first peek at the Durham book collection, a list of titles from s. xiii med., shows a very substantial interest in classical texts.[34] However, as Piper points out, when the collection next comes into view in catalogues of the 1390s, these books were no longer present and had presumably been deaccessioned. Yet, in the interim century and a half, the library had acquired a new run of classical texts, among them Valerius and a further source routinely pillaged by John of Wales, Aulus Gellius's *Noctes Atticae*.[35] These appear among books recorded in the "spendment" in 1392, a locale which Piper associates with the monastic chancery; he suggests that their value might have been in constructing ornate classical references in letters.

Yet one might suggest an alternate account. Peter of Kelloe's index to Valerius must predate the book recorded in the "spendment" by about half a century. And the effort of extending in detail a pre-existing *tabula* must indicate the presence of a (separate) copy, as well as a desire to reduce Valerius's rather list-like accounts of classical heroism to a tool readily accessible on a topical basis. One imagines that the tables exist to facilitate use of a book only belatedly recorded, and that this was a new library acquisition of the 1320s or 1330s.

These interests in classical materials, not patristics or theology, speak to well-documented contemporary developments at Durham Cathedral. Richard Aungerville/de Bury was the bishop between 1333 and 1345, although erratically in residence, being appointed to the post as a valued royal administrator, and apparently much more frequently resident in London. As his *Philobiblion* indicates, he was a prolific collector of books and particularly given to universal interests, including "pagan" ones. Moreover, between 1325 and 1335, the "classicising friar" Robert Holcot was a member of his household, and in the Middle Ages frequently taken to have written the *Philobiblion*.[36] In this context, one might see the provision of a text like *Compendiloquium* as addressing a gap in holdings that was of contemporary Durham interest. However, the appended annotations I have been describing would be sensible as feeding the interface between monastic and local Durham contacts, as highlighting anecdotal material useful in providing exempla for sermons. Further provocative hints appear in another indexed Durham volume, DCL A.III.27 (Holcot on Wisdom, s. xiv ex., a later outlier in these proceedings): this has column numbering, but lines identified by letters 'a–g' at seven-line intervals.[37]

I return, for a moment, to the other, unannotated text of MS Laud Misc. 603, Martin of Troppau's history. This text remained of continuing interest in the house. It was used extensively in the prior John Wessington's historical researches in the early fifteenth century. Moreover, from a record of about 1440, Durham owned at least one further copy of Martin's chronicle, apparently for ready use. This was not, however, part of the Priory's library stock, but kept in a collection attached to the shrine of St. Cuthbert, and, in Piper's account, useful to the "feretrar" or the keeper of the shrine (the Middle English word borrowed from Latin *feretrarius*) in explaining the Cathedral's various relics to those interested.[38]

As is the rule in monastic houses, property is not supposed to be personal. Bodleian, MS Laud Misc. 641 (Peter Chrysologus of Ravenna's sermons, s. xiii) explicitly states that Robert Brackenbury's ownership was only "pro tempore vite sue." Thus, on his death, his entire library returned to the common Cathedral library stock, housed in *armoria* in the cloister. His books were then shelved with other relevant sections of the collection, principally, and most pointedly, as one would expect, with "Libri medicinae" and "Libri historiales." This move back into general use occurred promptly after Brackenbury's death, since the books are appropriately noted in the 1395 catalogue; I have mentioned above the letter mark "I" in Laud misc. 643, for example.[39]

However, this was not MS Laud 603's last move in the house. As I have noted above, the book is also marked by two further, analogous but differing, library marks, "$2^a\ 7^i$ ff" and "$1a\ 7^{mi}$ ff." These indicate its placement, not in a cloister *armorium*, but a new library space, "the slype," or covered passage. Following Piper, this was constructed around 1410, although the shelfmarks in the books date from a good deal later in the century, perhaps after 1450.[40]

It is not clear what one is to make of the differing shelfmarks recorded here. On the whole, I would think the hand cataloguing the manuscript's contents and assigning to book to $2^a\ 7^i$ was apt to have been accurate on this score. But the disparity may mean that the book was originally placed on one side of "the slype" library's seventh lectern ('prima') and only later moved to the other ('secunda'). Given the evidence provided by Durham books with intact shelfmarks, this may have represented a change in perceptions of usefulness. The shelfmark "$1^a\ 7^i$" was clearly reserved for the subject of history, including surviving books like British Library, MS Burney 310 (Eusebius, copied for the house's great scholar, Uthred of Boldon, in 1381). Placing the Laud MS here would merely carry over its earlier shelving among "libri historiales," perhaps only reflecting its opening and longest text.

In contrast, the contents of "$2^a\ 7^i$," i.e., the second side of the seventh lectern, were a mix of medical and classical materials. From the surviving shelfmarks, which run up to "X," this side of the lectern must have held at least twenty-one volumes, of which nine marked examples survive. It shows a mixture of items reminiscent of Brackenbury's collection, although slightly differently poised. Here the combination is of medica and, apparently, grammatica. The latter group of books includes:

> as "C": now Cambridge, Trinity College, MS O.3.22 (1194): Claudian, s. xii ex.
> as "F": now the Laud MS
> as "N": now Oxford, St John's College, MS 154: Aelfric's grammar, s. xi in. and xi ex.
> as "P": now DCL, MS C.IV.5: "Cicero," rhetorics, i.e. *De inventione + Ad Herennium*, s. xii

This reshelving, if that is what it represents, suggests the John of Wales taking precedence over the longer initial historical text of the volume. And the Laud MS presumably remained here for as long as a century and a half, well past the Dissolution.[41]

As I suggested in my opening, following one's nose, while often leading to frustrating dead ends, may equally include benefits. Here a random study of an otherwise ignored book offers considerable gleanings about an understudied but prominent book-feature, the *tabula* or index, as well as subsidiary information about late medieval Durham library practices.

Keble College, Oxford

NOTES

1. 'Quod turpe est semper ex alieno sapere et nichil de suo proferre, 16, ubi bona', the annotator's summary, MS Laud Misc. 603, fol. 97ra. For the text here annotated, see John of Wales, *Compendiloquium* 9.7, edn. fol. 229ra/image 594. I refer to this edition throughout: see the online available *Summa de regimine vitae seu Margarita doctorum* (Venice: Georgius Arrivabenus, 30 July 1496) [ISTC ij00333000, Bod-inc J-161], fols. 167ra–232rb. For convenience, I add to this edition's foliation the image number in the copy reproduced on Proquest. In this printed edition, the *Breviloquium de sapientia* follows immediately, as it does in the manuscript discussed here.
2. See further "Adventures in Libraries," *Textual Cultures* 14.2 (Fall, 2021), 3–16.
3. The book owner Robert Brackenbury was first identified by N. R. Ker, *Medieval Libraries of Great Britain: A List of Surviving Books*, 2nd edn, Royal Historical Society Guides and Handbooks 3 (London: The Royal Historical Society, 1964), 253. Pollard's reference to the book appears at Bodleian Library, MS Pollard 224, fol. 73v; see further note 23.

4. On the text and its circulation, see Wolfgang-Valentin Ikas, *Martin von Troppau (Martinus Polonus), O. P. (d. 1278) in England: Überlieferungs- und Wirkungsgeschichtliche Studien zu dessen Papst- und Kaiserchronik* (Wiesbaden: Reichert, 2002), 33–46 (who misdates this manuscript as "s. xiv ex"). For comparable information on the remaining texts of the manuscript, see Jenny Swanson, *John of Wales: A Study of the Works and Ideas of a Thirteenth-Century Friar*, Cambridge Studies in Medieval Life and Thought, 4th ser. 10 (Cambridge: Cambridge University Press, 1989), 232–257 passim.
5. Otto Pächt and J. J. G. Alexander, *Illuminated Manuscripts in the Bodleian Library, Oxford*, 3 vols (Oxford: Clarendon Press, 1966–73), 3:57–58 (no. 632), apparently saw no inconsistency in the decorative pattern, merely commenting "Good penwork initials."
6. I would simply register a modest doubt as to whether the same individual was responsible for both (although I have difficulty imagining otherwise). Numerals cannot be assigned to a hand with anything like the facility by which one analyzes verbal materials. Moreover, the numeration has been provided with a different pen, with narrower nib, and probably different ink from that visible in the page-foot notations.
7. I ignore here some further textual annotation: a faded note, apparently in plummet (and thus probably extraneous to what I describe) on fol. 65vb; contemporary marginal glossing and identification of topics on fols. 61–62^v and 63^v. These latter examples are not clearly in the same hand as the page-foot notes, but they may represent an original annotative intention, rather sporadic, before a determination that the text deserved more extensive treatment.
8. This chapter—and uniquely John of Wales's discussion of Plato—includes one culturally important reference: "Vnde in dicto libro qui dicitur *Suda* dicitur..." ("Thus, it says in the book called *Suda*," fol. 193ra/522); see Tiziano Dorandi and Michele Trizio, "*Editio Princeps del Liber qui uocatur Suda di Roberto Grossatesta*," *Studia Graeco-Arabica* 4 (2014): 145–149, at 170–173, with extensive collations from *Compendiloquium*. See further "Lost Libraries: The Case of the Oxford Franciscans, c. 1330–40," *Journal of the Early Book Society* 24 (2021): 27–50, at 28–29 and 40 n.2; in contrast to the situation described there, evidence from the 1330s, John's citations must indicate the presence of Robert Grosseteste's autograph of his translation of the *Suda* at Oxford Greyfriars from a very early date, at the latest the 1260s.
9. 2 Nota (by "Et sequitur illud: Hanc mortem dicit Plato philosophis omne appetendum...")
   6 Capitulum 6m. De contemptu omnium mundalium a Platone
   15 De passione mundica Platonis

    20 De testimonio philosophorum
    26 Capitulum 7. De dominacione passionum interiorum. Nota
    39 Quod correccionem differenda tempore ire
10. Nota quod maximum remedium ire est dilacio 30 exemplum infra 35 Quod nichil in fluctu cernitur 35
    (cut off at the foot of the leaf:) Contra dulces ...dias <2>: actually referring to line 1, at the boundary between manuscript fols. 76rb and 76va: "Mori eciam dicitur tunc, cum anima adhuc in corpore constituta, corporeas illecebras, philosophia docente, contemnit et cupiditatem, **dulces insidias**, reliquasque anime exuit passiones" (For he is said to have died when the soul, while still attached to the body, disdains bodily enticements, following philosophy's teachings, and strips from the soul the emotions, other **pleasant attacks**, indeed desire itself).
11. There are a few exceptions, e.g., fol. 70va: the sequence 10, 5, 25, 30, 37; fol. 70vb: 6, 28, 17; fol. 74ra: 6, 13 et 16, 9, 38.
12. One should note that these decorative breaks cannot be associated with production process glitches. One's usual assumption is that "finishing" proceeded quire by quire. Such a view is based on widespread manuscripts' detail, by-the-quire counts (the number of supplied initials or paraphs) designed to facilitate computing the price for "finishing." Here, however, the breaks correspond to no overt codicological division. The only adjacent quire-boundary appears at fol. 84^v, which does correspond with leaves I have earlier mentioned as lineated, but lacking notes (perhaps a signal of incomplete annotation?).
13. Cf. Richard H. and Mary A. Rouse and R. A. B. Mynors, eds, *Registrum Anglie de libris doctorum et auctorum veterum*, Corpus of British Medieval Library Catalogues 2 (London: British Library, 1991), lxxxv–xcvii, a study of the production of the Greyfriars union catalogue of monastic manuscripts, the *Registrum Anglie*.
14. See Dennis Duncan, Index, *A History of the* (London: Allen Lane, 2021), as well as provocative comments in Siegfried Wenzel, "*Distinctiones* and Sermons: The *Distincciones Lathbury* (*Alphabetum morale*) and Other Collections in Fourteenth-Century England," *Mediaeval Studies* 78 (2016):181–202. On memory tools, see Mary Carruthers, *The Book of Memory: A Study of Memory in Medieval Culture*, 2nd edn, Cambridge Studies in Medieval Literature 70 (Cambridge: Cambridge University Press, 2008).
15. For a rough guide to the indexed text, see Swanson's account, *John of Wales*, 172–187. This, rather incongruously, resembles a Masterplots outline, and the text deserves more detailed scrutiny. Contrast Swanson's summary of *Compendiloquium* 8.3-6 (at 186–187) with "The Wisdom of Poetry: John of Wales's Defense," *Journal of Medieval Latin* 27 (2017): 303–326.

16. De Virgilio 18. Quod fuit poetarum preclarissimus et optimus 27.
    Quod Virgilius nomen habuit a uirga 35, et quomodo.
    Quomodo Neapolis, uexata peste sanguissugarum, liberata est per Virgilium proiciendo sanguissugam auream in puteo, etc. 1.
    Quomodo carnes seruauit Virgilius per quingentos annos 10.
    Quod Virgilius muniunt ortum suum aere immobili sicut muro 13.
    Quod Virgilius construxit palacium Rome in quo cuiuslibet regionis ymago campanam quam manu tenebat, quociens illa regio Romane magistati insidiari ausa est 17.
    Quod requisitus Virgilius quamdiu palacium ab eo constructum duraret, respondit quod stabit usque dum uirgo pariat 28.
    For Neckam's text, see *De naturis rerum libri duo...*, ed. Thomas Wright, Rolls Series 34 (London: Longman Green, 1863), 309–310 (2.174). For Virgil the necromancer, see Jan M. Ziolkowski, "Virgil," *The Oxford History of Classical Reception in English Literature: Volume 1: 800–1558*, ed. Rita Copeland (Oxford: Oxford University Press, 2016), 165–186, at 166–167, 176–178.
17. Quod ubi bonus uir est, ibi non est exilium, qui ubi est plura et breuis narr<acio> 39.
18. Et ibi bene de talibus, 'Defferebant enim secum bona sua, scilicet uirtutes; ideo nullum eis exilium erat graue'. Vnde Seneca ad Helbiam, 'Humile tugurium uirtutes recepit; ideo omnibus templis formosius erat cum illic iustitia conspecta erat, continentia, pietas, prudentia, et sic de aliis. Nullus angustus locus qui harum uirtutum magnam turbam capit; nullum graue exilium in quolibet cum tali comitatu ire. Brutus ait se Marcellum uidisse Miulenis exulantem et, quantum natura hominis pateretur, beatissime uiuentem, nec unquam cupidiorem bonarum artium quam eo tempore. Et adiecit uisum sibi se magis in exilium ire, qui sine illo rediturus esset, quam illum in exilium relinqui. Senatusque pro eo rogauit, ne exules essent si sine illo essent. Patria enim carere non est malum, quia forti animo omnis locus patria'.
19. 'Quod precepta faciunt longum iter; exempla breue et efficax 29' (= 3.3.9, fol. 188ra/512).
20. For Holcot's rendition, see Cambridge, Trinity College, MS R.8.16, fols 21^v–22.
21. One might also note the relatively long omission of annotation at fols 78–79 (= 3.4.14–4.5.9, edn fols 1[95]^{rb}–99va/526–34). This hiatus passes over materials on Plato's death, not his life, and ignores a largely canned biography of Aristotle that emphasizes his habits, rather than his teaching.
22. Until the late Alan Piper's extensive notes toward a Durham volume for the "Corpus of British Medieval Library Catalogues" have been edited for publication by Teresa Webber, one still relies upon James Raine jr,

ed., actually the work of Beriah Botfield, *Catalogi veteres librorum Ecclesiae cathedralis Dunelm....*, Surtees Society 7 (London: Nichols, 1838), 46–84 (here at 56). The catalogue entry indicates that the separately produced MS III was part of the book at that time.
23. See D. W. Rollason et al., eds, *The Durham Liber Vitae: London, British Library, MS Cotton Domitian A VII: Edition and Digital Facsimile* ..., 3 vols (London: British Library, 2007), here A. J. Piper, "Biographical Register of Durham Cathedral Priory (1083–1539)," at 3: 259–260; all the books Piper notes here, save one, already appeared in *MLGB* (see note 3).
24. Respectively, *VCH Durham* 3: 157–174 and 3: 321–343.
25. See further Michael Gullick, "The Hand of Simeon of Durham: Further Observations on the 'Durham Martyrology Scribe,'" and "The Two Earliest Manuscripts of the *Libellus de exordio*," *Symeon of Durham: Historian of Durham and the North*, ed. D. W. Rollason (Stamford: Shaun Tyas, 1998), 14–31 and 106–119, respectively; Julian Harrison, "The Mortuary Roll of Turgot of Durham," *Scriptorium* 58 (2004), 67–83.
26. For more detail, see M. B. Parkes, "*Folia librorum quaerere*: Medieval Experience of the Problems of Hypertext and the Index," *Pages from the Past: Medieval Writing Skills and Manuscript Books*, ed. Pamela Robinson and Rivkah Zim (Farnham: Ashgate, 2012), x.
27. For what follows, see "Graham Pollard and 'Oxford *Peciae*': False Starts and Discoveries," *The Library*, 7th ser. 25 (2024): 289–312. I simply note in passing the sole exception to Arabic numbers here: the Roman "xi," rather than "11," appears twice (of six total examples), at fols. 85rb and 96rb (= 4.6, fol. 208va/553; and 8.6, fol. 227^{rb-va}/590-91, respectively). Intermittently, the indexer sought to avoid confusion of the numeral with ".n.," i.e. "enim"?
28. See Rodney M. Thomson, *A Descriptive Catalogue of the Medieval Manuscripts of Merton College, Oxford* (Cambridge: Brewer, 2009), 39. The notes here are much more clearly "indexal" than those of Laud Misc. 603, references to actual entries that would appear in this aid, e.g., on fol. 64ra: "Miraculum 23 / <.>etidinacio 27 / Misericordia Dei, Ira Dei 43 / Oppressio 53 / Ignis, Punicio 57." Just as in the Laud MS, any prepared index is no longer part of this book.
29. Cf. Piper's suggestion, "The Historical Interests of the Monks of Durham," *Symeon of Durham*, 301–332, at 326, that the two copies of Martin of Troppau's chronicle Durham acquired s. xiv, "may well be the product of commercial workshops."
30. For what follows, see Meryl R. Foster, "Thomas of Westoe: A Monastic Book-Buyer at Oxford about 1300," *Viator* 23 (1992): 189–199. For the *tabulae* among his books, which I mention in the next paragraph, see 192 and 198–199 (items 9–10).

31. See Foster 192, 194–196 passim, and especially 195 note 40 and 197 note 53 (on Thomas's index in DCL A.III.31). I have surveyed Thomas's activity from DCL B.IV.41 (writing full text size notes, rendering comparisons difficult with the less than gloss-hand size in Laud) and the more readily comparable DCL C.III.14. I cite Piper, "The Historical Interests," 327. Comparable tables, generally to patristic authors, in more or less contemporary books appear in DCL B.III.27 and 28, B.IV.32; for the donor of the first of these, Thomas Lund, prior of Finchale and Durham subprior (floruit 1309–50) and another persistent annotator, see Piper, *Liber Vitae*, 3: 235–236.
32. The former, mentioned by Graham Pollard at Bodleian Library, MS Pollard 224, fol. 81, as an example of this indexing system, is not quite relevant. The affixed Arabic numerals at column heads that appeared to him column numbering are simply informal running titles identifying the psalm discussed on the leaf. These notations are nonetheless somewhat unusual, since customarily in manuscripts the psalms are unnumbered and recognised by readers, familiar from their liturgical use, by their incipits.
33. For him, see Piper, *Liber Vitae*, 3:239–240; he is recorded as about 1313–1345 or 1346, his index (the only thing Piper has to say of him) in a hand of comparable date.
34. See *Catalogi veteres*, 2 passim, 4 passim, 5–6, 8 passim, 9 ("Libri Guarini"). I am stimulated here by Piper's comments, "The Historical Interests," 312, 315, and 315 note77.
35. For these, see *Catalogi veteres*, 32, 109, "Libri Quintiliani A" (Valerius, marked as for the common armoire) and "Libri diversarum poetarum" D–E (a two-volume Gellius with table). The listing of classical materials in "the spendment" at 108–109 includes many further examples, multiple volumes with Cicero, Sydonius, Quintilian, and an assembly of poets and historians.
36. For Holcot, particularly in his relations with Richard de Bury, see William J. Courtenay, *Schools and Scholars in Fourteenth-Century England* (Princeton: Princeton University Press, 1987), 95–97, 104–106, 133–137.
37. Cited at MS Pollard 224, fol. 78v.
38. On Wessington's use of Martin in collecting historical materials, s. xv in., see Piper, "Historical Interests," 323; for more extensive discussion of Wessington, see R. B. Dobson, *Durham Cathedral Priory 1400-1450* (Cambridge: Cambridge University Press, 1973), esp. 81–113, 378–386. For the further copy of Martin's work (perhaps DCL, MS B.II.35?), see Piper, ibid. 307 and 313 n.65.

39. Ker, *Medieval Libraries*, passim; its materials inherited in the online mlgb3.bodleian.ox.ac.uk, reproduces all the shelfmarks, both 1395 (with page references to the catalogue), and later, the subject of my next paragraph.
40. See Piper, "The Libraries of the Monks of Durham," *Medieval Scribes, Manuscripts and Libraries: Essays Presented to N. R. Ker*, ed. Parkes and Watson (London: Scolar, 1978), 213–249, especially 223–226; and cf. his "Historical Interests," 316 and note 80 (where the cited shelfmark to Laud Misc. 604 is an error for our MS 603).
41. On early disruptions of the collections, see A. I. Doyle, "William Claxton and the Durham Chronicles," *Books and Collectors 1200-1700: Essays Presented to Andrew Watson*, ed. James P. Carley and Colin G. C. Tite (London: British Library, 1997), 335–355, esp. 350–351 (and 354 n.41 on the collection amassed by Christopher Watson in the 1560s or 1570s); and Hanna, "The Thomas Mans, Their Books, and Jesus College Librarianship," *The Library* 7th ser. 21 (2020), 46–73. For the book's passage to William Laud, see generally Coxe-Hunt, *Laudian Manuscripts*, x–xi.

An Unpublished Latin Quatrain of John Gower in a Lincoln College Manuscript

JAMES M. W. WILLOUGHBY AND DAVID R. CARLSON

Oxford, Lincoln College, MS Lat. 68 is a rather scrappy paper volume of *collectanea* on topics in civil law, which contains on folio 78v a short poem of the English poet John Gower (d. 1408) not previously noticed, a Latin quatrain in Leonine hexameters in unisonant disyllabic rhyme,[1] under the heading "H. quartus":[2]

> Electus Christi, pie Rex Henrice, fuisti,
> Qui bene venisti cum propria regna petisti:
> Tu mala vicisti que bonis bona restituisti.
> Det deus assisti tibi gaudia que meruisti.[3]

The copy is a stray, written by a scribe of the second quarter of the fifteenth century, reasonably soon after the poet's death in 1408, by contrast with the other evidence. It occurs on an otherwise blank verso at the end of one of the booklets of this composite manuscript, an assemblage of quires and individual leaves written by many different hands from the mid-fourteenth century to the early fifteenth. The contents throughout are glosses and commentary on the *tituli* and rubrics of the *Corpus iuris civilis*, and there is also a fragmentary copy of Bartolus de Saxoferrato, *De insigniis et armis* (fols. 79r–v, 94r–v). The volume has the appearance of a jurist's working collection, built up over time. The booklet at the end of which the Gower verses occur is largely in the hand of Richard Talvargh, who signed twice in this section (fols. 29v and 64r); he is probably to be identified as the Oxford clerk from the diocese of Exeter, who was admitted to the vicarage of Creed in Cornwall in November 1410.[4] Other names which occur in the manuscript help to identify Oxford as the probable place where this manuscript was assembled. Talvargh's is not, however, the hand of the Gower verses. These are written in a distinctive flourished Anglicana which aims at a Secretary styling. The hand is found again, at a slightly lower register, written on the inside of what was the book's original limp vellum cover (fol. 139v). This is now detached and positioned at the back of the modern binding, making in effect the final two leaves (fols. 138–139). On these leaves, our scribe copied two poems of legalistic interest: the common six lines on cases referred to the bishop, "Qui facit incestum deflorans aut homicida," and a less common poem beginning, "Si quis forte cupit consultus iuris haberi."[5] Other than the Gower verse, these juristic-mnemonic poems are the only near exceptions to the manuscript's concentration on the civilian codes.

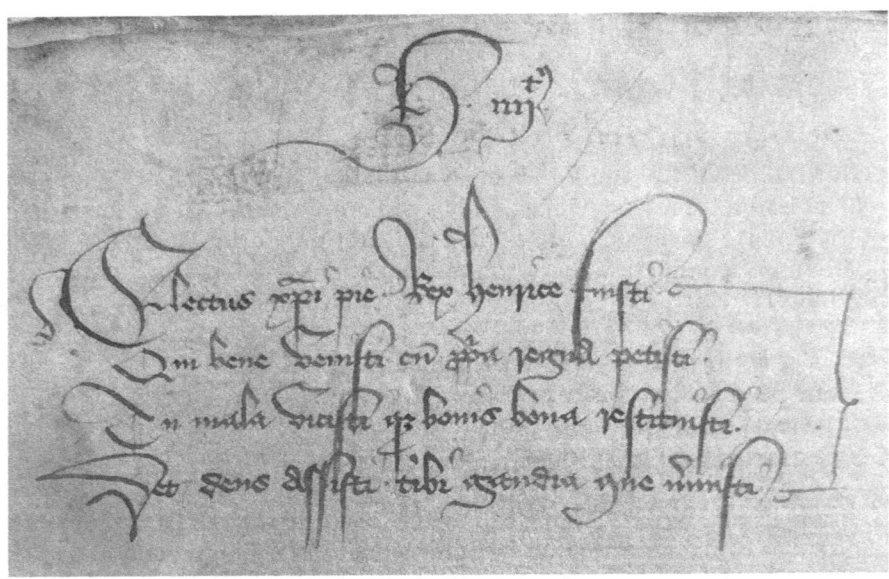

Figure 1. Oxford, Bodleian Library, Lincoln College MS Lat. 68, fol. 78v. Photograph by James M. W. Willoughby. Reproduced by kind permission of the Rector and Fellows of Lincoln College, Oxford.

AN UNPUBLISHED LATIN QUATRAIN 267

In the codicological circumstance, it is not possible to say how the Gower quatrain may have reached the Lincoln College manuscript. Gower's implication in legal practice is known;[6] also likewise attested are the peculiarly conservative-preservative revision-routines he used as a poet.[7] Although the fourth line of the poem in this Lincoln College manuscript copy, "Det deus assisti tibi gaudia que meruisti," is not otherwise known, its first three appear as the beginning of a related Gower item in other circulation. A poem likewise beginning "Electus Christi," but in seven lines, in a different configuration of meter and rhyme (the final seventh line is a pentameter, and its lines 5–7 have a different disyllabic Leonine rhyme in *-ata*), formed a part of the mutable Latin apparatus of Gower's substantial English poem—his only long predominantly English poem other than the *Confessio amantis*—now called *In Praise of Peace*, published to honor the accession of Henry IV probably in late 1399:[8]

Electus Christi, pie rex Henrice, fuisti
Qui bene venisti cum propria regna petisti:
Tu mala vicisti que bonis bona restituisti;
Et populo tristi noua gaudia contribuisti.
Est michi spes lata quod adhuc per te renouata
Succedent fata veteri probitate beata:
  Est tibi nam grata gracia sponte data.[9]

In the copy of *In Praise of Peace* in the "Trentham" manuscript (London, British Library MS Additional 59495)—a manuscript believed to be close to Gower, incorporating the poet's autograph[10]—the seven-line "Electus Christi" verses occur as head-verses (fol. 5r), prefacing the English poem (fols. 5r–10v); and then the poem's 385 lines of English stanzaic verse are followed by more Latin apparatus: Gower's "Rex celi deus" in fifty-six lines of unrhymed elegiacs (fols. 10v–11r), with "Quicquid homo scribat," a twelve-line version of Gower's valediction "in fine" again in unrhymed elegiacs, added on the manuscript's final page (fol. 39v).[11] The 1532 William Thynne edition of Chaucer has much the same matter but in different arrangement, evidently from a different line of textual descent: to begin, under the heading "Johan Gower / Unto the worthy and noble kynge Henry the fourth," the English alone of *In Praise of Peace* (fol. 375v–377v), followed by the seven-line "Electus Christi" (fol. 377v) and yet another version of the "Quicquid homo scribat" "in fine" verses (fols. 377v–378r), but nothing of or like the "Rex celi deus."

An hypothesis that Gower circulated something of these "Electus Christi" verses separately before their incorporation in the compound-complex *In Praise of Peace* may be corroborated by another stray copy, like that in the

Lincoln College manuscript and likewise un- or under-reported. For another copy of "Electus Christi," in seven lines again but without any of the English *In Praise of Peace*, occurs in the manuscript London, British Library, Cotton MS Julius F. vii, fol. 167r, one of the books in which the antiquary William Worcester (d. ca. 1482–1485) kept notes of his extensive miscellaneous researches:[12]

> Electus Christi pie rex Henrice fuisti
> Qui bene venisti cum propria regna petisti
> Tu mala vicisti que bonis bona restituisti
> Et populo tristi noua gaudia contribuisti
> Est michi spes lata quod adhuc parte revocata
> Succedent fata veteri probitate beata
>   Et tibi nam grata gracia sponte data.[13]

Although ordinarily Worcester provided information on his notes' provenance, including dates and places of his collections, there is none in the present case; and so again, though the hand is uniformly Worcester's own, the codicological circumstance (including the absence of the otherwise related *In Praise of Peace* matter again) makes it difficult to imagine how the copy reached the notebook.

The evidence of the Lincoln College manuscript and the Worcester notebook may suggest that these two stray "Electus Christi" copies were excerpted from an already compound-complex *In Praise of Peace*.[14] In other words, any putative revision in the case of Gower's "Electus Christi" verses may have been scribal, rather than authorial, making something brief and independent out of what had already formed a part of something grander, namely the *In Praise of Peace*, Latin and English, as in the varied configurations of the Trentham manuscript and Thynne's 1532 Chaucer edition. An impediment to this hypothesis of scribal intervention by way of excerption would be the anomalous but still properly rhymed fourth-line of the Lincoln College copy, otherwise unattested, but only if the line were written by Gower. The one line is too short a sample to admit certainly, however; and the line's rhyme, an easy one though odd, was given already by the first three lines, shared in all the versions.[15] The one line could have been fabricated by almost anyone familiar with the late-medieval verse-style of the sort that Gower was using late in his career, including the Oxford-trained legists who wrote the Lincoln College manuscript, copying other such verse into it.

On the other hand, another hypothesis might better avail. For the pattern of Gower's revisions of his own verse is clear, generally speaking. In rewriting, Gower's poems became longer, by accretion of lines, and came to be incorporated into grander poetic entities, compounded of multiple moveable parts. In revision, his poems changed from shorter to longer and from simple to compound-complex. To impose such a pattern on the evidence for the versions of Gower's "Electus Christi" presented herein would be relatively simpler: the "Electus Christi" verses grew from the four lines of the Lincoln College manuscript to seven all elsewhere, augmented in length and metrical complexity; also, from an independent, separate epigram-like poem, be it shorter or longer, in the Lincoln College manuscript and Worcester's notebook, to one component among others of the greater agglomeration, an English *In Praise of Peace* with its more and less extensive Latin apparatus.

Winchester College and Université d'Ottawa

NOTES

For much counsel, thanks are due Daniel Wakelin, Eric Weiskott, Stephanie Batkie, and Bard Swallow.

1. For the form's significance in Gower's Latin verse, see Eric Weiskott, "Gower's Quatrains: Language, Rhyme, Occasion," *English Studies* 103 (2022), 777–786.
2. "H." in the heading might well be expanded, too, as if it were an abbreviation for Henricus or the like, except that Gower used the same form causa metri in verse (where it scans as a *longum*), as for example in the quatrain "H. aquile pullus," in *Complete Works of John Gower*, ed. G.C. Macaulay, 4 vols. (Oxford: Clarendon Press, 1899–1902), 4.345, and *John Gower: The Minor Latin Works*, ed. R.F. Yeager (Kalamazoo, MI: Medieval Institute Publications, 2005), 46. For other instances of the usage in Gower, see Robert Epstein, "Literal Opposition: Deconstruction, History, and Lancaster," *Texas Studies in Literature and Language* 44 (2002), esp. 19–21.
3. "Elect of Christ thou wert, o pious king Henry; and thou didst well indeed when thou camest again into a realm already properly thine own: thou it wast who here overmastered wrongs and restored rights to the righteous. May God grant thee be adjudged the joys which thou hast merited." The edition of the verses in the manuscript (henceforth *L*) incorporates tacit expansions of the manuscript's abbreviations and editorial punctuation, as do all other quotations from early books herein.
4. A.B. Emden, *A Biographical Register of the University of Oxford to 1500*, 3 vols. (Oxford: Clarendon, 1957–1959), 3.1847.
5. Respectively, nos. 15482 and 17926 in Hans Walther, *Initia carminum ac versum Medii Aevi posterioris latinorum*, 2 vols. (Göttingen: Vandenhoeck & Ruprecht, 1959–1969). In Oxford, Merton College, MS 16,

fol. 219v, the former is preceded by a titulus, "Versus Willelmi in Clementinis capitulo duodecimo," identifying William of Mont Lauzun's commentary on the Clementines.

6. Gower's competence at law is established in Matthew Giancarlo, *Parliament and Literature in Late Medieval England* (Cambridge: Cambridge University Press, 2007), 92–112; for the literary consequence, see Candace Barrington, "John Gower's Legal Advocacy and 'In Praise of Peace,'" in John Gower, *Trilingual Poet*, ed. Elisabeth Dutton (Cambridge: Brewer, 2010), esp. 114–117, and "The Spectral Advocate in John Gower's Trentham Manuscript," in *Theorizing Legal Personhood in Late Medieval England*, ed. Andreea D. Boboc (Leiden: Brill, 2015), 94–118; also, Conrad van Dijk, *John Gower and the Limits of the Law* (Cambridge: Brewer, 2013).

7. See Weiskott, "Cumulative Revision in John Gower's *Quicquid homo scribat*," *English Studies* 103 (2022), 547–554, with Jonathan Hsy, "Blind Advocacy: Blind Readers, Disability Theory, and Accessing John Gower," *Accessus* 1.1.2 (2013), 12–18. Some other instances of recursive revision are analyzed in D. R. Carlson, "Gower on Henry IV's Rule: The Endings of the *Cronica tripertita* and its Texts," *Traditio* 62 (2007), 207–236.

8. For the date and context, see Weiskott, "'Loquela gravis iuvat:' Gower's *O deus immense* and the Place of Poetry, 1398–1400," *Studies in the Age of Chaucer* 45 (2023), 232–240. For Gower's development of such variable Latin apparatuses as occur with *In Praise of Peace*, see esp. D.A. Pearsall, "Gower's Latin in the *Confessio Amantis*," in *Latin and Vernacular: Studies in Late-Medieval Texts and Manuscripts*, ed. A.J. Minnis (Cambridge: Brewer, 1989), 13–25; also, Siân Echard, "With Carmen's Help: Latin Authorities in the *Confessio Amantis*," *Studies in Philology* 95 (1998), 1–40, and Richard K. Emmerson, "Reading Gower in a Manuscript Culture: Latin and English in Illustrated Manuscripts of the *Confessio Amantis*," *Studies in the Age of Chaucer* 21 (1999), 143–186.

9. "Elect of Christ thou wert, o pious king Henry; and thou didst well indeed when thou camest again into a realm already properly thine own: thou it wast who here overmastered wrongs and restored rights to the righteous; and, to a late mournful people, thou didst contribute joy anew. My broad-extending hope is that the fates shall raise up, equal to our blessed probity of old, what has as yet been renewed but through thee: for thankworthy divine favour has been thee freely granted." This version of the poem is ed. Macaulay, *Complete Works*, 3.481; also, ed. Michael Livingston, in Yeager, *John Gower The Minor Latin Works*, 107; and *The Chaucerian Apocrypha: A Selection*, ed. Kathleen Forni (Kalamazoo, MI: Medieval Institute Publications, 2005), 132. The text is

edited here in the orthography of the Trentham manuscript, London, British Library, Additional MS 59495, henceforth *T*, possibly as much as a century earlier than the 1532 printed edition, *The workes of Geffray Chaucer newly printed, with dyuers workes whiche were neuer in print before*, ed. William Thynne (London: Godfray, 1532 [= ESTC S106664]), henceforth *Thynne*, which uses a classicised spelling. The textual apparatus supplied (here as well as below) is exclusive: the *lemmata* are to be taken to represent all the textual witnesses not individually named after the bracket: 3 vicisti que] vicistique *Thynne* || 7 gracia] gratia *Thynne*.

10. On the manuscript, see Sebastian Sobecki, "*Ecce patet tensus*: The Trentham Manuscript, *In Praise of Peace*, and John Gower's Autograph Hand," *Speculum* 90 (2015), 925–959; also, Arthur W. Bahr, "Reading Codicological Form in John Gower's Trentham Manuscript," *Studies in the Age of Chaucer* 33 (2011), 219–262.

11. "Rex celi deus" in *Complete Works*, ed. Macaulay, 4.343–344; *Minor Latin Works*, ed. Yeager, 42–45 and 72–75; and see Carlson, "Gower's Early Latin Poetry," *Mediaeval Studies* 65 (2003), 299–304. The "Quicquid homo scribat" versions are *Complete Works*, ed. Macaulay, 4.365–366, and *Minor Latin Works*, ed. Yeager, 46–49 and 79; also, Carlson, "Rhyme Distribution Chronology of John Gower's Latin Poetry," *Studies in Philology* 104 (2007), 33–35.

12. For the biography, see Catherine Nall and Daniel Wakelin, *William Worcester, The Boke of Noblesse and the English Texts from its Codicil*, EETS OS 362 (Oxford: Early English Text Society, 2023), xv–xviii; and on Worcester's notebooks, see Wakelin, "William Worcester Writes a History of his Reading," *New Medieval Literatures* 7 (2005), esp. 57–67.

13. Although the copy's occurrence was noted by Macaulay, *Complete Works*, 4.lxxi; also, by Francis Aidan Gasquet, "The Note Books of William Worcester," *Downside Review* 13 (1894), 244, it has not been collated: 3 vicisti que] vicistique *Thynne* || 5 parte revocata] per te renouata *T Thynne* || 7 Et tibi] Est tibi *T Thynne* || gracia] gratia *Thynne*. The phrase here in 5, "quod adhuc parte revocata" ("what has as yet been but part-restored"), may be preferable to the phrase in the *In Praise of Peace* texts *T* and *Thynne*, "quod adhuc per te renouata" ("what has as yet been renewed but through thee"), for better sense.

14. Other excerptions of Gower are analyzed in Mimi Ensley, "'Profitable' Gower: Commonplacing and the Early Modern *Confessio Amantis*," *Journal of English and Germanic Philology* 121 (2022), 202–226.

15. The rhyme of the present passive infinitive in the last line of the Lincoln College "Electus Christi," "Det deus *assisti* tibi gaudia que meruisti," might be likened to the rhyme Gower uses in *Cultor in ecclesia* 7, "Qui pastor Cristi iusto cupit ordine *sisti*." But second-person singular per-

fect forms, otherwise relatively uncommon in consequence of the preference for more "polite" second-person plurals, are not much used for rhyme-making in Gower. Excepting the "Electus Christi" verses, having rhymes of the odd form six times in its first four lines, the same rhyme occurs elsewhere only three times in Gower: twice in *Cronica Tripertita*, 2.329, "Classem *fecisti* Francorum, quos *domuisti*" (amongst the *Cronica*'s 1062 rhymed lines); and once in the poorly attested *Confessio amantis* envoy beginning "Ad laudem Cristi, quem tu, virgo, *peperisti*," in *Complete Works*, ed. Macaulay, 3: 468; on it, see Siân Echard, "Last Words: Latin at the End of the *Confessio amantis*," in *Interstices: Studies in Middle English and Anglo-Latin Texts*, ed. R.F. Green and L.R. Mooney (Toronto: University of Toronto Press, 2004), 103–104. On the other hand, the odd rhyming of second-person singular perfect forms was used to excess by other contemporary Anglo-Latin poets. For example, the late fourteenth-century Anglo-Latin poem of the "Anonymous of Calais" known as *Crécy* has eighteen such rhymes in a single ten-line passage (*Crécy* 55–64), as well as a number of other rhymed lines built of them: 27–28, 276–277, and 293–294, "Que prius infame nomen fetens *habuisti*, | Insignis fame nomen sub eo *meruisti*" having the same rhyme as the fourth line of the Lincoln College "Electus Christi." *Crécy* is here cited from the edition in A.G. Rigg, "Propaganda of the Hundred Years War: Poems on the Battles of Crécy and Durham (1346): A Critical Edition," *Traditio* 54 (1999), 177–188; though on the authorship, see Bard Swallow, "Common Authorship and the 'Anonymous of Calais,'" *Journal of Medieval Latin* 33 (2023), 89–118.

Descriptive Reviews

SARA J. CHARLES
The Medieval Scriptorium: Making Books in the Middle Ages.
London: Reaktion Books, 2024.
352 pp. 47 color and 5 b&w plates.

Sara J. Charles closes her book *The Medieval Scriptorium: Making Books in the Middle Ages* with the wish that medieval manuscripts "may ... live on to delight further generations" (313). If delighting in a thing requires knowing something about it, this lively book is already calling forth those future generations, for between its engaging style and its encyclopedic scope, it opens the world of manuscript studies to a wide range of readers. I use the term "manuscript studies," but Charles's title claims the "medieval scriptorium" as her topic. That title alone may draw many readers to the book, conjuring, as it may, an image of a large tranquil space, probably in a monastery, in which rows of scribes labor in silence, all in the glow of shafts of heavenly light beaming in through the room's well-placed windows. Dispelling this image in the book's opening pages, Charles explains that if this kind of scriptorium existed at all, it was very uncommon. In its place, she posits a more expansive vision of a medieval scriptorium, a space that existed concretely, conceptually and even metaphysically. For Charles, the "medieval scriptorium" was extant on three levels: as any real-world place of writing, as a "centre of manuscript production" (71, 134), and as a "spiritual realm"

(136). As her book also makes clear, the medieval scriptorium was in many ways the engine of the intellectual, technological, and social changes that occurred during the European Middle Ages, changes that partook of both local and intercontinental networks.

The book's seven main chapters take a mostly chronological approach to developing Charles's layered concept of the medieval scriptorium. Thus, in chapter 1, "The Beginnings," we learn about the history of writing, writing surfaces, and the codex, noting its ties to Christianity. Chapter 2, "Monasticism and Manuscript Production in the West, 500–1050," takes us from Benedict's Monte Casino and Cassiodorus's Vivarium to the Irish monks and their far-reaching influence on book design, and to Charlemagne and the many book-related innovations he supported, including the standardization of Caroline minuscule and the founding of cathedral schools. Chapter 3, "*Locus scribendi*—The Place of Writing," lingers around the turn of the millennium, presenting a wealth of evidence indicating that monastic scribes worked primarily in solitude, thus elevating the *locus scribendi* to a "spiritual plane" (160). Inching forward in time, the next two chapters, "Material World: Parchment and Ink" and "Illumination," dive into the technical details of "Making Books in the Middle Ages," the subtitle of Charles's book. Together these chapters take us from sheep, goats, and goose feathers to bejeweled bindings with twenty-four pages on "painting and pigments" (201) along the way: two chapters that could stand alone as a book-making manual. In chapter 6, "The Twelfth-Century Renaissance," Charles takes us on a tour of a transformed "medieval scriptorium": the new centers of manuscript production situated in urban spaces near universities, spaces inhering in far-flung networks of exchange of physical, intellectual, and artistic materials, commercial spaces producing books on a broad spectrum of topics—with a range of new formats to match—for whole new categories of readers. Paradoxically, the flourishing demand for books that began in this period "sowed the seeds," Charles observes, for "the decline of manuscript production" (274). These seeds bore fruit in the form of Johannes Gutenberg's new machine, which is the story Charles takes up in chapter 7, "The End of the Scriptorium."

That Charles begins this book by debunking a popular image of a medieval scriptorium does not mean she is against images, imagination, or sensory details as tools for immersing readers in the multi-faceted medieval scriptorium. Most striking in this regard, she prefaces each chapter with a creative nonfiction vignette, putting readers in a minidrama pertaining to that chapter. In this way, before we read "The Beginnings," we follow a day in the writing life of Paula, Jerome's friend and collaborator, in which she deals with the trickiness of writing on papyrus. At the head of successive chapters, we meet Ciarán, an Irish monk transplanted to Luxeuil, who is struggling to fashion letters in the Merovingian script; the librarian of a tenth-century French convent as she prepares the cloister for the sisters' day of copying; William the parchment maker, who is proud to contribute to the "beautiful works" (162) the monks make; Gisela, an illuminator in a German convent who is beginning a painting of Mary and the infant Jesus; Sara, beginning her day managing a book workshop on Catte Street in Oxford; and, last but not least, one Johannes in his Mainz workshop in the year 1450, about to demonstrate his "new 'fast writing machine'" (275) to a group of curious townspeople. Charles brims each of these vignettes with appeals to readers' senses: for a few examples, Ciarán misses the "bracing air" (57) of Ireland; as Gisela grinds lapis lazuli grains she "feels them rub against the weight of the grinding stone, creating a rasping sound" (192); shopping for saffron for one of her pigments, Sara "lingers .... to inhale the mingling smells of ginger, cinnamon and pepper" (237). Apart from these vignettes, Charles takes every opportunity to flesh out the realities of making manuscripts, a process that was, as she puts it, "dirty, smelly, often boring and certainly back-breaking" (12). The book's fifty-two images—most of them in color—are a help as well.

While Charles's penchant for the sensory serves very well to bring the medieval scriptorium to life, several additional features of her book work both to demystify and to update the field of manuscript studies for a new generation—and to delight it as well. On the former score, Charles is careful throughout the book to gloss terms that might stump a general reader: the "Iberian Peninsula" is present day Spain and Portugal (75), for instance, and a "colophon" is "from the Greek word for 'finishing touch'" (145). She also supplies a generous glossary at the end of the book along with a list of further readings. In the category of updates, Charles notes the forced contributions to book making on the part of enslaved people, as scribes in the Greek and Roman periods and ongoingly as miners of orpiment—otherwise known as "arsenic sulphide" (213), a toxic ingredient for a yellow pigment. For a brighter update, female scribes are well represented in Charles's medieval scriptorium, as the list of vignettes may have already suggested. For readers' delight, Charles is a generous dispenser of fun or eye-opening facts: for just a few examples, earwax will get rid of bubbles in gesso, the late sixth-century Cathach of St. Columba likely required the skins of "18-27½ calves" (70), and the word "miniature" comes from the term for a red lead pigment called minium. These examples also hint at just how thoroughly this book was researched.

It is a shame that the book's many images do not have figure numbers to link them more clearly to the text and that their captions do not always include shelf marks and folio numbers. These problems are remedied, however, by the photo acknowledgements, which include the page numbers on which images appear along with their shelf marks and folio numbers.

Charles's *The Medieval Scriptorium* is bound to generate a new and fervent interest in medieval manuscripts. In whole or in parts, the book will also be useful in many pedagogical settings, from secondary school classrooms to graduate seminar rooms. For seasoned scholars, the two chapters on technical matters may be of particular interest.

Martha Rust, New York University

LAURA CLEAVER, DANIELLE MAGNUSSON, HANNAH MORCOS, AND ANGÉLINE RAIS, EDS.
The Pre-Modern Manuscript Trade and its Consequences, ca. 1890–1945.
Leeds: ARC Humanities, 2024. 471 pp.

The thirty essays in *The Pre-Modern Manuscript Trade and its Consequences, ca. 1890–1945* weave together an important narrative about the book trade in England, France, Germany, Italy, Canada, and the United States, one that is foundational to the formation of library collections and the development of medieval studies as a field of inquiry. This rich collection is the result of a symposium sponsored by the Cultural Values and the International Trade in Medieval European Manuscripts, ca. 1900–1945 (CULTIVATE MSS) project, funded by the European Research Council in 2020. A project aim was to examine the economic trade in medieval manuscripts and show how it shaped the development of private and public collections, including those in university libraries. Another aim was to illustrate how the trade in manuscripts directly shaped modern scholarship on the medieval period. For those invested in the history of books and the transmission of objects, there is much of to be gleaned among the case studies offered, which are divided into three sections. The following outlines the three parts with citation of chapters for each section.

Part I: "Dealers and the Market" has seven essays: Pierre-Louis Pinault, "Bernard Quaritch Ltd., Bibliophilic Clubs and the Trade in Medieval Manuscripts ca. 1878–1939"; A.S.G. Edwards, "Selling Middle English Manuscripts to North America up to 1945"; Danielle Magnusson, "Dollars and Drama: Early English Plays and the American Book Trade 1906–1926"; Livia Marcelli, "The Fates of the Manuscripts from the Vallicelliana Library of Rome at the nd of the Nineteenth Century"; Katharina Kaska and Christoph Egger, "Fuelling the Market: Sales from Austrian Monasteries 1919–1938"; Angéline Rais, "Jacques Rosenthal's Marketing Strategies: An Analysis of the *Bibliotheca medii aevi* Margaret Connolly, "From Drawing Room to Sale-room: Albums of Medieval Manuscript Cuttings in the 1920s"; and Lisa Fagin Davis, "Buying and Breaking with Philip and Otto."

Part 2: "Buyers" features thirteen essays: Francesca Manzari, "Illuminations from Northern and Central Italy in the Collection of the Dealer Vittorio Forti"; Rhiannon Lawrence-Francis, "The One That Got Away: How Lord Brotherton Lost Out on a Book and Founded a Library"; Karen Deslattes Winslow, "Becoming a Gentleman Collector: Alfred Chester Beatty's Influence on Calouste Sarkis Gulbenkian's Manuscript Collection"; Martina Lanza, "A Private Library and the Making of the Middle Ages in Florence: Piero Ginori Conti's Collection"; Paola Paesano, "The 'Calenzio Deal' and the Auction of the Oldest Vallicelliana Codices, 1874–1916"; Federico Botana, "The Acquisitions of Florentine Public Libraries 1900–1935"; Hannah Morcos, "Private Purses and 'National' Possessions: The French Acquisitions from the Phillipps Library (1908)"; Jérémy Delmulle and Hanno Wijsman, "Provenance Research on Lost Manuscripts: The Case of Louvain University Library"; James C.P. Ranahan, "To Buy, or Not to Buy? Market Forces and the Making of the Shakespeare Birthplace Trust's Collections"; Toby Burrows, "Women as Owners and Collectors in de Ricci's *Census of Medieval and Renaissance Manuscripts in the United States and Canada*"; Natalia Fantetti, "'A most fascinating and dangerous pursuit': The Book Collecting of Isabella Stewart Gardner"; Jill Unkel, "The Collector, Edith Beatty (1886–1952)"; and Nathalie Roman, "Paul Durrieu (1855–1925): Art Collecting and Scholarly Expertise."

Part 3: "Scholarly and Creative Engagements" offers nine essays: Nigel Ramsay, "Seymour de Ricci and William Roberts: Recorders and Analysts of the Market"; Christine Jakobi-Mirwald, "Stories of an Antiquary: The Legacy of M. R. James"; Kate Falardeau, "Phillipps MS 24275 and the Nineteenth- and Early Twentieth-Century Historiography of Bede's Martyrology"; Alan Mitchell, "Manuscripts and Meaning: The Biography and Value of John Ruskin's Blue Psalter, Brussels, Bibliothèque Royale de Belgique (KBR), MS IV 1013"; Nora Moroney, "Translation, Tradition, and Tracing the History of an Irish Manuscript Primer"; Dongwon Esther Kim,

"The Bedford Psalter and Hours: Making and Un-making National Identity in the Acquisition of an 'English' Manuscript"; Alexandra Plane, "The National Collection That Never Was: The 'Failure' of Henry Yates Thompson's Experimental National Gallery Exhibition"; Gaia Grizzi, "Exhibiting Italian Books Outside Italy: Tammaro De Marinis and the 1926 *Exposition du livre italien*"; and William P. Stoneman, "A Reference Book for Scholars and Collectors: Eric Millar's *English Illuminated Manuscripts*, 1926–1928."

This is a book I eagerly read—and enjoyed learning from. Highlights include insights about bibliographical societies, including the Roxburghe Club, Grolier Club, and Société des Bibliophiles français; dealers such as Philip Duschnes, Hans Peter Kraus, Bernard Quaritch, A.S.W. Rosenbach, and Jacques Rosenthal; and collecting families, including Alfred Chester Beatty, Henry Huntington, and J.P. Morgan. More engaging still are the descriptions of women collectors, including Edith Beatty, Dorothy Una Ratcliffe, and Isabella Stewart Gardner. Those who stole books and sold them are also documented. The most compelling essays are Pinault's investigation of Bernard Quaritch's work securing manuscripts for bibliographical society members and his efforts to control auction room prices; Rais's discussion of how Jacques Rosenthal's marketing practices shaped scholarship in the field; Connolly's use of sale catalogues for information about middle-class collecting and album making; Fagin Davis's discussion of Otto Ege and Philip C. Duschnes's collaboration in biblioclasm, and how Ege's widow continued his practices; Manzari's description of the illicit acquisition in Italy of fragments for the North American market; Paesano's presentation of how Fr. Generoso Calenzo appropriated and sold Vallicelliana manuscripts; Burrows's biographies of North American women owners and collectors; Unkel's study of Edith Beatty's robust collecting and giving of medieval manuscripts; Jakobi-Mirwald's account of the career of M.R. James, the cataloguer of so many English manuscript collections; Mitchell's investigation of John Ruskin as a collector; Kim's analysis of the Bedford Psalter and Hours; and Grizzi's discussion of how book exhibitions frame knowledge.

The Pre-Modern Manuscript Trade and its Consequences, ca. 1890–1945 is published as part of ARC Humanities' Collection Development, Cultural Heritage, and Digital Humanities book series. One other publication from this ARC project is also published in the series: *The Economics of the Manuscript and Rare Book Trade, ca. 1890–1939*, edited by Federico Botana and Laura Cleaver. This book series is an ideal venue to develop several complementary volumes that could broaden our understanding of the movement of books across time and geography. As this collection of essays demonstrates, trade in books and scrolls has much to teach us about colonialism, missionary movements, educational projects, and more. One hopes that this project can be emulated across southern and eastern Europe, with a focus on dealers and buyers and on collections development and dismemberment, and beyond into African, Middle Eastern, and Asian book collecting, as well as book dissemination in Central and South America.

    Virginia Blanton, University of Missouri Curators' Distinguished Professor

RICHARD GAMESON, ANDREW BEEBY, FLAVIA FIORILLO, CATHERINE NICHOLSON, PAOLA RICCIARDI, AND SUZANNE REYNOLDS
The Pigments of British Medieval Illuminators: A Scientific and Cultural Study.
London: Archetype Publications Ltd., 2023.
xvi + 471 pp. 287 color plates and graphs; 27 tables,

This reviewer has profited from the application of non-invasive scientific techniques in the course of her own research on British illuminated manuscripts, but has wondered how these procedures might be productively harnessed on a large scale. The volume under review provides an answer to this question. As the book's preface and introduction explain, *The Pigments of British Medieval Illuminators* is the product of a decade's worth of research undertaken by "Team Pigment" (Durham and Northumbria universities)—a group of manuscript scholars, research and heritage scientists, and curators led by Richard Gameson of Durham—sometimes working in collaboration with the MINIARE project led by Stella Panayotova and her former colleagues at the University of Cambridge.[1] Team Pigment analyzed the chemical composition and modes of application of colorants, metals, and glazes in over 300 manuscripts made between the sixth and late fifteenth century. Their findings are presented by integrating them, and the manuscripts themselves, into their larger historical, geographical, art historical, and cultural contexts. In addition to its chronological breadth and extensive evidentiary base, a further strength of this study is the investigators' decision to examine not just deluxe volumes but also more modestly produced ones. This approach allows them to identify norms and outliers in respect to the use of colorants and metals, and to pinpoint and contextualize the emergence or disuse of particular pigments and techniques.

Chapter I, "The Pigments, Dyes and Inks, and How Best to Identify Them," opens with lucid explanations of the scientific and imaging procedures employed to analyze the pigments, including fiber-optic reflectance spectroscopy (FORS), Raman spectroscopy, multispectral and hyperspectral imaging (MSI, HSI), X-ray fluorescence spectroscopy (XRF), and microscopy. The rest of the chapter comprises précis of the sources, structures, and methods of production of the various pigments, metals, glazes, and binding mediums, and explains which scientific techniques can be used to identify them. Chapters II to VI proceed chronologically. Each chapter opens with an overview of the main historical, religious, political, economic, and cultural developments and events that provide the context for the manuscripts. All but Chapter II include helpful tables that present key findings of the text. The chapters' conclusions are often used not merely to summarize their contents, but also to examine particular issues at greater length. Each chapter closes with a list of the manuscripts analyzed, the colorants and metals they contain, and helpful documentation.

Within this basic framework, each chapter organizes the material in a manner well-suited to the historical and art historical evidence. The manuscripts examined in Chapter II, "Conversion and Colour, c. 600–c. 900," few of which are securely dated, are grouped according to place or possible region of production: Northumbria, including Lindisfarne and Wearmouth-Jarrow; Kent, and specifically Canterbury; Mercia; Southumbria more generally; or Wales and Scotland. Chapter III, "Conquests and Chromophores, c. 900–c. 1066," presents the material in thematic sections that encompass the major events, developments, and personalities of the turbulent Anglo-Saxon period, including the reigns of the early kings Alfred, Edward the Elder, and Athelstan, the monastic reform movement and the revival of important ecclesiastical foundations that stimulated southern England's "bibliographic renaissance" (83), and the period of renewed Viking incursions and Danish rule. Because Chapter IV, "Normans, Angevins, Plantagenets and Pigments, c. 1066–c. 1250," eschews siloing the material by style-period, the reader gets a clear picture of continuities and developments in the use of pigments and gold across a wide selection of late Anglo-Saxon, Romanesque, and early Gothic books and genres, including herbals, saints' lives, patristic works, psalters, Bibles, and bestiaries. Among the key themes of Chapter V, "A Time of Expansion: Colour c. 1250–c. 1360," are the impact on illuminators' palettes of global trade and the emergence of mosaic gold as witnessed in a broad array of manuscripts produced in London-Westminster, Oxford, East Anglia, and elsewhere. Chapter VI, "Colour after the Black Death, c. 1360–c. 1485," presents the material in three roughly equal sub-periods: ca. 1360–ca. 1400, the first half of the fifteenth century, and the second half. The key development that distinguishes the fifteenth century from its predecessor is British artists' adoption in its early decades of highly-refractive lead-tin yellow, which appears in the pages of nearly every book type analyzed, from literary manuscripts and books of hours to statute collections. The conclusion offers a summary of the investigators' findings with respect to British artists' pigment use. There follow three appendices, the first of which provides a welcome edition and translation of the eleventh-century recipe collection traditionally known as *De coloribus et mixtionibus*, as well as indices and an extensive bibliography.

Among the most compelling contributions of this rich, dense study are the hypotheses it offers concerning the choices, preferences, and situations of the illuminators themselves, whose skills, knowledge, and resourcefulness are kept to the fore. For example, the illuminator of the frontispiece (now fol. 30v) in the early eighth-century Vespasian Psalter made in Canterbury varied his techniques to suit the material to be painted. While the artist used "some overpainting and much overdrawing" (57) to render the figures of David and his scribes and musicians, in executing the non-figural, ornamental elements he applied the pigments in areas of unblended color separated by "tiny reserved areas of blank parchment" (53)—a technique characteristic of the intricate ornamentation of Northumbrian books like the Lindisfarne Gospels. The ready availability and relative inexpensiveness of good-quality imported lapis lazuli during the tenth through twelfth centuries are affirmed by its liberal use in manuscripts as diverse as the copiously-illustrated Old English Hexateuch, Romanesque giant Bibles, and "ascetic" Cistercian books. That only one of the several artists of the Harley 603 Psalter employed azurite and vermilion for blue and red, rather than lapis and ochre, lends support to the idea that while the original team achieved their work before the Danish sack of Canterbury in 1011, the lone "continuator" (112) picked up the project sometime after that cataclysmic event. Readers will appreciate the characterization of the elaborate Beatus pages of some Gothic psalters as "laborator[ies] for coloristic and decorative experimentation" (220), and the many observations concerning the possible devotional, cognitive, or mimetic functions of different pigments and palettes. Equally valuable are the discussions of guide letters for colors, and the dramatic micrographs and details of the illuminations.

In the case of some topics, one wishes the authors had pushed further the implications of their analyses. In the discussion of "pigment choice and proximate location" of heraldry in the early fourteenth-century Pabenham-Clifford Hours, for instance, they might have considered not only how heraldic shields "express" "dynastic and individual piety" and "sacralise the space in which [donor and/or owner] figures pray" (257), but also how, in tandem with marginal imagery, the shields activate and inflect, and are activated and inflected by the texts and pictures they frame, thereby fusing the acts of prayer, meditation, reading, memorialization, and the construction of the social and political as well as devout self.[2] And, the overviews opening the later chapters occasionally paint aspects of the historical situation with too broad a brush. In this reviewer's view, for example, the statement that during the earliest waves of plague "the patronage and production of illuminated manuscripts of the highest quality continued unabated" (219) is not supported by the manuscript evidence. Overall, however, the overviews are solid introductions to the material.

While some scholars will prefer to consult only those portions of the book that are relevant to their research needs, this reviewer recommends reading it cover to cover. *The Pigments of British Medieval Illuminators* offers a history of British illumination from an important, previously understudied angle. It is recommended to all with an interest in medieval Britain's bibliophilic and artistic cultures.

Kathryn A. Smith, New York University.

NOTES

1. Stella Panayotova, ed., *The Art and Science of Illuminated Manuscripts: A Handbook* (London and Turnhout: Harvey Miller Publishers, 2020).
2. For this approach, see Kathryn A. Smith, *Art, Identity and Devotion in Fourteenth-Century England: Three Women and their Books of Hours* (London: British Library; Toronto: University of Toronto Press, 2003), 82–119, 167–184, and especially 172–176, which analyzes the heraldic and marginal decoration of the De Bois Hours (New York, Morgan Library & Museum MS M.700, c. 1325–1330) in relation to medieval sermons constructed around the theological, moral, political, and social meanings assigned to the tinctures and charges of heraldry.

KATHLEEN E. KENNEDY AND MELEK KARATAŞ, EDS.
Manuscripts in Bristol Collections: A Descriptive Catalogue.
Bristol Studies in Medieval Culture.
Cambridge: D. S. Brewer, 2025.
xiv + 184 pp. 25 color plates.

This volume attempts a difficult straddle (see 8). On the one hand, it supplements Neil Ker's account of Bristol manuscripts in *Medieval Manuscripts in British Libraries* and addresses specialists. Equally, it represents a laudable act of academic outreach, a revelation to local citizens of their culture. It is no bad thing to bring local history and topography to a general audience; this is highlighted in a series of essays of an introductory nature, useful to this imagined audience, but probably holding few surprises for readers of this journal. Everyone, however, will appreciate the provision of legible full-color illustrations, offering snapshots of all the manuscripts (and frequently accompanied by references to complete online images).

The address to professionals is, however, not altogether helpful, and readers will still need to compare Ker's partial record. For example, the catalogue fails to communicate two central features usually taken as obligatory in such efforts. It offers minimal identification of the texts included and usually lacks any reference to a standard edition. (For example, although there are several references to the copy of Uguccione of Pisa's *Derivationes* in Bristol Central Library, MS 8, none of the contributors seems aware of a fine printed edition, edited by Enzo Cecchini, et al., two volumes [Florence, 2004].) Similarly absent, but routine in recent descriptive catalogues, is any notation of piecemeal production, manuscripts composed of booklets or fascicles; and in a situation where apparently over-zealous bindings have rendered books difficult to collate, full reports of surviving signature systems should have been included. Nevertheless, we should be thankful for the extensive illustrations, and Bristolians should consider themselves effectively introduced to the local inflections of a general medieval book-culture.

Ralph Hanna, Keble College

STEVEN W. MAY

English Renaissance Manuscript Culture: The Paper Revolution.

Oxford: Oxford University Press, 2023.

xii + 273 pp. 13 b&w plates.

In this interesting and well-written book, Steven May aims to establish the connection between the introduction of paper in late medieval Britain and the advent of a Renaissance "hybrid" scribal tradition (4), where an informal but highly efficient network of professional and amateur scribes copied and, in some cases, composed a wide variety of texts. May regards traditional archival scholarship as less intellectually demanding than the systematic study of manuscript culture, which he argues only started after 1980 and is still in its infancy. He focuses on paper as a democratizing force that opened up textual production to the masses sitting in their ordinary homes, taverns and alehouses, and he questions the historic scholarly focus on elite scribal coteries emanating from the "triad" of court, inns of court, and university (5). After providing a historical introduction to the mechanics and technologies of textual production, May focuses primarily on manuscript production of Renaissance poetry, acknowledging repeatedly that the essential features of scribal compilation and distribution of manuscripts are sometimes a matter for speculation due to the dearth of supporting evidence.

After a survey of writing technologies (papyrus, clay tablets, animal hides, wax tablets, for example) and handwriting styles (the illustrative plates could have been better presented), May explores in detail a range of personal notebooks, commonplace books, recipe books, tracts on alchemy and various anthologies, before delving into the details of how the "hybrid" scribal culture worked, what texts were of interest to that culture, and how paper facilitated an exponential growth in manuscript production and circulation. He suggests that inns, taverns and alehouses may have been as significant loci of scribal activity as the rarified venues of the "triad," but acknowledges that evidence to support such a claim is scant because of the extremely high loss rate of paper manuscripts. The study then moves on to explore how Renaissance poetry circulated via informal scribal networks, often in notebooks whose origins do not always tally with their contents.

The high cost of parchment restricted medieval manuscript production to the wealthy secular and religious elites and discouraged creativity, note-taking, or drafting of writing; it also created a professional scribal coterie trained to work with such luxury materials. The result, May argues, was a marked decline in literacy, but the introduction of paper, wending its way from eighth-century China and the Middle East to southern Europe and finally England, galvanized revolutionary social change by opening up words, books, ideas and writing to the masses in the vernacular. Paper gradually became so inexpensive that ordinary citizens, in the privacy of their own homes, could produce manuscripts containing materials that interested them. Renaissance drama and Lollardy owe their success to paper, as does the rise in literacy and the growing prestige of the vernacular. By the mid-fifteenth century, a "hybrid" scribal culture was fully formed and for the next two centuries may have produced more books than the printing press (indeed some scribes copied from printed books). "The crucial technology is paper, not printing," May asserts (44).

The medieval focus on costly whole texts on parchment was replaced by vast numbers of single-sheet or bifolia paper "separates" that were later bound into miscellanies (56). Letter writing, rare on parchment, flourished on paper, revealing to us for the first time the social concerns and daily lives of ordinary people, as evidenced in the Stonor, Paston and Cely letters. Personal paper notebooks abounded among the growing educated population, featuring single-author works, anthologies, and miscellanies of practical and religious prose, household accounts, diaries, student notes, medical recipes, alchemical tracts, personal signatures, sententiae, coats of arms, portraits, maxims, records of births and deaths, devotional texts and much more. The format, content, sources, and compilation of these notebooks were entirely in the hands of their creators, and reflected their interests and abilities.

The idea that manuscript texts circulated only among elite coteries is, May contends, grossly incorrect. The vast majority of Renaissance manuscripts were produced by informal networks of scribal communities, often comprised of ordinary people pursuing ordinary interests. May thinks that taverns were "ideal environments for…making copies of manuscript texts" (112) and that they also widened scribal participation to include women. Manuscripts were posted across the country by carriers, and significant authors such as John Donne, Sir Walter Raleigh, Thomas Carew, Sir John Suckling, and Richard Lovelace were happy for their poems to circulate informally. Professional writers such as Michael Drayton, John Ford, George Gascoigne and John Lyly, on the other hand, went straight to print. Renaissance manuscript anthologies can seem somewhat *ad hoc* (in comparison to bespoke medieval compilations on parchment): they feature a range of contents that speak to the evolving tastes of the compilers, most of whom have never been identified. The rapid growth in official and personal correspondence on paper fueled a concomitant surge in carrier services and travel, but the Dissolution of the Monasteries, the Civil War, and the Great Fire of London ensured that manuscript survivals were rare. We owe what remains to visionary collectors who had suitable homes to preserve manuscripts and who subsequently donated their collections to the state or academic institutions for safekeeping.

The majority of manuscripts that have survived calamity, neglect and mismanagement is "weighted toward upper-class output and interests" (151). To understand Renaissance scribal culture "we must identify the extant manuscripts produced by the underclass" (151–2), May insists. Only around 400 Renaissance poetic manuscript miscellanies exist. Perhaps sixty times that number have been lost, making analysis of textual transmission extremely difficult. May explores rare testimony of compilers of manuscripts, and conducts textual criticism, biographical research and handwriting analysis in an attempt to establish the extent of "underclass" contributions, but acknowledges that much remains unknown and possibly unknowable about the identity of the compilers of these manuscripts.

May feels that the elite "triad" is unrepresentative of the bulk of scribal culture, as it amounted to only 10,000 of the half a million literate citizens in England between 1500 and 1620. He maintains that even if only 5% of women were literate "then women scribes outnumbered the total triad population by six to one" (196). "Exclusive courtier verse" (200) such as Sir Philip Sidney's reached remote geographical and social hinterlands; therefore one should not assume that the class of the compiler can be deduced from the contents of the compilation. Case studies undertaken demonstrate how the lack of solid evidence so often hamstrings attempts to discover the routes of transmission and the identities of compilers. Circumstantial evidence seems to support May's contention that "fast, voluminous and oblivious to social rank" scribal communities were primarily responsible for the dissemination of manuscript texts to ordinary people during the Renaissance (228). Ultimately, however, May concedes that "we do not know who copied the vast majority of Renaissance manuscripts or when, where, and how these scribes obtained their copy texts," but nevertheless he is convinced that "increasingly we will understand Renaissance scribal culture as a national phenomenon dominated by amateur scribes at all levels of society" (231).

Anyone who has conducted research on the transmission of manuscript texts will understand the difficulties May has faced in supporting his thesis with incontrovertible evidence. Far from invalidating his thinking, however, May's confident and worthwhile study challenges future researchers to keep digging for evidence and not to be discouraged by the uncanny ability of time and circumstance to erase precisely what we want to see.

Matthew Sullivan (Independent Scholar)

CORINNE SAUNDERS AND DIANE WATT, EDS.
Women and Medieval Literary Culture: From the Early Middle Ages to the Fifteenth Century. Cambridge: Cambridge University Press, 2023. xv + 487 pp.

This collection, which grew out of meetings of the Leverhulme Trust-funded International Network "Women's Literary Culture and the Medieval English Canon," which ran from 2015 to 2017, is wide-ranging, informative, and, I believe, essential for anyone working in English medieval women's texts and literary contexts. A thorough introduction to the volume written by the editors, Corinne Saunders and Diane Watt, lays out that, despite the typically narrow focus of English female authorship on Marie de France, Julian of Norwich, and Margery Kempe, when a wider view is taken—of other named women as translators/compilers, translated texts of continental women writers, women scribes, letters, patronage, and anonymous works—the picture of what women were reading, writing, and commissioning in medieval England is much more textured and complex than the work of the three usual suspects would indicate.

The collection is divided into five sections, each with several short essays. All of the essays are thoughtful and informative and straddle the line of being an introduction to a subject to a reader who may not know much and delving deeper into the specifics of the topic. The first section, "Patrons,

Owners, Writers, and Readers in England and Europe," looks at specific women and the traces of their literary culture that they have left behind. Elaine Treharne, in "'Misere, meidens': Abbesses and Nuns," examines additions and annotations to manuscripts made by a "Matilda" and another by an unnamed nun, both possibly from Barking Abbey. In "Creating Her Own Story: Queens, Noblewomen, and Their Cultural Patronage," Mary Dockray-Miller looks at books commissioned and owned by medieval English queens and the Continental women who were part of the English cultural court and milieu. This section closes with Mary C. Erler's "Woman-to-Woman Initiatives Between English Female Religious," focusing on the learning of late medieval nuns, especially those at Syon Abbey.

The second section, entitled "Circles and Communities in England," likewise has three strong essays, each looking at small groups of women and the texts that they shared among themselves. Michelle M. Sauer's "*Ancrene Wisse*, the Katherine Group, and the Wooing Group as Textual Communities, Medieval and Modern" looks at the ways in which critics over the last century have linked these texts and seen the way they circulated as part of a network of anchoritic texts, as well as the ways these texts get integrated into a broader devotional landscape of medieval England. We return to Syon Abbey with Laura Saetveit Miles's "Syon Abbey and the Birgittines," which looks at the way texts were connected and interconnected around the Abbey through patronage of women like Margaret Beaufort and the Abbey's abbesses, as well as the ways that St. Birgitta's writing and influence are infused in the textual output from the Syon. Finally, Diane Watt's "What the Paston Women Read" looks at the hints of book ownership and reading in the letters of the Pastons, who, while they may not have been literary, owned and borrowed books and hence participated in a literary culture.

Section Three, "Health, Conduct, and Knowledge," is the least coherent of the all the sections, although the individual essays are very strong. Naoë Kukita Yoshikawa's "Embracing the Body and the Soul: Women in the Literary Culture of Medieval Medicine" looks at how ancient tracts of medicine were rearticulated in the later middle ages, particularly in the work known as *The Trotula*. Kathleen Ashley examines the development of conduct books in "Gender and Class in the Circulation of Conduct Books," and how they incorporate literary texts and lessons for their female readers. In "Women's Learning and Lore: Magic, Recipes, and Folk Belief," Martha W. Driver looks at several different manuscripts and books across genres (conduct books, Dame Juliana Berners' *Book of Hawking, Hunting, and Blasing of Arms*, birth girdles, devotional manuscripts) to show the way charms and folk belief are reflected therein. The final essay in this section is Denis Renevey's "Women and Devotional Compilations," where he suggests some of the ways in which women may have played a part in compilatory activity, both as recipients of the texts and as writers whose work gets excerpted into them.

The fourth section, "Genre and Gender," is the largest, comprising seven different essays which all address different genres and the way women's writing or reading intersects with it. David Fuller writes about "Lyrics: Meditations, Prayers, and Praises; Songs and Carols," particularly those with Mary as its subject. Christiania Whitehead addresses women as both subjects and readers of saints' lives, such as Hild in Bede's work or Criseyde in Chaucer, in "'It satte me wel bet ay in a cave / To bidde and rede on holy seyntes lyves': Women and Hagiography." In "Tears, Meditation, and Literary Entanglement: The Writings of Medieval Visionary Women," Liz Herbert McAvoy looks at the way that medieval visionary women in their writing inform each other across temporal and geographical boundaries from Margery Kempe, the nuns of Helfta, to Hildegard of Bingen. Sue Niebrzydowski's "Convent and City: Medieval Women and Drama" also looks at the ways in which texts inform each other, from Hrotsvitha of Gandersheim through Katherine Sutton at Barking Abbey. We turn to the genre of romance with Corinne Saunders's "Women and Romance," where she looks at female protagonists in popular medieval romance and the way it reflects contemporary debates about women in society. Neil Cartlidge turns to fabliaux in "Trouble and Strife in the Old French *Fabliaux*," looking at the extreme depictions of men and women and how this creates a shared community of laughter in its readers. Finally, Venetia Bridges writes about "Chaucer and Gower," and what ethical questions about gender the authors raise in common.

The last and final section, "Women as Authors," in some sense returns us to the introduction where Saunders and Watt pointed out that there is much more to consider in women's literary culture than just the named and known authors. We close with these women, with each of the five chapters looking at medieval women writers and how they responded to and shaped the culture in which they participated. Emma Campbell, in "Marie de France: Identity and Authorship in Translation," looks at Marie as possibly not one sole woman but as a representation of a broader literary tradition within which women may have been writing. In "Julian of Norwich: A Woman's Vision, Book, and Readers," Barry Windeatt looks at the intersection of the short and long text and Julian's own awareness of how her gender infuses her theology and the afterlife of her texts. Anthony Bale's "The Communities of *The Book of Margery Kempe*" examines the textual, geographic, and spiritual influences that shape Margery's thought and text. We move to the Continent with Nancy Bradley Warren's "Christine de Pizan: Women's Literary Culture and Anglo-French Politics," where she looks at Christine's political savvy both in life and in her writing and how this aspect of Christine gets erased in later writings about her. Finally, closing both the section and the collection, we have Cathryn A. Charnell-White's "Beyond Borders: Women Poets in Ireland, Scotland, and Wales up to c. 1500" which opens up the British Isles beyond England, and the women poets whose work we know and the way they addressed and challenged gender roles.

Given space constraints and the sheer number of essays contained within this collection, it is impossible to go into detail on any of the essays. Overall, however, the collection has a good deal to offer members of the Early Book Society. The quality of the essays is notably high and the detailed and careful references to extant manuscripts and early printed materials here will give scholars a lot to work with.

Jennifer N. Brown, Marymount Manhattan College

ANNA DLABAČOVÁ, ANDREA VAN LEERDAM AND JOHN J. THOMPSON, EDS.
Vernacular Books and their Readers in the Early Age of Print (c. 1450 – 1600). Intersections: Interdisciplinary Studies in Early Modern Culture, Vol. 85
Leiden: Brill, 2023
xx + 410 pp. 82 figs. 3 tables.

This ambitious essay collection focuses on ways that readers interacted with early printed vernacular books published throughout Europe. The various essays offer considerable breadth, especially in their frequent incorporation of early print and manuscript studies not available in English translation. The volume's eighty-two plates, several in color, reinforce the contributors' arguments. Readers without nearby research libraries will appreciate the open access provided by the Dutch Research Council NOW: https://doi.org/10.1163/9789004520158.

Because early printers often published Latin and vernacular editions of the same books or employed Latin glosses and titles in some vernacular books, the vernacular emphasis does not exclude books printed in Latin but presents them in comparison to their vernacular counterparts. In the volume's introduction, Anna Dlabačová and Andrea van Leerdam, within three sections that avoid the usual geographic or genre groupings, lay out a convincing rationale that best reflects interactions between books and their readers in an attempt to offer a broader, more interdisciplinary spectrum in the scholarship of vernacular books: "Real and Imagined Readers," "Mobility of Texts and Images," and "Intermediality."

In Part 1, "Real and Imagined Readers," as Dlabačová and van Leerdam explain, "imagined" readers were potential rather than actual, appealed to through page design, illustrations, paratexts, and other elements. "Real" readers may have been those same imagined readers, but their physical interactions with their books are revealed only through their written notes or glosses, physical alterations, or traces such as stains or wax left on the pages (13). The five contributors to this longest section employ comparative methodologies to set up reading patterns which may have been distinct from publishers' or compilers' anticipated patterns, in order to show the differences between the two audiences in different regions and languages. Heather Bamford's lead essay examines handwritten magical recipes or talismans reproduced in secret manuscripts or hidden in wall inscriptions among the Muslim population forced to accept Christianity or leave Iberia after Islam was forbidden. In their decision to place Bamford's essay first, the editors likely hope that readers will apply her fascinating and useful insights on manuscript materiality to the parallel print materiality discussed throughout the volume, but without other essays mentioning vernacular print in Spain, the parallel remains less defined than it could be.

Tillmann Taape's study of the surgeon Hieronymus Brunschwig's book on medical distillation, *Das buoch der rechten kunst zü distilieren*, first published by the Strasbourg printer Johann Grüninger, presents Brunschwig as an author determined to write books for the "common man" portrayed in illustrations as the "striped layman." Woodcuts and textual directions for distillation mark this figure as a recipient and disseminator of "hybrid knowledge" (61). Grüninger also translated *Hortulus animae* from Latin into German and published *Der Wurtzgarten* in 1501, the first vernacular edition of the *Hortulus* and the basis of Stefan Matter's exploration of German prayer book printing. Grüninger relied upon apparatus such as biblical passages and glosses either indicating Latin texts or translating some words and phrases, prompting Matter to observe that "I know of no other case in which the process of translation itself is so systematically made evident" (100). Although Grüninger's first attempt did not find the audience he anticipated, a stream of later vernacular editions, including his own second edition, made the vernacular *Hortulus animae* the most popular printed prayer book in pre-Reformation Germany.

Suzan Folkerts examines another popular devotional genre, the Middle Dutch *Epistles and Gospels*, printed first in Deventer by Richard Pafraet and Jacob van Breda as an outgrowth of the Devotio Moderna movement that capitalized on the laity's interests in acquiring New Testament texts. The Deventer editions, first lightly illustrated and later containing woodcuts that may have been made for these printings, proved immensely successful, judging from the traces lay readers left—coloring in woodcuts, corrections and annotations, and autographs. Karolina Mroziewicz turns to Marcin Bielski's *Chronicle of the Whole World*, published in Cracow in 1551, 1554, and 1564, to explore how its noble Polish readers personalized the first printed Polish-language universal history in family copies passed down into the late eighteenth century. While some readers marked passages regarding ancient history gleaned from Latin sources, they reserved their most virulent interactions for Bielski's Protestant sympathies—cross-outs of the story of Pope Joan or defaced portraits of Martin Luther.

Part 2 is titled "The Mobility of Texts and Images." Three essays by Martha W. Driver, Alexa Sand, and Elisabeth de Bruijn offer a pan-European perspective encompassing English, French, Dutch, and German printed books. Admittedly, the essays by Driver and Sand focus heavily on how the transnational exchange enabled early English printers to reshape continental sources for their audiences. Driver's informative essay, with some tongue-in-cheek observations, details English woodcuts of the schoolmaster and students, especially those in grammars and other educational books printed by Wynkyn de Worde, Richard Pynson, and others to "recover" learning practices and "kinds of books. . . thought appropriate" (195) for schoolchildren as she traces their iconographic sources in Dutch and German books. She also presents an intriguing argument as to why John Lydgate's *The Churl and Bird* includes a schoolmaster woodcut in its earliest printed editions. Sand presents de Worde as a promoter of the *Ars moriendi* through a set of sometimes humorous woodcuts used in multiple editions of *The crafte to lyue well and to dye well* plus other books capitalizing on the good death for early Tudor audiences. Although he emulated and borrowed ideas from the French printer Antoine Vérard, de Worde's "learning to die" (1999) woodcuts not only created a profitable market for himself but widely disseminated a new genre, the "extensively illustrated spiritual instruction book" (216). De Bruijn's study of French, English, Dutch, and German romances printed before 1500 investigates their interconnectedness, circulation, and vernacular modifications. Significantly, de Bruijn points to manuscript culture, especially in Germany and France, for its "significant impact on the transregional dissemination of these romances" (235).

In Part 3, "Intermediality," Katell Lavéant, Margriet Hoogvliet, and Walter S. Melion explore how the printed book connected to other media such as manuscripts, broadsides, murals, and performances. Lavéant studies the tale of Bigorne and Chicheface, "merry monsters" with no known iconographic precedents before Guy Marchant printed a 1495 broadside, revealing how the story and illustrations circulated and transformed through what she calls "joyful books" (268), broadsides, small pamphlets, and prints published in France, Germany, the Netherlands, and England for entertainment. She makes a strong case for "intermedial transposition" (289) when she discusses how print images of Bigorne and Chicheface inspired wall murals in two French castles. Hoogvliet repositions Pierre Michault's *Danse aux aveugles*, an allegorical dream poem, as a humanist-inspired religious text that encouraged a reader to employ the "rational mind for religious matters" (297). The illustrations appearing in all printed versions function as paratexts to guide readers' behaviors but also to help them visualize the speakers if the text were to be read aloud or performed. Melion describes the textual and visual components of the *Groenendaal Passion*, a handwritten prayer book compiled in Brabant and illustrated with engravings and woodcuts, focusing on its intersectionality in languages (vernacular and Latin), medium (manuscript and print), and format (text and image). In the process, he presents the book's design as an intentional complement to the teaching and meditative practices of the Augustinian canons of the Groenendaal monastery.

John J. Thompson's "Afterword" presents a case study of William Caxton's first dated work, the 1474 Ghent printing of *The Game and Play of the Chesse*, to demonstrate and reinforce the premise of this essay collection. Caxton published books responding to what readers already wanted or might want in the future, but he and other early printers were limited by what they and their peers had read or were reading, their geographical networks, and the literacy of their audiences. In a fitting conclusion to the entire volume, Thompson suggests that, like the early printers, this volume's contributors must rely on a speculative mindset, this one constructed on "the materiality of books and reading practices" (403) to identify vernacular books and their readers because the limited evidence represents only a fraction of what likely was published.

This volume presupposes that its own readers will be well-versed in the history, terminology, and ongoing debates of early book scholarship. As more general readers are able to gain access to academic books through open access, I could wish for more attention to the needs of a general audience who may encounter this volume via the internet. Along the same lines, a comprehensive index that incorporates subjects, terminology, and titles (especially those referred to in several essays) rather than an index of names only, would help readers more easily navigate the wealth of information this volume provides (full disclosure: I am a professional indexer). Overall, however, this admirable essay collection expands our knowledge of Europe's early vernacular books, their publishers, and, of course, their real and imagined readers.

Mary Morse, Rider University (Emerita)

JOHN GOLDFINCH, TAKAKO KATO, SATOKO TOKUNAGA, EDS.
Production and Provenance. Copy-Specific Features of Incunabula.
Leiden, Boston: Brill, 2025.
xviii + 442 pp. 48 color plates, 56 figures, 8 tables.

The editors of this book come with a pedigree: until his retirement, John Goldfinch was curator of incunabula at the British Library, while his co-editors, Takako Kato and Satoko Tokunaga, academics at, respectively, De Montfort University and Keio University, will be well known to scholars of manuscripts and printed books, not least as members of the Early Book Society.[1] They are all ideally suited to have produced this important volume, and they have acquired some prestigious contributors.

The Introduction is by Kato, whose university hosted the 2015 conference which foregrounds this book: "Reading Copy-Specific Features: Producers, Readers and Owners of Incunabula." She lays out the salient and significant elements of copy-specific variation in manuscripts, especially incunabula, and details the rise in interest and research developing from databases such as GW (*Gesamtkatalog der Wiegendrucke*) and ISTC, which estimate that there are approaching half a million individual copies of incunabula. In addition, there are 250 incunabula catalogues. The earliest are the BMC (*Catalogue of Printed Books in the XVth Century now in the British Museum*) volumes (1908–2007) and the Uppsala catalogue of Isak Collijn

(1907). BMCXI (volume XI, for England) is full, rigorous, and of infinite value to members of EBS interested in studying individual British Library incunabula. The Cambridge History of the Book in Britain is rightly cited in the roll of honor, and one might (as Kato does not) cite the very early interest exhibited by the founding in 1987 of the Early Book Society by Martha Driver and Sarah Horrall. In addition, there are digital projects: 15cBOOKTRADE run by Cristina Dondi, MEI (Material Evidence in Incunabula) hosted by CERL (Consortium of European Research Libraries, which also hosts the image database, Provenance Digital Archives). In the course of the book, it is clear that researchers are now eagerly using the material available from Glasgow (the Glasgow Incunabula Project, GIP) and Cambridge (the Fitzwilliam Museum and the colleges in book form, the University Library as a database[2]).

After Kato's Introduction, the book is divided into five parts: Part 1: Perspectives on Incunabula Study; Part 2: Aspects of Early Printing; Part 3: Early Journeys and Producers; Part 4: Later Journeys and Provenances; Part 5: Provenances and Collections. The division is judicious and perhaps, unusually, all contributors fit well into the parts allotted them. One might say that no one is off-message. Also commendable (but of course essential in discussing copy-specific material) is that, apart from the two Part 1 essays and the last essay in Part 5, the twelve essays are illustrated with many color plates and figures, and some with useful tables. This is a carefully planned and carefully edited volume.

One of the questions which the book seeks to address is: "Should we still treat incunabula as a distinct category of books" (7)? In Part 1 (Perspectives on Incunabula Study), the Queen of the Incunabulum, Lotte Hellinga, in her semi-historical survey of the attitudes to, and interest in, incunabula ("Unique Features in Early Printed Books"), filtered through her own deeply experienced assessment of the value and limitations of copy-specific material, concedes that, although 1500 is a useful rather than categoric date, "yet there is a clear distinction between books printed in the first three decades of printing and those of the sixteenth century" (17). She and the next contributor, David Pearson ("Incunabula in Our New Book Historical Landscape"), deal with this and the other research questions posed in the Introduction: what can the study of copy-specific features tell us about the market, the use of books, the movement of books, and what extra values can this focus bring to studies in bibliography and book history? Both bring their vast experience to bear on these questions, Hellinga somewhat iconoclastic about the value of copy-specific features, but avowedly writing as a "historian of typography" (32, with several interesting observations), Pearson positive in his assessment, but basing his observations on his belief that the essence of the history of the book as a subject is "understanding the social impact of books; what we want to know is not just what was printed and produced, but what impact and influence it did or did not have" (39).[3] Both essays are wise and thought-provoking introductions to those that follow and defy excerption or summary when ten more essays await review.

Part 2 (Aspects of Early Printing) begins with Edward Potten writing on "A Succession of Uncertainties: Dating the Buxheim *Saint Christopher*."[4] Potten addresses the book's title, *Production and Provenance*, through a study of the copy-specific evidence of this problematically-dated woodcut, which survives, with an Annunciation, pasted to the front and rear boards of the *Laus Mariae* in Buxheim. His argument is detailed and forensic, admirably illustrated, and probably conclusive in its tentative conclusion that it dates from the 1430s, not (as the woodcut prints) 1423. Mary Kay Duggan next writes very interestingly on "Coping with Blank Spaces for Music in Incunabula," that is, the fact that, while nearly one thousand incunabula were designed to incorporate notation, the music was largely to be inserted by the owner himself (or herself, since there is an Appendix: "Female Ownership of Liturgical Psalters"). Here, copy-specificity is of course of fundamental importance, and Duggan's case-studies (with illustrations) of mostly liturgical printed books provide interesting details on how the owners addressed the blank spaces, the texts without notation, and other forms in which their printed books reached them.

Part 3 (Early Journeys and Producers) is art historical. Holly James-Maddocks, in "Illuminators of English and Continental Incunabula in England, c.1455-1500," highlights the opportunities offered by the Cambridge and Glasgow material (see above). Her case studies for English illumination (defined here as gold or silver decorated initials and flourishes) in English and Continental incunabula are the Gutenberg 42-line Bible, the Rufinus (*Expositio Symboli*) which was the first Oxford printed text, and the "Fitzjames Limner," who illuminated for Richard Fitzjames a Lyndwode, again printed in Oxford, but by Theodoric Rood. (The Fitzjames biography does not go beyond his Merton connections, but his positions as chaplain to Henry VII, and bishop of London and then of Chichester, seem relevant to the fact that he employed this limner to illuminate three manuscripts.) This is a full and detailed essay, very interesting on the Oxford connections, and mostly (but not fully) illustrated with color plates, ending with an appendix of thirty-six English-illuminated incunabula. The Cambridge material used by James-Maddocks, based on a study of 2,000 incunabula, was co-produced by the next contributor, Suzanne Reynolds, who investigates "Tracking Changes: Decoration, Binding, and Annotation in Incunabula Imported to England." The survey uncovered over 400 volumes with hand-illumination, in about eighty of which places of printing and illumination did not coincide, and which included many early imports to England. It is some of these which Reynolds studies, revealing valuable information about how Continental incunabula were acquired in England, and where and how they were illuminated. Finally, in this part, Daryl Green investigates the early journeys of printed books to Scotland before Scotland's first printing press (Chepman and Myllar) received royal assent in 1507 (it produced books for around five years). The sole external evidence for pre-1507 printed book purchases by Scots abroad is in the ledger of Andrew Halyburton, so that Green must use the evidence of copy-specific books in his essay "The first Printed Books to Arrive in Scotland: Fifteenth-Century St Andrean Owners of Fifteenth-Century Books." Acknowledging his use of Durkan and Ross (*Early Scottish Libraries*, 1961) and Margaret Ford (in *CHBB* III), as well as GIP, the Glasgow database that has featured in essays above, and the University of Aberdeen "Provenance Database," Green explains his methods in assembling his data, which reveal that only 128 extant incunabula were circulating in Scotland before 1501, almost half in Sammelbände, that thirty-one of fifty-five known book owners owned only one book, and that around a third of the books had gone into circulation beyond their original owners by 1500. A discussion of the data leads into a number of case studies of incunabula and their owners, including, of course, the St. Andrews bibliophile, William Scheves.

Part 4 (Later Journeys and Provenances) consists of three essays. John McQuillen traces three early editions, "From Mainz to Manhattan: the Morgan Library's Three Gutenberg Bibles." In the context of this book, his analysis is written so as to disrupt any notion (already belied by evidence and published research) of any "sameness" (208), and to reveal their copy-specific differences: "Printing practices, hand decoration, binding, provenance, and every action taken by a reader or owner of the book leaves an indelible mark" (208). These marks he details by a "series of temporal analyses" (208) of the bibles, from the vellum PML 13 and 818, through the paper Old Testament PML 12, to the paper PML 19206-7, purchased by Morgan in 1896, 1910, and 1911 respectively, the last in order to acquire a copy "free of the imperfections and modern interventions found in the vellum and paper Old Testament copies" (224). Eric Marshall White, in the next essay, "Context Specifics and the History of Collecting Ulrich Zel's 1466 Chrysostom," deals with the first book printed in what was to become the important printing center of Cologne, the quarto edition of the *Sermo super psalmum L*, identified by its colophon, the fourth earliest dated colophon printed outside Mainz. His is a fascinating collecting history (often involving considerable intervention) of each of the eleven recorded copies, two of which are his own discovery, Chatsworth Library DEV/000882 and Saint-Omer, Bibliothèque de la Ville 4807, n° 118. Finally in this section, one of the volume's editors, Takako Kato, undertakes the interventions involved in "Perfecting and Completing Caxton's *Golden Legend*: the Stratigraphy of Non-homogeneous Copies." The 1483/4 edition of the *Golden Legend* is extant in thirty-three copies (of which she has studied and collated thirty-one, the other two being in Dallas, Texas, and Auckland, New Zealand) and ten fragments. Study of the rubricated initials, paraph marks, and strokes, together with other material evidence, has revealed thirteen non-homogeneous copies (that have suffered both mutilation and conflation) and eighteen homogeneous copies (not free of mutilation, but containing only the leaves original to the volume). Moreover, Kato has located the lost leaves from both types of copy (as fragments or within other copies), and reconstructed the original collations of three of the homogeneous and all of the non-homogeneous copies. This is meticulous research displaying painstaking effort, evidenced by two appendices, one listing the copies with condition and collation, and the other listing reconstructed originals and their styles of rubrication. Two case-studies explain the stratigraphy ("historical layers added to a copy after it was originally produced by Caxton and his co-workers," 270) of George III's copy (British Library, C.ii.d.8) and the copy of the second Earl Spencer, founder of the Roxburghe Club, whose collection was bought by Enriqueta Rylands (the book is now University of Manchester, John Rylands Library, Incunable Collection, 12018.1-2).

Finally, Part 5 (Provenance and Collections) has two essays, both of which are about important databases: first the much-cited Glasgow Incunabula Project, second the project called "Durham Priory Library Recreated."[5] Julie Gardham (Senior Librarian, Special Collections, University of Glasgow) entitles her essay "'There ys in this olde Book many a good saying and Lesson': Copy-Specific Discoveries in the Glasgow Incunabula Project."[6] (This introductory essay to GIP might have served better nearer the front of the book, before one had read so much about the project.) Under headings which largely replicate the search categories of the database, Gardham discusses "Provenance," "Annotation," "Purchase Prices," "Bindings," "Decoration," and "Other Features" (e.g., index tabs, parchment editions, and so on).[7] It is "Provenance" (as in Part 5's title) and "Annotation" which are most discussed here. Of 720 recorded names, most are of "the middling sort," that is, clerics/vicars (80), scholars/academics (twenty-five), and so on, who are cited in around 160 of the books. There is some little evidence of female names (in five books), while those belonging to "the upper crust" feature in thirty-eight books, with owners such as George III, Charles VIII, Louis XV, and lesser aristocracy and gentry. "Monastic" provenance is found from all over Europe, including seven books from the Celestines of Metz, and one taken for Henry VIII from Ramsey Abbey. "Annotation" deals with "General Annotation," found in 80% of the books, fewer as the centuries pass, although "Practical Annotation" (headings, chapter numbers, corrections, bibliographic details, and so on) starts in the eighteenth century and reveals developing antiquarian and bibliophilic interests. The value of GIP has been shown by earlier essays in the volume, and in "What Next for GIP," Gardham notes that its data are now shared with the CERL Hand Press Book and the MEI databases.

In the next essay, Sheila Hingley (Head of Heritage Collections at Durham University Library) introduces the reader to "Durham Priory Library: Recent Initiatives towards the Reconstruction of a Medieval Cathedral Library" (the "Collections" part of the Part's title). The Durham holdings are remarkable, as was amply demonstrated in their time by Neil Ker, Alan Piper, and Ian Doyle, whom Hingley acknowledges. Early catalogues date from 1420 and from 1633 to 1676, but Durham hauled itself into the present day in 2014 with the digitization program "Durham Priory Library Recreated," established by the university together with the cathedral chapter. Amazingly, most of the extant books from the Priory Library are still to be found close to the cathedral, in the Cathedral Library and the Palace Green Library, or five miles away, at Ushaw College.[8] With the project still in progress, Hingley can offer only tentative results, such as that sixty-four pre-1540 Priory books survive in the Cathedral Library (thirty-four incunables, of which the library has eighty-one in total), sixty-five in Ushaw (twenty-two incunables of a total of 134), and just two in the University Library.

What I missed in this fine volume (but largely supplied above from my own knowledge and from the Internet) were any details of the contributors, and a general index which would direct me, for example, to all the references to GIP. After the bibliography, and three indices (manuscripts, early printed books, early printed books in STC), the general index deals with codicological and related terms (e.g., annotation, artist, and so on), followed by an index of auction and sales catalogues, and an index of names. All these are scholarly and of immense value, but a simple general index which was truly general would have been an added benefit in a book which overall it is impossible to fault.

Susan Powell, University of Salford

NOTES

1. See Susan Powell in *JEBS* 2015 for a review of Ed Potten and Satoko Tokunaga, *Incunabula on the Move: The Production, Circulation and Collection of Early Printed Books* (vol. 18, 298–301).
2. For Glasgow: https://www.gla.ac.uk/myglasgow/incunabula/. See too Jack Baldwin, *A Catalogue of Fifteenth-Century Printed Books in*

Glasgow Libraries and Museums, 2 vols (Woodbridge, 2020) (see Susan Powell, *JEBS* 2022, 265–268 for a review). For Cambridge: A.E. Andriolo and S. Reynolds, *A Catalogue of Western Book Illuminations in the Fitzwilliam Museum and the Cambridge Colleges, Part Five: Illuminated Incunabula*, vol. 1: *Books Printed in Italy before 1500* (London and Turnhout, 2017); www.lib.cam.ac.uk/collections/departments/rare-books/rare-books-collections/incunabula

3. See Susan Powell, *JEBS* 2019, for a review of David Pearson, *Provenance Research in Book History: A Handbook* (vol.22, 343–346).
4. See Susan Powell, *JEBS* 2019, for a review of Ed Potten and Toshiyuki Takamiya, *Association and Provenance: Essays in Memory of Eric G. Stanley* (vol. 22, 347–350). See also note 1 above.
5. https://www.durhampriory.ac.uk/
6. See Susan Powell, *JEBS* 2016 for a review of Julie Gardham, *Ingenious Impressions: Fifteenth-century printed books from the University of Glasgow Library* (vol. 19, 289–290).
7. The database itself, noted at note 1 above, should be consulted for the full range of search categories.
8. See *JEBS* 2016 for James Kelly, *Treasures of Ushaw College: Durham's Hidden Gem* (vol. 19, 305–306).

THOMAS C. SAWYER
*The Making and Meaning of a Medieval Manuscript:
Interpreting MS Bodley 851.*
Cambridge: Brewer, 2025.
xvi + 233 pp. 14 color plates.

MS Bodley 851 can scarcely be described as unknown or undiscussed, in a variety of contexts: the unique copy of Walter Map's *De nugis curialium*, an important collection of Oxonian Latin poetry, and (sigh!) the infamous Z-Text of *Piers Plowman*. Sawyer should be congratulated for a penetrating original discussion, one that should be of interest not simply to *afficionados* of the various texts assembled in the book but considerably more widely.

The guts of Sawyer's contribution are largely theoretical and argued out in a provocative opening chapter. His critique takes aim at what has been the conventional mode of discussing manuscripts and their texts ever since Derek Pearsall's edited volume, *Manuscripts and Readers in Fifteenth-Century England* (1983). In Sawyer's view, this conventional interest is too absorbed in a narrow range of manuscripts and texts and imbricated in modern constructions, not medieval ones. Here the bugbears under scrutiny concern the imposition of generic categories, the product of modern study, and the ahistorical myopia of English studies, with its concerted inattention to the multilingual culture of medieval England.

In contrast, Sawyer argues for broadening the discipline. He insists that any discussion of a manuscript's texts must be accompanied by basic descriptive bibliography, the construction of a production history. Consequently, one's interests should not be texts, but The Book (a useful, although generally text-centered, precursor is Stephen G. Nichols and Siegfried Wenzel's *The Whole Book* [1996]). In Sawyer's argument, discussions need to play off these two interests, in bibliography and text, against one another, taking full account of both synergies and disruptions. Such a study, Sawyer argues, creates what he calls "a codicological unconsciousness," that is, what is not overtly stated but inherent in compiling texts into a book.

One might think Bodley 851 a peculiar subject for such an innovation; as I have already indicated, the volume is surely one of the perhaps too-often-visited "old chestnuts" of English studies. However, Sawyer's analytical account, the instantiation of his theoretical principles, argued out through case studies in chapters 2 to 4, will quickly dispel any such doubts. Sawyer considers in detail how the assembly of diverse materials across two languages creates provocative interfaces. His discussions are attractively marked by open-endedness, a desire to provoke, rather than to insist upon definitive conclusions.

Sawyer turns his hand to three engaging intratextual collocations. Chapter 2 takes up "misogamy." This is a particularly prominent feature, since Walter Map absorbed a (revised) version of his ubiquitous *Dissuasio ... ne uxorem ducat* into *De nugis* and since Bodley 851 includes a widely-disseminated lyric with similar title—as well as a Latin lyric heralding the married Virgin. Chapter 3 considers the Bodley 851 compiler's effort to assemble Map's *De nugis* and the dis-/con-junction of these efforts with the author's own open-ended *contes*. Chapter 4 examines "the Z-text," not (as conventionally) as warped *Piers Plowman*, but in its manuscript siting as companion to Mappian Latinate satiric lyrics. These are sophisticated and richly suggestive analyses.

Although, as I have said, Sawyer's work should arouse protracted general interest, a few features seem to me to require further comment. The volume is richly illustrated—and in color—but the size of the manuscript and that of Sawyer's book do not readily interface. Nearly all the images are too small to support legibly the arguments they are illustrating. Further, although this does not in any way diminish or qualify Sawyer's fundamental contribution, his bibliographical discussion is often marked by an unfortunate definitiveness that goes against the grain of the usually constructive open-ended discussion.

First of all, dating the hands in Bodley 851 (40–42), Sawyer recognizes that the scribes share versions of *anglicana formata*. However, as Malcolm Parkes showed in his nigh biblically-authoritative discussion, *English*

Cursive Book Hands (1969), *anglicana* script had a rather rocky road in its transformation from an idiosyncratic business hand (first found in formal manuscripts about 1270) to a formal book hand. (Even the great M. R. James once dated a manuscript in *anglicana* including texts of the 1330s as s. xiii, on the basis of its script features.) As Parkes showed, a specifically "formata" variety (separated minims, consistent inking) is a development of the mid-fourteenth century. Thus Bodley 851 is unlikely to be any earlier. The only narrower specification (no one responsibly dates more narrowly than a twenty- to thirty-year span, without external evidence) would be to describe the book as of s. xiv ex. or xiv4/4, i.e. perhaps as late as 1400+/-. (One of the manuscript's great students, the late George Rigg, once went shamelessly palaeographer-shopping round Oxford, looking for someone who would date the book before the death of John of Wells in 1388; both Parkes and Jeremy Griffiths demurred.)

Second, there is an issue with the identification of hands.[1] In spite of Sawyer's efforts at accommodating them (56–58), the manuscript does have a scribe S, who is not X (see plate 10). More troubling is the effort to identify the production-separate bookplate/*ex* libris associating the book with John of Wells's ownership on the basis of script features (39–41, 62–64). All those adduced are merely examples of "script" rather than "hand" (a distinction Sawyer discusses at 37–38).

I would qualify these objections by affirming Sawyer's general account. I would be fairly certain that Bodley 851 was produced in an Oxonian monastic/Benedictine context, either Gloucester College and/or (using exemplars borrowed [?] from a similar institution) Christ Church priory's Canterbury College. The primary evidence, which Sawyer mentions (49–50 and n.39), is a deviant, unrevised version of Nigel Wireker's *Speculum stultorum* ("Dan Brunel the ass"). In its extensive general circulation, the text appears in a revised version, but Canterbury, where Nigel was a monk, surely had the minority, unrevised form of the text, only fully paralleled in another manuscript with strong Oxonian and (perhaps belatedly) Canterbury affiliations, MS Bodley 761.

Finally, all objections aside, as I have indicated, Sawyer's is a major contribution, one that should invite protracted study, and indeed (in spite of Boydell and Brewer's pricing) purchase.

Ralph Hanna, Keble College

NOTES

1. Here I simply reiterate arguments I have made previously: "Auchinleck 'Scribe 6' and Some Corollary Issues," in *The Auchinleck Manuscript: New Perspectives*, ed. Susanna Fein, York Medieval Press (Woodbridge:

Boydell, 2016), 209–221, at 215 n.17; "Famous Scribe, Unrecognised Stint," in *Scribal Cultures in Late Medieval England: Essays in Honour of Linne R. Mooney*, ed. Margaret Connolly, et al. (Woodbridge: Boydell, 2022), 67–81, at 71–72 and 71 n.13.

MISTY SCHIEBERLE, ED. WITH ASSISTANCE FROM
AMANDA BOHNE
Medieval Manuscripts, Readers & Texts.
Essays in Honour of Kathryn Kerby-Fulton.
York Manuscript and Early Print Studies, 7.
York Medieval Press in association with the Boydell Press.
Woodbridge: Boydell & Brewer, 2024.
291 pp. 8 illustrations.

Kathryn Kerby-Fulton's work has opened rich lines of inquiry, bringing to attention forms of visionary, prophetic, and revelatory writing that afford new insights into *Piers Plowman* and many other works. She has written on big topics such as apocalypticism and censorship and also on the material forms and reception of certain medieval texts—on their authors, and on the makers, commissioners, readers and annotators of particular manuscripts. The most recent of her single-authored books, *The Clerical Proletariat and the Resurgence of Medieval English Poetry* (2021), has drawn attention to the forms of literary production associated with clerks in minor orders, those without benefices or established positions, a concern that reflects her own personal sympathy for present-day early career scholars in need of support and encouragement. The collaborative nature of many of her books, edited collections, and articles is testimony to the active nature of this encouragement and to her ready collegiality. The twelve essays that Misty Schieberle and Amanda Bohne have brought together in *Medieval Manuscripts, Readers and Texts*, contributed by former students and colleagues in scholarship, illustrate the breadth of Kathryn Kerby-Fulton's interests and the productive areas of research prompted by her example.

Visionary writings of different kinds feature in three of the essays. Thomas Goodmann's "A Dream of John Bale? The *Catalogus Vetus* and the Lives of Ralph Strode," pursues Bale's assertion that Strode was the author of a *"fantasma"* (126), now lost, and reviews the likelihood that the Merton philosopher-logician Strode was the same individual as the London lawyer Strode, who with wife and son was resident for some time close to Chaucer in Aldgate. Barbara Newman's study of "Three English Otherworld Visions: Towards a Spirituality of Parish Life" compares three Latin accounts of visions recorded between 1196 and 1206: those of the Monk of Eynsham, experienced by Edmund, a novice at Eynsham abbey; Ailsi, a member of the rural gentry from Launceston, transmitted by his grandson Peter of Cornwall; and Thurkill, an Essex peasant, recorded by Ralph of Coggeshall. The three accounts offer absorbing detail of the contours of parish piety at different social levels.

In "Women's St Edmund: Envisioning a Saint and his Contemplative Legacy," Jocelyn Wogan-Browne looks at the involvement of women in the transmission and reception of St. Edmund of Abingdon's *Speculum Ecclesie*. Accounts of St. Edmund's life indicate connections between some of his own female relatives and court circles where devotional works constituted women's reading, and the later history of the *Speculum*, in various vernaculars, suggests continuing female interest.

The London circles in which *Piers Plowman* was produced and read are approached from different angles by three contributors. Misty Schieberle looks at the wills of selected late-fourteenth-century Londoners of mercantile status to assess attitudes to the city's clerical proletariat, the kinds of unbeneficed clerks who were the target of some of Langland's criticism. The evidence that Schieberle finds indicates that testators may well have appreciated the difficulties faced by these members of the city's "gig economy" (Kathryn Kerby-Fulton's phrase, 192), and have used bequests to offer various forms of support. In "Langland's Government Scribes at Home and at Work: A Brief Comparison of the HM 114 Scribe and the Fortescue Family," Karrie Fuller compares the role of *Piers Plowman* in two London manuscript anthologies, one (Huntington Library MS HM 114) produced in the early fifteenth century and the other (BodL MS Digby 145) a century later, but both involving scribes who worked in London administrative contexts. Comparison of the items with which *Piers* keeps company in the two compilations, and of the nature of readerly annotations, suggests a fluid, changing reception history. The Huntington HM 114 scribe (possibly to be identified as the government clerk Richard Osbarn) may have worked in the same circles as the individual discussed in Linne R. Mooney's essay on "The Trevisa-Gower Scribe: Another London Literary Scribe of the Early Fifteenth Century." Using palaeographical and art-historical detail, Mooney identifies and outlines this scribe's work in two copies of the *Con-*

fessio Amantis and one of the *Polychronicon*, and argues for his connection with John Marchaunt, John Carpenter, and other artisans associated with the work of London's Guildhall.

A number of the essays illustrate the results of larger-scale manuscript surveys. For "Ars Codicis: Marginalia, Meaning, and the Manuscript Book(s) of Chaucer's *House of Fame*," Sarah Baechle has looked at glosses in the three extant copies, finding that the presence of Latin commentary from a variety of sources underlines the poem's decentering of authority. In "Telling Tails: Pursuing the Trail of the Minstrel-Scribe in Manuscripts of *Sir Isumbras*," Andrew W. Klein reviews scribal handling of tail-rhyme in the eight surviving copies of this romance, arguing that some of the evidence might indicate consciousness of the work's potential for oral performance. Works surviving in much larger numbers of manuscripts prompt some methodological experiments. Of the 220 copies of Geoffrey of Monmouth's *Historia regum Britanniae/De gestis Britonum*, many are workaday, apparently undistinguished productions, but Siân Echard finds value in "The Pleasures of Plainness: Ordinary Manuscripts in Extraordinary Traditions," and considers some of their material features and signs of use. Rather differently, the potential of cultural mapping as a method of assessing textual production and consumption is explored in two essays: "Professional Reading Networks and the Reception of Nicholas Love's *Mirror of the Blessed Life of Jesus Christ*: Opportunities and Consequences," by John J. Thompson, tracks the provenance and transmission of some of the sixty-odd copies of Love's influential translation, while Jeremy J. Smith's "Function, Form and *The Lay Folks' Mass Book*," with only nine witnesses to investigate, is able to present details that hint at the spoken use of at least parts of the work. While the essays on manuscripts in this collection are mostly concerned with their production and aspects of their medieval use, Smith also broaches some editorial issues, and a jointly written essay by Christopher Cannon and James Simpson outlines some of the concerns facing modern editors who confront the many manuscripts of Chaucer's writings. Their essay on "Editing Chaucer's Works: Coherence and Collaboration" illustrates some of the ways in which the manuscript witnesses resist recension or best text or diplomatic editing, and describes their solution of a "pragmatic" (75) method that allows for editorial intervention, especially in metrical matters.

Brief accounts of these twelve essays do not do proper justice to their substance and the great range of methods with which they probe the questions that have prompted them. There is meat here for many tastes—consideration of pious practice from the twelfth to the fifteenth century, of female devotion, of the habits of scribes and annotators, and of the challenges facing editors. As the bibliography to the book makes clear, and as underlined in an appreciation contributed to the collection by Rosalynn Voaden, Kathryn Kerby-Fulton's interests are wide and valuably fruitful.

Julia Boffey, Queen Mary University of London

About the Authors

Chiara Benati is Professor of Germanic Philology at the University of Genoa, Italy. Her research interests include the earliest (Low) German surgical treatises and the vernacular rendering of their specialized terminology. She is currently coordinating a two-year research project founded by the European Union NextGeneration EU aimed at completion of the first critical edition of the German translation and a new critical edition of the English version of Lanfranc of Milan's *Chirurgia magna*.

Virginia Blanton is University of Missouri Curators' Distinguished Professor. Her research focuses on medieval women, especially nuns, and their relationship with books, as writers, readers, singers, patrons, and book owners.

Julia Boffey is Professor Emerita of Medieval Studies in the Department of English at Queen Mary, University of London. She works on the production, transmission and reception of late medieval and early sixteenth-century literature in Britain, especially poetry, and on late-medieval literary culture more generally. Her recent publications include a modern translation of part of *The Great Chronicle of London* and (with A. S. G. Edwards) an edition of *The Epitaffe of Jasper Tudor*.

Jennifer N. Brown is the Dean of Arts and Sciences at Bentley University in Waltham, Massachusetts. Her research and teaching interests are in medieval devotional literature for and about women. Her work includes the 2018 monograph *Fruit of the Orchard: Reading Catherine of Siena in Late Medieval and Early Modern England* (University of Toronto Press) and the 2021 co-edited volume, with Nicole Rice, *Manuscript Culture and Medieval Devotional Traditions* (York Medieval Press). She also has a forthcoming novel, *The Lost Book of Elizabeth Barton* (St. Martin's Press).

D. R. Carlson is *professeur émérite* in the University of Ottawa. His recent publications include "Statius' *Silvae* and Paracorporal Roman Elegy in Early Tudor England," *Classical Philology* 120 (2025): 224–243.

Lisa Fagin Davis received her PhD in Medieval Studies from Yale University and has catalogued medieval manuscript collections at Yale University, the University of Pennsylvania, the Walters Art Museum, Wellesley College, the Museum of Fine Arts Boston, the Boston Public Library, and several private collections. She regularly teaches an introduction to manuscript studies at the Simmons University School of Library and Information Science and has taught Latin paleography at Yale University and Rare Book School.

Martha W. Driver, FSA, is Distinguished Professor of English emerita at Pace University in New York City. A co-founder of the Early Book Society for the study of manuscripts and printing history, she writes about illustration from manuscript to print, the early history of publishing, and manuscript and book production. In addition to publishing several books and some 80 articles in these areas, she has edited thirty-two journals over twenty-eight years. Her website is marthawdriver.com

Ralph Hanna is Professor of Palaeography emeritus and emeritus fellow, Keble College, Oxford. His publications include editions for the Early English Text Society, *Richard Rolle: Uncollected Verse and Prose, with Related Northern Texts* (o.s. 329, 2007) and *Speculum Vitae: A Reading Edition*, 2 vols (o.s. 331–2, 2008) as well as *Editing Medieval Texts* (Liverpool, 2015), and with David Rundle, *A Descriptive Catalogue of the Western Manuscripts, to c. 1600, in Christ Church, Oxford* (Oxford Bibliographical Society, 2017). His *Richard Rolle: Unprinted Latin Writings* in the Exeter Medieval Texts and Studies series was published in 2019; *Malachy the Irishman, On Poison: A Study and an Edition* for the same series appeared in fall 2020; and again for the same series, his publication *Robert Holcot, Exegete: Selections from the Commentary on Minor Prophets* appeared in 2021. His most recent edition is John Ridewall, *Fulgencius Metaforalis* for Liverpool University Press (2023). He is currently at work in the libraries at Worcester and Lincoln Cathedrals, seeking evidence for Robert Holcot's *Convertimini* and its extensive Middle English progeny.

S.C. Kaplan is Assistant Professor of French at Louisiana Tech University and an academic editor. Her research combines interests in women's books with digital humanities in the Books of Duchesses project (booksofduchesses.com). She has recently published articles in *JEBS, Manuscript Studies, Manuscripta*, and *Le Moyen Français* and is now working on her second monograph, tentatively titled *Uninked Inscriptions: Almost-Invisible Readers' Marks in the Bourbons' Book Collection*.

Michael P. Kuczynski holds the Pierce Butler Chair in English in the School of Liberal Arts, Tulane University, New Orleans. He has published widely on medieval manuscripts and early printed books, especially psalters. His two-volume critical edition of a glossed Wycliffite

Psalter was published in 2019 by the Early English Text Society. He is currently completing a book-length study of the *Epistola Lentuli*, a Psalms-based medieval forgery that purports to describe the physical appearance and demeanor of Jesus Christ.

Sarah Dyer Magleby recently earned her PhD from the Kress Foundation Department of Art History at the University of Kansas in Late Medieval and Northern Renaissance Art and is currently a lecturer at the Kansas City Art Institute and the University of Kansas. Sarah's research interests lie in gender studies, material and visual culture, and inventories as a means of rematerializing past collections. Through the Jeanne Marandon Fellowship, she also studied in Paris at the Institut national d'histoire de l'art, where she conducted necessary research for her dissertation "The Turquam-Gilles Inventory: Reconstructing an Estate and Familial Status in Paris, c. 1500."

Mary Morse is Emeritus Professor of English and Past Director of the Gender and Sexuality Studies Program at Rider University. Her research focuses on late medieval Englishwomen's devotional and childbirth practices. She recently published *English Birth Girdles: Devotions for Women in "Travell of Childe"* (Medieval Institute Publications/De Gruyter, 2024).

Susan (Sue) Powell is Emeritus Professor of Medieval Texts and Culture (University of Salford), a Fellow of the Society of Antiquaries, and Chair of the Harlaxton Medieval Symposium steering committee. She is an editor and scholar of manuscripts and early printed books. Her research focusses on religious and devotional texts and institutions of the late Middle Ages and Tudor period. Latterly, she has published the household accounts of Lady Margaret Beaufort (1443–1509), mother of Henry VII.

Caleb Prus is a fourth-year MD candidate at the University of Rochester School of Medicine. He holds an MSt in English (650–1550) from the University of Oxford, and his research interests include Middle English medical texts and their manuscripts, the history of medicine, and psychiatry.

Martha Rust is Professor of English at New York University, specializing in late-medieval English literature and manuscript culture. Her first book, *Imaginary Worlds in Medieval Books: Exploring the Manuscript Matrix* (Palgrave, 2007), envisioned the confines of a medieval manuscript as the potential territory of a virtual world. Her second book, *Lists and the Poetics of Reckoning in Middle English Culture*, forthcoming from Peter Lang, theorizes the list as a device that functions within three signifying domains: those of words, pictures, and things.

Valerie Schutte is a historian of Tudor England, with a particular focus on royal women and book history. Her first monograph, *Mary I and the Art of Book Dedications: Royal Women, Power, and Persuasion*, was published in 2015, and her second, *Princesses Mary and Elizabeth Tudor and the Gift Book Exchange*, appeared in 2021. She has edited or co-edited seven volumes on Mary I, Shakespeare, and queenship. She consulted on the recent *Six Lives* exhibition at the National Portrait Gallery in London. Valerie is currently editing a volume on Tudor myths and another on Mary I and humanism. Her third monograph, a cultural biography of Anne of Cleves, will be published with Routledge in 2026.

Kathryn A. Smith, FSA, FRHistS, is Professor in the Department of Art History at New York University. Her most recent book is *The Painted Histories of the Welles-Ros Bible (Paris, BnF fr. 1): Scripture Transformed in Fourteenth Century England* (Boydell Press, 2025).

Elizaveta Strakhov is Associate Professor of English at Marquette University. She is the author of *Continental England: Form, Translation, and Chaucer in the Hundred Years War* (Ohio State University Press, 2022), co-editor with Megan L. Cook of *John Lydgate's Dance of Death and Related Works* (TEAMS, 2019), and co-editor with Carissa M. Harris and Sarah Baechle of *Rape Culture and Female Resistance in Late Medieval Literature* (Penn State University Press, 2022). She has published extensively on Middle English literature, Anglo-French relations and medieval manuscripts in *Medium Ævum, Studies in the Age of Chaucer, Huntington Library Quarterly, and New Literary History*, among others.

Matthew Sullivan, PhD, is a globally experienced international educator who has lived and worked in six countries, contributed to teaching and learning across the tertiary, secondary and primary sectors, and is now also active in promoting literacy and numeracy in UK prisons. He was an international school headmaster for seventeen years in Asia and has written a number of articles on educational, literary-historical and nautical topics. A specialist in medieval literature with a D.Phil. in English from Oxford University, Dr Sullivan has a strong interest in literary history.

ABOUT THE AUTHORS

Daniel Wakelin is Jeremy Griffiths Professor of Medieval English Palaeography in the Faculty of English, University of Oxford, and Fellow of St. Hilda's College. His recent publications include *Immaterial Texts in Late Medieval England* (Cambridge University Press, 2022), and with Catherine Nall, an edition of William Worcester's *The Boke of Noblesse and the English Texts from its Codicil*, EETS os 362 (Oxford University Press, 2023).

James Willoughby is Moberly Librarian at Winchester College, England, and follows research interests in medieval libraries and textual transmission. His co-authored volume on the English and Welsh secular cathedrals for the *Corpus of British Medieval Library Catalogues* series will be published in 2025. He is currently at work on a descriptive catalogue of the manuscripts of Lincoln College, Oxford.

Lucas Wood is Associate Professor of French at Texas Tech University. His research explores the hermeneutic, ideological, and aesthetic tensions that animate courtly and chivalric discourses and textualities in medieval Francophone culture. He is particularly interested in the intersections between questions of genre, gender, political thought, and allegorical poetics.

The twenty-eighth volume of the *Journal of the Early Book Society*
was published in Fall 2025 by Pace University Press

Cover and Interior Layouts by Kaitlyn Tenorio-Gravesande
The journal was typeset in Arno Pro
and printed by Lightning Source in La Vergne, Tennessee.

Pace University Press
Director: Manuela Soares
Faculty Advisor: Eileen Kreit
Production Consultant: Joseph Caserto
Production Associate: Rachel Gluckstern
Graduate Assistants: Kaitlyn Tenorio-Gravesande
and Vidhi Sampat
Student Aide: Kianna Swingle

www.ingramcontent.com/pod-product-compliance
Lightning Source LLC
Chambersburg PA
CBHW061427300426
44114CB00014B/1573